A Restoration Reader

CHARLES II

From an engraving by Blooteling after a painting by Sir Peter Lely.

A Restoration Reader

edited by
JAMES HOLLY HANFORD

THE BOBBS-MERRILL COMPANY, INC.
Publishers

Indianapolis   New York

First Edition

Introduction

A long age ago, when the wounds of the First World War were green, a young American instructor from the Middle West, calling on a Boston lady, found her new-risen from her drawing-room couch, where she had been reading Restoration drama. "It seemed to me," he writes, "very wonderful and sophisticated and non-Victorian, a sight not to be duplicated, except, perhaps, in some group of disillusioned ones in London."

Actually, mature interest in the culture of the English has always found it easy enough to embrace the age of Charles II, in spite of the political and moral case which Whig tradition tended to build up against it. Nell Gwyn we had always with us. The Count of Gramont was sooner or later discovered by every rambler among spicy memoirs. Pepys went like hot cakes as soon as the code was broken and a discreet abridgment of the diary published. And Dryden stood like a colossus, one of the seven wonders of literature, even if homage to his greatness warmed the cockles of few hearts.

It remains true, however, that the interest and appeal of this age have been obscured for most readers by the prejudice of history. The nineteenth century, with its great democratic, humanitarian and material achievements, acknowledged its debt to the Renaissance, to the Puritan revolution and to the eighteenth century but not to this moment of political and spiritual reaction. Its literary enthusiasms were reserved for the universality of Shakespeare and his fellow dramatists, for the grandeurs of the imagination in Milton, for the realistic exploration of human nature in the fathers of modern fiction, for the wit of Pope and Swift, the humor and urbanity of Addison and Steele, the wisdom and the wit of Burke and Johnson, above all for its own discovery of emotion and romance and the upreach of the soul. More recently critical taste has rediscovered the tortured greatness of Donne and the other metaphysicals. Seen in the perspective of this great tradition, the reign of Charles II was transitory and aberrant, both in politics and art. Except for Dryden, it produced no masterpieces, and Dryden was apt to be read and studied too much out of the context of his times to be really interesting. Charles himself was the amusing Merry Monarch about whom choice and scandalous anecdotes were rife. As King, he was a self-indulgent traitor who sold his country to a foreign power. The mind and manners of the time were characterized by an un-English cynicism, a blatancy of sexual misbehavior in literature and life which cried out for the moral reform of Anne.

All this, of course, is partly true. But the age is nonetheless intriguing and the study of it, in its full complexity, an exciting experience of the mind, giving a new sense of variety and contrast in English culture and even a sense of fresh discovery in the modes of human greatness. The present collection is intended to illustrate the manifold interest of the Restoration epoch and to give an idea of its dramatic patterning. The selections are both historic and literary, poetry and prose, with the latter predominating. The attempt has been made to take the age at its own valuation and to let it speak in its own language, but to make the setting and relevancy of the documents clear by the arrangement, the captions and the introductory notes. The texts are in general modernized but occasionally allowed to stand in their original form. Thus the slightly archaic spelling of Samuel Pepys, as given in Wheatley's text, serves to illustrate the irregular practices of the time, while giving no great trouble to the reader. The same is true of Dryden, the great practitioner of the new versification, whose elisions are a part of his technique.

Bowdlerization has hitherto been an all but universal practice in the reprinting of Restoration literature and cannot wholly be avoided. The juicier passages in Pepys are still locked up in cipher and represented by dots in print. The Earl of Rochester's four-letter words were altered or omitted in the first collected edition and generally thereafter. It would be good fun to restore him to his original bawdiness, but I have not done so.

Enough remains to represent this side of the mores of the time.

It is to be remembered in this connection that much of the characteristic behavior of Restoration society was a deliberate reply to Puritan hypocrisy. The old regime was to be discredited and one way of doing it was to defy its standard values. Charles's openness as regards his mistresses proclaimed the mentionability of such things in other than moralistic terms. On the other hand, it will not do to take all this at more than its face value or to let it too much color the total picture. People love to talk when free to do so— and there are doubtless in the annals of Restoration gallantry many more words than deeds. The really interesting things are to be sought elsewhere. They are to be sought in the great religious and political struggle which carried over from the preceding age and mounted in intensity as the forces regained the balance which had been lost in the downfall of the Puritan regime, in the national recovery from the disasters of plague and fire, in the hysteria of the Popish Plot, in the advance of science, the modernization of expression, the settlement of national and international policy, the re-establishment of an English way of life.

One thing which makes the record of this time more interesting to the modern reader than those of an earlier, if greater, time is the development of biographical curiosity and the habit of gratifying it. It is no accident that the great secular and religious diaries belong to this period, no accident that personal correspondence is richer and more gossipy, no accident that the great collections of lives by Wood and Aubrey contain anecdotes of a sort that would not have been thought worth recording a generation earlier. No Restoration writer, to be sure, explores the ranges of human personality as did the Elizabethan dramatists, but their representations were a work of poetry and fiction. The seventeenth century and particularly the Restoration pulled back the draperies of truth. If the dignity of God's image in his creature, man, suffers some impairment in the process, its rich complexity does not, and the nobler aspects of human nature stand out no less clearly amid the spotted actualities of the daily scene. This is obvious enough in the instances of domestic loyalty and love in the families of Sir Richard Fanshawe and Lady Russell, the integrity and public spirit of John Evelyn, the professional devotion of Dr. Thomson dissecting the body of a victim of the Plague, the unwavering endurance of religious persecution by Baxter, Fox and Bunyan. It is to be found also mixed with baser matter in personalities of whom history has recorded mainly the unworthiness. There are, for example, real patriotism and a capacity for unselfish affection in Charles II which belie the ordinary picture of him. And Samuel Pepys spent nine tenths of his time living a good, an honest and an efficient life which the journalistic featuring of his weaknesses obscures.

This book is not offered as a piece of edification, but edification may nevertheless be derived from it. The great thing is to take the world as it is without getting overexcited about it. It is easier to do this in retrospect. The issues of the past are still alive, but the fact that they wear another garb invites us to look at them with an outsider's eye. We are undisturbed even when the lineaments of personality in history seem very like our own. And this is not mere escape, for consciously or unconsciously we are measuring ourselves against them. At least, we are making some new and curious acquaintances in a world the same and not the same, and our pia maters are being a little expanded, presumably to their advantage. Our own immoralists are too busy with their immoralities and our own witch-hunters with their witch-hunting to read the sad story of Rochester's repentance or Titus Oates's whipping at cart's tail. But more reflective persons can ponder profitably on these things. If there is any general observation to be made, it is that while the pendulum of action swings back and forth and around meaninglessly enough, the written record becomes part of the cumulative and progressive experience of mankind.

Contents

II

THE EMPIRE OF LOVE

IV

OLD AND NEW SCIENCE

V

GRACE ABOUNDING

VI

HIC JACET

List of Illustrations

Acknowledgments

The editor wishes to express his gratitude for permission to reprint from:

Bell, Walter G., *The Great Plague in London in 1665* (The Bodley Head, London, 1951), excerpt from George Thomson's *Loimotomia* and a photostat of "Diseases and Casualties of the Week"

Bryant, Arthur, ed., *The Letters, Speeches and Declarations of Charles II* (Cassell & Company, Ltd., London, 1951), three letters to Clarendon, excerpts from three letters to Henrietta, and one letter to Prince Rupert

Clark, Evart Mordecai, ed., *English Literature: The Seventeenth Century* (Charles Scribner's Sons, Inc., New York, 1929), Charles Cotton's lyrics, excerpt from Thomas Ellwood's *Autobiography*, and Charles Sackville's "Song Written at Sea"

Coffin, R. P. T., and A. M. Witherspoon, eds., *A Book of Seventeenth-Century Prose* (Harcourt, Brace & Company, Inc., New York, 1929), excerpts from John Dryden's *Essay of Dramatic Poesy* and Sir William Temple's *Discourse of Health and Long Life*

Comfort, W. W., ed., *William Penn, Fruits of an Active Life* (Friends Book Store, Philadelphia, 1945), "Letter to the Indians" and "Prayer for Philadelphia"

Dobell, Bertram, ed., *Thomas Traherne, Centuries of Meditation* (Dobell, Ltd., London, 1948), excerpt

Moore, Cecil A., ed., *Restoration Literature, Poetry and Prose* (Appleton-Century-Crofts, Inc., New York, 1934), excerpts from Aphra Behn's *Oroonoko*; John Bunyan's *Grace Abounding*, Abraham Cowley's "Of Solitude"; John Dryden's "Absalom and Achitophel," "Alexander's Feast," "Anne Killegrew," "Astraea Redux" and "The Hind and the Panther"; Charles Sedley's lyrics; and John Wilmot's "Satire against Mankind"

————, *Twelve Famous Plays of the Restoration and Eighteenth Century* (Modern Library, Random House, Inc., New York, 1933), excerpts from William Congreve's *Love for Love* and *The Way of the World*, and William Wycherley's *The Country Wife*

Turner, Francis C., *James II* (Eyre & Spottiswoode, Ltd., London, 1948), Barillon's letter to Louis XIV

Wade, Gladys I., ed., *Thomas Traherne, Poetical Works* (Dobell, Ltd., London, 1932), "Wonder"

Wilson, John H., *Nell Gwyn: Royal Mistress* (Farrar, Strauss & Young, Inc., New York, 1952), letter to Lawrence Hyde, letter to Mrs. Francis Jennings

I *Chronicles of the Realm*

1 *Happy Return*

The return of Charles II, on May 26, 1660, was a signal for mad rejoicing. England was heartily sick of the confusion of the last days of the Puritan regime. A legitimate monarch and a re-established church seemed more desirable than all the hard-won freedoms, which turned out not to be such freedoms after all, and Charles's own policies and personality were such as to minimize the fears of all but the leaders of the Great Rebellion. Now was the time for all good men not too deeply dyed in collaboration to proclaim their loyalty. Now was the time for those who had suffered for the royal cause in mind, body or estate to present their claims. Now was the time for the sharers of Charles's poverty-stricken exile to smile in their long-awaited dignities and prepare to enjoy the benefits of power.

ANONYMOUS

The journey from Holland and the progress to London were the really important incidents in Charles's career, more memorable, even, than his coronation a year later. A contemporary writer reports them in the clumsy but effective pamphleteering manner of the day. Great hero of the occasion was the Lord General Monk, shortly to be made the Duke of Albemarle. His well-timed decision had forwarded the Restoration by many months and insured its taking place without a battle. Edward Montagu, like Monk a loyal instrument of Cromwell's victories, had also gone with the tide while there was yet time. He resigned his naval command, was promptly reinstated, escorted Charles to England and was rewarded by an earldom.

England's Joy

THE LANDING

Being come aboard one of the fairest of those ships which attended at Sluce for wafting him over from the Hague in Holland and therein having taken leave of his sister, the Princess royal, he set sail for

3

England on Wednesday evening, May 23rd, 1660. And having, during his abode at sea, given new names to that whole navy, consisting of twenty-six goodly vessels, he arrived at Dover on the Friday following, about two o'clock in the afternoon.

Ready on the shore to receive him stood the Lord General Monk, as also the Earl of Winchelsea, Constable of Dover Castle, with diverse persons of quality on the one hand, and the mayor of Dover, accompanied by his bretheren of that corporation, on the other, with a rich canopy. As soon as he had set foot on the shore the Lord General, presenting himself on his knee and kissing his royal hand, was embraced by his Majesty and received diverse gracious expressions of the great sense he had of his loyalty and in being so instrumental in his restoration. There also did the corporation of Dover and the Earl of Winchelsea do their duties to him in like sort, all the people making joyful shouts, the great guns from the ships and castle telling aloud the happy news of this entrance upon English ground.

THE ROAD TO LONDON

From Canterbury he came on Monday to Rochester, where the people had hung up over the midst of the streets, as he rode, many beautiful garlands, curiously made up with costly scarfs and ribbons, decked with spoons and bodkins of silver and small plate of various sorts, and some with gold chains in like sort as at Canterbury, each striving to outdo the other in all expressions of joy. On Tuesday, May 29th, which happily fell out to be his Majesty's birthday, he set forth from Rochester in his coach, but afterwards took horse on the farther side of Blackheath. On which spacious plain he found diverse great and eminent troops of horse in a most splendid and glorious equipage, and a kind of rural triumph expressed by the country swains in a morris dance with the old music of tabor and pipe, which was performed with all agility and cheerfulness imaginable.

THE HOME-COMING

In this magnificent fashion his Majesty entered the borough of Southwark about half past three o'clock in the afternoon and within an hour after, the City of London at the bridge, where he found the windows and streets exceedingly thronged with people to behold him and the wall adorned with hangings and carpets of tapestry and other costly stuff, and in many places sets of loud music, all the conduits, as he passed, running claret wine, and the several companies in their liveries, with the ensigns belonging to them. As also the trained bands of the city standing along the streets as he passed, welcoming him with loyal acclamations. And within the rails where Charing Cross formerly was, a stand of six hundred pikes, consisting of knights and gentlemen as had been officers in the armies of his late Majesty of blessed memory, the truly noble and valiant Sir John Stowell, Knight of the honorable order of the Bath, a person famous for his eminent actings and sufferings, being at the head of them.

From which place the citizens in velvet coats and gold chains being drawn up on each hand and diverse companies of foot soldiers, his Majesty passed between them and entered Whitehall at seven o'clock, the people making loud shouts and the horse and foot several volleys of shots at this his happy arrival. Where the House of Lords and Commons of Parliament received him and kissed his royal hand.

At the same time likewise the Reverend Bishops of Ely, Salisbury, Rochester, and Chichester in their episcopal habits, with diverse of the long oppressed orthodox clergy, met in the royal chapel of Henry the Seventh of Westminster and there sung Te Deum etc. in praise and thanks to Almighty God for his unspeakable mercy in the deliverance of his Majesty from many dangers and so happily restoring him to rule these kingdoms according to his just and undoubted right.

JOHN DRYDEN

Far beyond the sphere of mere journalism is the magnificent rhetoric with which John Dryden salutes the restored monarch and voices the common enthusiasm of the new age. It is a circumstance to be buried in oblivion that he has recently paid tribute to the dead Protector. Loyalty and patriotism of a happier sort well up in him. There is no reserve in his conviction that a golden age for England is at hand. He is later to learn that all is not gold that glitters and to bear a hand in beating back the old menace of rebellion in its successive forms. But to whatever use he puts his pen, whether to flatter or denounce or to illuminate and delight, he is the outstanding poet of the time. A friend of Milton and a sharer in the

*great tradition of English literature, he cares in the end more for art
than for politics. If he sometimes prostitutes the muse, he knows
how to make the noblest amends. The issues of the day are glorified
in his hands and a new standard set for the kind of writing which
is of its time and yet above it. The high moments of Dryden's long
career are represented in the succeeding pages. He had a living to
earn and he turned to the stage, as Shakespeare had done before
him, but his greatness is in the identification of his genius with a
cause—the cause at once of order and good sense, of loyalty to
established traditions of excellence in personality, art and institutions,
but also of freshness of expression and vitality of mind. He found
occasional poetry brick and left it marble. In the present passage he
gives voice to the hope of a united nation, great in the arts of peace,
but mighty enough to impose the Pax Britannica upon the world.
The allusion to Dutch aggression in the East suggests the dominant
commercial rivalry of the time, a rivalry which had already led to
one war and was to be the occasion of two more.*

Astraea Redux

And welcome now, great monarch, to your own!
Behold th' approaching cliffs of Albion.
It is no longer motion cheats your view;
As you meet it, the land approacheth you.
The land returns, and in the white it wears
The marks of penitence and sorrow bears.
But you, whose goodness your descent doth shew,
Your heav'nly parentage and earthly too,
By that same mildness which your father's crown
Before did ravish shall secure your own.
Not tied to rules of policy, you find
Revenge less sweet than a forgiving mind.
Thus, when th' Almighty would to Moses give
A sight of all he could behold and live,
A voice before His entry did proclaim
Long-suff'ring, goodness, mercy, in His name.
Your pow'r to justice doth submit your cause,
Your goodness only is above the laws,
Whose rigid letter, while pronounc'd by you,
Is softer made. So winds, that tempests brew,
When through Arabian groves they take their flight,
Made wanton with rich odors, lose their spite.

And as those lees that trouble it refine
The agitated soul of gen'rous wine,
So tears of joy, for your returning spilt,
Work out and expiate our former guilt.
Methinks I see those crowds on Dover's strand,
Who in their haste to welcome you to land
Chok'd up the beach with their still growing store
And made a wilder torrent on the shore:
While, spurr'd with eager thoughts of past delight,
Those who had seen you court a second sight,
Preventing still your steps and making haste
To meet you often, wheresoe'er you pass'd.
How shall I speak of that triumphant day
When you renew'd th' expiring pomp of May!
A month that owns an int'rest in your name;
You and the flow'rs are its peculiar claim.
That star that at your birth shone out so bright
It stain'd the duller sun's meridian light,
Did once again its potent fires renew,
Guiding our eyes to find and worship you.
   And now Time's whiter series is begun,
Which in soft centuries shall smoothly run;
Those clouds that overcast your morn shall fly,
Dispell'd to farthest corners of the sky.
Our nation, with united int'rest blest,
Not now content to poise, shall sway the rest.
Abroad your empire shall no limits know,
But, like the sea, in boundless circles flow;
Your much-lov'd fleet shall with a wide command
Besiege the petty monarchs of the land;
And as old Time his offspring swallow'd down,
Our ocean in its depths all seas shall drown.
Their wealthy trade from pirates' rapine free,
Our merchants shall no more advent'rers be;
Nor in the farthest East those dangers fear
Which humble Holland must dissemble here.
Spain to your gift alone her Indies owes,
For what the pow'rful takes not he bestows;
And France that did an exile's presence fear
May justly apprehend you still too near.
At home the hateful names of parties cease,

And factious souls are wearied into peace.
The discontented now are only they
Whose crimes before did your just cause betray:
Of those your edicts some reclaim from sins,
But most your life and blest example wins.
O happy Prince, whom Heav'n hath taught the way
By paying vows to have more vows to pay!
O happy age! O times like those alone
By fate reserv'd for great Augustus' throne,
When the joint growth of arms and arts foreshew
The world a monarch, and that monarch you!

SAMUEL PEPYS

The first years of Charles's reign were, in spite of many problems, prosperous sailing for the new regime. They were prosperous also for the young naval clerk, Samuel Pepys, who set down in shorthand from day to day the spicy record of what he had seen and done. His story begins just before the King's return, when Pepys was rejoicing in the bright prospects of his patron and employer, Sir Edward Montagu, later Earl of Sandwich, and ends in 1669, when failing eyesight compelled him to give up both his public office and his beloved journal. His appetite for life, his curiosity, his naïve egotism, half boastful and half furtive, and his increasing breadth of interest and contact make the diary one of the richest of all human documents. It may be read as the intimate confession of an individual or as the mirror of an age. Actually it is both. Pepys has something to say about almost every public event and personality. He is a creature of the life around him and his reactions give us the tone, the smell, of what is happening to society as no objective history could do. It would be a great mistake to accept his version as the only or even the most normal one. He is too emotional for that. His fellow diarist, John Evelyn, has more dignity and a better sense of values. But it is precisely the combination of the trivial and the important which makes the reportorial validity of Pepys.

The selections which follow cover the period before the great catastrophes of the middle '60s and before the more dramatic episodes in Pepys's personal life. They show him a bit dazed by the spectacles he is called on to witness but becoming rapidly at home in a world of new experiences. We shall hear from him again in other contexts.

The Year 1660

BLESSED be God, at the end of the last year I was in very good health, without any sense of my old pain, but upon taking of cold. I lived in Axe Yard, having my wife, and servant Jane, and no more in family than us three. My wife . . . gave me hopes of her being with child, but on the last day of the year . . . [the hope was belied].

The condition of the State was thus; viz. the Rump, after being disturbed by my Lord Lambert, was lately returned to sit again. The officers of the Army all forced to yield. Lawson lies still in the river, and Monk is with his army in Scotland. Only my Lord Lambert is not yet come into the Parliament, nor is it expected that he will without being forced to it. The new Common Council of the City do speak very high; and had sent to Monk their sword-bearer, to acquaint him with their desires for a free and full Parliament, which is at present the desires, and the hopes, and expectation of all. Twenty-two of the old secluded members having been at the House-door the last week to demand entrance, but it was denied them; and it is believed that [neither] they nor the people will be satisfied till the House be filled. My own private condition very handsome, and esteemed rich, but indeed very poor; besides my goods of my house, and my office, which at present is somewhat uncertain. Mr. Downing master of my office.

January 1 (Lord's day). This morning (we living lately in the garret,) I rose, put on my suit with great skirts, having not lately worn any other clothes but them. Went to Mr. Gunning's chapel at Exeter House, where he made a very good sermon upon these words:—"That in the fulness of time God sent his Son, made of a woman," &c.; showing, that, by "made under the law," is meant his circumcision, which is solemnized this day. Dined at home in the garret, where my wife dressed the remains of a turkey, and in the doing of it she burned her hand.

January 26. Home from my office to my Lord's lodgings where my wife had got ready a very fine dinner—viz. a dish of marrow bones; a leg of mutton; a loin of veal; a dish of fowl, three pullets, and two dozen of larks all in a dish; a great tart, a neat's tongue, a dish of anchovies; a dish of prawns and cheese. . . . The news this day is a letter that speaks absolutely Monk's concurrence with this Parliament, and nothing else, which yet I hardly believe.

January 30. This morning, before I was up, I fell a-singing of my song, "Great, good, and just," &c. and put myself thereby in mind that this was the fatal day, now ten years since, his Majesty died. Scull the waterman came and brought me a note from the Hope from Mr. Hawly with direction, about his money, he tarrying there till his master be gone. To my office, where I received money of the excise of Mr. Ruddyer, and after we had done went to Will's and staid there till 3 o'clock and then I taking my £12 10s. od. due to me for my last quarter's salary, I went with them by water to London to the house where Sign^r Torriano used to be and staid there awhile with Mr. Ashwell, Spicer and Ruddier. Then I went and paid £12 17s. 6d. due from me to Captn Dick Matthews according to his direction the last week in a letter. After that I came back by water playing on my flageolette and not finding my wife come home again from her father's I went and sat awhile and played at cards with Mrs. Jem, whose maid had newly got an ague and was ill thereupon. So homewards again, having great need to do my business, and so pretending to meet Mr. Shott the wood monger of Whitehall I went and eased myself at the Harp and Ball, and thence home where I sat writing till bed-time and so to bed. There seems now to be a general cease of talk, it being taken for granted that Monk do resolve to stand to the Parliament, and nothing else. Spent a little time this night in knocking up nails for my hat and cloaks in my chamber.

March 3. To Westminster Hall, where I found that my Lord was last night voted one of the Generals at Sea, and Monk the other. I met my Lord in the Hall, who bid me come to him at noon. . . . Then I, by coach with my Lord, to Mr. Crew's, in our way talking of public things, and how I should look after getting of his Commissioner's despatch. . . . Returning, met Mr. Gifford, who took me and gave me half a pint of wine, and told me, as I hear this day from many, that things are in a very doubtful posture, some of the Parliament being willing to keep the power in their hands. After I had left him, I met with Tom Harper, who took me into a place in Drury Lane, where we drank a great deal of strong water, more than ever I did in my life at one time before. He talked huge high that my Lord Protector would come in place again, which indeed is much discoursed of again, though I do not see it possible.

March 6 (Shrove Tuesday). I called Mr. Sheply and we both

went up to my Lord's lodgings at Mr. Crew's, where he bade us to
go home again, and get a fire against an hour after. Which we
did at White Hall, whither he came, and after talking with him and
me about his going to sea, he called me by myself to go along with
him into the garden, where he asked me how things were with me,
and what he had endeavoured to do with my uncle to get him to do
something for me, but he would say nothing too. He likewise bade
me look out now at his turn some good place, and he would use all
his own, and all the interest of his friends that he had in England,
to do me good. And asked me whether I could, without too much
inconvenience, go to sea as his secretary, and bid me think of it.
He also began to talk things of State, and told me that he should
want one in that capacity at sea, that he might trust in, and therefore he would have me to go. He told me also, that he did believe
the King would come in, and did discourse with me about it, and
about the affection of the people and City, at which I was full glad.
After he was gone, I waiting upon him through the garden till he
came to the Hall, where I left him and went up to my office, where
Mr. Hawly brought one to me, a seaman, that had promised £10
to him if he get him a purser's place, which I think to endeavour
to do. Here comes my uncle Tom, whom I took to Will's and
drank with, poor man, he comes to inquire about the knights of
Windsor, of which he desires to get to be one. While we were
drinking, in comes Mr. Day, a carpenter in Westminster, to tell me
that it was Shrove Tuesday, and that I must go with him to their
yearly Club upon this day, which I confess I had quite forgot. So I
went to the Bell, where were Mr. Eglin, Veezy, Vincent a butcher,
one more, and Mr. Tanner, with whom I played upon a viall, and
he a viallin, after dinner, and were very merry, with a special good
dinner, a leg of veal and bacon, two capons and sausages and fritters,
with abundance of wine. After that I went home, where I found
Kate Sterpin who hath not been here a great while before. She gone
I went to see Mrs. Jem, at whose chamber door I found a couple of
ladies, but she not being there, we hunted her out, and found that
she and another had hid themselves behind a door. Well, they all
went down into the dining-room, where it was full of tag, rag, and
bobtail, dancing, singing, and drinking, of which I was ashamed, and
after I had staid a dance or two I went away. . . .

My Lord told me, that there was great endeavours to bring in the
Protector again; but he told me, too, that he did believe it would
not last long if he were brought in; no, nor the King neither (though

he seems to think that he will come in), unless he carry himself
very soberly and well. Every body now drinks the King's health
without any fear, whereas before it was very private that a man dare
do it. Monk this day is feasted at Mercers' Hall, and is invited one
after another to all the twelve Halls in London. Many think that
he is honest yet, and some or more think him to be a fool that
would raise himself, but think that he will undo himself by endeavouring it. My mind, I must needs remember, has been very
much eased and joyed at my Lord's great expressions of kindness
this day, and in discourse thereupon my wife and I lay awake an
hour or two in our bed.

March 8. This noon I met at the Dog tavern Captain Philip
Holland, with whom I advised how to make some advantage of my
Lord's going to sea, which he told me might be by having of five
or six servants entered on board, and I to give them what wages I
pleased, and so their pay to be mine; he was also very urgent to
have me take the Secretary's place, that my Lord did proffer me.

April 8 (Lord's day). Very calm again, and I pretty well, but my
head aked all day. About noon set sail; in our way I see many
vessels and masts, which are now the greatest guides for ships. We
had a brave wind all the afternoon, and overtook two good mer-
chantmen that overtook us yesterday, going to the East Indies. The
lieutenant and I lay out of his window with his glass, looking at the
women that were on board them, being pretty handsome. This
evening Major Willoughby, who had been here three or four days
on board with Mr. Pickering, went on board a catch for Dunkirk.
We continued sailing when I went to bed, being somewhat ill again,
and Will Howe, the surgeon, parson, and Balty supped in the Lieutenant's cabin and afterwards sat disputing, the parson for and I
against extempory prayers, very hot.

May 16. Soon as I was up I went down to be trimmed below in
the great cabin, but then come in some with visits, among the rest
one from Admiral Opdam, who spoke Latin well, but not French
nor English, to whom my Lord made me to give his answer and to
entertain; he brought my Lord a tierce of wine and a barrel of
butter, as a present from the Admiral. After that to finish my trim-
ming, and while I was doing of it in comes Mr. North very sea-sick
from shore, and to bed he goes. After that to dinner, where Commissioner Pett was come to take care to get all things ready for the
King on board. My Lord in his best suit, this the first day, in expectation to wait upon the King. But Mr. Edw. Pickering coming

from the King brought word that the King would not put my Lord
to the trouble of coming to him; but that he would come to the
shore to look upon the fleet to-day, which we expected, and had our
guns ready to fire, and our scarlet waistcloathes out and silk pend-
ants, but he did not come. My Lord and we at ninepins this afternoon upon the Quarter-deck, which was very pretty sport. This
evening came Mr. John Pickering on board, like an ass, with his
feathers and new suit that he had made at the Hague. My Lord very
angry for his staying on shore, bidding me a little before to send to
him, telling me that he was afraid that for his father's sake he might
have some mischief done him, unless he used the General's name.
To supper, and after supper to cards. I stood by and looked on till
11 at night and so to bed. This afternoon Mr. Edwd. Pickering told
me in what a sad, poor condition for clothes and money the king
was, and all his attendants, when he came to him first from my
Lord, their clothes not being worth forty shillings the best of them.
And how overjoyed the King was when Sir J. Greenville brought
him some money; so joyful, that he called the Princess Royal and
Duke of York to look upon it as it lay in the portmanteau before
it was taken out. My Lord told me, too, that the Duke of York is
made High Admiral of England.

May 23. In the morning came infinity of people on board from
the King to go along with him. My Lord, Mr. Crew, and others, go
on shore to meet the King as he comes off from shore, where Sir
R. Stayner bringing His Majesty into the boat, I hear that His
Majesty did with a great deal of affection kiss my Lord upon his
first meeting. The King, with the two Dukes and Queen of Bo-
hemia, Princess Royal, and Prince of Orange, came on board, where
I in their coming in kissed the King's Queen's, and Princess's hands,
having done the other before. Infinite shooting off of the guns, and
that in a disorder on purpose, which was better than if it had been
otherwise. All day nothing but Lords and persons of honour on
board, that we were exceeding full. Dined in a great deal of state,
the Royall company by themselves in the coach, which was a blessed
sight to see. . . . After dinner the King and Duke altered the name
of some of the ships, viz. the Nazeby into Charles; the Richard,
James; the Speaker, Mary; the Dunbar (which was not in company
with us), the Henry; Winsly, Happy Return; Wakefield, Richmond;
Lambert, the Henrietta; Cheriton, the Speedwell; Bradford, the
Success. That done, the Queen, Princess Royal, and Prince of
Orange, took leave of the King, and the Duke of York went on

board the London, and the Duke of Gloucester, the Swiftsure. Which done, we weighed anchor, and with a fresh gale and most happy weather we set sail for England. All the afternoon the King walked here and there, up and down (quite contrary to what I thought him to have been), very active and stirring. Upon the quarter-deck he fell into discourse of his escape from Worcester, where it made me ready to weep to hear the stories that he told of his difficulties that he had passed through. . . . In the evening I went up to my Lord to write letters for England, which we sent away with word of our coming, by Mr. Edw. Pickering. The King supped alone in the coach; after that I got a dish, and we four supped in my cabin, as at noon. About bed-time my Lord Bartlett (who I had offered my service to before) sent for me to get him a bed, who with much ado I did get to bed to my Lord Middlesex in the great cabin below, but I was cruelly troubled before I could dispose of him, and quit myself of him. So to my cabin again, where the company still was, and were talking more of the King's difficulties; as how he was fain to eat a piece of bread and cheese out of a poor boy's pocket; how, at a Catholique house, he was fain to lie in the priest's hole a good while in the house for his privacy. After that our company broke up, and the Doctor and I to bed. We have all the Lords Commissioners on board us, and many others. Under sail all night, and most glorious weather.

May 25. By the morning we were come close to the land, and every body made ready to get on shore. The King and the two Dukes did eat their breakfast before they went, and there being set some ship's diet before them, only to show them the manner of the ship's diet, they eat of nothing else but pease and pork, and boiled beef. I had Mr. Darcy in my cabin and Dr. Clerke, who eat with me, told me how the King had given £50 to Mr. Sheply for my Lord's servants, and £500 among the officers and common men of the ship. I spoke with the Duke of York about business, who called me Pepys by name, and upon my desire did promise me his future favour. Great expectation of the King's making some Knights, but there was none. About noon (though the brigantine that Beal made was there ready to carry him) yet he would go in my Lord's barge with the two Dukes. Our Captain steered, and my Lord went along bare with him. I went, and Mr. Mansell, and one of the King's footmen, and a dog that the King loved, in a boat by ourselves, and so got on shore when the King did, who was received by General Monk with all imaginable love and respect at his entrance upon the land at Dover.

July 15. Lay long in bed to recover my rest. Going forth met with Mr. Sheply, and went and drank my morning draft with him at Wilkinson's, and my brother Spicer. After that to Westminster Abbey, and in Henry the Seventh's Chappell heard part of a sermon, the first that ever I heard there. To my Lord's and dined all alone at the table with him. After dinner he and I alone fell to discourse, and I find him plainly to be a sceptic in all things of religion, and to make no great matter of anything therein, but to be a perfect Stoic.

October 7. To my Lord's and dined with him; he all dinner time talking French to me, and telling me the story how the Duke of York hath got my Lord Chancellor's daughter with child, and that she do lay it to him, and that for certain he did promise her marriage, and had signed it with his blood, but that he by stealth had got the paper out of her cabinet. And that the King would have him to marry her, but that he will not. So that the thing is very bad for the Duke, and them all; but my Lord do make light of it, as a thing that he believes is not a new thing for the Duke to do abroad. Discoursing concerning what if the Duke should marry her, my Lord told me that among his father's many old sayings that he had wrote in a book of his, this is one—that he that do get a wench with child and marry her afterwards is as if a man should——in his hat and then clap it on his head. I perceive my Lord is grown a man very indifferent in all matters of religion, and so makes nothing of these things.

October 10. Office day all the morning. In the afternoon with the upholster seeing him do things to my mind, and to my content he did fit my chamber and my wife's. At night comes Mr. Moore, and staid late with me to tell me how Sir Hards. Waller (who only pleads guilty), Scott, Coke, Peters, Harrison, &c. were this day arraigned at the bar at the Sessions House, there being upon the bench the Lord Mayor, General Monk, my Lord of Sandwich, &c.; such a bench of noblemen as had not been ever seen in England! They all seem to be dismayed, and will all be condemned without question. In Sir Orlando Bridgman's charge, he did wholly rip up the unjustness of the war against the King from the beginning, and so it much reflects upon all the Long Parliament, though the King had pardoned them, yet they must hereby confess that the

King do look upon them as traitors. To-morrow they are to plead
what they have to say. At night to bed.

October 13. To my Lord's in the morning, where I met with Captain Cuttance, but my Lord not being up I went out to Charing
Cross, to see Major-general Harrison hanged, drawn, and quartered;
which was done there, he looking as cheerful as any man could do
in that condition. He was presently cut down, and his head and
heart shown to the people, at which there was great shouts of joy.
It is said, that he said that he was sure to come shortly at the right
hand of Christ to judge them that now had judged him; and that
his wife do expect his coming again. Thus it was my chance to see
the King beheaded at White Hall, and to see the first blood shed
in revenge for the blood of the King at Charing Cross. From thence
to my Lord's, and took Captain Cuttance and Mr. Sheply to the
Sun Tavern, and did give them some oysters. After that I went by
water home, where I was angry with my wife for her things lying
about, and in my passion kicked the little fine basket, which I
bought her in Holland, and broke it, which troubled me after I had
done it. Within all the afternoon setting up shelves in my study. At
night to bed.

October 14 (Lord's day). Early to my Lord's, in my way meeting
with Dr. Fairbrother, who walked with me to my father's back
again, and there we drank my morning draft, my father having gone
to church and my mother asleep in bed. Here he caused me to put
my hand among a great many honorable hands to a paper or certificate in his behalf. To White Hall chappell, where one Dr. Crofts
made an indifferent sermon, and after it an anthem, ill sung, which
made the King laugh. Here I first did see the Princess Royal since
she came into England. Here I also observed, how the Duke of
York and Mrs. Palmer did talk to one another very wantonly
through the hangings that parts the King's closet and the closet
where the ladies sit.

October 20. To my Lord's by land, calling at several places about
business, where I dined with my Lord and Lady; when he was very
merry, and did talk very high how he would have a French cook,
and a master of his horse, and his lady and child to wear black
patches; which methought was strange, but he is become a perfect
courtier; and, among other things, my Lady saying that she could
get a good merchant for her daughter Jem., he answered, that he
would rather see her with a pedlar's pack at her back, so she married

a gentleman, than she should marry a citizen. This afternoon, going through London, and calling at Crowe's the upholster's, in Saint Bartholomew's, I saw the limbs of some of our new traitors set upon Aldersgate, which was a sad sight to see; and a bloody week this and the last have been, there being ten hanged, drawn, and quartered. Home, and after writing a letter to my uncle by the post, I went to bed.

November 4 (Lord's day). In the morn to our own church, where Mr. Mills did begin to nibble at the Common Prayer, by saying "Glory be to the Father, &c." after he had read the two psalms; but the people had been so little used to it, that they could not tell what to answer. This declaration of the King's do give the Presbyterians some satisfaction, and a pretence to read the Common Prayer, which they would not do before because of their former preaching against it. After dinner to Westminster, where I went to my Lord's, and having spoke with him, I went to the Abbey, where the first time that ever I heard the organs in a cathedral.

November 22. This morning came the carpenters to make me a door at the other side of my house, going into the entry, which I was much pleased with. At noon my wife and I walked to the Old Exchange, and there she bought her a white whisk and put it on, and I a pair of gloves, and so we took coach for Whitehall to Mr. Fox's, where we found Mrs. Fox within, and an alderman of London paying £1,000 or £1,400 in gold upon the table for the King, which was the most gold that ever I saw together in my life. Mr. Fox came in presently and did receive us with a great deal of respect; and then did take my wife and I to the Queen's presence-chamber, where he got my wife placed behind the Queen's chair, and I got into the crowd, and by and by the Queen and the two Princesses came to dinner. The Queen a very little plain old woman, and nothing more in her presence in any respect nor garb than any ordinary woman. The Princess of Orange I had often seen before. The Princess Henrietta is very pretty, but much below my expectation; and her dressing of herself with her hair frized short up to her ears, did make her seem so much the less to me. But my wife standing near her with two or three black patches on, and well dressed, did seem to me much handsomer than she.

December 4. This day the Parliament voted that the bodies of Oliver, Ireton, Bradshaw, &c., should be taken up out of their graves in the Abbey, and drawn to the gallows, and there hanged and buried under it: which (methinks) do trouble me that a man of so great courage as he was, should have that dishonour, though otherwise he might deserve it enough.

The Year 1661

January 7. This morning, news was brought to me to my bedside, that there had been a great stir in the City this night by the Fanatiques, who had been up and killed six or seven men, but all are fled. My Lord Mayor and the whole City had been in arms, above 40,000.

January 9. Waked in the morning about six o'clock, by people running up and down in Mr. Davis's house, talking that the Fanatiques were up in arms in the City. And so I rose and went forth; where in the street I found every body in arms at the doors. So I returned (though with no good courage at all, but that I might not seem to be afeared), and got my sword and pistol, which, however, I had no powder to charge; and went to the door, where I found Sir R. Ford, and with him I walked up and down as far as the Exchange, and there I left him. In our way, the streets full of Train-band, and great stories, what mischief these rogues have done; and I think near a dozen have been killed this morning on both sides. Seeing the city in this condition, the shops shut, and all things in trouble, I went home and sat, it being office day, till noon.

January 10. Among other things Mr. Davis told us the particular examinations of these Fanatiques that are taken: and in short it is this, of all these Fanatiques that have done all this, viz., routed all the Train-bands that they met with, put the King's lifeguards to the run, killed about twenty men, broke through the City gates twice; and all this in the day-time, when all the City was in arms; —are not in all about 31. Whereas we did believe them (because they were seen up and down in every place almost in the City, and had been about Highgate two or three days, and in several other places) to be at least 500. A thing that was never heard of, that so few men should dare and do so much mischief. Their word was, "The King Jesus, and the heads upon the gates." Few of them would receive any quarter, but such as were taken by force and kept alive; expecting Jesus to come here and reign in the world presently, and will not believe yet but their work will be carried on though they do die. The King this day came to town.

January 19. To the Comptroller's, and with him by coach to White Hall; in our way meeting Venner and Pritchard upon a sledge, who with two more Fifth Monarchy men were hanged to-day, and the two first drawn and quartered.

April 23 (Coronation Day). About 4 I rose and got to the Abbey, where I followed Sir J. Denham, the Surveyor, with some company that he was leading in. And with much ado, by the favour of Mr. Cooper, his man, did get up into a great scaffold across the North end of the Abbey, where with a great deal of patience I sat from past 4 till 11 before the King came in. And a great pleasure it was to see the Abbey raised in the middle, all covered with red, and a throne (that is a chair) and footstool on the top of it; and all the officers of all kinds, so much as the very fidlers, in red vests. At last comes in the Dean and Prebends of Westminster, with the Bishops (many of them in cloth of gold copes), and after them the Nobility, all in their Parliament robes, which was a most magnificent sight. Then the Duke, and the King with a scepter (carried by my Lord Sandwich) and sword and mond before him, and the crown too. The King in his robes, bare-headed, which was very fine. And after all had placed themselves, there was a sermon and the service; and then in the Quire at the high altar, the King passed through all the ceremonies of the Coronačon, which to my great grief I and most in the Abbey could not see. The crown being put upon his head, a great shout begun, and he came forth to the throne, and there passed more ceremonies: as taking the oath, and having things read to him by the Bishop; and his lords (who put on their caps as soon as the King put on his crown) and bishops come, and kneeled before him. And three times the King at Arms went to the three open places on the scaffold, and proclaimed, that if any one could show any reason why Charles Stewart should not be King of England, that now he should come and speak. And a Generall Pardon also was read by the Lord Chancellor, and meddalls flung up and down by my Lord Cornwallis, of silver, but I could not come by any. But so great a noise that I could make but little of the musique; and indeed, it was lost to every body. But I had so great a lust to . . . that I went out a little while before the King had done all his ceremonies, and went round the Abbey to Westminster Hall, all the way within rayles, and 10,000 people, with the ground covered with blue cloth; and scaffolds all the way. Into the Hall I got, where it was very fine with hangings and scaffolds one upon another full of brave ladies; and my wife in one little one, on the

right hand. Here I staid walking up and down, and at last upon one
of the side stalls I stood and saw the King come in with all the
persons (but the soldiers) that were yesterday in the cavalcade; and
a most pleasant sight it was to see them in their several robes. And
the King came in with his crown on, and his sceptre in his hand,
under a canopy borne up by six silver staves, carried by Barons
of the Cinque Ports, and little bells at every end. And after a long
time, he got up to the farther end, and all set themselves down at
their several tables; and that was also a brave sight: and the King's
first course carried up by the Knights of the Bath. And many fine
ceremonies there was of the Heralds leading up people before him,
and bowing; and my Lord of Albemarle's going to the kitchin and
eat a bit of the first dish that was to go to the King's table. But,
above all, was these three Lords, Northumberland, and Suffolk, and
the Duke of Ormond, coming before the courses on horseback, and
staying so all dinner-time, and at last to bring up [Dymock] the
King's Champion, all in armour on horseback, with his spear and
targett carried before him. And a Herald proclaims "That if any
dare deny Charles Stewart to be lawful King of England, here was
a Champion that would fight with him;" and with these words, the
Champion flings down his gauntlet, and all this he do three times in
his going up towards the King's table. At last when he is come, the
King drinks to him, and then sends him the cup which is of gold,
and he drinks it off, and then rides back again with the cup in his
hand. I went from table to table to see the Bishops and all others
at their dinner, and was infinitely pleased with it. And at the Lord's
table, I met with William Howe, and he spoke to my Lord for me,
and he did give me four rabbits and a pullet, and so I got it and
Mr. Creed and I got Mr. Michell to give us some bread, and so we
at a stall eat it, as every body else did what they could get. I took a
great deal of pleasure to go up and down, and look upon the ladies,
and to hear the musique of all sorts, but above all, the 24 violins.
About six at night they had dined, and I went up to my wife, and
there met with a pretty lady (Mrs. Frankleyn, a Doctor's wife, a
friend of Mr. Bowyer's), and kissed them both, and by and by took
them down to Mr. Bowyer's. And strange it is to think, that these
two days have held up fair till now that all is done, and the King
gone out of the Hall; and then it fell a-raining and thundering and
lightening as I have not seen it do for some years: which people did
take great notice of; God's blessing of the work of these two days,
which is a foolery to take too much notice of such things. I observed

little disorder in all this, but only the King's footmen had got hold of the canopy, and would keep it from the Barons of the Cinque Ports, which they endeavoured to force from them again, but could not do it till my Lord Duke of Albemarle caused it to be put into Sir R. Pye's hand till tomorrow to be decided. At Mr. Bowyer's; a great deal of company, some I knew, others I did not. Here we staid upon the leads and below till it was late, expecting to see the fire-works, but they were not performed to-night: only the City had a light like a glory round about it with bonfires. At last I went to King-street, and there sent Crockford to my father's and my house, to tell them I could not come home to-night, because of the dirt, and a coach could not be had. And so after drinking a pot of ale alone at Mrs. Harper's I returned to Mr. Bowyer's, and after a little stay more I took my wife and Mrs. Frankleyn (who I proffered the civility of lying with my wife at Mrs. Hunt's to-night) to Axe-yard, in which at the further end there were three great bonfires, and a great many great gallants, men and women; and they laid hold of us, and would have us drink the King's health upon our knees, kneeling upon a faggot, which we all did, they drinking to us one after another. Which we thought a strange frolique; but these gallants continued thus a great while, and I wondered to see how the ladies did tipple. Thus did the day end with joy every where; and blessed be God, I have not heard of any mischance to any body through it all, but only to Serj.^t Glynne, whose horse fell upon him yesterday, and is like to kill him, which people do please themselves to see how just God is to punish the rogue at such a time as this; he being now one of the King's Serjeants, and rode in the caval-cade with Maynard, to whom people wish the same misfortune. There was also this night in King-Street, a woman had her eye put out by a boy's flinging a firebrand into the coach. Now, after all this, I can say that, besides the pleasure of the sight of these glorious things, I may now shut my eyes against any other objects, nor for the future trouble myself to see things of state and show, as being sure never to see the like again in this world.

The Year 1662

April 6 (Lord's day). By water to White Hall. Thence to the Chappell, and there, though crowded, heard a very honest sermon before the King by a Canon of Christ Church, upon these words,

"Having a form of goodliness, but denying," &c. Among other things, did much insist upon the sin of adultery: which methought might touch the King, and the more because he forced it into his sermon, methinks, besides his text. So up and saw the King at dinner.

May 15. At night, all the bells of the town rung, and bonfires made for the joy of the Queen's arrival, who came and landed at Portsmouth last night. But I do not see much thorough joy, but only an indifferent one, in the hearts of people, who are much discontented at the pride and luxury of the Court, and running in debt.

June 14. Up by four o'clock in the morning and up on business at my office. Then we sat down to business, and about 11 o'clock, having a room got ready for us, we all went out to the Tower-hill; and there, over against the scaffold, made on purpose this day, saw Sir Henry Vane brought. A very great press of people. He made a long speech, many times interrupted by the Sheriff and others there; and they would have taken his paper out of his hand but he would not let it go. But they caused all the books of those that writ after him to be given the Sheriff; and the trumpets were brought under the scaffold that he might not be heard. Then he prayed, and so fitted himself, and received the blow; but the scaffold was so crowded that we could not see it done. But Boreman, who had been upon the scaffold, came to us and told us, that first he began to speak of the irregular proceeding against him; that he was, against the Magna Charta, denied to have his exceptions against the indictment allowed; and that there he was stopped by the Sheriff. Then he drew out his paper of notes, and begun to tell them first his life; that he was born a gentleman, that he was bred up and had the quality of a gentleman, and to make him in the opinion of the world more a gentleman, he had been, till he was seventeen years old, a good fellow, but then it pleased God to lay a foundation of grace in his heart, by which he was persuaded, against his worldly interest, to leave all preferment and go abroad, where he might serve God with more freedom. Then he was called home, and made a member of the Long Parliament; where he never did, to this day, any thing against his conscience, but all for the glory of God. Here he would have given them an account of the proceedings of the Long Parliament, but they so often interrupted him, that at last he was forced to give over: and so fell into prayer for England in generall, then for the churches in England, and then for the

City of London: and so fitted himself for the block, and received the blow. He had a blister, or issue, upon his neck, which he desired them not hurt: he changed not his colour or speech to the last, but died justifying himself and the cause he had stood for; and spoke very confidently of his being presently at the right hand of Christ; and in all things appeared the most resolved man that ever died in that manner, and showed more heat than cowardize, but yet with all humility and gravity. One asked him why he did not pray for the King. He answered, "Nay," says he, "you shall see I can pray for the King: I pray God bless him!" The King had given his body to his friends; and, therefore, he told them that he hoped they would be civil to his body when dead; and desired they would let him die like a gentleman and a Christian, and not crowded and pressed as he was.

July 16. This day I was told that my Lady Castlemaine (being quite fallen out with her husband) did yesterday go away from him, with all her plate, jewels, and other best things; and is gone to Richmond to a brother of her's; which, I am apt to think, was a design to get out of town, that the King might come at her the better. But strange it is how for her beauty I am willing to construe all this to the best and to pity her wherein it is to her hurt, though I know well enough she is a whore.

September 7. Here I also saw Madam Castlemaine, and, which pleased me most, Mr. Crofts, the King's bastard, a most pretty spark of about 15 years old, who, I perceive, do hang much upon my Lady Castlemaine, and is always with her; and I hear, the Queens, both of them are mighty kind to him. By and by in comes the King, and anon the Duke and his Duchess; so that, they being all together, was such a sight as I never could almost have happened to see with so much ease and leisure. They staid till it was dark, and then went away; the King and his Queen, and my Lady Castlemaine and young Crofts, in one coach and the rest in other coaches. Here were great store of great ladies, but very few handsome. The King and Queen were very merry; and he would have made the Queen-Mother believe that his Queen was with child, and said that she said so. And the young Queen answered, "You lye;" which was the first English word that I ever heard her say: which made the King good sport; and he would have taught her to say in English, "Confess and be hanged."

September 21 (Lord's day). The Queen coming by in her coach, going to her chappell at St. James's (the first time it hath been ready for her), I crowded after her, and I got up to the room where her closet is; and there stood and saw the fine altar, ornaments, and the fryers in their habits, and the priests come in with their fine copes and many other very fine things. I heard their musique too; which may be good, but it did not appear so to me, neither as to their manner of singing, nor was it good concord to my ears, whatever the matter was. The Queene very devout: but what pleased me best was to see my dear Lady Castlemaine, who, tho' a Protestant, did wait upon the Queen to chappell. By and by, after mass was done, a fryer with his cowl did rise up and preach a sermon in Portuguese; which I not understanding, did go away, and to the King's chappell.

December 31. Thence merry back, Mr. Povy and I, to White Hall; he carrying me thither on purpose to carry me into the ball this night before the King. All the way he talking very ingeniously, and I find him a fine gentleman, and one that loves to live nobly and neatly, as I perceive by his discourse of his house, pictures, and horses. He brought me first to the Duke's chamber, where I saw him and the Duchess at supper; and thence into the room where the ball was to be, crammed with fine ladies, the greatest of the Court. By and by comes the King and Queen, the Duke and Duchess and all the great ones; and after seating themselves, the King takes out the Duchess of York; and the Duke, the Duchess of Buckingham; the Duke of Monmouth, my Lady Castlemaine; and so other lords other ladies; and they danced the Bransle. After that, the King led a lady a single Coranto; and then the rest of the lords, one after another, other ladies; very noble it was, and great pleasure to see. Then to country dances; the King leading the first, which he called for; which was, says he, "Cuckolds all awry," the old dance of England. Of the ladies that danced, the Duke of Monmouth's mistress, and my Lady Castlemaine, and a daughter of Sir Harry de Vicke's, were the best. The manner was, when the King dances, all the ladies in the room, and the Queen herself, stand up; and indeed he dances rarely, and much better than the Duke of York.

Thus ends this year with great mirth to me and my wife. Our condition being thus:—we are at present spending a night or two at my Lord's lodgings at White Hall. Our home at the Navy office, which is and hath a pretty while been in good condition, finished and made very convenient. My purse is worth about £650, besides my goods of all sorts, which yet might have been more but for my late layings out upon my house and public assessment, and yet would not have been so much if I had not lived a very orderly life all this year by virtue of the oaths that God put into my heart to take against wine, plays, and other expenses, and to observe for these last twelve months, and which I am now going to renew, I under God owing my present content thereunto. My family is myself and wife, William, my clerk; Jane, my wife's upper mayde, but, I think, growing proud and negligent upon it: we must part, which troubles me; Susan, our cook-mayde, a pretty willing wench, but no good cook; and Wayneman, my boy, who I am now turning away for his naughty tricks. We have had from the beginning our healths to this day, very well, blessed be God! Publique matters stand thus: The King is bringing, as is said, his family, and Navy, and all other his charges, to a less expence. In the mean time, himself following his pleasures more than with good advice he would do; at least, to be seen to all the world to do so. His dalliance with my Lady Castlemaine being publique, every day, to his great reproach; and his favouring of none at Court so much as those that are the confidants of his pleasure, as Sir H. Bennet and Sir Charles Barkeley; which, good God! put it into his heart to mend, before he makes himself too much contemned by his people for it! The Duke of Monmouth is in so great splendour at Court, and so dandled by the King, that some doubt, if the King should have no child by the Queen (which there is yet no appearance of), whether he would not be acknowledged for a lawful son; and that there will be a difference follow upon it between the Duke of York and him; which God prevent! My Lord Chancellor is threatened by people to be questioned, the next sitting of the Parliament, by some spirits that do not love to see him so great; but certainly he is a good servant to the King. My Lord Sandwich is still in good esteem, and now keeping his Christmas in the country; and I in good esteem, I think, as any man can be, with him. In fine, for the good condition of myself, wife, family, and estate, in the great degree that it is, and for the public state of the nation, so quiett as it is, the Lord God be praised!

The Year 1663

May 15. After dinner I went up to Sir Thomas Crew, who lies there not very well in his head, being troubled with vapours and fits of dizziness: and there I sat talking with him all the afternoon from one discourse to another, the most was upon the unhappy posture of things at this time; that the King do mind nothing but pleasures, and hates the very sight or thoughts of business; that my Lady Castlemaine rules him, who, he says, hath all the tricks of Aretin that are to be practised to give pleasure. In which he is too able . . . , but what is the unhappiness is that, as the Italian proverb says, "lazzo dritto non vuolt consiglio." If any of the sober counsellors give him good advice, and move him in anything that is to his good and honour, the other part, which are his counsellers of pleasure, take him when he is with my Lady Castlemaine, and in a humour of delight, and then persuade him that he ought not to hear nor listen to the advice of those old dotards or counsellors that were heretofore his enemies: when, God knows! it is they that now-a-days do most study his honour. It seems the present favourites now are my Lord Bristol, Duke of Buckingham, Sir H. Bennet, my Lord Ashley, and Sir Charles Barkeley; who, among them, have cast my Lord Chancellor upon his back, past ever getting up again. . . . It is made very doubtful whether the King do not intend the making of the Duke of Monmouth legitimate; but surely the Commons of England will never do it, nor the Duke of York suffer it, whose lady, I am told, is very troublesome to him by her jealousy.

October 27. Mr. Coventry tells me to-day that the Queen had a very good night last night; but yet it is strange that still she raves and talks of little more than of her having of children, and fancys now that she hath three children, and that the girle is very like the King. And this morning about five o'clock waked (the physician feeling her pulse, thinking to be better able to judge, she being still and asleep, waked her) and the first word she said was, "How do the children?"

November 9. Thence to Westminster Hall, where I met with Mr. Pierce, chyrurgeon; and among other things he asked me seriously whether I knew anything of my Lord's being out of favour with the King; and told me, that for certain the King do take mighty notice of my Lord's living obscurely in a corner not like himself, and becoming the honour that he is come to. I was sorry to hear, and the truth is, from my Lord's discourse among his people (which I am told) of the uncertainty of princes' favours, and his melancholy keeping from Court, I am doubtful of some such thing; but I seemed wholly strange to him in it, but will make my use of it. He told me also how loose the Court is, nobody looking after business, but every man his lust and gain; and how the King is now become besotted upon Mrs. Stewart, that he gets into corners, and will be with her half an houre together kissing her to the observation of all the world; and she now stays by herself and expects it, as my Lady Castlemaine did use to do; to whom the King, he says, is still kind, so as now and then he goes to have a chat with her as he believes; but with no such fondness as he used to do. But yet it is thought that this new wench is so subtle, that she lets him not do any thing than is safe to her, but yet his doting is so great that, Pierce tells me, it is verily thought if the Queene had died, he would have married her.

December 31. I home and supped, and so had a good fire in my chamber and there sat till 4 o'clock in the morning making up my accounts and writing this last Journall of the year. And first I bless God I do, after a large expense, even this month, by reason of Christmas, and some payments to my father, and other things extraordinary, find that I am worth in money, besides all my household stuff, or any thing of Brampton, above £800, whereof in my Lord Sandwich's hand, £700, and the rest in my hand. So that there is not above £15 of all my estate in money at this minute out of my hands and my Lord's. For which the good God be pleased to give me a thankful heart and a mind careful to preserve this and increase it. I do live at my lodgings in the Navy Office, my family being, besides my wife and I, Jane Gentleman, Besse, our excellent, good-natured cook-mayde, and Susan, a little girle, having neither man nor boy, nor like to have again a good while, living now in most perfect content and quiett, and very frugally also; my health pretty good, but only that I have been much troubled with a costiveness which I am labouring to get away, and have hopes of doing it. At the office I am well, though envied to the devil by Sir William Batten, who hates me to death, but cannot hurt me. The rest either love me, or at least do not show otherwise, though I know Sir W. Pen to be a false knave touching me, though he seems fair. My father and mother well in the country; and at this time the young ladies of Hinchingbroke with them, their house having the small-pox in it. The Queene after a long and sore sickness is become well again; and the King minds his mistresse a little too much, if it pleased God! but I hope all things will go well, and in the Navy particularly, wherein I shall do my duty whatever comes of it. The great talke is the designs of the King of France, whether against the Pope or King of Spayne nobody knows; but a great and a most promising Prince he is, and all the Princes of Europe have their eye upon him. . . . The Duchesse of York, at this time, sicke of the meazles, but is growing well again. The Turke very far entered into Germany, and all that part of the world at a losse what to expect from his proceedings. Myself, blessed be God! in a good way, and design and resolution of sticking to my business to get a little money with doing the best service I can to the King also; which God continue! So ends the old year.

SAMUEL BUTLER

The literary game of ridiculing militant Puritanism was a popular one in the heyday of reaction against its power. Samuel Butler's mock-heroic portrait of a pulpit-pounding Cromwellian warrior did as much to secure the nation against a revival of the Good Old Cause as any display of the carcasses of its leaders in the London streets. Charles II delighted in this witty satire. Samuel Pepys, hearing it talked of, ran out to buy it but was disappointed. "It is so silly an abuse of the Presbyter knight going to the wars that I am ashamed of it." He never really became acclimated to the fashionable belittling of things that he had once thought great.

Butler's Characters belongs to a once popular but not often entertaining literary genre. The Fifth Monarchists, whose brand of fanaticism he analyzes in our second selection, attempted a rising in January 1661, with the results mentioned by Pepys above. They had rested their faith on Daniel 2 (see also Revelation 16-17), identifying the last of the kingdoms therein described with the thousand years reign of Christ on earth—a dangerous doctrine, since the Saints proposed to bring in this kingdom at once by force of arms. Sir Henry Vane, whose execution followed six months later, was of this persuasion, but his character little resembled Butler's portrait.

Hudibras

THE ARGUMENT OF THE FIRST CANTO

Sir Hudibras his passing worth,
The manner how he sallied forth:
His arms and equipage are shown;
His horse's virtues, and his own.

Th' adventure of the bear and fiddle,
Is sung, but breaks off in the middle.

THE PRESBYTERIAN KNIGHT

When civil fury first grew high,
And men fell out, they knew not why;
When hard words, jealousies, and fears
Set folks together by the ears,
And made them fight, like mad or drunk,
For Dame Religion as for punk,
Whose honesty they all durst swear for,
Though not a man of them knew wherefore;
When Gospel Trumpeter, surrounded
With long-eared rout, to battle sounded,
And pulpit, drum ecclesiastic,
Was beat with fist instead of a stick,
Then did Sir Knight abandon dwelling,
And out he rode a-colonelling.
  A wight he was whose very sight would
Entitle him Mirror of Knighthood,
That never bowed his stubborn knee
To anything but chivalry,
Nor put up blow but that which laid
Right Worshipful on shoulder blade;
Chief of domestic knights and errant,
Either for chartel or for warrant;
Great on the bench, great in the saddle,
That could as well bind o'er as swaddle;
Mighty he was at both of these
And styl'd of War, as well as Peace:
(So some rats, of amphibious nature,
Are either for the land or water).
But here our Authors make a doubt
Whether he were more wise or stout:
Some hold the one, and some the other,
But, howsoe'er they make a pother,
The diff'rence was so small, his brain
Outweigh'd his rage but half a grain;
Which made some take him for a tool
That knaves do work with, call'd a Fool. . . .

He was in logic a great critic,
Profoundly skill'd in analytic;
He could distinguish, and divide
A hair 'twixt south and southwest side;
On either which he would dispute,
Confute, change hands, and still confute:
He'd undertake to prove, by force
Of argument, a man's no horse;
He'd prove a buzzard is no fowl,
And that a lord may be an owl;
A calf an alderman, a goose a justice,
And rooks Committee-men and Trustees.
He'd run in debt by disputation,
And pay with ratiocination:
All this by syllogism, true
In mood and figure he would do. . . .
    For his religion, it was fit
To match his learning and his wit:
'Twas Presbyterian true blue;
For he was of that stubborn crew
Of errant saints, whom all men grant
To be the true Church Militant;
Such as do build their faith upon
The holy text of pike and gun;
Decide all controversies by
Infallible artillery;
And prove their doctrine orthodox,
By Apostolic blows and knocks;
Call fire and sword, and desolation,
A godly, thorough Reformation,
Which always must be carry'd on,
And still be doing, never done;
As if Religion were intended
For nothing else but to be mended:
A sect whose chief devotion lies
In odd perverse antipathies;
In falling out with that or this,
And finding somewhat still amiss;
More peevish, cross, and splenetic,
Than dog distract, or monkey sick:

That with more care keep holyday
The wrong, than others the right way;
Compound for sins they are inclin'd to,
By damning those they have no mind to:
Still so perverse and opposite,
As if they worship'd God for spite:
The self-same thing they will abhor
One way, and long another for:
Freewill they one way disavow,
Another, nothing else allow:
All piety consists therein
In them, in other men all sin:
Rather than fail, they will defy
That which they love most tenderly;
Quarrel with minc'd-pies, and disparage
Their best and dearest friend, plum-porridge;
Fat pig and goose itself oppose,
And blaspheme custard through the nose.

THE INDEPENDENT SQUIRE

A Squire he had whose name was Ralph,
That in the adventure went his half.
Though writers, for more statlier tone,
Do call him Ralpho, 'tis all one,
And when we can, with meter safe,
We'll call him so; if not, plain Rafe;
For rhyme the rudder is of verses,
With which, like ships, they steer their courses.
An equal stock of wit and valor
He had laid in, by birth a tailor. . . .
His knowledge was not far behind
The Knight's, but of another kind,
And he another way came by't;
Some call it gift, and some New Light,
A liberal art, that costs no pains
Of study, industry, or brains.
His wits were sent him for a token,
But in the carriage cracked and broken.
Like commendation nine-pence crooked,

With to and from my Love, it looked.
He ne'er considered it, as loth
To look a gift-horse in the mouth;
And very wisely would lay forth
No more upon it than 'twas worth.
But as he got it freely, so
He spent it frank and freely too.
For saints themselves will sometimes be,
Of gifts that cost them nothing, free.
By means of this, with hem and cough,
Prolongers to enlightened snuff,
He could deep mysteries unriddle,
As easily as thread a needle;
For as of vagabonds we say
That they are ne'er beside their way,
Whate'er men speak by this New Light,
Still they are sure to be in the right.
'Tis a dark-lanthorn of the spirit,
Which none see by but those that bear it,
A light that falls down from on high
For spiritual trades to cozen by,
An *ignis fatuus* that bewitches,
And leads men into pools and ditches,
To make them *dip* themselves, and sound
For Christendom in dirty pond;
To dive, like wild-fowl for salvation,
And fish to catch regeneration.
This light inspires and plays upon
The nose of saint like bagpipe drone,
And speaks through hollow empty soul,
As through a trunk or whisp'ring hole,
Such language as no mortal ear
But spiritual eaves-droppers can hear.
So Phœbus or some friendly muse
Into small poets song infuse,
Which they at second-hand rehearse,
Through reed or bagpipe, verse for verse.
Thus Ralph became infallible,
As three- or four-legged oracle,
The ancient cup, or modern chair;
Spoke truth point-blank, though unaware.

A FIFTH-MONARCHY MAN

Is one that is not contented to be a privy counselor of the Kingdom of Heaven, but would fain be a minister of state of this world, and translate the Kingdom of Heaven to the Kingdom of Earth. His design is to make Christ king, as his forefathers the Jews did, only to abuse and crucify him, that he might share his lands and goods, as he did his vicegerents' here. He dreams of a fool's paradise without a serpent in it, a golden age all of saints, and no hypocrites, all holy-court princes, and no subjects but the wicked; a government of Perkin Warbeck and Lambert Simnel saints, where every man that had a mind to it might make himself a prince and claim a title to the crown. He fancies a Fifth Monarchy as the quintessence of all governments, abstracted from all matter and consisting wholly of revelations, visions, and mysteries. John of Leyden was the first founder of it, and though he miscarried, like Romulus in a tempest, his posterity have revelations every full moon, that there may be a time to set up his title again, and with better success; though his brethren that have attempted it since had no sooner quartered his coat with their own but their whole outward men were set on the gates of the city; where a head and four quarters stand as types and figures of the Fifth Monarchy.

JOHN MILTON

Milton's image of the Hebrew champion Samson, blind and help-less among the Philistines, has commonly been taken as symbolic of his own situation in the Restoration. How conscious he was of the analogy we cannot say, but the following chorus comes too near to the realities to allow us to think it anything but a reflection on the downfall of the Puritan ideal and the tragic fates of its great leaders, men like Vane, whom Milton had worked with and admired.

The Ways of God to Man

God of our fathers, what is man!
That thou towards him with hand so various,
Or might I say contrarious,

Temperest thy providence through his short course,
Not evenly, as thou rulest
The angelic orders and inferior creatures mute,
Irrational and brute.
Nor do I name of men the common rout,
That wandering loose about
Grow up and perish, as the summer fly,
Heads without name, no more remembered,
But such as thou hast solemnly elected,
With gifts and graces eminently adorned
To some great work, thy glory,
And people's safety, which in part they effect;
Yet toward these thus dignified, thou oft
Amidst their height of noon,
Changest thy countenance and thy hand, with no regard
Of highest favors past
From thee on them, or them to thee of service.
  Nor only dost degrade them, or remit
To life obscured, which were a fair dismission,
But throwest them lower than thou didst exalt them high,
Unseemly falls in human eye,
Too grievous for the trespass or omission,
Oft leavest them to the hostile sword
Of heathen and profane, their carcasses
To dogs and fowls a prey, or else captived,
Or to the unjust tribunals, under change of times,
And condemnation of the ingrateful multitude.
If these they scape, perhaps in poverty
With sickness and disease thou bowest them down,
Painful diseases and deformed,
In crude old age;
Though not disordinate, yet causeless suffering
The punishment of dissolute days; in fine,
Just or unjust, alike seem miserable,
For oft alike, both come to evil end.
So deal not with this once thy glorious champion,
The image of thy strength, and mighty minister.
What do I beg? how hast thou dealt already?
Behold him in this state calamitous, and turn
His labors, for thou canst, to peaceful end.

RICHARD BAXTER

The author of Saints' Everlasting Rest, *a book once famous but now forgotten, was the most humane of Puritans and the most reasonable of nonconformists. Like other Presbyterian preachers in the Great Rebellion he backed the struggle against tyranny in church and state till the fanatics rose to the ascendant; then he retired to his pastorate at Kidderminster and took no part in king-killing or usurpation. "Anabaptists, Antinomians, Seekers" were worse than prelates. The offer of a bishopric at the Restoration was for him the parting of the ways. He did his best to secure the comprehension of moderates within the church, but, failing this, elected the lot of an unlicensed preacher. He managed to carry on against persecution during the reign of indulgent Charles, but was tried with great brutality by Jeffreys in 1685 and released from prison only because of illness and old age. The selections are from* Reliquiae Baxterianae, *a voluminous autobiography.*

The Problem of Toleration

The most of the time being spent thus in speaking to particulars of the Declaration as it was read, when we came to the end the Lord Chancellor drew out another paper and told us that the king had been petitioned also by the Independents and Anabaptists, and though he knew not what to think of it himself and did not very well like it, yet something he had drawn up which he would read to us and desire us also to give our advice about it. Thereupon he read, as an addition to the Declaration, that "others also be permitted to meet for religious worship and that no justice of peace or officer disturb them." When he had read it, he again desired them all to think on it and give their advice. But all were silent. The Presbyterians all perceived, as soon as they heard it, that it would secure the liberty of the Papists; and one of them whispered me in the ear and entreated me to say nothing, for it was an odious business, but let the bishops speak to it. But the bishops would not speak a word, nor any one of the Presbyterians neither and so we were like to have ended in that silence. I knew if we consented to it it would be charged on us that we spake for a toleration of Papists and sectaries. (But yet it might have lengthened out our own.) And if we spake against it, all sects and parties would be set against us as the causers of their sufferings, and as a partial people that would have liberty ourselves but would have no others have it with us. At last, seeing the silence continue, I thought our very silence would be charged on us a consent if it went on and therefore I only said this, that "this reverend brother, Dr. Gunning, even now speaking against sects, had named the Papists and the Socinians. For our parts we desired not favor to ourselves alone and rigorous severity we desired against none. As we humbly thanked his Majesty for his indulgence to ourselves, so we distinguish the tolerable parties from the intolerable. For the former we humbly crave just lenity and favor; but for the latter, such as the two sorts named before by that reverend brother, for our parts we cannot make their toleration our request." To which his Majesty said that "There were laws enough against the Papists"; and I replied that "We understood the question to be whether those laws should be executed on them or not." And so his Majesty broke up the meeting of that day. And here you may note by the way the fashion of these times and the state of the Presbyterians. Any man that was for a spiritual, serious way of worship (though he were for moderate Episcopacy and liturgy), and that lived according to his profession, was called commonly a Presbyterian, as formerly he was called a Puritan, unless he joined himself to Independents, Anabaptists, or some other sect which might afford him a more odious name. And of the lords, he that was for Episcopacy and the liturgy was called a Presbyterian if he endeavoured to procure any abatement of their impositions, for the reconciling of the parties or the ease of the ministers and people that disliked them. And of the ministers, he was called a Presbyterian that was for Episcopacy and liturgy if he conformed not so far as to subscribe or swear to the English diocesan frame and all their impositions. I knew not of any one lord at court that was a Presbyterian; yet were the Earl of Manchester (a good man) and the Earl of Anglesey, and the Lord Hollis called Presbyterians and as such appointed to direct and help them, when I have heard them plead for moderate Episcopacy and liturgy myself; and they would have drawn us to yield further than we did.

The Suppression of Dissent

And as we were forbidden to preach, so we were vigilantly watched in private, that we might not exhort one another or pray together;

and (as I foretold them often they would use us when they had silenced us) every meeting for prayer was called a dangerous meeting for sedition, or a conventicle at least. I will now give but one instance of their kindness to myself. One Mr. Beale, in Hatton Garden, having a son (his only child and very towardly and hopeful) who had been long sick of a dangerous fever (as I remember, a quartan), and by relapse brought so low that the physicians thought he would die, desired a few friends, of whom I was one, to meet at his house to pray for him; and because it pleased God to hear our prayers and that very night to restore him, his mother shortly after falling sick of a fever, we were desired to meet to pray for her recovery (the last day when she was near to death). Among those that were to be there, it fell out, through some other occasions, that Dr. Bates and I did fail them and could not come. But it was known at Westminster that we were appointed to be there. Whereupon two justices of the peace were procured from the distant parts of the town, one from Westminster and one from Clerkenwell to come with the Parliament's sergeant-at-arms to apprehend us. They came in the evening when part of the company were gone (there were only a few of their kindred there, besides two or three ministers to pray). They came upon them into the room where the gentlewoman lay ready to die and drew the curtains and took some of their names, but missing of their prey returned disappointed. What a joy would it have been to them that reproached us as Presbyterian seditious schismatics to have found but such an occasion as *praying with a dying woman* to have laid us up in prison. Yet that same week there was published a witty malicious invective against the silenced ministers, in which it was affirmed that Dr. Bates and I were at Mr. Beale's house such a day keeping a conventicle. But the liar had so much extraordinary modesty as within a day or two to print a second edition in which those words (so easily to be disproved) were left out. Such eyes were everywhere then upon us.

Many holy, excellent ministers were about these times laid in the jails in many counties for private meetings to preach and pray and some for venturing to preach publicly in churches which had no ministers (for so many were cast out that all their places could not presently be supplied).

2 Three Horsemen: *War, Plague, Fire*

ANDREW MARVELL

As a lyric poet Andrew Marvell, Milton's friend and fellow worker, does not belong to the Restoration, but he was still young when it began. He accepted the change and interested himself, with high-minded patriotism, in the business of politics. Like many far plainer Englishmen who were neither worldlings nor fanatics, he suffered increasingly under the reactionary tendencies in church and state. For a time he was Member of Parliament from Hull. Later he became disgusted at the management of public affairs and expressed his disillusionment in satires, not less intense than his early idealistic lyrics. In the early enthusiasm for the Dutch war the court poet, Edmund Waller, had written Instructions to a Painter, *glorifying the progress of the navy and describing the partial victory of July 3, 1665. We shall learn from Pepys how, within two years, England had wearied of the war against her commercial rivals, who were nevertheless Protestants. Many English had taken service with the Dutch Navy; some of the greater ships had been laid up for lack of funds. Then occurred the event, one of the most humiliating in British naval annals, which Marvell made the central incident in a sort of parody on Waller.*

The Dutch fleet under De Ruyter attacked Sheerness and Chatham, sailed with impunity up the river Medway and towed away the Royal Charles, *flagship of the English Navy. Popular resentment centered on the Earl of Clarendon. Charles himself remained popular, but the docility which had characterized the English people since the happy return was at an end.*

Britain's Shame

Ruyter the while, that had our ocean curb'd,
Sail'd now among our rivers undisturb'd:
Survey'd their crystal streams, and banks so green,
And beauties ere this never naked seen.

Through the vain sedge the bashful nymphs he ey'd;
Bosoms, and all which from themselves they hide.
The sun much brighter, and the skies more clear,
He finds the air, and all things, sweeter here.
The sudden change, and such a tempting sight,
Swells his old veins with fresh blood, fresh delight.
Like am'rous victors he begins to shave,
And his new face looks in the English wave.
His sporting navy all about him swim,
And witness their complaisance in their trim.
Their streaming silks play through the weather fair,
And with inveigling colors court the air.
While the red flags breathe on their topmasts high
Terror and war, but want an enemy.
Among the shrouds the seamen sit and sing,
And wanton boys on ev'ry rope do cling.
Old Neptune springs the tides, and water lent:
(The gods themselves do help the provident).
And, where the deep keel on the shallows cleaves,
With trident's lever, and great shoulder heaves.
Æolus their sails inspires with eastern wind,
Puffs them along, and breathes upon them kind.
With pearly shell the Tritons all the while
Sound the sea-march, and guide to Sheppy Isle.
  So have I seen in April's bud, arise
A fleet of clouds, sailing along the skies:
The liquid region with their squadrons fill'd,
The airy sterns the sun behind does gild;
And gentle gales them steer, and Heaven drives,
When, all on sudden, their calm bosom rives
With thunder and lightning from each armed cloud;
Shepherds themselves in vain in bushes shroud.
Such up the stream the Belgic navy glides,
And at Sheerness unloads its stormy sides. . . .
  There our sick ships unrigg'd in summer lay,
Like molting fowl, a weak and easy prey.
For whose strong bulk earth scarce could timber find,
The ocean water, or the heavens wind.
Those oaken giants of the ancient race,
That rul'd all seas, and did our Channel grace.
The conscious stag, so once the forest's dread,

Flies to the wood, and hides his armless head.
Ruyter forthwith a squadron does untack,
They sail securely through the River's track.
An English pilot too (O shame, O sin!),
Cheated of pay, was he that show'd them in.

Our wretched ships within their fate attend,
And all our hopes now on frail chain depend:
Engine so slight to guard us from the sea,
It fitter seem'd to captivate a flea.
A skipper rude shocks it without respect,
Filling his sails, more force to recollect.
Th' English from shore the iron deaf invoke
For its last aid: "Hold, chain, or we are broke."
But with her sailing weight, the Holland keel,
Snapping the brittle links, does thorow reel;
And to the rest the open'd passage shew.

Monk from the bank the dismal sight does view.
Our feather'd gallants, which came down that day
To be spectators safe of the *new play*,
Leave him alone when first they hear the gun,
(Comb'ry the fleetest) and to London run.
Our seamen, whom no danger's shape could fright,
Unpaid, refuse to mount our ships for spite:
Or to their fellows swim on board the Dutch,
Which show the tempting metal in their clutch.
Oft had he sent, of Duncombe and of Legge
Cannon and powder, but in vain, to beg:
And Upnor Castle's ill-deserted wall,
Now needful, does for ammunition call.
He finds, wheres'e'er he succor might expect,
Confusion, folly, treach'ry, fear, neglect.

But when the *Royal Charles*, what rage, what grief,
He saw seiz'd, and could give her no relief!
That sacred keel, which had, as he, restor'd
His exil'd sov'reign on its happy board;
And thence the British admiral became;
Crown'd, for that merit, with their master's name.
That pleasure-boat of war, in whose dear side
Secure so oft he had this foe defied:
Now a cheap spoil, and the mean victor's slave,
Taught the Dutch colors from its top to wave;

Of former glories the reproachful thought,
With present shame compar'd, his mind distraught.
Such from Euphrates bank, a tigress fell,
After the robbers, for her whelps does yell:
But sees, enrag'd, the river flow between.
Frustrate revenge, and love, by loss more keen,
At her own breast her useless claws does arm;
She tears herself since him she cannot harm.
The guards, plac'd for the chain's and fleet's defense,
Long since were fled on many a feign'd pretense.
Daniel had there adventur'd, man of might;
Sweet Painter, draw his picture while I write.
Paint him of person tall, and big of bone,
Large limbs, like ox, not to be kill'd but shown.
Scarce can burnt iv'ry feign an hair so black,
Or face so red, thine ochre and thy lack.
Mix a vain terror in his martial look,
And all those lines by which men are mistook.
But when, by shame constrain'd to go on board,
He heard how the wild cannon nearer roar'd;
And saw himself confin'd, like sheep in pen;
Daniel then thought he was in lions' den.
But when the frightful fire-ships he saw,
Pregnant with sulphur, to him nearer draw,
Captain, lieutenant, ensign, all make haste,
Ere in the fiery furnace they be cast.
Three children tall, unsing'd, away they row,
Like Shadrack, Meshek, and Abednego.
Not so brave Douglas; on whose lovely chin
The early down but newly did begin;
And modest beauty yet his sex did veil,
While envious virgins hope he is a male.
His yellow locks curl back themselves to seek,
Nor other courtship knew but to his cheek.
Oft has he in chill Esk or Seine, by night,
Harden'd and cool'd his limbs, so soft, so white;
Among the reeds, to be espied by him,
The nymphs would rustle; he would forward swim.
They sigh'd and said, "Fond boy, why so untame,
That fli'st love fires, reserv'd for other flame?"
Fix'd on his ship, he fac'd that horrid day,

And wond'red much at those that run away:
Nor other fear himself could comprehend,
Than lest Heav'n fall, ere thither he ascend.
But entertains, the while, his time too short
With birding at the Dutch, as if in sport:
Or waves his sword, and could he them conjure
Within its circle, knows himself secure.
The fatal bark him boards with grappling fire,
And safely through its port the Dutch retire:
That precious life he yet disdains to save,
Or with known art to try the gentle wave.
Much him honors of his ancient race
Inspire, nor would he his own deeds deface.
And secret joy in his calm soul does rise,
That Monk looks on to see how Douglas dies.
Like a glad lover, the fierce flames he meets,
And tries his first embraces in their sheets.
His shape exact, which the bright flames enfold,
Like the sun's statue stands of burnish'd gold.
Round the transparent fire about him glows,
As the clear amber on the bee does close:
And, as on angels' heads their glories shine,
His burning locks adorn his face divine.
But, when in his immortal mind he felt
His alt'ring form, and solder'd limbs to melt,
Down on the deck he laid himself, and died,
With his dear sword reposing by his side.
And, on the flaming plank, so rests his head
As one that's warm'd himself and gone to bed.
His ship burns down, and with his relics sinks,
And the sad stream beneath his ashes drinks.
Fortunate boy! if either pencil's fame,
Or if my verse, can propagate thy name;
When Œta and Alcides are forgot,
Our English youth shall sing the valiant Scot.
  Each doleful day still with fresh loss returns;
The *Loyal London* now a third time burns.
And the true *Royal Oak*, and *Royal James*,
Allied in fate, increase, with theirs, her flames.
Of all our navy none should now survive,
But that the ships themselves were taught to dive:

And the kind River in its creek them hides,
Fraughting their pierced keels with oozy tides.
    Up to the Bridge contagious terror strook:
The Tow'r itself with the near danger shook.
And were not Ruyter's maw with ravage cloy'd,
Ev'n London's ashes had been then destroy'd.
Officious fear, however, to prevent
Our loss, does so much more our loss augment.
The Dutch had robb'd those jewels of the crown:
Our merchant-men, lest they should burn, we drown
So when the fire did not enough devour,
The houses were demolish'd near the Tow'r.
Those ships that yearly from their teeming hole
Unloaded here the birth of either pole;
Furs from the north, and silver from the west,
From the south perfumes, spices from the east;
From Gambo gold, and from the Ganges gems;
Take a short voyage underneath the Thames,
Once a deep river, now with timber floor'd,
And shrunk, lest navigable, to a ford.
    Now (nothing more at Chatham left to burn)
The Holland squadron leisurely return:
And spite of Rupert and of Albemarles,
To Ruyter's triumph lead the captive *Charles*.
The pleasing sight he often does prolong:
Her masts erect, tough cordage, timbers strong,
Her moving shape, all these he does survey,
And all admires, but most his easy prey.
The seamen search her all, within, without:
Viewing her strength, they yet their conquest doubt.
Then with rude shouts, secure, the air they vex;
With gamesome joy insulting on her decks.
Such the fear'd Hebrew, captive, blinded, shorn,
Was led about in sport, the public scorn.
    Black day accurs'd! On thee let no man hale
Out of the port, or dare to hoist a sail,
Or row a boat in thy unlucky hour:
Thee, the year's monster, let thy dam devour.
And constant Time, to keep his course yet right,
Fill up thy space with a redoubled night.
When aged Thames was bound with fetters base,

And Medway chaste ravish'd before his face,
And their dear offspring murder'd in their sight;
Thou, and thy fellows, 'heldst the odious light.
Sad change, since first that happy pair was wed,
When all the rivers grac'd their nuptial bed;
And Father Neptune promis'd to resign
His empire old, to their immortal line!
Now with vain grief their vainer hopes they rue,
Themselves dishonor'd, and the gods untrue:
And to each other, helpless couple, moan,
As the sad tortoise for the sea does groan.
But most they for their darling *Charles* complain:
And were it burnt, yet less would be their pain.
To see that fatal pledge of sea-command
Now in the ravisher De Ruyter's hand,
The Thames roar'd, swooning Medway turn'd her tide,
And were they mortal, both for grief had died. . . .
  Paint last the King, and a dead shade of night,
Only dispers'd by a weak taper's light;
And those bright gleams that dart along and glare
From his clear eyes, yet these too dark with care.
There, as in the calm horror all alone,
He wakes and muses of th' uneasy throne:
Raise up a sudden shape with virgin's face,
Though ill agree her posture, hour, or place:
Naked as born, and her round arms behind,
With her own tresses interwove and twin'd:
Her mouth lock'd up, a blind before her eyes,
Yet from beneath the veil her blushes rise;
And silent tears her secret anguish speak,
Her heart throbs, and with very shame would break.
The object strange in him no terror mov'd:
He wonder'd first, then pitied, then he lov'd:
And with kind hand does the coy vision press,
Whose beauty greater seem'd by her distress;
But soon shrunk back, chill'd with her touch so cold,
And th' airy picture vanish'd from his hold.
In his deep thoughts the wonder did increase,
And he divin'd 'twas *England* or the *Peace*.
  Express him startling next with list'ning ear,
As one that some unusual noise does hear.

With cannon, trumpets, drums, his door surround,
But let some other painter draw the sound:
Thrice did he rise, thrice the vain tumult fled,
But again thunders when he lies in bed;
His mind secure does the known stroke repeat,
And finds the drums Lewis's march did beat.
   Shake then the room, and all his curtains tear,
And with blue streaks infect the taper clear:
While the pale ghosts his eye does fix'd admire
Of grandsire Harry, and of Charles his sire.
Harry sits down, and in his open side
The grisly wound reveals, of which he died.
And ghastly Charles, turning his collar low,
The purple thread about his neck does show:
Then, whisp'ring to his son in words unheard,
Through the lock'd door both of them disappear'd.
The wondrous night the pensive King revolves,
And rising, straight on Hyde's disgrace resolves.
   At his first step, he Castlemaine does find,
Bennet, and Coventry as't were design'd.
And they, not knowing, the same thing propose,
Which his hid mind did in its depths enclose.
Through their feign'd speech their secret hearts he knew;
To her own husband, Castlemaine, untrue;
False to his master Bristol, Arlington;
And Coventry falser than anyone,
Who to the brother, brother would betray;
Nor therefore trusts himself to such as they.
His father's ghost too whisper'd him one note,
That who does cut his purse will cut his throat.
But in wise anger he their crimes forbears,
As thieves repriev'd for executioners;
While Hyde, provok'd, his foaming tusk does whet,
To prove them traitors, and himself the Pett.
   Painter adieu, how well our arts agree;
Poetic picture, painted poetry.
But this great work is for our monarch fit,
And henceforth Charles only to Charles shall sit.
His master-hand the ancients shall outdo,
Himself the poet and the painter too. . . .

SAMUEL PEPYS

The dramatic events of the middle '60s—the partial victories and outstanding disasters of the war with Holland, the plague of 1665 and the fire of 1666, the dismissal of Lord Chancellor Clarendon from his position as Charles's instrument of government, leaving the nation exposed to the intrigues of royal mistresses and weak or dubious ministers (Buckingham and Shaftesbury, Arlington, Clifford and Lauderdale)—these events are among the sensations of English history. They produced a profound effect on the public mind and prepared the way for the political and religious excitements which heralded the end of the Stuart regime. Pepys's diary is the most vivid day-by-day record of the impact of these happenings. Pepys was far advanced in his career and was involved as a public official in the problems of the nation. His feelings and interpretations are, however, very much those of the average Englishman. Interlarded with his commentary on public affairs is the everlasting record of his private doings. The amazing story of his domestic life in this period is reserved for a later section of the present volume.

The Year 1664

February 15. This afternoon Sir Thomas Chamberlin came to the office to me, and showed me several letters from the East Indys, showing the height that the Dutch are come to there, showing scorn to all the English, even in our only Factory there of Surat, beating several men, and hanging the English Standard St. George under the Dutch flagg in scorn; saying, that whatever their masters do or say at home, they will do what they list, and will be masters of all the world there; and have so proclaimed themselves Soveraigne of all the South Seas; which certainly our King cannot endure, if the Parliament will give him money. But I doubt and yet do hope they will not yet, till we are more ready for it.

June 22. At noon to the 'Change and Coffee-house, where great talke of the Dutch preparing of sixty sayle of ships. The plague grows mightily among them, both at sea and land.

November 21. I to the 'Change and there staid long doing business, and this day for certain newes is come that Teddiman hath brought in eighteen or twenty Dutchmen, merchants, their Bour-

The Manner of Dissecting
the
PESTILENTIALL BODY.

AUTOPSY OF A PLAGUE VICTIM

Frontispiece to George Thomson's *Loimotomia* reproduced in W. G.
Bell, *The Great Plague*. By Permission of John Lane and Mr. Bell.

LONDON ON FIRE

Old painting believed to be contemporary, reproduced in W. G. Bell, *The Great Fire*. By permission of John Lane and Mr. Bell.

deaux fleete, and two men of warr to Portsmouth. And I had letters this afternoon, that three are brought into the Downes and Dover; so that the warr is begun: God give a good end to it!

The Year 1665

March 4. This day was proclaimed at the 'Change the war with Holland.

April 17. Up and to the Duke of Albemarle's, where he shewed me Mr. Coventry's letters, how three Dutch privateers are taken, in one whereof Everson's son is captaine. But they have killed poor Captaine Golding in The Diamond. Two of them, one of 32 and the other of 20 odd guns, did stand stoutly up against her, which hath 46, and the Yarmouth that hath 52 guns, and as many more men as they. So that they did more than we could expect, not yielding till many of their men were killed. And Everson, when he was brought before the Duke of Yorke, and was observed to be shot through the hat, answered, that he wished it had gone through his head, rather than been taken. Thence to White Hall; where the King seeing me, did come to me, and calling me by name, did discourse with me about the ships in the River; and this is the first time that ever I knew the King did know me personally; so that hereafter I must not go thither, but with expectation to be questioned, and to be ready to give good answers.

June 3. All this day by all people upon the River, and almost every where else hereabout were heard the guns, our two fleets for certain being engaged; which was confirmed by letters from Harwich, but nothing particular: and all our hearts full of concernment for the Duke, and I particularly for my Lord Sandwich and Mr. Coventry after his Royall Highnesse.

June 7. The hottest day that ever I felt in my life. This day, much against my will, I did in Drury Lane see two or three houses marked with a red cross upon the doors, and "Lord have mercy upon us!" writ there; which was a sad sight to me, being the first of the kind that, to my remembrance, I ever saw. It put me into an ill conception of myself and my smell, so that I was forced to buy some roll-tobacco to smell to and chaw, which took away the apprehension. By water home, where weary with walking, and with the mighty heat of the weather, and for my wife's not coming home, I staying walking in the garden till twelve at night, when it begun to lighten exceedingly, through the greatness of the heat. Then, despairing of her coming home, I to bed.

June 8. Alone at home to dinner, my wife, mother, and Mercer dining at W. Joyce's; I giving her a caution to go round by the Half Moone to his house, because of the plague. I to my Lord Treasurer's by appointment of Sir Thomas Ingram's, to meet the Goldsmiths; where I met with the great news at last newly come, brought by Bab May from the Duke of Yorke, that we have totally routed the Dutch; that the Duke himself, the Prince, my Lord Sandwich and Mr. Coventry are all well which did put me into such joy, that I forgot almost all other thoughts. Admirall Opdam blown up, Trump killed, and said by Holmes; all the rest of their admiralls, as they say, but Everson are killed: we having taken and sunk, as is believed, about 24 of their best ships; killed and taken near 8 or 10,000 men, and lost, we think, not above 700. A great[er] victory never known in the world. They are all fled, some 43 got into the Texell, and others elsewhere, and we in pursuit of the rest. Thence, when my heart full of joy, home, and to my office a little; then to my Lady Pen's, where they are all joyed and not a little puffed up at the good successe of their father; and good service indeed is said to have been done by him. Had a great bonfire at the gate; and I with my Lady Pen's people and others to Mrs. Turner's great room, and then down into the streete. I did give the boys 4s. among them, and mighty merry. So home to bed, with my heart at great rest and quiett, saving that the consideration of the victory is too great for me presently to comprehend.

August 10. By and by to the office, where we sat all the morning; in great trouble to see the Bill this week rise so high, to above 4,000 in all, and of them above 3,000 of the plague. And an odd story of Alderman Bence's stumbling at night over a dead corps in the street, and going home and telling his wife, she at the fright, being with child, fell sicke and died of the plague. Thence to the office and, after writing letters, home, to draw over anew my will, which I had bound myself by oath to dispatch by to-morrow night; the town growing so unhealthy, that a man cannot depend upon living two days to an end.

August 31. Up; and, after putting several things in order to my removal, to Woolwich; the plague having a great encrease this week, beyond all expectation of almost 2,000, making the general Bill 7,000, odd 100; and the plague above 6,000. Thus this month ends with great sadness upon the publick, through the greatness of the plague every where through the kingdom almost. Every day sadder and sadder news of its encrease. In the City died this week 7,496, and of them 6,102 of the plague. But it is feared that the true number of the dead this week is near 10,000; partly from the poor that cannot be taken notice of, through the greatness of the number, and partly from the Quakers and others that will not have any bell ring for them. Our fleete gone out to find the Dutch, we having about 100 sail in our fleete, and in them the Soveraigne one; so that it is a better fleete than the former with the Duke was.

October 5. The Bill, blessed be God! is less this week by 740 of what it was the last week. Being come to my lodging I got something to eat, having eat little all the day, and so to bed, having this night renewed my promises of observing my vowes as I used to do; for I find that, since I left them off, my mind is run a' wool-gathering and my business neglected.

October 16. Thence I walked to the Tower; but, Lord! how empty the streets are and melancholy, so many poor sick people in the streets full of sores; and so many sad stories overheard as I walk, every body talking of this dead, and that man sick, and so many in this place, and so many in that. And they tell me that, in Westminster, there is never a physician and but one apothecary left, all being dead; but that there are great hopes of a great decrease this week: God send it!

October 26. The 'Change pretty full, and the town begins to be lively again, though the streets very empty, and most shops shut.

The Year 1666

June 2. Up, and to the office, where certain newes is brought us of a letter come to the King this morning from the Duke of Albemarle, dated yesterday at eleven o'clock, as they were sailing to the Gunfleete, that they were in sight of the Dutch fleete, and were fitting themselves to fight them; so that they are, ere this, certainly engaged; besides, several do averr they heard the guns all yesterday in the afternoon. This put us at the Board into a tosse. Presently come orders for our sending away to the fleete a recruite of 200 soldiers. After dinner having nothing else to do till flood, I went and saw Mrs. Daniel, to whom I did not tell that the fleets were engaged, because of her husband, who is in the R. Charles. Very pleasant with her half an hour, and so away and down to Blackewall, and there saw the soldiers (who were by this time gotten most of them drunk) shipped off. But, Lord! to see how the poor fellows kissed their wives and sweethearts in that simple manner at their going off, and shouted, and let off their guns, was strange sport.

June 5. Thence after the Duke into the Parke, walking through to White Hall, and there every body listening for guns, but none heard, and every creature is now overjoyed and concludes upon very good grounds that the Dutch are beaten because we have heard no guns nor no news of our fleete. By and by walking a little further, Sir Philip Frowde did meet the Duke with an expresse to Sir W. Coventry (who was by) from Captain Taylor, the Storekeeper at Harwich, being the narration of Captain Hayward of The Dunkirke; who gives a very serious account, how upon Monday the two fleetes fought all day till seven at night, and then the whole fleete of Dutch did betake themselves to a very plain flight, and never looked back again. That Sir Christopher Mings is wounded in the leg; that the Generall is well. That it is conceived reasonably, that of all the Dutch fleete, which, with what recruits they had, come to one hundred sayle, there is not above fifty got home, and of them, few if any of their flags. We were all so overtaken with this good newes, that the Duke ran with it to the King, who was gone to chappell, and there all the Court was in a hubbub, being rejoiced over head and ears in this good newes. The joy of the City was this night exceeding great.

June 7. Up betimes, and to my office about business. But my Lord Bruncker and Sir T. H. that come from Court, tell me quite contrary newes, which astonishes me: that is to say, that we are beaten, lost many ships and good commanders; have not taken one ship of the enemy's; and so can only report ourselves a victory; nor is it certain that we were left masters of the field. Then to my office and anon to White Hall, late, to the Duke of York to see what commands he hath, which I did and do find the Duke much damped in his discourse, touching the late fight, and all the court talk sadly of it. And as to news, I do find great reason to think that we are beaten in every respect, and that we are the losers. The Duke of Albemarle writes that he never fought with worse officers in his life, not above twenty of them behaving themselves like men.

September 2 (Lord's day). Some of our mayds sitting up late last night to get things ready against our feast to-day, Jane called us up about three in the morning, to tell us of a great fire they saw in the City. So I rose and slipped on my night-gowne, and went to her window, and thought it to be on the back-side of Marke-lane at the farthest; but, being unused to such fires as followed, I thought it far enough off; and so went to bed again and to sleep. About seven rose again to dress myself, and there looked out at the window, and saw the fire not so much as it was and further off. So to my closett to set things to rights after yesterday's cleaning. By and by Jane comes and tells me that she hears that above 300 houses have been burned down to-night by the fire we saw, and that it is now burning down all Fish-street, by London Bridge. So I made myself ready presently, and walked to the Tower, and there got up upon one of the high places, Sir J. Robinson's little son going up with me; and there I did see the houses at that end of the bridge all on fire, and an infinite great fire on this and the other side the end of the bridge; which, among other people, did trouble me for poor little Michell and our Sarah on the bridge. So down, with my heart full of trouble, to the Lieutenant of the Tower, who tells me that it begun this morning in the King's baker's house in Pudding-lane, and that it hath burned St. Magnus's Church and most part of Fish-street already. So I down to the water-side, and there got a boat and through bridge, and there saw a lamentable fire. Poor Michell's house, as far as the Old Swan, already burned that way, and the fire running further, that in a very little time it got as far as the Steele-yard, while I was there. Everybody endeavouring to remove their goods, and flinging into the river or bringing them into lighters that lay off; poor people staying in their houses as long as till the very fire touched them, and then running into boats, or clambering from one pair of stairs by the water-side to another. And among other things, the poor pigeons, I perceive, were loth to leave their houses, but hovered about the windows and balconys till they were, some of them burned, their wings, and fell down. Having staid, and in an hour's time seen the fire rage every way, and nobody, to my sight, endeavouring to quench it, but to remove their goods, and leave all to the fire, and having seen it get as far as the Steele-yard, and the wind mighty high and driving it into the City; and every thing, after so long a drought, proving combustible, even the very stones of churches, and among other things the poor steeple by which pretty Mrs. —— lives, and whereof my old schoolfellow Elborough is parson, taken fire in the very top, and there burned till it fell down: I to White Hall (with a gentleman with me who desired to go off from the Tower, to see the fire, in my boat); to White Hall, and there up to the King's closett in the Chappell, where people come about me, and I did give them an account dismayed them all, and word was carried in to the King. So I was called for, and did tell the King and Duke of Yorke what I saw, and that unless his Majesty did command houses to be pulled down nothing could stop the fire. They seemed much troubled, and the King commanded me to go to my Lord Mayor from him, and command him to spare no houses, but to pull down before the fire every way. The Duke of York bid me tell him that if he would have any more soldiers he shall; and so did my Lord Arlington afterwards, as a great secret. Here meeting with Captain Cocke, I in his coach, which he lent me, and Creed with me to Paul's, and there walked along Watling-street, as well as I could, every creature coming away loaden with goods to save, and here and there sicke people carried away in beds. Extraordinary good goods carried in carts and on backs. At last met my Lord Mayor in Canning-street, like a man spent, with a handkercher about his neck. To the King's message he cried, like a fainting woman, "Lord! what can I do? I am spent: people will not obey me. I have been pulling down houses; but the fire overtakes us faster than we can do it." That he needed no more soldiers; and that, for himself, he must go and refresh himself, having been up all night. So he left me, and I him, and walked home, seeing people all almost distracted, and no manner of means used to quench the fire. The houses, too, so very thick thereabouts, and full of matter for burning, as pitch and tarr, in Thames-street; and warehouses of oyle, and wines, and brandy, and other things. Here I saw Mr. Isaake Houblon, the handsome man, prettily dressed and dirty, at his door at Dowgate, receiving some of his brothers' things, whose houses were on fire; and, as he says, have been removed twice already; and he doubts (as it soon proved) that they must be in a little time removed from his house also, which was a sad consideration. And to see the churches all filling with goods by people who themselves should have been quietly there at this time. By this time it was about twelve o'clock; and so home, and there find my guests, which was Mr. Wood and his wife Barbary Sheldon, and also Mr. Moone: she mighty fine, and her husband, for aught I see, a likely man. But Mr. Moone's design and mine, which was to look over my closett and please him with the sight thereof, which he hath long desired, was wholly disappointed; for we were in great trouble and disturbance at this fire, not knowing what to think of it. However, we had an extraordinary good dinner, and as merry as at this time we could be. While at dinner Mrs. Batelier come to enquire after Mr. Woolfe and Stanes (who, it seems, are related to them), whose houses in Fish-street are all burned, and they in a sad condition. She would not stay in the fright. Soon as dined, I and Moone away, and walked through the City, the streets full of nothing but people and horses and carts loaden with goods, ready to run over one another, and removing goods from one burned house to another. They now removing out of Canning-streete (which received goods in the morning) into Lumbard-streete, and further; and among others I now saw my little goldsmith, Stokes, receiving some friend's goods, whose house itself was burned the day after. We parted at Paul's; he home, and I to Paul's Wharf, where I had appointed a boat to attend me, and took in Mr. Carcasse and his brother, whom I met in the streete, and carried them below and above bridge to and again to see the fire, which was now got further, both below and above, and no likelihood of stopping it. Met with the King and Duke of York in their barge, and with them to Queenhithe, and there called Sir Richard Browne to them. Their order was only to pull down houses apace, and so below bridge at the water-side; but little was or could be done, the fire coming upon them so fast. Good hopes there was of stopping it at the Three Cranes above, and at Buttolph's Wharf below bridge, if care be used; but the wind carries it into the City, so as we know not by the water-side what it do there. River full of lighters and boats taking in goods, and good goods swimming in the water, and only I observed that hardly one lighter or boat in three that had the goods of a house in, but there was a pair of Virginalls in it. Having seen as much as I could now, I away to White Hall by appointment, and there walked to St. James's Parke, and there met my wife and Creed and Wood and his wife, and walked to my boat; and there upon the water again, and to the fire up and down, it still encreasing, and the wind great. So near the fire as we could for smoke; and all over the Thames, with one's face in the wind, you were almost burned with a shower of fire-drops. This is very true; so as houses were burned by these drops and flakes of fire, three or four, nay, five or six houses, one from another. When we could endure no more upon the water, we to a little ale-house on the Bankside, over against the Three Cranes, and there staid till it was dark almost, and saw the fire grow; and, as it grew darker, appeared more and more, and in corners and upon steeples, and between churches and houses, as far as we could see up the hill of the City, in a most horrid malicious bloody flame, not like the fine flame of an ordinary fire. Barbary and her husband away before us. We staid till, it being darkish, we saw the fire as only one entire arch of fire from this to the other side the bridge, and in a bow up the hill for an arch of above a mile long: it made me weep to see it. The churches, houses, and all on fire and flaming at once; and a horrid noise the flames made, and the crack-

ing of houses at their ruine. So home with a sad heart, and there find
every body discoursing and lamenting the fire; and poor Tom Hater
come with some few of his goods saved out of his house, which is
burned upon Fish-streete Hill. I invited him to lie at my house,
and did receive his goods, but was deceived in his lying there, the
newes coming every moment of the growth of the fire; so as we were
forced to begin to pack up our owne goods, and prepare for their
removal; and did by moonshine (it being brave dry, and moonshine,
and warm weather) carry much of my goods into the garden, and
Mr. Hater and I did remove my money and iron chests into my
cellar, as thinking that the safest place. And got my bags of gold into
my office, ready to carry away, and my chief papers of accounts also
there, and my tallys into a box by themselves. So great was our fear,
as Sir W. Batten hath carts come out of the country to fetch away his
goods this night. We did put Mr. Hater, poor man, to bed a little;
but he got but very little rest, so much noise being in my house, taking down of goods.

September 3. About four o'clock in the morning, my Lady Batten
sent me a cart to carry away all my money, and plate, and best
things, to Sir W. Rider's at Bednall-greene. Which I did, riding myself in my night-gowne in the cart; and, Lord! to see how the streets
and the highways are crowded with people running and riding, and
getting of carts at any rate to fetch away things. I find Sir W. Rider
tired with being called up all night, and receiving things from several
friends. His house full of goods, and much of Sir W. Batten's and
Sir W. Pen's. I am eased at my heart to have my treasure so well
secured. Then home, with much ado to find a way, nor any sleep all
this night to me nor my poor wife. But then and all this day she and
I, and all my people labouring to get away the rest of our things,
and did get Mr. Tooker to get me a lighter to take them in, and we
did carry them (myself some) over Tower Hill, which was by this
time full of people's goods, bringing their goods thither; and down to
the lighter, which lay at the next quay, above the Tower Docke. And
here was my neighbour's wife, Mrs. ——, with her pretty child, and
some few of her things, which I did willingly give way to be saved
with mine; but there was no passing with anything through the
postern, the crowd was so great. The Duke of Yorke come this day
by the office, and spoke to us, and did ride with his guard up and
down the City to keep all quiet (he being now Generall, and having
the care of all). This day, Mercer being not at home, but against
her mistress's order gone to her mother's, and my wife going thither

to speak with W. Hewer, met her there, and was angry; and her mother saying that she was not a 'prentice girl, to ask leave every time she goes abroad, my wife with good reason was angry, and, when she came home, bid her be gone again. And so she went away, which troubled me, but yet less than it would, because of the condition we are in, fear of coming into in a little time of being less able to keepe one in her quality. At night lay down a little upon a quilt of W. Hewer's in the office, all my owne things being packed up or gone; and after me my poor wife did the like, we having fed upon the remains of yesterday's dinner, having no fire nor dishes, nor any opportunity of dressing any thing.

September 4. Up by break of day to get away the remainder of my things; which I did by a lighter at the Iron gate: and my hands so few, that it was the afternoon before we could get them all away. Sir W. Pen and I to Tower-streete, and there met the fire burning three or four doors beyond Mr. Howell's, whose goods, poor man, his trayes, and dishes, shovells, &c., were flung all along Tower-street in the kennels, and people working therewith from one end to the other; the fire coming on in that narrow streete, on both sides, with infinite fury. Sir W. Batten not knowing how to remove his wine, did dig a pit in the garden, and laid it in there; and I took the opportunity of laying all the papers of my office that I could not otherwise dispose of. And in the evening Sir W. Pen and I did dig another, and put our wine in it; and I my Parmazan cheese, as well as my wine and some other things. The Duke of Yorke was at the office this day, at Sir W. Pen's; but I happened not to be within. This afternoon, sitting melancholy with Sir W. Pen in our garden, and thinking of the certain burning of this office, without extraordinary means, I did propose for the sending up of all our workmen from Woolwich and Deptford yards (none whereof yet appeared), and to write to Sir W. Coventry to have the Duke of Yorke's permission to pull down houses, rather than lose this office, which would much hinder the King's business. So Sir W. Pen he went down this night, in order to the sending them up to-morrow morning; and I wrote to Sir W. Coventry about the business, but received no answer. This night Mrs. Turner (who, poor woman, was removing her goods all this day, good goods into the garden, and knows not how to dispose of them), and her husband supped with my wife and I at night, in the office, upon a shoulder of mutton from the cook's, without any napkin or any thing, in a sad manner, but were merry. Only now and then walking into the garden, and saw how horridly

the sky looks, all on a fire in the night, was enough to put us out
of our wits; and, indeed, it was extremely dreadful, for it looks just
as if it was at us, and the whole heaven on fire. I after supper walked
in the darke down to Tower-streete, and there saw it all on fire, at the
Trinity House on that side, and the Dolphin Taverne on this side,
which was very near us; and the fire with extraordinary vehemence.
Now begins the practice of blowing up of houses in Tower-streete,
those next the Tower, which at first did frighten people more than
any thing; but it stopped the fire where it was done, it bringing
down the houses to the ground in the same places they stood, and
then it was easy to quench what little fire was in it, though it kindled
nothing almost. W. Hewer this day went to see how his mother did,
and comes late home, telling us how he hath been forced to remove
her to Islington, her house in Pye-corner being burned; so that the
fire is got so far that way, and all the Old Bayly, and was running
down to Fleete-streete; and Paul's is burned, and all Cheapside. I
wrote to my father this night, but the post-house being burned, the
letter could not go.

September 5. I lay down in the office again upon W. Hewer's quilt,
being mighty weary, and sore in my feet with going till I was hardly
able to stand. About two in the morning my wife calls me up and
tells me of new cryes of fire, it being come to Barkeing Church, which
is the bottom of our lane. I up, and finding it so, resolved presently
to take her away, and did, and took my gold, which was about
£2,350, W. Hewer, and Jane, down by Proundy's boat to Woolwich;
but Lord! what a sad sight it was by moone-light to see the whole
City almost on fire, that you might see it plain at Woolwich, as if
you were by it. There, when I come, I find the gates shut, but no
guard kept at all, which troubled me, because of discourse now
begun, that there is plot in it, and that the French had done it.
I got the gates open, and to Mr. Shelden's, where I locked up my
gold, and charged my wife and W. Hewer never to leave the room
without one of them in it, night or day. So back again, by the way
seeing my goods well in the lighters at Deptford, and watched well
by people. Home, and whereas I expected to have seen our house
on fire, it being now about seven o'clock, it was not. But to the
fyre, and there find greater hopes than I expected; for my confidence
of finding our Office on fire was such, that I durst not ask any body
how it was with us, till I come and saw it not burned. But going to
the fire, I find by the blowing up of houses, and the great helpe given
by the workmen out of the King's yards, sent up by Sir W. Pen,

there is a good stop given to it, as well as at Marke-lane end as ours; it having only burned the dyall of Barking Church, and part of the porch, and was there quenched. I up to the top of Barking steeple, and there saw the saddest sight of desolation that I ever saw; every where great fires, oyle-cellars, and brimstone, and other things burning. I became afeard to stay there long, and therefore down again as fast as I could, the fire being spread as far as I could see it; and to Sir W. Pen's, and there eat a piece of cold meat, having eaten nothing since Sunday, but the remains of Sunday's dinner. Here I met with Mr. Young and Whistler; and having removed all my things, and received good hopes that the fire at our end is stopped, they and I walked into the town, and find Fanchurch-streete, Gracious-streete, and Lumbard-streete all in dust. The Exchange a sad sight, nothing standing there, of all the statues or pillars, but Sir Thomas Gresham's picture in the corner. Walked into Moorefields (our feet ready to burn, walking through the towne among the hot coles), and find that full of people, and poor wretches carrying their goods there, and every body keeping his goods together by themselves (and a great blessing it is to them that it is fair weather for them to keep abroad night and day); drank there, and paid twopence for a plain penny loaf. Thence homeward, having passed through Cheapside and Newgate Market, all burned, and seen Anthony Joyce's house in fire. And took up (which I keep by me) a piece of glasse of Mercers' Chappell in the streete, where much more was, so melted and buckled with the heat of the fire like parchment. I also did see a poor cat taken out of a hole in the chimney, joyning to the wall of the Exchange, with the hair all burned off the body, and yet alive. So home at night, and find there good hopes of saving our office; but great endeavours of watching all night, and having men ready; and so we lodged them in the office, and had drink and bread and cheese for them. And I lay down and slept a good night about midnight, though when I rose I heard that there had been a great alarme of French and Dutch being risen, which proved nothing. But it is a strange thing to see how long this time did look since Sunday, having been always full of variety of actions, and little sleep, that it looked like a week or more, and I had forgot almost the day of the week.

December 8. Mr. Pierce did also tell me as a great truth, as being told it by Mr. Cowly, who was by, and heard it, that Tom Killigrew should publiquely tell the King that his matters were coming into a very ill state; but that yet there was a way to help all, which is, says he, "There is a good, honest, able man, that I could name, that if your Majesty would employ, and command to see all things well executed, all things would soon be mended; and this is one Charles Stuart, who now spends his time in employing his lips . . . about the Court, and hath no other employment; but if you would give him this employment, he were the fittest man in the world to perform it."

December 31. Rising this day with a full design to mind nothing else but to make up my accounts for the year past, I did take money, and walk forth to several places in the towne as far as the New Exchange, to pay all my debts, it being still a very great frost and good walking. Our enemies, French and Dutch, great, and grow more by our poverty. The Parliament backward in raising, because jealous of the spending of the money; the City less and less likely to be built again, every body settling elsewhere, and nobody encouraged to trade. A sad, vicious, negligent Court, and all sober men there fearful of the ruin of the whole kingdom this next year; from which, good God deliver us! One thing I reckon remarkable in my owne condition is, that I am come to abound in good plate, so as at all entertainments to be served wholly with silver plates, having two dozen and a half.

The Year 1667

June 8. Up, and to the office, where all the news this morning is, that the Dutch are come with a fleete of eighty sail to Harwich, and that guns were heard plain by Sir W. Rider's people at Bednall-greene, all yesterday even. The King hath sent down my Lord of Oxford to raise the countries there; and all the Westerne barges are taken up to make a bridge over the River, about the Hope, for horse to cross the River, if there be occasion.

June 10. Up; and news brought us that the Dutch are come up as high as the Nore; and more pressing orders for fire-ships. W. Batten, W. Pen, and I to St. James's; where the Duke of York gone this morning betimes, to send away some men down to Chatham. So we three to White Hall, and met Sir W. Coventry, who presses all that is possible for fire-ships. So we three to the office presently; and thither comes Sir Fretcheville Hollis, who is to command them all in some exploits he is to do with them on the enemy in the River. So we all down to Deptford, and pitched upon ships and set men at work: but, Lord! to see how backwardly things move at this pinch. I find the Duke of Albemarle just come, with a great many idle lords and gentlemen, with their pistols and fooleries; and the bulwarke not able to have stood half an hour had they come up; but the Dutch are fallen down from the Hope and Shell-haven as low as Sheernesse, and we do plainly at this time hear the guns play.

June 12. When I come to Sir W. Coventry's chamber, I find him abroad; but his clerk, Powell, do tell me ill news is come to Court of the Dutch breaking the chain at Chatham, which struck me to the heart. And to Whitehall to hear the truth of it; and there, going up the back stairs I did hear some laquies speaking of sad newes come to Court, saying, that hardly anybody in the Court but do look as if he cried, for the newes is true, that the Dutch have broken the chaine and burned our ships, and particularly "The Royal Charles:" other particulars I know not, but most sad to be sure. And, the truth is, I do fear so much that the whole kingdom is undone, that I do this night resolve to study with my father and wife what to do with the little that I have in money by me, for I give [up] all the rest that I have in the King's hands, for Tangier, for lost. So God help us! I have in my own person, done my full duty, I am sure.

June 13. No sooner up but hear the sad newes confirmed of the Royall Charles being taken by them, and now in fitting by them—and turning several others; and that another fleete is come up into the Hope. Upon which newes the King and Duke of York have been below since four o'clock in the morning, to command the sinking of ships at Barking-Creeke, and other places, to stop their coming up higher: which put me into such a fear, that I presently resolved of my father's and wife's going into the country; and, at two hours' warning, they did go by the coach this day, with about £1,300 in gold in their night-bag. Pray God give them good passage, and good care to hide it when they come home! but my heart is full of fear. They gone, I continued in fright and fear what to do with the rest. W. Hewer hath been at the banker's, and hath got £500 out of Backewell's hands of his own money; but they are so called upon that they will be all broke, hundreds coming to them for money: and their answer is, "It is payable at twenty days—when the days are out, we will pay you." In the evening, I sent for my cousin Sarah [Gyles] and her husband, who come; and I did deliver them my chest of writings about Brampton, and my brother Tom's papers, and my journalls, which I value much; and did sent my two silver flaggons to Kate Joyce's: that so, being scattered what I have, something might be saved. I have also made a girdle, by which, with some trouble, I do carry about me £300 in gold about my body, that I may not be without something in case I should be surprised: for I think, in any nation but our's, people that appear (for we are not indeed so) so faulty as we, would have their throats cut. Late at night comes Mr. Hudson, the cooper, my neighbour, and tells me that he come from Chatham this evening at five o'clock, and saw this afternoon "The Royal James," "Oake," and "London" burnt by the enemy with their fire-ships: that two or three men-of-war come up with them, and made no more of Upnor Castle's shooting, than of a fly. I made my will also this day, and did give all I had equally between my father and wife, and left copies of it in each of Mr. Hater and W. Hewer's hands, who both witnessed the will, and so to supper and then to bed, and slept pretty well, but yet often waking.

June 14. The hearts as well as affections of the seamen are turned away; and in the open streets in Wapping, and up and down, the wives have cried publickly, "This comes of your not paying our husbands; and now your work is undone, or done by hands that understand it not." And Sir W. Batten told me that he was himself affronted with a woman, in language of this kind, on Tower Hill publickly yesterday; and we are fain to bear it, and to keep one at the office door to let no idle people in, for fear of firing of the office and doing us mischief. Mr. Hater tells me at noon that some rude people have been, as he hears, at my Lord Chancellor's, where they have cut down the trees before his house and broke his windows; and a gibbet either set up before or painted upon his gate, and these three words writ: "Three sights to be seen; Dunkirke, Tangier, and a barren Queene." Most people that I speak with are in doubt how we shall do to secure our seamen from running over to the Dutch; which is a sad but very true consideration at this day.

August 24 (St. Bartholomew's day). This morning was proclaimed the peace between us and the States of the United Provinces, and also of the King of France and Denmarke; and in the afternoon the Proclamations were printed and come out; and at night the bells rung, but no bonfires that I hear of any where, partly from the dearness of firing, but principally from the little content most people have in the peace.

November 11. To Captain Cocke's (he out of doors), and there drank their morning draught, and thence [Sir] G. Carteret and I toward the Temple in coach together; and there he did tell me how the King do all he can in the world to overthrow my Lord Chancellor, and that notice is taken of every man about the King that is not seen to promote the ruine of the Chancellor; and that this being another great day in his business, he dares not but be there. He tells me that as soon as Secretary Morrice brought the Great Seale from my Lord Chancellor, Bab. May fell upon his knees, and catched the King about the legs, and joyed him, and said that this was the first time that ever he could call him King of England, being freed from this great man: which was a most ridiculous saying.

The Year 1668

January 17. Up, and by coach to White Hall to attend the Council there, and here I met first by Mr. Castle the shipwright, whom I met there, and then from the whole house the discourse of the duell yesterday between the Duke of Buckingham, Holmes, and one Jenkins, on one side, and my Lord of Shrewsbury, Sir John Talbot, and one Bernard Howard, on the other side: and all about my Lady Shrewsbury, who is a whore, and is at this time, and hath for a great while been, a whore to the Duke of Buckingham. And so her husband challenged him, and they met yesterday in a close near Barne-Elmes, and there fought: and my Lord Shrewsbury is run through the body, from the right breast through the shoulder: and Sir John Talbot all along up one of his armes; and Jenkins killed upon the place, and the rest all, in a little measure, wounded. This will make the world think that the King hath good councillors about him, when the Duke of Buckingham, the greatest man about him, is a fellow of no more sobriety than to fight about a whore. And this may prove a very bad accident to the Duke of Buckingham, but that my Lady Castlemayne do rule all at this time as much as ever she did, and she will, it is believed, keep all matters well with the Duke of Buckingham: though this is a time that the King will be very backward, I suppose, to appear in such a business.

February 17. Some mutterings I did hear of a design of dissolving the Parliament; but I think there is no ground for it yet, though Oliver would have dissolved them for half the trouble and contempt these have put upon the King and his councils. I did spend a little time at the Swan, and there did kiss the maid, Sarah.

February 18. Up by break of day, and walked down to the old

Swan. I drank, but did not see Betty, and so to Charing Cross stairs, and thence walked to Sir W. Coventry's, and talked with him, who tells me how he hath been persecuted. I will remember what, in mirth, he said to me this morning, when upon this discourse he said, if ever there was another Dutch war, they should not find a Secretary; "Nor," said I, "a Clerk of the Acts, for I see the reward of it; and, thanked God! I have enough of my own to buy me a good book and a good fiddle, and I have a good wife." I stepped to the Dog Taverne, and thither come to me Doll Lane, and there we did drink together, and she tells me she is my valentine.

April 30. Thus ends this month; my wife in the country, myself full of pleasure and expense; and some trouble for my friends, my Lord Sandwich, by the Parliament, and more for my eyes, which are daily worse and worse, that I dare not write or read almost anything. The Parliament going in a few days to rise. The kingdom in an ill state through poverty; a fleete going out, and no money to maintain it, or set it out; seamen yet unpaid, and mutinous when pressed to go out again. So we are all poor, and in pieces—God help us! while the peace is like to go on between Spain and France; and then the French may be apprehended able to attack us. So God help us!

May 15. I am told also that the Countess of Shrewsbury is brought home by the Duke of Buckingham to his house, where his Duchess saying that it was not for her and the other to live together in a house, he answered, "Why, Madam, I did think so, and, therefore, have ordered your coach to be ready, to carry you to your father's," which was a devilish speech, but, they say, true; and my Lady Shrewsbury is there, it seems.

September 9. To Westminster, to Sir R. Long's office; and, going, met Mr. George Montagu, who talked and complimented me mightily. He tells me that now Buckingham does rule all; and the other day, in the King's journey he is now on, at Bagshot, and that way, he caused Prince Rupert's horses to be turned out of an inne, and caused his own to be kept there, which the Prince complained of to the King, and the Duke of York seconded the complaint: but the King did over-rule it for Buckingham, by which there are high displeasures among them; and Buckingham and Arlington rule all. So, after a little supper, vexed, and spending a little time melancholy in making a base to the Lark's song, I to bed.

THOMAS VINCENT

The great visitations of plague and fire are nowhere so powerfully described as by the nonconformist preacher, Thomas Vincent, in his long pamphlet entitled God's Terrible Voice in the City. *Remaining at his post throughout the plague, he made the most of an occasion such as few exhorters have ever had, first to carry his followers through the crisis, then to castigate the city for its sins and bid it repent before it should be utterly destroyed. There can be no question of the fidelity of his account. Defoe made use of it in his realistic fiction,* A Journal of the Plague Year, *and, though little known, the earlier record deserves to rank with that masterpiece as a monument to the pity and terror of the time. Vincent must have taken up his pen when the ruins of God's second act of judgment were still smoldering.*

The Flight from London

It was in the month of May that the plague was first taken notice of. Our bill of mortality did let us know but of three which died of the disease in the whole year before, but in the beginning of May the bill tells us of nine which fell by the plague, one just in the heart of the City, the other eight in the suburbs. This was the first arrow of warning that was shot from Heaven amongst us, and fear quickly begins to creep upon people's hearts. Great thoughts and discourse there is in the town about the plague, and they cast in their minds whither they should go if the plague should increase. Yet when the next week's bill signifieth to them the disease from nine to three their minds are something appeased; discourse of that subject cools; fears are hushed; and hopes take place that the black cloud did but threaten and give few drops, but the wind would drive it away. But when in the next bill the number of the dead by the plague is mounted from three to fourteen, and in the next to seventeen, and in the next to forty-three, and the disease begins so much to increase and disperse:—

Now secure sinners begin to be startled, and those who would have slept at quiet in their nests are unwillingly awakened. Now a great consternation seizeth upon most persons and fearful bodings of a desolating judgment. Now guilty sinners begin to look about

The Difeafes and Cafualties this Week.

Abortive	4	Impofthume	8
Aged	45	Infants	22
Bleeding	1	Kingfevil	4
Broken legge	1	Lethargy	1
Broke her fcull by a fall in the ftreet at St. Mary VVoolchurch	1	Livergrown	1
		Meagrome	1
		Palfie	1
Childbed	28	Plague	4237
Chrifomes	9	Purples	2
Confumption	126	Quinfie	5
Convulfion	89	Rickets	23
Cough	1	Rifing of the Lights	18
Drophe	53	Rupture	1
Feaver	348	Scurvy	3
Flox and Small-pox	11	Shingles	1
Flux	1	Spotted Feaver	166
Frighted	2	Stilborn	4
Govvt	1	Stone	2
Grief	3	Stopping of the ftomach	17
Griping in the Guts	79	Strangury	3
Head-mould-fhot	1	Suddenly	2
Jaundies	7	Surfeit	74
		Teeth	111
		Thrufh	6
		Tiffick	9
		Ulcer	1
		Vomiting	10
		Winde	4
		Wormes	20

Chriftned	Males	90	Buried	Males	2777	Plague	4237
	Females	81		Females	2791		
	In all	171		In all	5568		

Increafed in the Burials this Week ——— 249

Parifhes clear of the Plague ——— 27   Parifhes Infected ——— 103

The Affize of Bread fet forth by Order of the Lord Maior and Court of Aldermen, A penny Wheaten Loaf to contain Nine Ounces and a half, and three half-penny White Loaves the like weight.

THE SAME BILL OF MORTALITY. (REVERSE)

them and think with themselves into what corner of the land they might fly to hide them. Now the profane and sensual, if they have not remorse for their sins, yet dread and terrors, the effects of guilt, they could not drive from them. And if by company and carousing and soft pleasures they do intoxicate and smoothen their spirits in the day, yet we must guess what dread doth return upon them if they give any room for retirement, and what hideous thoughts such persons have in the silent nights, through fears of death which they are in danger of. Now those who did not believe in an unseen God's threatenings of eternal judgments do tremble at the beginning of his execution of one (and not the greatest) temporal judgment. Now those which had, as it were, challenged the God of Heaven and defied him by their horrid oaths and blasphemies, when he begins to appear, they retreat, yea fly away with terror and amazement. The great Orbs begin first to move. The lords and gentry retire into their countries; their remote houses are prepared, goods removed, and London is quickly upon their backs. Few ruffling gallants walk the streets; few spotted ladies to be seen at windows. A great forsaking there was of the adjacent places where the plague did first rage.

Death Rides Triumphant

In August how dreadful is the increase! From 2010 the number amounts up to 2817 in one week; and thence to 3880 the next; thence to 4237 the next; thence to 6102 the next. And all those of the plague, besides other diseases.

Now the cloud is very black, and the storm comes down upon us very sharp. Now Death rides triumphantly on his pale horse through our streets and breaks into every house almost where any inhabitants are to be found. Now people fall as thick as leaves from the trees in Autumn when they are shaken by a mighty wind. Now there is a dismal solitude in the London streets. Every day looks like the face of a Sabbath day, observed with greater solemnity than is used to be in the city. Now shops are shut in, people rare, and very few that walk about, insomuch that the grass begins to spring up in some places, and a deep silence almost in every place, especially within the walls. No rattling coaches, no prancing horses, no calling in customers nor offering wares, no London cries sounding in the ears. If any voice be heard it is the groans of dying persons

breathing forth their last and the funeral knells of them that are
ready to be carried to their graves.

The Plague among God's People

It was generally observed amongst us that God's people who died
by the plague amongst the rest, died with such peace and comfort
as Christians do not ordinarily arrive unto except when they are
called forth to suffer martyrdom for the testimony of Jesus Christ.
Some who have been full of doubts and fears and complaints while
they have lived and been well have been filled with assurance and
comfort and praise and joyful expectation of glory when they have
lain on their deathbeds with the disease. And not only more grown
Christians, who have been more ripe for glory, have had these
comforts, but also some younger Christians, whose acquaintance with
the Lord hath been of no long standing.

I can speak something of my own knowledge concerning some of
my friends whom I have been withal. I shall instance only in the
house where I lived. We were eight in the family, three men, three
youths, an old woman, and a maid, all which came to me hearing
of my stay in town, some to accompany me, others to help me. It
was the latter end of September before any of us were touched.
The young ones were not idle but improved their time in praying
and hearing, and were ready to receive instruction, and were strangely
borne up against the fears of the disease death, every day so familiar
to their view. But at last we were visited and the plague came in
dreadfully upon us. The cup was put into our hand to drink after
a neighbor family had tasted it, with whom we had much sweet
society in this time of sorrow. And first our maid was smitten. It
began with a shivering and trembling in her flesh and quickly seized
on her spirits. It was a sad day which I believe I shall never forget.
I had been abroad to see a friend in the City whose husband was
newly dead of the plague and she herself visited with it. I came
back to see another whose wife was dead of the plague and he
himself under apprehensions that he should die within a few hours.
I came home and the maid was on her death bed, and another crying
out for help, being left alone in a sweating fainting fit. What was an
interest in Christ worth then! What a privilege to have a title in
the Kingdom of Heaven!

But I proceed. It was Monday when the maid was smitten; on

Thursday she died full of tokens; on Friday one of the youths had a swelling in his groin; and on the Lord's day died with the marks of the distemper upon him; on the same day another youth did sicken; and on the Wednesday following he died; on the Thursday night his master fell sick of the disease and within a day or two was full of spots, but strangely, beyond his own and others' expectations, recovered. Thus did the plague follow us and came upon us one by one. As Job's messengers came one upon the heels of another so the messengers of death came so close one after another in dreadful manner, as if we must all follow one another immediately into the Pit. Yet the Lord in mercy put a stop to it and the rest were preserved. But that which was very remarkable in this visitation was the carriage especially of those youths that died, who, I believe, were less troubled themselves than others were troubled for them. The first youth that was visited, being asked by his father concerning the provision he had made for his death and eternity, told him he hoped, if he died, he should go to Heaven. Being asked the grounds of his hopes, said the Lord had enabled him to look beyond this world, and when he was drawing near to his end boldly inquired whether the tokens did yet appear, saying he was ready for them. And so a hopeful bud was nipped. But let not the father or the mother weep and be in sadness for him. He is no doubt with their father and with his heavenly Father, which may be their comfort. The other also was a very sweet hopeful youth, so loving and towardly that it could not choose but attract love from those that were acquainted with him. But the grace he had gotten in those years, being, I suppose, under seventeen, did above all beautify him and stand him in the greatest stead. In his sickness he had much quietness and serenity upon his spirit and lay so unconcerned at the thoughts of approaching death, that I confess I marvelled to see it. The sting and fear of death were strangely taken out through the hopes which he had of future glory. Yet once he told his mother he could desire to live a little longer, if it were the will of God. She asked him why he desired it? He told her he desired to live till fire and faggot came and above all he would fain die a martyr. She said if he died now he should have a crown. He answered but if he died a martyr he should have a more glorious crown, yet he was not unwilling to receive his crown presently, and went away with great peace and sweetness in his looks to his Father's house. And I could not blame the mother's grief for the loss of such an only son, but to be so immoderate was not well. Now I am sure it is time to dry up tears and lay aside sorrows for the loss of him who hath been so long filled with joys in the heavenly mansions.

God's Hand in Plague and Fire

But if we further enquire into the reason why the plague was sent the last year . . . and why the fire was sent this year . . . what shall we say was the cause of these extraordinary national judgments but the extraordinary national sins? It was an extraordinary hand of God which brought the plague, of which no natural cause can be assigned why it should be so great this year more than in former years but that sin was grown to greater height, and that a fire should prevail against all attempts to quench it, to burn down the city, and that judgment just following on the heels of the other, what reason can be assigned but that England's sins and God's displeasure have been extraordinary?

A Catalogue of London's Sins

The first sin of London is slighting of the gospel. . . .

The second sin of London is unfruitfulness in such a fertile soil. . . .

A third sin of London is hypocrisy in the profession of religion. This sin exceedingly prevailed in the late times, when profession of religion was grown into fashion. Religion was near the mouths of most but far from their reins. . . . London hath formerly abounded with hypocrites and more lately it hath not been free. If hell fire be the portion of hypocrites hereafter (Matt. 24:51) no wonder then if God be angry with a place for this sin here. . . .

A fifth sin of London is division among professors. . . .

A seventh sin of London is fearful apostacy and a spirit of compliance with the sins of the times. . . .

A ninth sin of London is profaneness and a loose and frothy spirit, especially in the youth and springing generation. . . .

A thirteenth sin of London is unmercifulness. . . . I shall not blame the whole for this sin, for the charity of London hath sounded throughout the world. . . . But Oh what marble bowels have some had toward the poor! So that they could as freely part with so many drops of blood as pieces of money. . . .

A fourteenth sin of London is uncleanness, another sin of Sodom.

Their sin was unnatural uncleanness. I would hope that this sin hath been little known and practiced in the City, but fornication and adultery have been too common. . . . And hath this been the practice only of the court and Westminster side? Hath not the cursed leaven of this sin spread itself also in the City?

The twenty fourth sin of London is murmuring, and that not only in want and under losses and crosses but also in fulness and plenty. Many farmers in the country have murmured at the plenty and cheapness of corn; many traders in the City have murmured at the plenty of the commodities they have dealt in, because, however such plenty is a public and unspeakable mercy, yet they have had the less private advantage, which hath been chiefly regarded by them. Yea, some in their murmuring have wished for a plague that the survivors might have the better trade.

The twenty fifth and last sin of London which I shall speak of is carnal security, another of Sodom's sins. . . . When London had provoked God so highly by so many sins, yet how secure were they before his judgment broke forth upon them. They ate and drank, they bought, they sold, they planted, they builded. They sate at ease and put from them the evil day. . . . And I might add here as a cause of the security of some the presumptious confidence of future events which belong only to God to foreknow. . . . Great expectations many had of the fall of Antichrist and Babylon in the year 1666 and other events, limiting times which God hath not clearly revealed, which is entrenching on God's prerogative and, I believe, a greater provocation than such persons are aware of. This may be one reason why London is fallen instead of Babylon in this year of such expectation and presumption.

By this time it may be the reader may be wearied with reading as I am with thinking and writing of London's sins. But how hath the Lord been wearied with the bearing of them, as a cart is pressed that is full of sheaves (Amos 2:13). If when you read of London's judgments withal you consider London's provocations, you must acknowledge that God is righteous in that he hath punished London no more than they have deserved for their sins.

GEORGE THOMSON

Many physicians fled London with the court and the wealthier classes when the plague was raging, but an impressive number re-

*mained. Among these latter was George Thomson, who contracted
the disease, but survived to write* Loimotomia, *or the Pest Anato-
mized. He was perhaps the only doctor to dissect the body of a
victim. We give the opening of his post-mortem and one later
sentence which apparently describes the moment of discovery illus-
trated in the picture.*

Autopsy on a Victim of the Plague

In the year 1665, a most rueful, lamentable time as ever London
suffered in this kind, when the Sickness swept away many thousands
in a week in the month of August, I visited a lusty, proper man
by name Mr. William Pick, living in Petticoat Lane. Grievously
wounded by one of those poisonous arrows that flew thick about poor
mortals so that his condition seemed to be almost desperate and
finding no relief at all from those frivolous and vain preparations a
Galenist had exhibited to him *usque ad nauseam,* [he] was in some
short space preserved by chemical remedies, the poison being therewith excluded and the Archeus of the stomach redeemed from captivity. At the same time, there lay a servant of Mr. Pick's, a youth
of about 15 years of age, laboring under most horrid symptoms,
raving as it were extimulated by some fury, which tragical interlude
was quickly terminated by a mortal catastrophe. Upon this, I took
occasion to request my then recovering patient, his master, to grant
me liberty to open this defunct body for my own instruction and
the satisfaction of all inquisitive persons. To which, having given
him some persuasive reasons to that purpose, he straight conde-
scended, yet not without some jealousy and kind fear lest I should
do myself injury. Upon his concession, I, being much exhilarated in
my spirits, having obtained that desire which was often denied me
by those who pretended several slight excuses—I girt up myself with
all expedition, getting in readiness what instruments were fitting, with
a porringer containing sulphur to burn under the corpse which was at
that time placed in the open air in a yard there adjacent, which
for several respects was very convenient. And for my better accomodation, a servant by the permission of the foresaid master was
ready to afford me his service in opening the coffin nailed up, and
administering some other things necessary for my design.

The head of the coffin being taken off and the linen cleared away,

I could not but admire to behold a skin so beset with spots black and blue, more remarkable for multitude and magnitude than any I have yet seen. . . . Then, having opened the right cavity of the heart, I therein found a white congealed matter, extracting which with my fingers and narrowly viewing it, I could not compare it to anything more like than a lamb-stone cut in two, which the servant beholding, standing near, easily assented to in his judgment. . . .

JOHN DRYDEN

Annus Mirabilis was written after the fire but before the Dutch raid on the English naval bases in June 1667. There had been a succession of engagements which could be interpreted as victories, though they were not really so since De Ruyter saved his fleet. The loyal and patriotic court poet uses these as the theme of a rousing glorification of the war at about the last moment when even official propaganda could speak this language. In recording the events of 1666, Dryden passes over the plague with a mere mention and describes the great fire as a timely castigation of England for its pride of victory. These were wonders indeed but woeful ones, intelligible only on the principle that whom God loveth he chastiseth. At the intercession of King Charles God stayed his hand. The people have recovered hope. The image of a new city, capital of an empire too mighty to be challenged by its commercial rivals, rises above the ruins to possess all hearts.

Dryden calls his poem historical rather than heroic, but he has Virgil in mind and deliberately echoes him in style and imagery.

London Redivivus

And now four days the sun had seen our woes;
    Four nights the moon beheld th' incessant fire:
It seem'd as if the stars more sickly rose,
    And farther from the fev'rish north retire.

In th' empyrean heaven (the blest abode),
    The Thrones and the Dominions prostrate lie,
Not daring to behold their angry God;
    And an hush'd silence damps the tuneful sky.

At length th' Almighty cast a pitying eye,
 And mercy softly touch'd his melting breast:
He saw the town's one half in rubbish lie,
 And eager flames drive on to storm the rest.

An hollow crystal pyramid he takes,
 In firmamental waters dipp'd above;
Of it a broad extinguisher he makes
 And hoods the flames that to their quarry strove.

The vanquish'd fires withdraw from every place,
 Or, full with feeding, sink into a sleep:
Each household genius shews again his face,
 And from the hearts the little Lares creep.

Our king this more than natural change beholds;
 With sober joy his heart and eyes abound:
To the All-good his lifted hands he folds,
 And thanks him low on his redeemed ground.

As when sharp frosts had long constrain'd the earth,
 A kindly thaw unlocks it with mild rain;
And first the tender blade peeps up to birth,
 And straight the green fields laugh with promis'd grain:

By such degrees the spreading gladness grew
 In every heart which fear had froze before;
The standing streets with so much joy they view,
 That with less grief the perish'd they deplore.

The father of the people open'd wide
 His stores, and all the poor with plenty fed:
Thus God's anointed God's own place supplied,
 And fill'd the empty with his daily bread.

This royal bounty brought its own reward,
 And in their minds so deep did print the sense,
That if their ruins sadly they regard,
 'Tis but with fear the sight might drive him thence.

But so may he live long, that town to sway,
 Which by his auspice they will nobler make,
As he will hatch their ashes by his stay,
 And not their humble ruins now forsake.

They have not lost their loyalty by fire;
 Nor is their courage or their wealth so low,
That from his wars they poorly would retire,
 Or beg the pity of a vanquish'd foe.

Not with more constancy the Jews of old,
 By Cyrus from rewarded exile sent,
Their royal city did in dust behold,
 Or with more vigor to rebuild it went.

The utmost malice of their stars is past,
 And two dire comets, which have scourg'd the town,
In their own plague and fire have breath'd their last,
 Or, dimly, in their sinking sockets frown.

Now frequent trines the happier lights among,
 And high-rais'd Jove, from his dark prison freed,
(Those weights took off that on his planet hung,)
 Will gloriously the new-laid works succeed.

Methinks already, from this chymic flame,
 I see a city of more precious mold,
Rich as the town which gives the Indies name,
 With silver pav'd, and all divine with gold.

Already, laboring with a mighty fate,
 She shakes the rubbish from her mounting brow,
And seems to have renew'd her charter's date,
 Which Heav'n will to the death of time allow.

More great than human, now, and more *august*,
 New-deified she from her fires does rise:
Her widening streets on new foundations trust,
 And, opening, into larger parts she flies.

Before, she like some shepherdess did show,
  Who sate to bathe her by a river's side;
Not answering to her fame, but rude and low,
  Nor taught the beauteous arts of modern pride.

Now, like a maiden queen, she will behold,
  From her high turrets, hourly suitors come:
The East with incense, and the West with gold,
  Will stand, like suppliants, to receive her doom.

The silver Thames, her own domestic flood,
  Shall bear her vessels like a sweeping train;
And often wind, (as of his mistress proud,)
  With longing eyes to meet her face again.

The wealthy Tagus, and the wealthier Rhine,
  The glory of their towns no more shall boast;
And Seine, that would with Belgian rivers join,
  Shall find her luster stain'd, and traffic lost.

The vent'rous merchant, who design'd more far,
  And touches on our hospitable shore,
Charm'd with the splendor of this northern star,
  Shall here unlade him, and depart no more.

Our pow'rful navy shall no longer meet,
  The wealth of France or Holland to invade;
The beauty of this town, without a fleet,
  From all the world shall vindicate her trade.

And, while this fam'd emporium we prepare,
  The British ocean shall such triumphs boast,
That those who now disdain our trade to share,
  Shall rob like pirates on our wealthy coast.

Already we have conquer'd half the war,
  And the less dang'rous part is left behind;
Our trouble now is but to make them dare,
  And not so great to vanquish as to find.

Thus to the eastern wealth thro' storms we go,
    But now, the Cape once doubled, fear no more;
A constant trade-wind will securely blow,
    And gently lay us on the spicy shore.

3 *Plot and Counterplot: The End of an Era*

JOHN EVELYN

Pepys's diary having ended in 1669, John Evelyn is our chronicler for the next epoch of Restoration history. The initial event was Charles II's secret agreement with Louis XIV (May 22, 1670), which naturally does not appear in Evelyn. The Treaty of Dover bound the English monarch to declare war again on Holland, to assist Louis in his plan to seize the Spanish Netherlands and finally to announce his own conversion to the Catholic faith, "as soon as the welfare of the realm shall permit"—all this in return for a large subsidy designed to free him from the control of an increasingly restive Parliament. There followed in due course the second Dutch war (the third, counting the one waged by Cromwell), the great outbreak of popular feeling against Catholicism, the attempt of Shaftesbury to exclude James from the succession, the failure of Whig plotting, Charles's death at the moment of his triumph, the Monmouth rebellion, bloodily suppressed, and finally the Glorious Revolution.

Evelyn's reaction to these events is characteristic of a loyal supporter of the House of Stuart who is nevertheless staunchly Protestant. He is troubled at the execution of the Whig lords but also full of anxiety over the revolutionary settlement. "God of his infinite mercy compose these things, that we may be at last a Nation and a Church under some fixed and sober establishment."

As is apparent in these extracts, Evelyn's diary is a more studied composition than that of his friend and fellow member of the Royal Society, Samuel Pepys. The two men live in the same world and engage in many of the same activities, but the distance between them as human beings is immense. This is nowhere more apparent than in Evelyn's great affair of the heart, the true character of which could hardly be guessed from the diary entries but is fully revealed in other private papers. It was a case of "seraphic love" between an older man and a religious-minded girl, one of the maids of honor, who finally broke away from the exclusive demands of her spiritual friend to marry her fiancé, Sidney Godolphin.

In his public activity Evelyn was a virtuoso in the best sense of the word, interested in all the arts and sciences and in every program for their advancement, his special skills being in architecture, forestry and numismatics. He was a man of great integrity and became a trusted adviser of Charles in technical matters. Throughout the Dutch wars he was commissioner for the sick and wounded; he also served as member of the council for plantations. He took a leading part with Robert Boyle in the founding of the Royal Society and became its most honored member.

The Year 1671

May 10. Dined at Mr. Treasurer's, where dined Monsieur De-Grammont and several French noblemen and one Blood, that impudent, bold fellow who had not long before attempted to steal the imperial crown itself out of the Tower, pretending only curiosity of seeing the regalia there, when, stabbing the keeper though not mortally, he boldly went away with it through all the guards, taken only by the accident of his horse falling down. How he came to be pardoned and even received into favor, not only after this but several other exploits almost as daring, both in Ireland and here, I could never come to understand. Some believed he became a spy of several parties, being well with the sectaries and enthusiasts, and did his Majesty services that way, which none alive could do so well as he. But it was certainly, as the boldest attempt, so the only treason of this sort that was ever pardoned. The man had not only a daring but a villainous, unmerciful look, a false countenance, but very well spoken and dangerously insinuating.

August 3. A full appearance at the Council. The matter in debate was whether we should send a deputy to New England requiring them of Massachusetts to restore such to their limits and respective possessions as had petitioned the Council; this to be the open commission only but in truth with secret instructions to inform the Council of the conditions of those Colonies and whether they were of such power as to be able to resist his Majesty and declare for themselves as independent of the Crown, which we are told and which of late years made them refractory. Colonel Middleton being called in, assured us they might be curbed by a few of his Majesty's first-rate frigates, to spoil their trade with the islands. But though my Lord President was not satisfied, the rest were, and we did resolve to advise his Majesty to send commissioners with a formal commission for adjusting boundaries, etc., with some other instructions.

The Year 1672

March 12. Now was the first blow given by us to the Dutch convoy of the Smyrna fleet, by Sir Robert Holmes and Lord Ossorie, in which we received little save blows and a worthy reproach for attacking our neighbors before any war was proclaimed, and then pretending the occasion to be that, some time before, the Merlin yacht chancing to sail through the whole Dutch fleet, their Admiral did not strike to that trifling vessel. Surely this was a quarrel slenderly grounded and not becoming Christian neighbors. We are like to thrive accordingly. . . .

A few days before this, the Treasurer of the Household, Sir Thomas Clifford hinted to me, as a confidant, that his Majesty would shut up the Exchequer (and accordingly his Majesty made use of infinite treasure there to prepare for an intended rupture). But, says he, it will soon be open again and everybody satisfied, for this bold man, who had been the sole adviser of the King to invade that sacred stock (though some pretend it was Lord Ashley's counsel, then Chancellor of the Exchequer), was so over-confident of the success of this unworthy design against the Smyrna merchants as to put his Majesty on an action which not only lost the hearts of his subjects and ruined many widows and orphans whose stocks were lent him, but the reputation of his Exchequer forever, it being before in such credit that he might have commanded half the wealth of the nation.

The credit of this bank being thus broken did exceedingly discontent the people and never did his Majesty's affairs prosper to any purpose after it for, as it did not supply the expense of the meditated war, so it melted away, I know not how. . . .

To this succeeded the King's declaration for a universal toleration; Papists and swarms of sectaries now boldly showing themselves in their public meetings. This was imputed to the same council, Clifford warping to Rome as was believed, nor was Lord Arlington clear of suspicion to gratify that party, but, as since it has proved and was then evidently foreseen, to the extreme weakening of the Church of England and its episcopal government as it was projected. . . .

April 4. I went to see the fopperies of the Papists at Somerset House and York House where now the French Ambassador had caused to be represented our Blessed Savior at the paschal supper

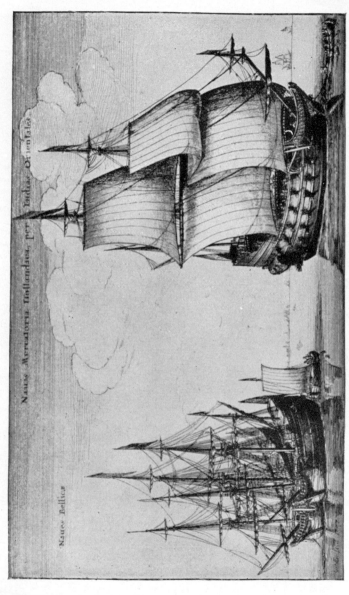

Naues Mercatoriæ Hollandicæ, per Indias Orientales

Naues Bellicæ

THE DUTCH FLEET

From a print by Wenceslaus Hollar, reproduced from the original in Princeton University Library. By permission of Princeton University Library.

SAMUEL PEPYS SINGING

From a portrait by John Hayles. Reproduced by permission of The National Portrait Gallery.

with his disciples, in figures and puppets made as big as life of waxwork, curiously clad and sitting around a large table, the room nobly hung and shining with innumerable lamps and candles. This was exposed to all the world. All the city came to see it; such liberty had the Roman Catholics at this time obtained.

May 14. To Dover, but the fleet did not appear till the sixteenth, when the Duke of York with his and the French squadron, in all 170 ships (of which above 100 were men of war) sailed by after the Dutch who were newly withdrawn. Such a gallant and formidable navy never, I think, spread sail upon the seas. It was a goodly yet terrible sight to behold them as I did, passing Eastward by the straights between Dover and Calais in a glorious day. . . .

May 31. I received another command to repair to the seaside. So I went to Rochester where I found many wounded, sick, and prisoners newly put on shore after the engagement on the 28th, in which the Earl of Sandwich, that incomparable person and my particular friend, and divers more whom I loved, were lost. My Lord (who was Admiral of the Blew) was in the Prince, which was burned, one of the best men of war that ever spread canvas on the sea. . . . My Lord Sandwich was prudent as well as valiant and always governed his affairs with success and little loss. He was for deliberation and reason, they [Albemarle and Clifford] for action and slaughter without either, and for this, whispered as if my Lord Sandwich was not so gallant because he was not so rash and knew how fatal it was to lose a fleet such as was that under his conduct, and for which these very persons would have censured him on the other side. This it was, I am confident, grieved him and made him enter like a lion and fight like one, too, in the midst of the hottest service where the stoutest of the rest, seeing him engaged and so many ships upon him, dared not or would not come to his succor, as some of them whom I know might have done. Thus this gallant person perished to gratify the pride and envy of some I named. . . .

The Year 1673

July 25. I went to Tunbridge Wells to visit my Lord Clifford, late Lord Treasurer, who was there to divert his mind more than his body. It was believed that he had so engaged himself to the Duke that rather than take the test, without which he was not capable of holding any office, he would resign that great and honorable station. This, I am confident, grieved him to the heart and at last broke it. For though he carried with him music and people to divert him and, when I came to see him, lodged me in his own apartment and would not let me go from him, I found he was struggling in his mind, and being of a rough and ambitious nature, he could not long brook the necessity he had brought on himself of submission to this conjuncture. Besides he saw the Dutch war, which was made much by his advice as well as the shutting up of the Exchequer, very unprosperous. These things his high spirit could not support. Having stayed here two or three days, I obtained leave of my Lord to return. . . .

The Year 1678

October 1. The Parliament and the whole nation were alarmed about a conspiracy of some eminent Papists for the destruction of the King and introduction of Popery, discovered by one Oates and Dr. Tongue, which last I knew, being the translator of the 'Jesuits' Morals'. I went to see and converse with him at Whitehall, with Mr. Oates, one that was lately an apostate to the church of Rome and now returned again with this discovery. He seemed to be a bold man and, in my thoughts, furiously indiscreet, but everybody believed what he said and it quite changed the genius and motions of the Parliament, growing now corrupt and interested with long sitting and court practices, but with all this Popery would not go down. This discovery turned them all as one man against it, and nothing was done but to find out the depth of this. Oates was encouraged, and everything he affirmed taken for gospel. The truth is, the Roman Catholics were exceedingly bold and busy everywhere since the Duke forebore to go any longer to the Chapel.

October 21. The murder of Sir Edmonbury Godfrey, found strangled about this time, as was manifest by the Papists, he being a justice of the peace and one who knew much of their practices, as conversant with Coleman (a servant of the . . . now accused), put the whole nation into a new ferment against them.

November 5. Dr. Tillotson preached before the Commons at St. Margaret's. He said the Papists were now arrived at that impudence as to deny that there ever was any such thing as the gunpowder conspiracy. But he affirmed that he himself had several letters written by Sir Everard Digby (one of the traitors), in which he gloried that

he was to suffer for it, and that it was so contrived that of the
Papists not above two or three should have been blown up and
they such as were not worth saving.

November 15. The Queen's birthday. I never saw the Court more
brave nor the nation in more apprehension and consternation. Coleman and one Staly had now been tried, condemned, and executed.
On this, Oates grew so presumptuous as to accuse the Queen of
intending to poison the King, which certainly that pious and virtuous
lady abhorred the thoughts of, and Oates his circumstances made it
utterly unlikely, in my opinion. He probably thought to gratify some
who would have been glad his Majesty should have married a fruitful
lady, but the King was too kind a husband to let any of these make
an impression on him. However, divers of the Popish peers were sent
to the Tower, accused by Oates, and all the Roman Catholic Lords
were by a new act forever excluded the Parliament, which was a
mighty blow. The King's, Queen's, and Duke's servants were banished and a test to be taken by everybody who pretended to enjoy
any office of public trust, and who would not be suspected of
Popery. I went with Sir William Godolphin, a member of the
Commons House, to the Bishop of Ely (Dr. Peter Gunning) to be
resolved whether masses were idolatry, as the test expressed it, which
was so worded that several good Protestants scrupled and Sir William, though a learned man and excellent divine himself, had some
doubts about it. The Bishop's opinion was that he might take it,
though he wished it had been otherwise worded in the test.

The Year 1679

July 18. I went early to the Old Bailey Sessions House to the
famous trial of Sir George Wakeman, one of the Queen's physicians,
and three Benedictine monks; the first (whom I was well acquainted
with and take to be a worthy gentleman abhorring such a fact) for
intending to poison the King; the others, as accomplices to carry out
the plot to subvert the government and introduce Popery. . . . For
my part, I look on Oates as a vain, insolent man, puffed up with
the favor of the Commons for having discovered something really
true, more especially as detecting the dangerous intrigue of Coleman,
proved out of his own letters and of a general design which the
Jesuited party of the Papists ever had and still have, to ruin the
Church of England. But that he was trusted with those great

secrets he pretended or had any solid grounds for what he accused divers noblemen of, I have many reasons to induce my contrary belief. . . . But indeed the murder of Sir Edmund Godfrey, suspected to have been compassed by the Jesuit party for his intimacy with Coleman (a busy person whom I also knew) and the fear they had that he was able to have discovered some things to their prejudice, did so exasperate not only the Commons but all the nation that much of these sharpnesses against the more honest Roman Catholics who lived peaceably is to be imputed to that horrid fact. . . .

November 28. Came over the Duke of Monmouth from Holland unexpectedly to his Majesty while the Duke of York was on his journey to Scotland, whither the King sent him to reside and govern. The bells and bonfires of the City at this arrival of the Duke of Monmouth publishing their joy, to the no small regret of some at Court. This Duke, whom for distinction they called the Protestant Duke (though the son of an abandoned woman), the people made their idol.

The Year 1680

November 30. . . . This signal day begun the trial (at which I was present) of my Lord Viscount Stafford for conspiring the death of the King; second son to my Lord Thomas Howard, Earl of Arundel and Surry, Earl Marshall of England and grandfather to the present Duke of Norfolk, whom I so well knew and from which excellent person I received so many favors. . . . The principal witnesses were Mr. Oates (who called himself Dr.), Mr. Dugdale, and Turberville. Oates swore that he delivered a commission to Viscount Stafford from the Pope, to be Paymaster General to an army intended to be raised; Dugdale, that being at Lord Aston's, the prisoner dealt with him plainly to murder his Majesty; and Turberville, that at Paris he had also proposed the same to him.

December 7. On Tuesday I was again at the trial when judgment was demanded; and after my Lord had spoken what he could in denying the fact, the managers answering the objections, the peers adjourned to their house and within two hours returned again. There was in the meantime this question put to the judges, "whether there being but one witness to any single crime or act, it could amount to convict a man of treason." They gave an unanimous opinion that in case of treason they all were overt acts, for though no man should be condemned by one witness for any one act, yet for several acts to the same intent it was valid, which was my Lord's case. This being passed and the peers in their seats again, the Lord Chancellor Finch (this day the Lord High Steward) removing to the woolsack next his Majesty's state, after summoning the Lieutenant of the Tower to bring forth his prisoner and proclamation made for silence, demanded of every peer (who were in all 86) whether William Lord Viscount Stafford were guilty of the treason laid to his charge, or not guilty. Then the peer spoken to, standing up and laying his right hand on his breast, said Guilty or Not Guilty, upon my honor, and then sat down, the Lord Steward noting their suffrages as they answered upon a paper, when all had done the number of Not Guilty being but 31, the Guilty 55. And then after the proclamation for silence again, the Lord Steward directing his speech to the prisoner against whom the ax was turned edgeways, and not before, in aggravation of his crime. . . . He then pronounced sentence of death by hanging, drawing and quartering, according to form, with great solemnity and dreadful gravity, and, after a short pause, told the prisoner that he believed the Lords would intercede for the omission of some circumstances of his sentence, beheading only excepted; and then breaking his white staff, the court was dissolved. My Lord Stafford, during all this latter part, spoke but little, and only gave their Lordships thanks after the sentence was pronounced; and indeed behaved himself modestly and as became him.

The Year 1683

June 28. After the Popish Plot, there was now a new and (as they called it) a Protestant Plot discovered, that certain Lords and others should design the assassination of the King and the Duke as they were to come from Newmarket, with a general rising of the nation and especially of the City of London, disaffected to the present government. Upon which were committed to the Tower the Lord Russell, eldest son of the Earl of Bedford, the Earl of Essex, Mr. Algernon Sidney, son to the old Earl of Leicester, Mr. Trenchard, Hampden, Lord Howard of Escrick, and others. A proclamation was issued against my Lord Grey, the Duke of Monmouth, Sir Thomas Armstrong, and one Ferguson who had escaped beyond the sea. Of these some were said to be for killing the King, others for only

seizing on him and persuading him to new counsels, on the pretence
of the danger of Popery should the Duke live to succeed, who was
now again admitted to the councils and cabinet secrets. The Lords
Essex and Russell were much deplored, few believing they had any
evil intention against the King or the Church. Some thought they
were cunningly drawn in by their enemies for not approving some
late counsels and management relating to France, to Popery, to the
persecution of the dissenters, etc. They were discovered by the Lord
Howard of Escrick and some false brethren of the club, and the
design happily broken. Had it taken effect, it would, to all appearance, have exposed the government to unknown and dangerous
events, which God avert!

July 13. As I was visiting Sir Thomas Yarbrow and his Lady in
Covent Garden, the astonishing news was brought to us of the
Earl of Essex having cut his throat, having been but three days a
prisoner in the Tower and this happening on the very day and instant
that Lord Russell was on his trial and had sentence of death. This
accident exceedingly amazed me, my Lord Essex being so well known
by me to be a person of such sober and religious deportment, so
well at his ease, and so much obliged to the King. . . . What might
instigate him to this devilish fact, I am not able to conjecture. My
Lord Clarendon, his brother-in-law, who was with him but the day
before, assured me he was then very cheerful and declared it to be
the effect of his innocence and loyalty, and must believe that his
Majesty had no severe intentions against him, though he was altogether inexorable as to Lord Russell and some of the rest. For my
part, I believe the crafty and ambitious Earl of Shaftesbury had
brought them into some dislike of the present carriage of matters
at Court, not with any design of destroying the Monarchy (which
Shaftesbury has in confidence and for unanswerable reasons told me
he would support to his last breath, as having seen and felt the
misery of being under mechanic tyranny), but perhaps of setting up
some other whom he might govern and frame to his own platonic
fancy without much regard to the religion established under the
hierarchy for which he had no esteem. But when he perceived those
whom he had engaged to rise fail of his expectations and the day
passed, reproaching his accomplices that a second day for an exploit
of this nature was never successful, he gave them the slip and got into
Holland, where the fox died three months before these unhappy
Lords and others were discovered or suspected. Everyone deplored
Essex and Russell, especially the last, as being thought to have been

drawn in on pretence only of endeavoring to rescue the King from his present counselors and secure religion from Popery and the nation from arbitrary government, now so much apprehended; while the rest of those who were fled, especially Ferguson and his gang, had doubtless some bloody design to set up a Commonwealth and turn all things topsy-turvy. Of the same tragic principles is Sidney.

July 21. Lord Russell was beheaded in Lincoln's Inn Fields, the executioner giving him three butcherly strokes. The speech he made and paper which he gave the Sheriff declaring his innocence, the nobleness of the family, the piety and worthiness of the unhappy gentleman, wrought much pity and occasioned various discourses on the plot.

November 23. The Duke of Monmouth, till now proclaimed traitor on the pretended plot for which Lord Russell was lately beheaded, came this evening to Whitehall and rendered himself, on which were various discourses.

December 5. . . . The Duke of Monmouth, now having his pardon, refuses to acknowledge there was any treasonable plot, for which he is banished Whitehall. . . .

The Year 1685

February 4. I went to London, hearing his Majesty had been the Monday before (2nd February) surprised in his bedchamber with an apoplectic fit, so that if, by God's providence, Dr. King (that excellent chirurgeon as well as physician) had not been accidentally present to let him blood (having his lancet in his pocket), his Majesty had certainly died that moment; which might have been of direful consequence, there being nobody else present with the King save this doctor and one more, as I am assured. . . . On Thursday hopes of recovery were signified in the public Gazette, but that day about noon, the physicians thought him feverish. This they seemed glad of, as being more easily allayed and methodically dealt with than his former fits, so as they prescribed the famous Jesuit's powder; but it made him worse, and some very able doctors who were present did not think it a fever, but the effect of his frequent bleeding and other sharp operations used by them about his head, so that probably the powder might stop the circulation, and renew his former fits, which now made him very weak. Thus he passed Thursday night with great difficulty, when, complaining of a pain in his side, they drew twelve ounces more of blood from him; this was by six in the morning on Friday, and it gave him relief, but it did not continue, for being now in much pain, and struggling for breath, he lay dozing, and, after some conflicts, the physicians despairing of him, he gave up the ghost at half an hour after eleven in the morning, being the sixth of February, 1685, in the 36th year of his reign, and 54th of his age. . . .

Thus died King Charles II, of a vigorous and robust constitution, and in all appearance promising a long life. He was a prince of many virtues, and many great imperfections; debonaire, easy of access, not bloody nor cruel; his countenance fierce, his voice great, proper of person, every motion became him; a lover of the sea, and skillful in shipping; not affecting other studies, yet he had a laboratory, and knew of many empirical medicines and the easier mechanical mathematics; he loved planting and building, and brought in a politer way of living, which passed to luxury and intolerable expense. He had a particular talent in telling a story, and facetious passages, of which he had innumerable; this made some buffoons and vicious wretches too presumptuous and familiar, not worthy the favor they abused. He took delight in having a number of little spaniels follow him and lie in his bedchamber, where he often suffered the bitches to puppy and give suck, which rendered it very offensive, and indeed made the whole court nasty and stinking. He would doubtless have been an excellent prince, had he been less addicted to women, who made him uneasy, and always in want to supply their unmeasurable profusion, to the detriment of many indigent persons who had signally served both him and his father. He frequently and easily changed favorites to his great prejudice.

As to other public transactions, and unhappy miscarriages, 'tis not here I intend to number them; but certainly never had king more glorious opportunities to have made himself, his people, and all Europe happy, and prevented innumerable mischiefs, had not his too easy nature resigned him to be managed by crafty men, and some abandoned and profane wretches who corrupted his otherwise sufficient parts, disciplined as he had been by many afflictions during his banishment, which gave him much experience and knowledge of men and things; but those wicked creatures took him from off all application becoming so great a king. The history of his reign will certainly be the most wonderful for the variety of matter and accidents, above any extant in former ages: the sad tragical death of his father, his banishment and hardships, his miraculous restoration, conspiracies against him, parliaments, wars, plagues, fires, comets, revolutions abroad happening in his time, with a thousand other particulars. He was ever kind to me, and very gracious upon all occasions, and therefore I cannot without ingratitude but deplore his loss, which for many respects, as well as duty, I do with all my soul.

March 5. To my grief, I saw the new pulpit set up in the Popish Oratory at Whitehall for the Lent preaching, mass being publicly said and the Romanists swarming at Court with greater confidence than had ever been seen in England since the Reformation, so as everybody grew jealous to what this would tend.

June 14. There was now certain intelligence of the Duke of Monmouth landing at Lyme in Dorsetshire and of his having set up his standard as King of England. I pray God deliver us from the confusion which these beginnings threaten!

June 17. The Duke landed with but 150 men, but the whole Kingdom was alarmed, fearing that the disaffected would join them, many of the trained bands flocking to him. At his landing he published a declaration, charging his Majesty with usurpation and several horrid crimes on pretence of his own title and offering to call a free Parliament. This declaration was ordered to be burned by the hangman, the Duke proclaimed a traitor and a reward of £5,000 to any man who should kill him.

At this time the words engraved on the monument in London, intimating that the Papists fired the City, were erased and cut out.

July 15. Monmouth was this day brought to London and examined before the King, to whom he made great submission, acknowledged his seduction by Ferguson the Scot, whom he named the bloody villain. He was sent to the Tower, had an interview with his late Duchess whom he received coldly, having lived dishonestly with the Lady Henrietta Wentworth for two years. He obstinately asserted his conversation with that debauched woman to be no sin, whereupon, seeing he could not be persuaded to his last breath, the divines who were sent to assist him thought not fit to administer the Holy Communion to him. For the rest of his faults he professed great sorrow and so died without any apparent fear. He would not make use of a cap or other circumstance but, lying down, bid the fellow do his office better than to the late Lord Russell, and gave him gold. But the wretch made five chops before he had his head off, which so incensed the people that, had he not been guarded and got away, they would have torn him to pieces.

The Year 1688

September 18. I went to London where I found the Court in the utmost consternation on report of the Prince of Orange's landing, which put Whitehall into so panic a fear that I could hardly believe it possible to find such a change.

December 18. I saw the King take barge to Gravesend at 12 o'clock—a sad sight! The Prince comes to St. James's, and fills Whitehall with Dutch guards. A council of peers meet about an expedient to call a parliament; adjourn to the House of Lords. The Chancellor, Earl of Peterborough, and divers others taken. The Earl of Sunderland flies. Sir Edward Hales, Walker and others, taken and secured.

All the world go to see the Prince at St. James's where there is a great Court. There I saw him and several of my acquaintance who came over with him. He is very stately, serious, and reserved. The English soldiers sent out of town to disband them; not well pleased.

December 24. The King passes into France, whither the Queen and child were gone a few days before.

CHARLES II

To his contemporaries Charles II was the most interesting thing in England. As the historian or critic looks back from our own point of vantage he is neither the hero nor the villain of the piece. There are no heroes except men of genius and of virtue; there are no villains except meanness, passion and self-deception—the fury and the mire of human veins. The real memorabilia of the time are in society itself, in the shaping forces which we see to have been at work in business, politics, religion, in the words and actions of a thousand individuals in every walk of life. Charles, resplendent in his Garter robes or relaxing in Lady Castlemaine's boudoir, is only an accident, whose role and character are still a matter of dispute. He remains, however, a fascinating figure, the one and only Merry Monarch, easygoing, urbane, amoral, selfish, unreliable, but immensely experienced in the ways of men and women and uncannily astute in his dealings with them. No one better understood how to manage the clash of party and individual to his own advantage. He was capable of sacrificing the best and most loyal of his supporters and of betraying causes to which he had sworn the deepest allegiance, yet he was not without a certain brand of patriotism. He went with the tide but he always steered the boat. His aim was to do just this at any cost, for only so could he undo the work of revolution which had kept him for years a royal mendicant. The secret deal with France, which Whigs from then till now have looked at as a great betrayal and Tories as a piece of justifiable diplomacy, was but an incident in the total program of restoring the royal authority and securing the succession of his family to the throne. There was in his mind no alternative but continued turmoil and disruption. Yet his judgment in this as in other things was partly swayed by women. He triumphed, finally, at what seemed the moment of defeat and left a solid situation which might have endured for many reigns but for the inflexibility of James.

The character of Charles, both as a sovereign and as a man, is well represented in his correspondence, particularly in the famous letters to his sister, Henriette, the Duchess of Orléans, from which brief extracts are given below. The proclamation regarding the rebuilding of London and the speech to his last Parliament illustrate the quality of his public utterance. His deathbed scene is a classic episode which no one reports so faithfully as the French ambassador, Barillon. Other observations and opinions regarding Charles by those who knew him well afford the reader opportunity to weigh, if not to pass judgment on, the contradictions, real and apparent, in his personality and behavior.

Letters

TO THE LORD CHANCELLOR CLARENDON

1.

Portsmouth, May 21, 1662. 8 in the morning.

I arrived here yesterday about two in the afternoon, and as soon as I had shifted myself, I went to my wife's chamber, who I found in bed, by reason of a little cough, and some inclination to a fever, which was caused, as we physicians say, by having certain things stopped at sea which ought to have carried away those humours. But now all is in their due course, and I believe she will find herself very well in the morning as soon as she wakes.

It was happy for the honor of the nation that I was not put to the consummation of the marriage last night; for I was so sleepy by having slept but two hours in my journey as I was afraid that matters would have gone very sleepily. I can now only give you an account of what I have seen a-bed; which, in short, is, her face is not so exact as to be called a beauty though her eyes are excellent good and not anything in her face that in the least degree can shock one. On the contrary, she has as much agreeableness in her looks altogether, as ever I saw: and if I have any skill in physiognomy, which I think I have, she must be as good a woman as ever was born. Her conversation, as much as I can perceive, is very good; for she has wit enough and a most agreeable voice. You would much wonder to see how well we are acquainted already. In a word, I think myself very happy; but am confident our two humors will agree very well together. I have not time to say any more. My Lord Lieutenant will give you an account of the rest.

2.

June 7, 1662

The relation that has been made to me of Sir H. Vane's carriage yesterday in the Hall is the occasion of this letter, which, if I am rightly informed, was so insolent as to justify all he had done, acknowledging no supreme power in England but a Parliament, and many things to that purpose. You have had a true account of all, and, if he has given new occasion to be hanged, certainly he is too dangerous a man to let live if we can honestly put him out of the way. Think of this and give me some account of it tomorrow and till when I have no more to say to you.

3.

July or August 1662

I forgot, when you were here last, to desire you to give Broderick good counsel, not to meddle any more with what concerns my Lady Castlemaine and to let him have a care how he is the author of any scandalous reports. For if I find him guilty of any such thing I will make him repent it to the last moment of his life. And now I am entered on this matter, I think it necessary to give you a little good counsel in it, lest you may think that by making a further stir in the business, you may divert me from my resolution, which all the world shall never do. And I wish I may be unhappy in this world and the world to come if I fail in the least degree of what I have resolved, which is, of making my Lady Castlemaine of my wife's bedchamber. And whosoever I find use any endeavor to hinder this resolution of mine (except it be only to myself), I will be his enemy to the last moment of my life.

You know how true a friend I have been to you. If you will oblige me eternally, make this business as easy as you can, of what opinion soever you are of, for I am resolved to go through with this matter let what will come on it; which again I solemnly swear before Almighty God. Therefore, if you desire to have the continuance of my friendship, meddle no more with this business, except it be to beat down all false and scandalous reports and to facilitate what I am sure my honor is so much concerned in. And whosoever I find to be my Lady Castlemaine's enemy in this matter, I do promise, upon my word, to be his enemy as long as I live. You may show this letter to my Lord Lieutenant; and if you both have a mind to oblige me, carry yourselves like friends to me in this matter.

TO HIS SISTER HENRIETTA

1.

November 2, 1663

My wife is now out of all danger though very weak, and it was a very strange fever, for she talked idly four or five days after the fever had left her. But now that is likewise past and she will do herself as soon as she gets strength. And so, my dearest sister, I will trouble you no more at this time, but beg of you to love him who is entirely yours. c.

2.

January 18, 1664

My wife thanks you very kindly for the images you sent her; they are very fine ones, and she never saw such before. I have not had yet time to talk with the Comte de Gramont; he is so taken up with his wife, as I have scarce seen him these two days that he has been here. But that fury continues not long and I believe he will be as reasonable in that point as most men are and then I will give you a further account of our conversation. . . .

3.

February 1664

I was in great pain to hear of the fall you had lest it might have done you prejudice in the condition you are in, but I was as glad to find by your letter that it had done you no harm. We have the same disease of Sermons that you complain of there, but I hope you have the same convenience that the rest of the family had, of sleeping out most of the time, which is a great ease to those who are bound to hear them.

4.

March 17, 1664

The Queen showed me your letter about the operation done upon Mademoiselle Montausier, and by her smile, I believe she had no more guess at the meaning than you had at the writing of the letter. I am confident that this will be the only operation of that kind that will be done in our age, for, as I have heard, most husbands had rather make use of a needle and thread than of a knife. It may be you will understand this no more than what you writ in your own letter, but I do not doubt you will very easily get it to be explained without going to the Sorbonne. Therefore I need add no more but that I am entirely yours. c.

5.

August 26, 1667

I do assure you I am very much troubled that I cannot in everything give you that satisfaction I could wish, especially in this business of the Duchess of Richmond, wherein you may think me ill natured. But if you consider how hard a thing 'tis to swallow an injury done by a person I had so much tenderness for you will in some degree excuse the resentment I use towards her. You know my good nature enough to believe that I could not be so severe, if I had not great provocation and I assure you her carriage towards me has been as bad as breach of friendship and faith can make it. Therefore I hope you will pardon me if I cannot so soon forget an injury which went so near my heart.

6.

May 7, 1668

I did receive your letter by Fitzgerald the same day that the physicians were doing the very prescriptions you advise in your letter. But now that matter is over for my wife miscarried this morning. And though I am troubled at it, yet I am glad that 'tis evident she was with child, which I will not deny to you till now I did fear she was not capable of. The physicians do intend to put her into a course of physic which they are confident will make her hold faster next time. . . .

TO PRINCE RUPERT

June 1, 1673

Having had the news of an engagement the last week by the guns heard from all parts on the 28th, you may easily guess in what pain I was till I received yours of the 29th, which was brought me on the 31st in the morning, whereby I see you have done all that was possible with those circumstances the enemies afforded you. I assure myself that when our letters come from the other side of the water we shall know in spite of their teethes [sic] that they have had a considerable loss. In a word, I am very well pleased with your success.

Immediately upon the receipt of your letters I gave order for all those things which you writ for and I hope the ten fire ships will be ready very soon. The Straights fleets are in the Downs and as fast as they come up these men shall be sent to you. The particular account of all these things you will receive from my brother and the officers of the navy, so I shall add nothing to this only to thank you for what you have done and to wish you more success, assuring you of the continuance of my kindness to you in all occasions.

I hope you will punish those captains of the fire ships who did ill, as severely as you can. And pray send those Englishmen who were taken in the Dutch service in some safe vessel that they may be sure to be hanged here but there must be sent two or three witnesses with them.

Proclamation to Prohibit the Rebuilding of Houses after the Great Fire

September 13, 1666

As no particular man hath sustained any loss or damage by the late terrible and deplorable fire in his fortune or estate in any degree to be compared with the loss and damage we ourself have sustained, so it is not possible for any man to take the same more to heart and to be more concerned and solicitous for the rebuilding this famous city with as much expedition as is possible. And since it hath pleased God to lay this heavy judgment upon us all this time as an evidence of His displeasure for our sins, we do comfort ourself with some hope that He will, upon our due humiliation before Him, as a new

instance of His signal blessing upon us, give us life, not only to see
the foundations laid but the buildings finished, of a much more
beautiful city than is at this time consumed; and that as the seat
and situation of it is the most convenient and noble for the advancement of trade of any city in Europe, so that such care will be taken
for the re-edification of it, both for use and beauty, and such provision made for the future against the ordinary and casual accidents by
fire, as may, as far as human wisdom can provide . . . reasonably
secure the same, and make it rather appear to the world as purged
by fire (in how lamentable a manner soever) to a wondrous beauty
and comeliness than consumed by it.

. . . The woeful experience in this late heavy visitation hath sufficiently convinced all men of the pernicious consequences which
have attended the building with timber and even with stone itself,
and the notable benefit of brick, which in so many places has resisted
and even extinguished the fire: and we do therefore hereby declare
our express will and pleasure that no man whatsoever shall presume to
erect any house or building, great or small, but of brick or stone;
and if any man shall do the contrary, the next magistrate shall
forthwith cause it to be pulled down and such further course shall
be taken for his punishment as he deserves. And we suppose that the
notable benefit many men have received from those cellars, which
have been well and strongly arched, will persuade most men, who
build good houses, to practice that good husbandry by arching all
convenient places.

We do declare that Fleet Street, Cheapside, Cornhill and all other
eminent and notorious streets, shall be of such a breadth as may,
with God's blessing, prevent the mischief that one side may suffer if
the other be on fire; which was the case lately in Cheapside; the
precise breadth of which several streets shall be, upon advice with
the Lord Mayor and aldermen, shortly published, with many other
particular orders and rules, which cannot yet be adjusted. In the
meantime we resolve, though all streets cannot be of equal breadth,
yet none shall be so narrow as to make the passage uneasy or inconvenient, especially towards the water-side. Nor will we suffer any
lanes or alleys to be erected but where, upon mature deliberation, the
same shall be found absolutely necessary; except such places shall be
set aside, which shall be designed only for buildings of that kind,
and from whence no public mischief may probably arise.

Speech to Both Houses on Opening the Session

March 20, 1681

My Lords and Gentlemen: The unwarrantable proceedings of the last House of Commons were the occasion of my parting with the last Parliament. For I, who will never use arbitrary government myself, am resolved not to suffer it in others. I am unwilling to mention particulars because I am desirous to forget faults; but whosoever shall calmly consider what offers I have formerly made and what assurances I renewed to the last Parliament: how I recommended nothing so much to them as the alliances I had made for preservation of the general peace in Christendom and the further examination of the Popish Plot and how I desired their advice and assistance concerning the preservation of Tangier; and shall then reflect upon the strange, unsuitable returns made to such propositions . . . perhaps may wonder more, that I had patience so long, than that at last I grew weary of their proceedings.

I have thought it necessary to say thus much to you, that I may not have any new occasion given me to remember more of the late miscarriages. It is as much my interest and it shall be as much my care as yours to preserve the liberty of the subject; because the Crown can never be safe when that is in danger. And I would have you likewise be convinced that neither your liberties nor properties can subsist long when the just rights and prerogatives of the Crown are invaded, or the honor of the government brought low and into disreputation.

I conclude with this one advice to you, that the rules and measures of all your votes may be the known and established laws of the land; which neither can, nor ought to be departed from, nor changed, but by Act of Parliament. And I may the more reasonably require that you make the laws of the land your rule, because I am resolved they shall be mine.

GILBERT BURNET

Gilbert Burnet, though a Scot of Covenanter parentage, chose the way of conformity in youth and became after the Restoration an influential minister in his native land. He urged the members of the

Scottish clergy to accept the establishment but sought to mitigate extreme measures against those of Presbyterian leaning. As King's chaplain, preacher in London and voluminous writer on political and religious subjects, he became the greatest liberal churchman of his time. His sympathy with the Whigs' cause finally sent him into exile, but he returned to power with William and was made a bishop. The letter to Charles, written in 1680, is characteristic of the role which he played consistently as a loyal but independent spokesman of the Christian conscience. It is recorded that Charles tore the letter up and threw it in the fire. But he at least received it, and Burnet, though he lost favor, did not lose his head.

Plain Speech to Royalty

29 *January,* 1679

May it please your Majesty,

I have not presumed to trouble your Majesty for some months, not having anything worthy your time to offer; and now I choose rather this way, since the infinite duty I owe you puts me under restraints in discourse which I cannot so easily overcome. What I shall now suggest to your Majesty, I do it as in the presence of Almighty God, to whom I know I must give an account of all my actions. I therefore beg you will be graciously pleased to accept this most faithful zeal of your poor subject, who has no other design in it than your good and the discharge of his own conscience.

I must then first assure your Majesty, I never discovered anything like a design of raising rebellion among all those with whom I converse; but I shall add, on the other hand, that most people grow sullen, and are highly dissatisfied with you and distrustful of you. Formerly your ministers, or his royal highness, bore the blame of things that were ungrateful; but now it falls upon yourself, and time, which cures most other distempers, increases this. . . .

There is one thing, and indeed the only thing, in which all honest men agree as that which can easily extricate you out of all your troubles; it is not the change of a minister or of a council, a new alliance, or a session of Parliament, but it is (and suffer me, sir, to speak it with a more than ordinary earnestness) a change in your own heart and in your course of life. And now sir, if you do not with indignation throw this paper from you, permit me (with all the humility of a subject prostrate at your feet) to tell you, that all the distrust your people have of you, all the necessities you now are under, all the indignation of Heaven that is upon you, and appears in the defeating all your counsels, flow from this, that you have not feared nor served God, but have given yourself up to so many sinful pleasures. Your Majesty may perhaps justly think that many of those that oppose you have no regard for religion, but the body of your people consider it more than you can imagine. I do not desire your Majesty to put on a hypocritical show of religion, as Henry the third of France did, hoping thereby to have weathered the storms of those times. No! that would be seen through, and as it would provoke God more, so it would increase jealousies. No, sir, it must be real, and the evidences of it signal. All those about you who are the occasions of sin, chiefly the women, must be removed and your court be reformed. Sir, if you will turn you to religion sincerely and seriously, you shall quickly find a serene joy of another nature possess your mind than what arises from gross pleasures. God would be at peace with you and direct and bless all your counsels; all good men would presently turn to you, and ill men would be ashamed and have a thin party. For I speak it knowingly, there is nothing has so alienated the body of your people from you as what they have heard of your life, which disposes them to give an easy belief to all other scandalous reports.

Sir, this counsel is now almost as necessary for your affairs as it is for your soul; and though you have highly offended that God who has been infinitely merciful to you in preserving you at Worcester fight and during your long exile, and who brought you back so miraculously, yet he is still good and gracious; and will, upon your sincere repentance and change of life, pardon all your sins and receive you into his favour. Oh! sir, what if you should die in the midst of all your sins? At the great tribunal where you must appear, there will be no regard to the crown you now wear; but it will aggravate your punishment that, being in so eminent a station, you have so much dishonoured God. Sir, I hope you believe there is a God and a life to come, and that sin shall not pass unpunished. If your Majesty will reflect upon your having now been twenty years upon the throne, and in all that time how little you have glorified God, how much you have provoked him, and that your ill example has drawn so many after you to sin, that men are not now ashamed of their vices, you cannot but think that God is offended with you; and if you consider how ill your counsels at home and your wars abroad have succeeded and how much you have lost the hearts of your people, you may reasonably conclude this is of God, who will not turn away his anger from you till you turn to him with your whole heart.

I am no enthusiast either in opinion or temper; yet I acknowledge I have been so pressed in my mind to make this address to you, that I could have no ease till I did it; and since you were pleased to direct me to send you, through Mr. Chiffinch's hands, such informations as I thought fit to convey to you, I hope your Majesty will not be offended if I have made this use of that liberty. I am sure I can have no other design in it but your good; for I know very well this is not the method to serve any ends of my own. I therefore throw myself at your feet, and once more, in the name of God whose servant I am, do most humbly beseech your Majesty to consider of what I have written, and not to despise it for the meanness of the person who has sent it; but to apply yourself to religion in earnest. And I dare assure you of many blessings both temporal and spiritual in this life and of eternal glory in the life to come: but if you will go on in your sins, the judgements of God will probably pursue you in this life, so that you may be a proverb to after-ages; and after this life you will be forever miserable; and I, your poor subject that now am, shall be a witness against you in the great day, that I gave you this free and faithful warning.

Sir, no person alive knows that I have written to you to this purpose; and I chose this evening, hoping that your exercise tomorrow may put you into a disposition to weigh it more carefully. I hope your Majesty will not be offended with this sincere expression of my duty to you; for I durst not have ventured on it, if I had not thought myself bound to it both by the duty I owe to God and that which will ever oblige me to be,

May it please your Majesty, etc.

PAUL BARILLON, MARQUIS DE BRANGE

The correspondence of the French ambassador at the English court with his royal master, Louis XIV, contains this minute account of the intrigue which provided the dying Charles with his viaticum. It had been one of the provisions of the Treaty of Dover that the English King should announce his conversion at some propitious time. There was no propitious time, not even this. Left to himself, Charles might have kept still and jumped the life to come.

Ambassador's Report

The letter which I have the honor this day to address to Your Majesty, is solely to transmit to Your Majesty an exact account of the most important events which took place at the death of the late King of England. His illness, which began on the morning of Monday, February 12, took different turns during the following days; sometimes he was thought to be out of danger, but afterwards some circumstance happened which gave reason to believe his disorder was mortal; at length, about noon on Thursday, February 15, I was informed from a good quarter that there was no longer any hope and that his physicians did not think he could survive the night. I immediately after went to Whitehall; the Duke of York had given orders to the officers who kept the door of the ante-chamber to allow me to pass at all hours; he remained constantly in the King's chamber, except when he came out to give orders respecting what was passing in the town. The report was several times spread during the day that the King was dead. As soon as I arrived the Duke of York said to me, "The physicians think the King is in the greatest danger; I beg you will assure your master that in me he will always find a faithful and a grateful servant." I remained in the King's ante-chamber till five o'clock; the Duke of York invited me several times into the room and conversed with me about what was passing without doors, and of the assurances he had received from all quarters that everything was very quiet in the town and that he would be proclaimed King the instant his brother should expire. I retired for some time to the apartments of the Duchess of Portsmouth; I found her overwhelmed with grief, for the physicians had deprived her of all hopes. Nevertheless, instead of speaking to me of her sorrow and of the loss she was about to sustain, she led me into a closet, and said, "Monsieur l'Ambassadeur, I am going to tell you one of the greatest secrets in the world, and if it were known it would cost me my head. At the bottom of his heart the King is a Catholic, but he is surrounded by Protestant bishops, and nobody informs him of his situation or speaks to him of God. I cannot with decency again enter his room, besides the Queen is always there. The Duke of York is busied with his affairs, and these are too important to allow him to take that care which he ought about the conscience of the King. Go and tell him that I have conjured you to advise him to think on what can be done to save the King's soul: he is master of the King's room and he can cause to withdraw whoever he pleases. Lose no time, for if there be the least hesitation it will be too late."

I immediately returned to the Duke of York. I begged him to pretend to go to the apartment of the Queen who had quitted the King's room; she had just been bled because she had fainted; the room communicates with both the apartments; I followed him to the Queen's and told him what the Duchess of Portsmouth had said to me. He roused himself as it were from a profound lethargy; "You are right," he said, "there is no time to lose. I would sooner hazard everything than not do my duty on this occasion." He returned to me an hour after, under pretence of again visiting the Queen, and told me he had spoken to the King his brother and that he had found him determined not to receive the sacrament to which the Protestant bishops were pressing him; that this had very much surprised them; but that some of them would always remain in the King's room, unless he found a pretext to cause everybody to retire in order that he might speak to the King his brother with more freedom and induce him to make a formal abjuration of heresy and to confess himself to a Catholic priest.

We discussed various expedients: the Duke of York proposed that I should ask to speak with the King his brother, as if to communicate something in secret to him from Your Majesty, and that everybody should be ordered to withdraw. This I offered to do, but I represented to him that, besides the noise such a proceeding would make, there was no colourable pretext to justify my remaining in private with the King of England and him alone so long a time as was required for the accomplishment of what we had to do. The Duke next thought of bringing the Queen, as if to take a last farewell of the King and to beg his forgiveness if she had disobeyed him in anything, and that he should perform the same ceremony. At last the Duke of York determined to speak to his brother before all that were present, but in such a way that no one should understand what he said, because this would remove all suspicion and it would be imagined that he was only consulting him about State affairs and what he wished should be done after his death; therefore, without any more precaution, the Duke, after having forbidden anyone to come nigh, stooped down to his brother's ear: I was in the room, and more than twenty persons at the door which was open; what the Duke said was not heard, but the King said aloud from time to time, "Yes, with all my heart." He made the Duke sometimes repeat his words because he did not hear very well; this lasted about a quarter of an hour. The Duke of York then left the room as if to go to the Queen, and said to me, "The King has consented to my bringing him a priest; I dare not send any of the Duchess's, they are too well known; send quickly and seek one." I told him I would do it with pleasure but that I thought too much time would be lost, and that I had just seen all the Queen's priests in a closet near to her chamber. He replied, "You are right." He perceived at the same time the Count of Castelmelhor, who warmly embraced the proposition I made him and took upon him to speak to the Queen. He returned in an instant and said, "Though I were to endanger my head in this business I would do it with pleasure, but I know none of the Queen's priests who understands and speaks English." Upon this we resolved to send in search of an English priest to the Venetian Resident's, but as the time admitted no delay the Count of Castelmelhor went to the room where the Queen's priests were and found among them a Scotch priest named Huddlestone, the man who saved the King after the battle of Worcester and who had been excepted by Act of Parliament in all the laws enacted against the Roman Catholics and the priests. They gave him a wig and cassock to disguise him and led him to the door of an apartment which communicated by a small flight of steps with that of the King.

The Duke of York whom I had informed that all was ready sent Chiffinch to receive and conduct Mr. Huddlestone; he said next aloud, "Gentlemen, it is the King's wish that everybody should retire except the Earls of Bath and Feversham": the former is First Lord of the Bedchamber and the latter was this week in waiting. The physicians withdrew into a closet the door of which was shut when Chiffinch brought in Mr. Huddlestone. In presenting him the Duke of York said, "Sire, here is a man who saved your life and who comes at this moment to save your soul." The King replied, "He is welcome." He then confessed himself with sentiments of great piety and repentance. The Count of Castelmelhor had taken care to have Huddlestone instructed by a Portuguese bare-footed Carmelite what he was to say to the King on such an occasion, for of himself he was a man of no great acquirements. But the Duke of York told me he acquitted himself very well and made the King formally promise, in case of his recovering, to declare himself openly to be a Catholic. The King next received absolution, the Communion and even the extreme unction. All this lasted about three-quarters of an hour. The persons in the ante-chamber looked at one another, but nothing was expressed except in looks or whispers. The presence of the Earls of Bath and Feversham, who are Protestants, had somewhat removed the apprehensions of the bishops, but nevertheless the Queen's women and the other priests saw so much coming and going that I do not imagine the secret will be long kept.

After the King had received the Sacrament he had a slight respite of his illness. It is certain that he spoke more intelligibly and had more strength; we had already begun to hope that God was willing to work a miracle in curing him, but it was the opinion of the physicians that his malady was not diminished and that he could not survive the night. However, he appeared much easier and talked with more feeling and understanding than he had yet done from six o'clock in the evening till eight o'clock next morning. He spoke several times aloud to the Duke of York in terms full of affection and friendship, he twice recommended to him the Duchess of Portsmouth and the Duke of Richmond, as also all his other children. He made no mention of the Duke of Monmouth, neither good nor bad; he often testified his confidence in God's mercy. The Bishop of Bath and Wells, who was his private chaplain, said some prayers and spoke to him of God. The King moved his head to show he heard him. The Bishop was not over-officious in telling him anything particularly nor in proposing to him to make a confession of his faith: he was apprehensive of a refusal, and feared still more, as I think, to irritate the Duke of York.

The King retained his senses throughout the whole of the night and talked of several things with great calmness; at six o'clock he asked what hour it was and said, "Open the curtains, that I may once more see the day." He suffered great pain, and at seven o'clock was bled under an idea that it would alleviate his sufferings; at half-past eight he spoke with great difficulty, about ten was senseless, and calmly expired at noon without any convulsions. The new King retired to his chamber, was unanimously acknowledged and afterwards proclaimed.

I have thought it my duty to send Your Majesty an exact account of what passed on this occasion, and I esteem myself very happy that God has bestowed upon me the favour of having a part therein.

WILLIAM, LORD RUSSELL

*William, Lord Russell, has come down in history with Algernon
Sidney as one of the heroes of the Parliamentary opposition to
Charles II. His politics were those of Shaftesbury, whom he joined
in the effort to exclude James from the succession, but he was, like
Sidney, a man of higher character and of a sincere conviction. Sent
to the Tower on the charge of complicity in the Rye House Plot,
he was convicted of high treason and executed at Lincoln's Inn
Fields on July 21, 1683.*

The Paper Delivered by Lord Russell
to the Sheriffs

I thank God I find myself so composed and prepared for death
and my thoughts so fixed on another world that I hope in God I
am quiet from setting my heart on this. Yet I cannot forbear now
the setting down in writing a further account of my condition, to be
left behind me, than I will venture to say at the place of execution,
in the noise and clutter that is likely to be there. I bless God heartily
for those many blessings which He in his infinite mercy hath bestowed upon me through the whole course of my life: that I was born
of worthy and good parents and had the advantage of a religious education, which are invaluable blessings. For even when I minded it
least, it still hung about me and gave me checks, and has now for
many years so influenced and possessed me that I feel the happy
effects of it in this my extremity, in which I have been so wonderfully (I thank God) supported that neither my imprisonment nor
fear of death have been able to discompose me in any degree. But on
the contrary, I have found the assurances of the love and mercy of
God in and through my blessed Redeemer, in whom only I trust; and
I do not question but I am going to partake of that fulness of joy
which is in his presence. These hopes, therefore, do so wonderfully
delight me that I think this is the happiest time of my life, though
others may look upon it as the saddest.

I have lived and now am of the reformed religion, a true and
sincere Protestant and in the communion of the Church of England,
though I could never yet comply with or rise up to all the heights
of many people. I wish with all my soul all our differences were re-

moved and that all sincere Protestants would so far consider the
danger of Popery as to lay aside their heats and agree against the
common enemy, and that the Churchmen would be less severe and
the dissenters less scrupulous; for I think bitterness and persecution
are at all times bad, but much more now. . . .

As for my present condition, I bless God I have no repining in
my heart at it. I know, for my sins, I have deserved much worse at
the hands of God, so that I cheerfully submit to so small a punishment as the being taken off a few years sooner and the being made
a spectacle to the world. I do freely forgive all the world, particularly
those concerned in taking away my life, and I desire and conjure all
my friends to think of no revenge but to submit to the holy will of
God, into whose hands I resign myself entirely. . . .

Since my sentence, I have had few thoughts but preparatory ones
for death. Yet the importunity of my friends, and particularly the
best and dearest wife in the world, prevailed with me to sign petitions
and make an address for my life, to which I was ever averse. For (I
thank God) though in all respects I have lived the happiest and
contentedest man in the world (for now very near fourteen years),
yet I am so willing to leave all that it was not without difficulty
that I did anything for the saving of my life, that was begging. But
I was willing to let my friends see what power they had over me, and
that I was not obstinate nor sullen but would do anything that an
honest man could do for their satisfaction, which was the only motive
that swayed or had any weight with me.

And now, to sum up all, as I had not any design against the
King's life, or the life of any man whatsoever, so I never was in any
contrivance of altering the government. What the heats, passions,
and vanities of other men have occasioned, I ought not be responsible
for, nor could I help them though I now suffer for them. But the
will of the Lord be done, into whose hands I commend my
spirit! . . .

JOHN DRYDEN

Absalom and Achitophel, *the greatest of Dryden's political satires,
was published in 1681 in the midst of the excitement over the Duke
of Monmouth's first attempt to make himself successor to the throne
of England. The poet finds in the Biblical story of Absalom's
rebellion against David a rough parallel to the contemporary situa-*

tion. David, having no son by his wife Michal, King Saul's daughter, is Charles II; Absalom, beloved by his father and all too easily forgiven for disloyal action, is the illegitimate Duke of Monmouth; Achitophel, Absalom's evil councilor, is Shaftesbury, the restless leader of the Parliamentary effort to exclude James; Zimri, imported from a different episode in Scripture, is the versatile and corrupt Duke of Buckingham, who played on both sides in politics and was alternately in and out of Charles's favor. The Jebusites are the English Catholics. The opening lines of the poem and the brilliant satirical portraits which follow it in our selection illustrate the method of the allegory and its extraordinary ingenuity and effectiveness.

Absalom

In pious times, ere priestcraft did begin,
Before polygamy was made a sin,
When man on many multiplied his kind,
Ere one to one was cursedly confin'd,
When nature prompted and no law denied
Promiscuous use of concubine and bride,
Then Israel's monarch after Heav'n's own heart
His vig'rous warmth did variously impart
To wives and slaves, and, wide as his command,
Scatter'd his Maker's image through the land.
Michal, of royal blood, the crown did wear,
A soil ungrateful to the tiller's care:
Not so the rest; for sev'ral mothers bore
To godlike David sev'ral sons before.
But since like slaves his bed they did ascend,
No true succession could their seed attend.
Of all this num'rous progeny was none
So beautiful, so brave, as Absalon:
Whether, inspir'd by some diviner lust,
His father got him with a greater gust,
Or that his conscious destiny made way
By manly beauty to imperial sway.
Early in foreign fields he won renown,
With kings and states allied to Israel's crown;
In peace the thoughts of war he could remove,
And seem'd as he were only born for love.
Whate'er he did was done with so much ease,

In him alone 'twas natural to please;
His motions all accompanied with grace,
And Paradise was open'd in his face.
With secret joy indulgent David view'd
His youthful image in his son renew'd;
To all his wishes nothing he denied;
And made the charming Annabel his bride.
What faults he had (for who from faults is free?)
His father could not, or he would not see.
Some warm excesses, which the law forbore,
Were construed youth that purg'd by boiling o'er;
And Amnon's murder, by a specious name,
Was call'd a just revenge for injur'd fame.
Thus prais'd and lov'd, the noble youth remain'd,
While David undisturb'd, in Sion reign'd.

The Jebusites

Th' inhabitants of old Jerusalem
Were Jebusites; the town so call'd from them,
And theirs the native right.
But when the chosen people grew more strong,
The rightful cause at length became the wrong;
And ev'ry loss the men of Jebus bore,
They still were thought God's enemies the more.
Thus worn and weaken'd, well or ill content,
Submit they must to David's government:
Impov'rish'd and depriv'd of all command,
Their taxes doubled as they lost their land;
And, what was harder yet to flesh and blood,
Their gods disgrac'd, and burnt like common wood.
This set the heathen priesthood in a flame,
For priests of all religions are the same:
Of whatsoe'er descent their godhead be,
Stock, stone, or other homely pedigree,
In his defense his servants are as bold,
As if he had been born of beaten gold.
The Jewish Rabbins, though their enemies,
In this conclude them honest men and wise:
For 'twas their duty, all the learned think,

T' espouse his cause by whom they eat and drink.
From hence began that Plot, the nation's curse,
Bad in itself, but represented worse,
Rais'd in extremes, and in extremes decried,
With oaths affirm'd, with dying vows denied,
Not weigh'd or winnow'd by the multitude,
But swallow'd in the mass, unchew'd and crude.
Some truth there was, but dash'd and brew'd with lies,
To please the fools and puzzle all the wise.

Achitophel

Of these the false Achitophel was first,
A name to all succeeding ages curst:
For close designs and crooked counsels fit,
Sagacious, bold, and turbulent of wit,
Restless, unfix'd in principles and place,
In pow'r unpleas'd, impatient of disgrace;
A fiery soul, which, working out its way,
Fretted the pigmy body to decay,
And o'er-inform'd the tenement of clay.
A daring pilot in extremity,
Pleas'd with the danger, when the waves went high,
He sought the storms; but, for a calm unfit,
Would steer too nigh the sands to boast his wit.
Great wits are sure to madness near allied,
And thin partitions do their bounds divide;
Else, why should he, with wealth and honor blest,
Refuse his age the needful hours of rest?
Punish a body which he could not please,
Bankrupt of life, yet prodigal of ease?
And all to leave what with his toil he won
To that unfeather'd two-legg'd thing, a son,
Got, while his soul did huddled notions try,
And born a shapeless lump, like anarchy.
In friendship false, implacable in hate,
Resolv'd to ruin or to rule the State;
To compass this the triple bond he broke,
The pillars of the public safety shook,
And fitted Israel for a foreign yoke;

Then, seiz'd with fear, yet still affecting fame,
Usurp'd a patriot's all-atoning name.
So easy still it proves in factious times
With public zeal to cancel private crimes.
How safe is treason, and how sacred ill,
Where none can sin against the people's will!
Where crowds can wink and no offense be known,
Since in another's guilt they find their own!
Yet fame deserv'd no enemy can grudge;
The statesman we abhor, but praise the judge.
In Israel's courts ne'er sat an Abbethdin
With more discerning eyes or hands more clean,
Unbrib'd, unsought, the wretched to redress;
Swift of dispatch and easy of access.
Oh! had he been content to serve the crown
With virtues only proper to the gown,
Or had the rankness of the soil been freed
From cockle that oppress'd the noble seed,
David for him his tuneful harp had strung
And Heav'n had wanted one immortal song.
But wild Ambition loves to slide, not stand,
And Fortune's ice prefers to Virtue's land.
Achitophel, grown weary to possess
A lawful fame and lazy happiness,
Disdain'd the golden fruit to gather free,
And lent the crowd his arm to shake the tree.
Now, manifest of crimes contriv'd long since,
He stood at bold defiance with his prince,
Held up the buckler of the people's cause
Against the crown, and skulk'd behind the laws.
The wish'd occasion of the Plot he takes;
Some circumstances finds, but more he makes;
By buzzing emissaries fills the ears
Of list'ning crowds with jealousies and fears
Of arbitrary counsels brought to light,
And proves the King himself a Jebusite.
Weak arguments! which yet he knew full well
Were strong with people easy to rebel.
For, govern'd by the moon, the giddy Jews
Tread the same track when she the prime renews:
And once in twenty years, their scribes record,

By natural instinct they change their lord.
Achitophel still wants a chief, and none
Was found so fit as warlike Absalon.
Not that he wish'd his greatness to create,
(For politicians neither love nor hate):
But, for he knew his title not allow'd,
Would keep him still depending on the crowd,
That kingly pow'r, thus ebbing out, might be
Drawn to the dregs of a democracy.

Zimri

A num'rous host of dreaming saints succeed,
Of the true old enthusiastic breed:
'Gainst form and order they their pow'r employ,
Nothing to build, and all things to destroy.
But far more num'rous was the herd of such
Who think too little and who talk too much.
These, out of mere instinct, they knew not why,
Ador'd their fathers' God and property,
And by the same blind benefit of fate,
The Devil and the Jebusite did hate:
Born to be sav'd ev'n in their own despite,
Because they could not help believing right.
Such were the tools; but a whole Hydra more
Remains, of sprouting heads too long to score.
Some of their chiefs were princes of the land;
In the first rank of these did Zimri stand,
A man so various that he seem'd to be
Not one, but all mankind's epitome:
Stiff in opinions, always in the wrong,
Was ev'rything by starts, and nothing long;
But in the course of one revolving moon
Was chemist, fiddler, statesman, and buffoon;
Then all for women, painting, rhyming, drinking,
Besides ten thousand freaks that died in thinking.
Bless'd madman, who could ev'ry hour employ
With something new to wish or to enjoy!
Railing and praising were his usual themes,
And both (to show his judgment) in extremes:
So over violent or over civil

That ev'ry man with him was God or Devil.
In squand'ring wealth was his peculiar art;
Nothing went unrewarded but desert.
Beggar'd by fools, whom still he found too late,
He had his jest, and they had his estate.
He laugh'd himself from Court; then sought relief
By forming parties, but could ne'er be chief:
For spite of him, the weight of bus'ness fell
On Absalom and wise Achitophel;
Thus wicked but in will, of means bereft,
He left not faction, but of that was left.

At the precise moment of James II's accession to the throne John
Dryden, hitherto an ardent defender of the Church of England,
became a Catholic. Temperamentally, he was the reverse of a
religious man, but he had already accepted the principle of authority
against reason in matters of faith and his latest change was in the
direction he had been moving in since the Puritan beginnings of his
career. That this step was made easy by the fact that the court
itself was now Catholic and the prospects good for a return of the
national church to the fold is obvious enough. Loyalty was Dryden's
main profession. Every drop of his blood was Tory. In this poem in
support of the royal religion he uses the language he has always
used, the language of conformity against dissent, or order against
chaos, of unity in church and state against the hydra-headed monster
of rebellion. That he is no mere timeserver is shown by the fact that
when the Protestant and Parliamentary cause triumphed in the
Revolution he made no attempt to win favor by retreating from his
new position. The accession of William and Mary went uncelebrated
by his pen. But the deeper inspiration of the present poem is neither
religious nor political. Dryden is here more than ever the matchless
journalist in verse; his passion is for effectiveness of utterance, for
finality of word and meaning fitted to each other as glove to hand.
In the passage quoted he immortalizes the images of sectarian error
as seen against the changeless truth. The Hind is, of course, the
Roman Catholic Church, the Panther the Anglican, the lion Henry
VIII and the other beasts the various dissenting sects.

The Hind and the Panther

A milk-white Hind, immortal and unchang'd,
Fed on the lawns and in the forest rang'd;

Without unspotted, innocent within,
She fear'd no danger, for she knew no sin.
Yet had she oft been chas'd with horns and hounds
And Scythian shafts; and many winged wounds
Aim'd at her heart; was often forc'd to fly,
And doom'd to death, though fated not to die.
  Not so her young; for their unequal line
Was hero's make, half human, half divine.
Their earthly mold obnoxious was to fate,
Th' immortal part assum'd immortal state.
Of these a slaughter'd army lay in blood,
Extended o'er the Caledonian wood,
Their native walk; whose vocal blood arose,
And cried for pardon on their perjur'd foes.
Their fate was fruitful, and the sanguine seed,
Endued with souls, increas'd the sacred breed.
So captive Israel multiplied in chains,
A num'rous exile, and enjoy'd her pains.
With grief and gladness mix'd, their mother view'd
Her martyr'd offspring and their race renew'd;
Their corps to perish, but their kind to last,
So much the deathless plant the dying fruit surpass'd.
  Panting and pensive now she rang'd alone,
And wander'd in the kingdoms once her own.
The common hunt, though from their rage restrain'd
By sov'reign pow'r, her company disdain'd,
Grinn'd as they pass'd, and with a glaring eye
Gave gloomy signs of secret enmity.
'Tis true, she bounded by and tripp'd so light,
They had not time to take a steady sight;
For Truth has such a face and such a mien
As to be lov'd needs only to be seen.
  The bloody Bear, an *Independent* beast,
Unlick'd to form, in groans her hate express'd.
Among the tim'rous kind the *Quaking* Hare
Profess'd neutrality, but would not swear.
Next her the buffoon Ape, as atheists use,
Mimick'd all sects, and had his own to choose;
Still when the Lion look'd, his knees he bent,
And paid at church a courtier's compliment.
The bristled Baptist Boar, impure as he,

But whiten'd with the foam of sanctity,
With fat pollutions fill'd the sacred place,
And mountains level'd in his furious race;
So first rebellion founded was in grace.
But, since the mighty ravage which he made,
In German forests had his guilt betray'd,
With broken tusks and with a borrow'd name,
He shunn'd the vengeance and conceal'd the shame;
So lurk'd in sects unseen. With greater guile
False Reynard fed on consecrated spoil;
The graceless beast by Athanasius first
Was chas'd from Nice, then by Socinus nurs'd,
His impious race their blasphemy renew'd,
And Nature's King through Nature's optics view'd;
Revers'd, they view'd him lessen'd to their eye,
Nor in an infant could a God descry.
New swarming sects to this obliquely tend,
Hence they began, and here they all will end. . . .
    These are the chief; to number o'er the rest,
And stand, like Adam, naming ev'ry beast,
Were weary work; nor will the Muse describe
A slimy-born and sun-begotten tribe,
Who, far from steeples and their sacred sound,
In fields their sullen conventicles found.
These gross, half-animated lumps I leave;
Nor can I think what thoughts they can conceive.
But if they think at all, 'tis sure no high'r
Then matter put in motion may aspire;
Souls that can scarce ferment their mass of clay,
So drossy, so divisible are they,
As would but serve pure bodies for allay,
Such souls as shards produce, such beetle things
As only buzz to heav'n with ev'ning wings,
Strike in the dark, offending but by chance,
Such are the blindfold blows of ignorance.
They know not beings, and but hate a name;
To them the Hind and Panther are the same.
    The Panther, sure the noblest next the Hind,
And fairest creature of the spotted kind;
Oh, could her inborn stains be wash'd away,
She were too good to be a beast of prey!

How can I praise or blame, and not offend,
Or how divide the frailty from the friend?
Her faults and virtues lie so mix'd that she
Nor wholly stands condemn'd, nor wholly free.
Then, like her injur'd Lion, let me speak;
He cannot bend her, and he would not break.
Unkind already, and estrang'd in part,
The Wolf begins to share her wand'ring heart.
Though unpolluted yet with actual ill.
She half commits who sins but in her will.
If, as our dreaming Platonists report,
There could be spirits of a middle sort,
Too black for Heav'n and yet too white for Hell,
Who just dropp'd half-way down, nor lower fell;
So pois'd, so gently she descends from high,
It seems a soft dismission from the sky.
Her house not ancient, whatsoe'er pretense
Her clergy heralds make in her defense;
A second century not half-way run,
Since the new honors of her blood begun.
A Lion, old, obscene, and furious made
By lust, compress'd her mother in a shade;
Then, by a left-hand marriage, weds the dame,
Cov'ring adult'ry with a specious name;
So Schism begot; and Sacrilege and she,
A well match'd pair, got graceless Heresy.

ANONYMOUS

Here is a sample of the topical verse which flourished far below the level of Dryden and Marvell, finding its occasion, as their poems also did, in Restoration politics. There was a rumor that the male heir of James was a suppositious child. Bishop Burnet in his history solemnly recounts the questionable circumstances of the royal lying-in: evidence of a miscarriage a few days before ("Undone, undone," the Queen was heard to murmur), the timing of the blessed event when all the Protestant ladies about the court were at church, private delivery with the curtains of the bed drawn close and none within but the midwife and an under-dresser, a warming pan called for and brought in haste with no inspection of its contents. "The child was not heard to cry, nor was he shown to any in the room, but the under-dresser huddled away something in her arms, pretending more air was necessary, into a dressing-room hard by, that had communication with other apartments."

Mary of Modena was a member of the Este family, not therefore necessarily a bastard. Why "the blood of Southesk" for the King I do not know. James had cuckolded Lord Southesk, as we learn from the Gramont selection given below. The date is October 1688, James himself having two months more of rule and the bonnie bairn, the "Old Pretender" of aftertimes, being fated never to enjoy his own.

An excellent new Song, call'd,
THE PRINCE OF DARKNESS:
Shewing how three Kingdoms may be set on fire by a Warming-Pan

As I went by St. James's I heard a bird sing,
"Of a certain the Queen will have a boy in the spring."
But one of the chairmen did laugh and did say,
"It was born one night and brought forth the next day."
This bantling was heard at St. James's to squall,
Which made the Queen make so much haste from Whitehall.
"Peace, peace, little Master, and hold up thy head;
There's money bid for thee," the true mother said.
But nobody knows from what parish it came
And that is the reason it has not the name.
Good Catholics all were afraid it was dying,
There was such abundance of skreeching and crying,
Which is a good token by which we may swear
It is the Queen's own and the Kingdom's right heir.
Now if we should happen to have a true lad
From the loins of so wholesome a mother and dad,
'Twould be hard to distinguish which blood was the best,
Or that of Southesk or the bastard of Est.
But now we have cause of Thanksgiving indeed;
There was no other way of mending the creed.

HENRY PITMAN

Henry Pitman was transported to Barbados as a penalty for his part in the Monmouth rising. His relatives were unable to buy his freedom, but the money they supplied him enabled him to get a small boat and make his escape, together with seven of his fellow bond servants. The narrative of their hardships reads at times like Robinson Crusoe, and, indeed, Defoe is thought to have been familiar with Pitman's story, published after his return to England in 1689. The first island is Margarita, the second, here called Saltatudos, is Tortuga. Pitman was a doctor and a good observer. He describes at some length the turtles which multiplied on the island and the herbs which he converted to medicinal and other uses. By the time Pitman actually reached England, William was on the throne and the danger of his being sent back to the Indies over. Not all who escaped hanging fared so well. Bond servitude in America was the Siberian exile of those times.

Escape of a White Slave

May 15. We had fair weather and very pleasant sailing down the north side of this island. But when we had got about the middle of the island, my companions were no less importunate than before to go ashore for fresh water. To which I, at length, consented, partly because I saw that part of the island free from inhabitants, and partly enticed by the fair appearance of a sandy bay and that the water seemed so smooth that I thought we could not injure our boat by running her ashore, in regard we had neither anchor nor grapling to ride her off.

But contrary to our expectations, and to our great surprisal, we found the ground near the shore extremely foul; and the sea heaved us so fast in that we could not possibly have avoided being split on the rocks had not I leaped into the sea to fend her off, which whilst I laboured to do with my feet against the rock till I was almost spent, my companions with their two oars rowed her off. At which our hearts were filled with joy and our mouths with praises to the Lord who had so wonderfully preserved us from being cast away on this island, where probably we must either have been starved ourselves or have become food for those inhuman man-eaters.

From the west end of this island we directed our course for Saltatudos; but that afternoon the wind increased and a white ring encircled the moon, which I thought presaged ill weather, and to our great sorrow proved too true. For about nine at night a dreadful storm arose which made us despair of ever seeing the morning sun. And now the sea began to foam and to turn its smooth surface into mountains and vales. Our boat was tossed and tumbled from one side to the other and so violently driven and hurried away by the fury of the wind and sea that I was afraid we should be driven by the island in the night time; and therefore we brought our boat to with her head against the sea, but the wind and sea still increasing, we were forced to bear up before it with only sail sufficient to give her steerage way.

And now in vain we began to wish ourselves at the Barbadoes again or (which was worse) on that island on which we were so lately like to have been wrecked, believing that a misery then which now we should have thought a happiness, and that which confirmed us the more in the certainty of our approaching ruin was an unexpected voice which (to our thinking) seemed to hallow to us at a great distance. But the Omnipotent (who is never unmindful of the cries of his people in distress) heard our prayers; so that when all our hopes were given over and we had resigned ourselves into his hands, expecting every moment when the wide gaping sea would devour and swallow us up, God, of his infinite mercy and unspeakable goodness, commanded the violence of the winds to cease and allayed the fury of the raging waves. Eternal praises to his name for evermore!

May 16. This morning at break of day we saw the island of Saltatudos just before us and when it was sufficiently light that we could discern how the land lay, we steered down the north side of it intending to go ashore at some convenient place to refresh ourselves after that dreadful storm, and to take on board some fresh water, and if possible to stop the leaks of our boat in order to proceed in our voyage for Curaçoa; and accordingly when we came to the leeward of a small island hard by the other, we stood in directly for the shore, thinking it a convenient place to land. Which we had no sooner done but we saw a canoe coming thence, directing her course towards us. At which sight, being a little surprised, my companions provided their arms and charged their muskets and blunderbusses with glass bottles, for we coming from Barbadoes in so great hurry and fear, through forgetfulness they left their bag of bullets on the wharf.

When they were come somewhat nearer that we could perceive them to paddle like Indians, we bore up and were running from them. Which as soon as they preceived, they waved their hats and hailed us; by which we knew they were not Indians as we supposed, and therefore we permitted them to come nearer, and perceiving them to be white men, we enquired what they were. They told us they were Englishmen in distress, and waited for an opportunity to go off the island. The account we gave them of ourselves was very short: that we came from one of the Windward Islands, by which they supposed we had fled for debt and should have continued in that belief had not Thomas Waker, one of my companions, privately informed them that there were only he and John Nuthall that were debtors, the rest of us being rebels, for he thought thereby to ingratiate himself and friend in their friendship. But these privateers, for so they were, as we afterwards understood, hated them the more for their treachery and loved us the better, confessing that they were rebels, too, adding that if the Duke of Monmouth had 1,000 of them, they would soon have put to flight the King's army.

After we had sufficiently refreshed ourselves with rest and sleep, and returned to the Lord the praises due to his name for his wonderful and miraculous deliverance, we thought it time to consider how to stop the leaks of our boat and to raise a deck over her with rinds of trees etc., that we might proceed on our intended voyage for Curaçoa. Our intentions were no sooner perceived by the privateers but they endeavored to persuade us from it, alleging the insufficiency of our boat and the dangers we were so lately exposed unto, and advising us rather to go with them in their piraguas a privateering than to hazard our lives in a second attempt. With the like argument they would have easily prevailed with my companions to consent to go with them, had I not persuaded them to the contrary.

But when the privateers saw it was in vain to persuade us from it they thought to compel us by burning our boat. But this contrivance answered not their expectations. For notwithstanding they burnt our boat and took our sails and other utensils from us, I continued my resolution and chose rather to trust Divine Providence on that desolate and uninhabitable island than to partake or be any ways concerned with them in their piracy, having confidence in myself that God, who had so wonderfully preserved us on the sea and brought us to this island, would in like manner deliver us hence if we continue faithful to him. And in order to our better accomodation and preservation I gave the privateers thirty pieces of eight for the Indian they took on the Main but were not so true to their promise as to set at liberty, who I expected would be serviceable to us in catching fish etc.

About the 25th of May twenty-two of the privateers, having raised the sides of their piraguas with boards, fastened them with the nails they saved in the burning of our boat, and fitted them for sea, they set sail, leaving four of their company behind that refused to go with them, as also a Spanish boat that was of no service to them, neither could be of any use to us unless we had sails for her and a rudder to guide her, both of which we wanted.

The privateers had no sooner left us but we found ourselves of necessity obliged to seek out for provisions. Being led by the example of those four privateers that stayed behind we walked along the seashore to watch for tortoises or turtle, which when they came out of the sea to lay their eggs in the sand we turned on their backs. And they being incapable of turning themselves again we let them remain so till the day following or until we had conveniency of killing them, for if they were sufficiently defended from the heat of the sun by a shade which we usually built over them, they would live several days out of the water.

And thus we walked to and fro in the night time to turn turtle, and in the daytime we were employed in killing them, whose flesh was the chiefest of our diet, being roasted by the fire on wooden spits. And sometimes, when we designed a festival, we left some part of the flesh on the calapatch and calapee, that is, the back and breast shells, which we roasted by setting them upright in two forked sticks thrust into the sand before a large fire. What we did not eat we cut into long and slender pieces, and after we had salted it very well we dried it carefully in the sun on ranges of sticks set up for that purpose, for we found no other way of preserving it, having nothing to wet salt in. But we found it so difficult to divide their shells that we broke our knives and were forced to make new ones out of the swords my companions brought with them. Which we did after this manner. First, we broke them into suitable lengths and softened them in the fire and then rubbed them on a stone to a fit shape and thinness. And after we had hardened them again we fixed them in hafts and made them more serviceable than our former. . . .

After we had spent about three months on this desolate and disconsolate island, we saw a ship, attended by a small sloop, steering toward the shore. At which we were at once possessed with hopes and fears; with hopes that it was some English vessel in which we might probably get a passage thence, and with fear lest it should be a Spaniard, who doubtless would make us prisoners if they could take us, supposing that we were privateers.

The four privateers that remained with us all this time drew near the seaside where the ship was at anchor, and after they had discovered them to be privateers made signs to them to send their boat ashore, which accordingly they did. And after they had carried them on board, the captain of the man-of-war sent up the sloop to that part of the island where I and my companions were. And when they came ashore unto us they inquired, "Which was the doctor?" My companions informed them that it was I. One of them therefore addressed himself particularly to me, desiring me in the name and on the behalf of their captain to go with them on board the man-of-war, where I should be kindly entertained and have liberty to come ashore when I pleased. I readily embraced this kind invitation but could not procure liberty for any of my companions to go with me. When we came to the man-of-war I was very honorable handed over the side, the trumpets in the meantime sounding, and very kindly received and welcomed aboard by the captain and doctor, who invited me aft into the great cabin, where I was not only feasted with wine and choice provisions, but had given me by the doctor a pair of silk stockings, a pair of shoes, and a great deal of linen cloth to make me shirts etc.

After a long discourse concerning the affairs of England, more particularly of the progress and defeat of the Duke of Monmouth, which they seemed to deplore, I addressed myself to the captain in behalf of myself and companions, humbly entreating them to permit us to go with them either to that port to which they were bound or otherwise to put us on board of some English ship they should accidentally meet withal. For I understood by their discourse that they had taken a rich prize and were bound directly for a port to spend their money, as they usually do, so that I apprehended no danger in going with them.

But the captain not being able to take us aboard without the consent of the company, having but two votes and as many shares in the ship and cargo, the company were called together and, after some debates, they voted that they would take me with them but none of my companions. However, they were so kind that they sent them a cask of wine, some bread and cheese, a gammon of bacon, some linen cloth, thread and needles to make them shirts etc. And the next day they permitted them to come on board and entertained them very courteously. In about two days time we set sail, leaving my companions on the island, not a little grieved at my departure.

II *The Empire of Love*

ANTHONY HAMILTON

Philibert, Count of Gramont, spent a few lively years at the English court and returned to his native France in 1664 with one of its prize beauties, Elizabeth Hamilton, as his wife. His adventures as soldier, gambler and lover were narrated in French by his brother-in-law, Anthony Hamilton, son of a Scottish Royalist who enjoyed Charles's favor at the Restoration. Besides the incidents in which Gramont himself was concerned, the book includes many of the most celebrated scandals in high life belonging to the years of its coverage, elaborated with great skill and exhibiting a connoisseurship in such matters unmatched in the literature of gallantry. Hamilton professed to have set down the incidents exactly as they were related by Gramont in his later years. This statement is more than doubtful, but the memoirs are by no means wholly fiction, the main facts being often substantiated by other records. The spirit in which they are written is that of comedy and no scenes from Restoration drama are more happily conceived or brilliantly executed than the best of the Gramont episodes.

The Devil Makes a Slip

The Duke of York, having quieted his conscience by the declaration of marriage, thought that he was entitled by this generous effort to give way a little to his inconstancy; He therefore immediately seized upon whatever he could first lay his hands upon: this was Lady Carnegy, who had been in several other hands. She was still tolerably handsome and her disposition, naturally inclined to tenderness, did not oblige her new lover long to languish. Everything coincided with their wishes for some time. Lord Carnegy, her husband, was in Scotland; but his father dying suddenly, he as suddenly returned with the title of Southesk, which his wife detested; but which she took more patiently than she received the news of his return. Some private intimation had been given him of the honor that was done him in his absence; nevertheless he did not show his jealousy at first; but as he was desirous to be satisfied of the reality of the fact he kept a strict watch over his wife's actions. The Duke of York and her ladyship had for some time been upon such terms of intimacy as not to pass their time in frivolous amusements; however, the husband's return obliged them to maintain some decorum: he therefore never went to her house but in form, that is to say always accompanied by some friend or other, to give his amours at least the appearance of a visit.

About this time Talbot returned from Portugal: this connection had taken place during his absence; and without knowing who Lady Southesk was, he had been informed that his master was in love with her.

A few days after his arrival he was carried, merely to keep up appearances, to her house by the Duke; and after being introduced and some compliments having been paid on both sides, he thought it his duty to give his Royal Highness an opportunity to pay his compliments and accordingly retired into the ante-chamber which looked into the street and placed himself at the window to view the people as they passed.

He was one of the best-meaning men in the world on such occasions; but was so subject to forgetfulness and absence of mind that he once forgot, and left behind him at London, a complimentary letter which the Duke had given him for the Infanta of Portugal and never recollected it till he was going to his audience.

He stood sentry, as we have before said, very attentive to his instructions, when he saw a coach stop at the door without being in the least concerned at it, and still less at a man whom he saw get out of it, and whom he immediately heard coming upstairs.

The devil, who ought to be civil upon such occasions, forgot himself in the present instance and brought up Lord Southesk *in propria persona*: his Royal Highness's equipage had been sent home because my lady had assured him that her husband was gone to see a bear and a bull-baiting, an entertainment in which he took great delight, and from whence he seldom returned until it was very late; so that Southesk, not seeing any equipage at the door, little imagined that he had such good company in his house; but if he was surprised to see Talbot carelessly lolling in his wife's ante-chamber, his surprise was soon over. Talbot, who had not seen him since they were in Flanders and never supposing that he had changed his name: "Welcome, Carnegy, welcome, my good fellow," said he, giving him his hand, "where the devil have you been that I have never been able to set eyes on you since we were at Brussels? What business brought you here? Do you likewise wish to see Lady Southesk? If this is your intention, my poor friend, you may go away again; for I must inform you the Duke of York is in love with her, and I will tell you in confidence that, at this very time, he is in her chamber."

Southesk, confounded as one may suppose, had no time to answer all these fine questions. Talbot, therefore, attended him downstairs as his friend; and as his humble servant, advised him to seek for a mistress elsewhere. Southesk, not knowing what else to do at that time, returned to his coach; and Talbot, overjoyed at the adventure, impatiently waited for the Duke's return that he might acquaint him with it; but he was very much surprised to find that the story afforded no pleasure to those who had the principal share in it and his greatest concern was that Carnegy had changed his name, as if only to draw him into such a confidence.

This accident broke off a commerce which the Duke of York did not much regret; and indeed it was happy for him that he became indifferent; for the traitor Southesk meditated a revenge whereby, without using either assassination or poison, he would have obtained some satisfaction upon those who had injured him if the connection had continued any longer.

Lady Muskerry's Pillow

There was dancing every day at the Queen's apartments because the physicians recommended it, and no person thought it amiss, for even those who cared least for it chose that exercise to digest the waters rather than walking. Lord Muskerry thought himself secure against his lady's rage for dancing for, although he was ashamed of it, the princess of Babylon was, by the Grace of God, six or seven months advanced in pregnancy and, to complete her misfortune, the child had fallen all on one side so that even Euclid would have been puzzled to say what her figure was. The disconsolate lady seeing Miss Hamilton and Mrs. Wetenhall set out every morning—sometimes on horseback and sometimes in a coach, but ever attended by a gallant troop to conduct them to court and to convey them back— she fancied a thousand times more delights at Tunbridge than in reality there were and she did not cease, in her imagination, to dance over at Summerhill all the country dances which she thought had been danced at Tunbridge. She could no longer support the racking torments which disturbed her mind, when relenting Heaven, out of pity to her pains and sufferings, caused Lord Muskerry to repair to London and kept him there two whole days. As soon as ever he had turned his back, the Babylonian princess declared her resolution to make a trip to court.

She had a domestic chaplain who did not want sense, and Lord

Muskerry, for fear of accidents, had recommended her to the whole-some counsels and good prayers of this prudent divine. But in vain were all his preachings and exhortations to stay at home. In vain did he set before her eyes her husband's commands and the dangers to which she would expose herself in her present condition. He likewise added that, her pregnancy being a particular blessing from heaven, she ought therefore to be so much the more careful for its preservation since it cost her husband perhaps more trouble than she was aware of to obtain it. These remonstrances were altogether ineffectual. Miss Hamilton and her cousin Wetenhall having the complaisance to confirm her in her resolution, they assisted in dress-ing her the next morning and set out along with her. All their skill and dexterity were requisite to reduce her shape into some kind of symmetry, but, having at last pinned a small cushion under her petticoat on the right side to counteract the untoward appearance the little infant occasioned by throwing itself on the left, they almost split their sides with laughter, assuring her at the same time that she looked perfectly charming.

As soon as she appeared, it was generally believed that she had dressed herself in a farthingale in order to make her court to the Queen, but every person was pleased at her arrival. Those who were unacquainted with the circumstances assured her in earnest that she was pregnant with twins, and the Queen, who envied her condition notwithstanding the ridiculous appearance she then made, being made acquainted with the motive of her journey, was determined to gratify her inclinations.

As soon as the hour for country dances arrived, her cousin Hamil-ton was appointed her partner. She made some faint excuses at first on account of the inconvenient situation she was then in but soon suffered them to be overcome, in order, as she said, to show her duty to the Queen—and never did a woman in this world enjoy such complete satisfaction.

We have already observed that the greatest prosperity is liable to the greatest change. Lady Muskerry, trussed up as she was, seemed to feel no manner of uneasiness from the motion in dancing. On the contrary, being only apprehensive of the presence of her husband, which would have destroyed all her happiness, she danced with un-common briskness lest her ill stars should bring him back before she had fully satisfied herself with it. In the midst, therefore, of her capering in this indiscreet manner, her cushion came loose without her perceiving it and fell to the ground in the middle of the first round. The Duke of Buckingham, who watched her, took it up instantly, wrapped it up in his coat and, mimicking the cries of a newborn infant, he went about inquiring for a nurse for the young Muskerry among the maids of honor.

This buffoonery, joined to the strange figure of the poor lady, had almost thrown Miss Stewart into hysterics, for the princess of Babylon after this accident was quite flat on one side and immoderately protuberant on the other. All those who had before suppressed their inclinations to laugh, now gave themselves free scope when they saw that Miss Stewart was ready to split her sides. The poor lady was greatly disconcerted. Every person was officious to console her, but the Queen, who inwardly laughed more heartily than any, pretended to disapprove of their taking such liberties.

While Miss Hamilton and Mrs. Wetenhall endeavoured to refit Lady Muskerry in another room, the Duke of Buckingham told the King that if the physicians would permit a little exercise immediately after a delivery, the best way to recover Lady Muskerry was to renew the dance as soon as ever her infant was replaced. This advice was approved and accordingly put in execution. The Queen proposed, as soon as she appeared, a second round of country dances; and Lady Muskerry accepting the offer, the remedy had its desired effect and entirely removed every remembrance of her late mishap.

King's Gambit Declined

This good-natured king began now to be rather peevish; nor was it altogether without reason: he disturbed no person in their amours and yet others had often the presumption to encroach upon his. Lord Dorset, first lord of the bedchamber, had lately debauched from his service Nell Gwyn, the actress: Lady Cleveland, whom he now no longer regarded, continued to disgrace him by repeated infidelities with unworthy rivals and almost ruined him by the immense sums she lavished on her gallants, but that which most sensibly affected him was the late coldness and threats of Miss Stewart. He long since had offered her all the settlements and all the titles she could desire, until he had an opportunity more effectually to provide for her, which she had pretended only to decline for fear of the scandal they might occasion on her being raised to a rank which would attract the public notice; but since the return of the court she had given herself other airs. Sometimes she was for retiring from court to appease the continual uneasiness her presence gave the queen: at other times it was to avoid temptations by which she wished to insinuate that her innocence was still preserved. In short, the king's heart was continually distracted by alarms or oppressed by humor and caprice.

As he could not for his life imagine what Miss Stewart wished him to do or what she would be at, he thought upon reforming his establishment of mistresses to try whether jealousy was not the real occasion of her uneasiness. It was for this reason that, after having solemnly declared he would have nothing more to say to the Duchess of Cleveland, since her intrigue with Churchill, he discarded without any exception all the other mistresses which he had in various parts of the town. The Nell Gwyns, the Miss Davis's, and the joyous train of singers and dancers in his majesty's theatre were all dismissed. All these sacrifices were ineffectual: Miss Stewart continued to torment and almost to drive the king to distraction: but his majesty soon after found out the real cause of this coldness.

This discovery was owing to the officious Duchess of Cleveland who, ever since her disgrace, had railed most bitterly against Miss Stewart as the cause of it and against the king's weakness who, for an inanimate idiot, had treated her with so much indignity. As some of her grace's creatures were still in the king's confidence, by their means she was informed of the king's uneasiness and that Miss Stewart's behavior was the occasion of it; and as soon as she had found the opportunity she had so long wished for, she went directly into the king's cabinet through the apartment of one of his pages called Chiffinch. This was not new to her.

The king was just returned from visiting Miss Stewart, in a very ill humor: the presence of the Duchess of Cleveland surprised him and did not in the least diminish it. She, perceiving this, accosted him in an ironical tone and with a smile of indignation: "I hope," said she, "I may be allowed to pay you my homage, although the angelic Stewart has forbid you to see me at my own house. I will not make use of reproaches and expostulations which would disgrace myself, still less will I endeavor to excuse frailities which nothing can justify, since your constancy for me deprives me of all defense, considering I am the only person you have honored with your tenderness who has made herself unworthy of it by ill-conduct. I come now, therefore, with no other intent than to comfort and to condole with you upon the affliction and grief into which the coldness or new-fashioned chastity of the inhuman Stewart has reduced your majesty." These words were attended by a fit of laughter as unnatural and

strained as it was insulting and immoderate, which completed the
king's impatience: he had, indeed, expected that some bitter jest
would follow this preamble; but he did not suppose she would have
given herself such blustering airs, considering the terms they were
then upon; and as he was preparing to answer her, "Be not offended,"
said she, "that I take the liberty of laughing at the gross manner in
which you are imposed upon: I cannot bear to see that such particular affectation should make you the jest of your own court and that
you should be ridiculed with such impunity. I know that the
affected Stewart has sent you away under pretence of some indisposition or perhaps some scruple of conscience; and I come to acquaint
you that the Duke of Richmond will soon be with her, if he is not
there already. I do not desire you to believe what I say since it might
be suggested either through resentment or envy: only follow me to
her apartment, either that, no longer trusting calumny and malice,
you may honor her with a just preference if I accuse her falsely; or,
if my information be true, you may no longer be the dupe of a
pretended prude who makes you act so unbecoming and ridiculous
a part."

As she ended this speech, she took him by the hand while he
was yet undecided and pulled him away towards her rival's apartments. Chiffinch being in her interest, Miss Stewart could have no
warning of the visit, and Babiani, who owed all to the Duchess of
Cleveland and who served her admirably well upon this occasion,
came and told her that the Duke of Richmond had just gone into
Miss Stewart's chamber. It was in the middle of a little gallery which,
through a private door, led from the king's apartments to those of
his mistresses. The Duchess of Cleveland wished him good-night as
he entered her rival's chamber and retired, in order to wait the
success of the adventure of which Babiani, who attended the king,
was charged to come and give her an account.

It was near midnight: the king, in his way, met his mistress's
chambermaids, who respectfully opposed his entrance and in a very
low voice, whispered his majesty that Miss Stewart had been very
ill since he left her; but that, being gone to bed, she was, God be
thanked, in a very fine sleep. "That I must see," said the king,
pushing her back, who had posted herself in his way. He found Miss
Stewart in bed, indeed, but far from being asleep: the Duke of
Richmond was seated at her pillow and in all probability was less
inclined to sleep than herself. The perplexity of the one party and
the rage of the other were such as may easily be imagined upon such

a surprise. The king, who of all men, was one of the most mild and gentle, testified his resentment to the Duke of Richmond in such terms as he had never before used. The duke was speechless and almost petrified: he saw his master and his king justly irritated. The first transports which rage inspires on such occasions are dangerous: Miss Stewart's window was very convenient for a sudden revenge, the Thames flowing close beneath it: he cast his eyes upon it; and, seeing those of the king more incensed and fired with indignation than he thought his nature capable of, he made a profound bow and retired, without replying a single word to the vast torrent of threats and menaces that were poured upon him.

Miss Stewart, having a little recovered from her first surprise, instead of justifying herself, began to talk in the most extravagant manner and said everything that was most capable to inflame the king's passion and resentment; that, if she were not allowed to receive visits from a man of the Duke of Richmond's rank, who came with honorable intentions, she was a slave in a free country; that she knew of no engagement that could prevent her from disposing of her hand as she thought proper; but, however, if this was not permitted her in his dominions, she did not believe that there was any power on earth that could hinder her from going over to France and throwing herself into a convent, to enjoy there that tranquillity which was denied her in his court. The king, sometimes furious with anger, sometimes relenting at her tears and sometimes terrified at her menaces, was so greatly agitated that he knew not how to answer either the nicety of a creature who wanted to act the part of Lucretia under his own eye, or the assurance with which she had the effrontery to reproach him. In this suspense, love had almost entirely vanquished all his resentments and had nearly induced him to throw himself upon his knees and entreat pardon for the injury he had done her, when she desired him to retire and leave her in repose, at least for the remainder of that night without offending those who had either accompanied him or conducted him to her apartments by a longer visit. This impertinent request provoked and irritated him to the highest degree: he went out abruptly, vowing never to see her more, and passed the most restless and uneasy night he had ever experienced since his restoration.

The next day the Duke of Richmond received orders to quit the court and never more to appear before the king; but it seems he had not waited for those orders, having set out early that morning for his country seat.

Miss Stewart, in order to obviate all injurious constructions that might be put upon the adventure of the preceding night, went and threw herself at the queen's feet; where, acting the new part of an innocent Magdalen, she entreated her majesty's forgiveness for all the sorrow and uneasiness she might have already occasioned her: she told her majesty that a constant and sincere repentance had induced her to contrive all possible means for retiring from court; that this reason had inclined her to receive the Duke of Richmond's addresses, who had courted her a long time; but since this courtship had caused his disgrace and had likewise raised a vast noise and disturbance, which perhaps might be turned to the prejudice of her reputation, she conjured her majesty to take her under her protection and endeavor to obtain the king's permission for her to retire into a convent, to remove at once all those vexations and troubles her presence had innocently occasioned at court. All this was accompanied with a proper deluge of tears.

It is a very agreeable spectacle to see a rival prostrate at our feet, entreating pardon, and at the same time justifying her conduct. The queen's heart not only relented but she mingled her own tears with those of Miss Stewart: after having raised her up and most tenderly embraced her, she promised her all manner of favor and protection either in her marriage or in any other course she thought fit to pursue and parted from her with the firm resolution to exert all her interest in her support; but, being a person of great judgment, the reflections which she afterwards made induced her to change her opinion.

She knew that the king's disposition was not capable of an obstinate constancy: she therefore judged that absence would cure him or that a new engagement would by degrees entirely efface the remembrance of Miss Stewart: and that, since she could not avoid having a rival, it was more desirable she should be one who had given such eminent proofs of her prudence and virtue. Besides, she flattered herself that the king would ever think himself eternally obliged to her for having opposed the retreat and marriage of a girl whom at that time he loved to distraction. This fine reasoning determined her conduct. All her industry was employed in persuading Miss Stewart to abandon her schemes; and what is most extraordinary in this adventure is that, after having prevailed upon her to think no more either of the Duke of Richmond or of a nunnery, she charged herself with the office of reconciling these two lovers.

Indeed it would have been a thousand pities if her negotiation had miscarried: but she did not suffer this misfortune; for never were the king's addresses so eager and passionate as after this peace, nor ever better received by the fair Stewart.

WILLIAM OLDYS

The picturesque antiquary William Oldys was a great accumulator of fact and gossip about the English stage. This account of Eleanor Gwyn is probably his, though the Grub Street publication from which it is taken bears the name of the actor Betterton. Nell's story was already a source of much amusement when this early version of it was written, and such it has remained. "Rowley" or "Old Rowley" was the familiar appellation of Charles II. Hart is Charles Hart, who is said to have introduced Nell Gwyn to the stage. She called him her Charles the First.

Some Account of Mrs. Gwyn

Mrs. Ellen Gwyn, though mistress of a monarch, was the daughter of a fruiterer in Covent Garden.

> This shows that sultans, emperors, and kings,
> When blood boils high, will stoop to meanest things.

Nelly, for by that name she was universally known, came into the theater in the way of her profession, as a fruiteress, that is.

> The orange basket her fair arm did suit
> Laden with pippins and Hesperian fruit.
> This first step raised, to the wondering pit she sold
> The lovely fruit smiling with streaks of gold.
> Fate now for her did his whole force engage,
> And from the pit she's mounted to the stage.
> There in full lustre did her glories shine,
> And, long eclipsed, spread forth their light divine.
> There Hart's and Rowley's soul she did ensnare,
> And made a king the rival to a player.

Such is Lord Rochester's account. And Mr. Langbain tells us that Mrs. Ellen Gwyn spoke a new prologue to an old play called *The Knight of the Burning Pestle*. We find her afterward acting the parts of Queen Almahide in the *Conquest of Grenada*, Florimel in *The Maiden Queen*, Donna Jacintha in *The Mock Astrologer*, Valeria in *The Royal Martyr*, in which tragedy Mrs. Boutel played the part of Saint Catherine. Mrs. Gwyn, besides her own part of Valeria, was likewise appointed, in that character, to speak the Epilogue, in performing which she so captivated the King (who was present the first night of the play) by the humorous turns she gave it, that his Majesty, when she had done, went behind the scenes and carried her off to an entertainment that night.

In the tragedy of *Tyrranic Love* or *The Royal Martyr*, Valeria is daughter to the Roman emperor, Maximin. She, being forced by her father to marry Placidius, stabs herself for the love of Porphyrius, who thus condoles her loss:

> Our arms no more let Aquileia fear,
> But to her gates our peaceful ensigns bear,
> While I mix cypress with my myrtle wreath,
> Joy for my life, and mourn Valeria's death.

As Valeria is carried off the stage dead, she thus accosts the bearer:

> Hold, are you mad? You damned confounded dog,
> I am to rise and speak the epilogue!

She then addresses herself to the audience:

> I come, kind gentlemen, strange news to tell ye;
> I am the ghost of poor departed Nelly.
> Sweet ladies, be not frighted, I'll be civil;
> I'm what I was, a little harmless devil.
> For after death we spirits have such natures
> We had, for all the world, when human creatures;
> And therefore I, that was an actress here,
> Play all my tricks in hell, a goblin there.
> Gallants, look to it! you say there are no sprites,
> But *I'll* come, dance about your beds at nights;
> And, faith, you'll be in a sweet kind of taking
> When I surprise you between sleep and waking. . . .
> But farewell, Gentlemen, make haste to me;
> I'm sure ere long to have your company.
> As for my epitaph when I am gone,
> I'll trust no poet but will write my own:
> Here Nelly lies, who though she lived a slattern
> Yet died a princess, acting in Saint Cattern. . . .

Nelly was eased of her virginity by Mr. Hart. . . . But his Majesty carrying off the prize we must leave her under the royal protection.

There are many comical passages reported of Nell Gwyn, she being of a gay, frolicsome and humorous disposition; but some are a little too loose and others a little too long to be here inserted. This story may perhaps be excused: that having once by an unlucky run of ill luck at gaming lost all her money and run in debt with

Sir John Germain he took the advantage of making such a proposal
for easy payment as may be well guessed at from her answer, when
she replied, with equal smartness and fidelity to her royal keeper,
that truly she was no such sportswoman as to lay the dog where
the deer should lie. Many sharp satires were written on her, rather
through envy at her sudden advancement from such a mean origin
than any unworthiness in her of the station to which she was
advanced. . . . For she troubled not her head with religion and was
no popish mistress, nor with politics, and did no mischief. And
though she might be alike chargeable with the rest to his majesty,
nevertheless, as she had more spirit, wit, and pleasantry, so had she
the more justice, charity, and generosity in her than all the king's
other mistresses. The haughty and imperious air she left to them;
hers was free and degagé, which rendered her more amiable because
less awful. . . . His majesty had issue by her, Charles, surnamed
Beauclerc, born about the middle of May, 1670, who was created
Earl of Burford and afterwards Duke of St. Albans [and] another
son, named James, born about Christmas day, 1671. As for herself,
she died at her house in Pall Mall in 1691 and was pompously
interred in the Parish Church of St. Martin's in the fields, where Dr.
Thomas Tenison, then vicar thereof and late Archbishop of Canterbury, preached her funeral sermon, or a panegyric, rather, upon her
and her profession as some thought it, giving a more mild and
favorable character of such a woman than was then deemed to
become his cloth. . . . Among her donations one was a sum of
money for a weekly entertainment of the ringers at St. Martin's aforesaid, which they enjoy to this day.

ELEANOR GWYN

*The letters of Nell Gwyn confirm the legend of her relaxed
and relaxing personality. Of the two here given, the first is addressed
to one of a group of political intriguers of the party of Buckingham
and Shaftesbury, who tried to use her influence with the King.
Though her rival, the Duchess of Portsmouth, is on the other side,
Nell's mind is too full of things in general to be a very heavy
plotter. The second letter gives instructions and the news to an old
friend who was working for her in London, while Nell and her royal
son were in residence on the confines of the court at Windsor. The
letters are dictated, the first probably to her maid, Bridget. We sadly
correct the spelling and supply punctuation, leaving, however, one*

passage in its original state as a specimen of seventeenth-century
English as it was sometimes written.

Letters

TO LAWRENCE HYDE

Pray, dear Mr. Hyde, forgive me for not writing to you before now, for the reason is I have been sick three months and since I recovered I have had nothing to entertain you withal. Nor have nothing now worth writing, but that I can hold no longer to let you know I never have been in any company without drinking your health, for I love you with all my soul.

The Pall Mall is now to me a dismal place since I have utterly lost Sir Carr Scroope never to be recovered again, for he told me he could not live always at this rate and so began to be a little uncivil, which I could not suffer from an ugly *beau garçon.* Mrs. Knight's Lady mother is dead and she has put up a scutcheon no bigger than my Lady Green's scutcheons. My Lord Rochester has gone in the country. Mr. Savile has got a misfortune, but is upon recovery and is to marry an heiress who, I think, won't have an ill time of it if he holds up his thumb. My Lord of Dorset appears once in three months, for he drinks ale with Shadwell and Mr. Harris at the Duke's house all day long. My Lord Burford remembers his service to you.

my Lord Bauclair is is goeing into France we are a goeing to supe with the king at whithale & my Lady Harvie the king remembers his sarvis to you now lets talk of state affairs for we never caried things so cunningly as now for we dont know whether we shall have pesce or war but I am for war and for no other reason but that you may come home I have a thousand merry conseets but I cant make her write um & therfore you must take the will for the deed god bye your most loveing obedient faithful & humbel

sarvant
E G

TO MRS. FRANCES JENNINGS

I have received your letter, and I desire you would speak to my Lady Williams to send me the gold stuff and a note with it because I must sign it. Then she shall have her money the next day of Mr.

Trant. Pray tell her Ladyship that I will send her a note of what quantity of things I'll have bought if her Ladyship will put herself to the trouble to buy them. When they are bought, I will sign a note for her to be paid. Pray, Madam, let the man go on with my sedan and send Potvin and Mr. Coker down to me, for I want them both. The bill is very dear to boil the plate, but necessity has no law. I am afraid, Madam, you have forgot my mantle which you were to line with musk-colored satin and all my other things, for you send me no patterns nor answer. Monsieur Lainey is going away. Pray send me word about your son Griffin, for his Majesty is mighty well pleased that he will go along with my Lord Duke [her son, the Duke of St. Albans]. I am afraid you are so much taken up with your own house that you forget my business. My service to dear Lord Kildare, and tell him I love him with all my heart. Pray, Madam, see that Potvin brings now all my things with him, my Lord Duke's bed, etc. If he has not made them all up, he may do that here, for if I do not get my things out of his hands now, I shall not have them until this time twelve-month. The Duke brought me down with him my crochet of diamonds and I love it the better because he brought it. Mr. Lumley and everybody else will tell you that it is the finest thing that ever was seen. Good Madam, speak to Mr. Beaver to come down, too, that I may bespeak a ring for the Duke of Grafton before he goes into France.

I have continued extreme ill ever since you left me, and I am so still. I have sent to London for a doctor. I believe I shall die. My service to the Duchess of Norfolk, and tell her I am as sick as her Grace, but do not know what I ail although she does, which I am overjoyed that she goes on with her great belly.

Pray tell my Lady Williams that the King's mistresses are accounted ill pay-masters, but she shall have her money the next day after I have the stuff.

Here is sad slaughter at Windsor, the young men taking their leaves and going to France, and although they are none of them my lovers, yet I am loth to part with the men. Mrs. Jennings, I love you with all my heart, so good-bye.

E.G.

Let me have an answer to this letter.

ANONYMOUS

A Panegyric on Nelly

Of a great heroine I mean to tell
And by what just degrees her titles swell
To Mistress Nelly, grown from Cinder Nell.
Much did she suffer, first on bulk and stage,
From the blackguards and bullies of the age.
Much more her growing virtue did sustain
While dear Charles Hart and Buckhurst sued in vain.
In vain they sued. Cursed be the envious tongue
That her undoubted chastity would wrong.
For should we Fame believe, we then might say
That thousands lay with her as well as they.
But Fame, thou liest, for her prophetic mind
Foresaw her greatness fate had well designed,
And her ambition chose to be, before
A virtuous countess, an imperial whore.
Even in her native dirt, her soul was high
And did at Crowns and shining Monarchs fly.
Even while she cinders raked, her swelling breast
With thoughts of glorious whoredom was possessed.
Still did she dream (nor could her birth withstand)
Of dangling scepters in her dirty hand. . . .
Less famed that Nelly was whose cuckold's rage
In ten years' wars did half the world engage.
She's now the darling strumpet of the crowd,
Forgets her state and talks to them aloud,
Lays by her greatness and descends to prate
With those 'bove whom she's raised by wondrous fate.
True to the Protestant interest and cause,
True to the established government and laws,
The choice delight of the whole mobile,
Scarce Monmouth's self is more beloved than she.
Was this the cause that did their quarrel move
That both are rivals in the people's love?
No, it was her matchless loyalty alone
That bid Prince Perkin pack up and be gone.

"Ill bred thou art," says Prince. Nell does reply,
"Was Mrs. Barlow better bred than I?"
Thus sneaked away the nephew overcome,
By his aunt-in-law's severer wit struck dumb.
    Her virtue, loyalty, wit, and noble mind
In the foregoing doggerel you may find.
Now for her piety one touch, and then
To Rymer I'll resign my muse and pen.
'Twas this that raised her charity so high
To visit those that did in durance lie.
From Oxford prison many did she free.
There died her father and there gloried she
In giving others life and liberty.
So pious a remembrance still she bore
Even to the fetters that her father wore.
Nor was her mother's funeral less her care.
No cost, no velvet did the daughter spare.
Fine gilded scutcheons did the hearse enrich
To celebrate this martyr of the ditch.
Burnt brandy did in flaming brimmers flow
Drunk at her funeral, while her well pleased shade
Rejoiced even in the sober fields below
At all the drunkenness her death had made.
Was ever child with such a mother blessed?
Or ever mother such a child possessed? . . .
Thus we in short have all the virtues seen
Of the incomparable Madam Gwinn.
Nor wonder others are not with her shown.
She who no equal has, must be alone.

SAMUEL PEPYS

Pepys in his own small way began early to follow the pattern of sexual promiscuity set by his sovereign lord, the King. The record of his philanderings runs throughout the diary, ranging from mere ogling to downright wife stealing. Pepys was by nature the most amorous of men. He sets down his sensual experiences as he sets down the increase of his wealth, his book buying, his playgoing or his pleasant conversations with his wife, but with a ludicrous use of French and Spanish for the key words. As the diary progresses and Pepys becomes an increasingly important figure in public life the appetite for every sort of pleasure seems to grow on him, until the pace becomes very fast indeed. There is something hectic about his self-indulgence, and he does not hold his emotions at arm's length. He is at times on edge with jealousy of his abused wife, once because of the purely professional ministrations of a dancing master. Conversely he is troubled in his amours by a sense of guilt to which a French education had made those placed above him happily immune. Obviously a plain Englishman of Puritan upbringing plays the game of adultery unlimited only at his peril. Nor was Mrs. Pepys any better trained to put up with her husband's infidelities and perhaps pay him back in kind. She bore it after a fashion till Samuel succumbed to a real infatuation within the household. What followed is comedy or tragedy as one chooses to regard it. The Deb Willet episode interlaces with other matter in the last two years of the diary. Trivial in itself it has the shape of drama. Pepys seems, to be sure, to have been on the way toward surviving the storm which so shook his little state of man, and Deb's final wink is a rather impotent conclusion. But one cannot tell. The impairment of his eyesight and the cessation of paper confidences suggest the possibility of a real catastrophe in store for him. As it was, Mrs. Pepys died shortly after the diary period. A respectable gentlewoman, herself a former servant in the Pepysian menage, came to share his hearth, his tea table and perhaps his bed. His troubles in later life were mainly political, and he died in peaceful and interested retirement in the reign of Anne.

The Affaire Deb Willett

September 30, 1667. So by coach home, and there found our pretty girl Willet come, brought by Mr. Batelier, and she is very pretty, and so grave as I never saw a little thing in my life. Indeed, I think her a little too good for my family, and so well carriaged as I hardly ever saw. I wish my wife may use her well.

October 5. Took my wife and Willet to the Duke of York's playhouse, but the house so full, it being a new play, "The Coffee House," that we could not get in, and so to the King's house: and there, going in, met with Knepp, and she took us up into the tireing-rooms: and to the women's shift, where Nell was dressing herself, and was all unready, and is very pretty, prettier than I thought. And so walked all up and down the house above, and then below into the scene-room, and there sat down, and she gave us fruit: and here I read the questions to Knepp, while she answered me, through all her part of "Flora's Figary's" which was acted to-day. But, Lord!

to see how they were both painted would make a man mad, and did make me loath them; and what base company of men comes among them, and how lewdly they talk! and how poor the men are in clothes, and yet what a shew they make on the stage by candle-light, is very observable. But to see how Nell cursed, for having so few people in the pit, was pretty; the other house carrying away all the people at the new play, and is said, now-a-days, to have generally most company, as being better players. By and by into the pit, and there saw the play, which is pretty good, but my belly was full of what I had seen in the house, and so, after the play done, away home, and there to the writing my letters, and so home to supper and to bed.

December 7. All the morning at the office, and at noon home to dinner with my clerks, and while we were at dinner comes Willet's aunt to see her and my wife; she is a very fine widow and pretty handsome but extraordinary well carriaged and speaks very handsomely and with extraordinary understanding, so as I spent the whole afternoon in her company with my wife, she understanding all the things of note touching plays and fashions and Court and everything and speaks rarely, which pleases me mightily, and seems to love her niece very well, and was so glad (which was pretty odde) that since she came hither her breasts begin to swell, she being afeard before that she would have none, which was a pretty kind of content she gave herself.

December 22 (Lord's day). Up, and my wife, poor wretch, still in pain, and then to dress myself and down to my chamber to settle some papers, and thither come to me Willet with an errand from her mistress, and this time I first did give her a little kiss, she being a very pretty humoured girle, and so one that I do love mightily.

March 24, 1668. To White Hall, where great talk of the tumult at the other end of the town, about Moore-fields, among the 'prentices, taking the liberty of these holydays to pull down bawdy-houses. And Lord! to see the apprehensions which this did give to all people at Court, that presently order was given for all the soldiers, horse and foot, to be in armes! and forthwith alarmes were beat by drum and trumpet through Westminster, and all to their colours, and to horse, as if the French were coming into the town! So Creed, whom I met her, and I to Lincolne's Inn-fields, thinking to have gone into the fields to have seen the 'prentices; but here we found these fields full of soldiers all in a body, and my Lord Craven commanding of them, and riding up and down to give orders, like a madman. And some young men we saw brought by soldiers to the Guard at White Hall, and overheard others that stood by say, that it was only for pulling down the bawdy-houses; and none of the bystanders finding fault with them, but rather of the soldiers for hindering them. And we heard a Justice of the Peace this morning say to the King, that he had been endeavouring to suppress this tumult, but could not; and, that, imprisoning some [of them] in the new prison at Clerkenwell, the rest did come and break open the prison and release them; and that they do give out that they are for pulling down the bawdy-houses, which is one of the greatest grievances of the nation. To which the King made a very poor, cold, insipid answer: "Why, why do they go to them, then?" and that was all, and had no mind to go on with the discourse. So home and there to my chamber, to prick out my song "It is Decreed," intending to have it ready to give Mr. Harris on Thursday, when we meet, for him to sing, believing that he will do it more right than a woman that sings better, unless it were Knepp, which I cannot have opportunity to teach it to.

March 25. Up, and walked to White Hall, there to wait on the Duke of York, which I did. The Duke of York and all with him this morning were full of the talk of the 'prentices, who are not yet [put] down, though all the guards and militia of the town have been in armes all this night and the night before; and the 'prentices have made fools of them, sometimes by running from them and flinging stones at them. Some blood hath been spilt, but a great many houses pulled down; and, among others, the Duke of York was mighty merry at that of Damaris Page's, the great bawd of the seamen; and the Duke of York complained merrily that he hath lost two tenants, by their houses being pulled down, who paid him for their wine licenses £15 a year. But here it was said how these idle fellows have had the confidence to say that they did ill in contenting themselves in pulling down the little bawdy-houses, and did not go and pull down the great bawdy-house at White Hall. And some of them have the last night had a word among them, and it was "Reformation and Reducement." This do make the courtiers ill at ease to see this spirit among people, though they think this matter will not come to much: but it speaks people's minds; and then they do say that there are men of understanding among them, that have been of Cromwell's army: but how true that is, I know not.

March 31. I called Deb. to take pen, ink, and paper and write down what things come into my head for my wife to do in order to her going into the country, and the girl, writing not so well as she would do, cried, and her mistress construed it to be sullenness, and so away angry with her too, but going to bed she undressed me, and there I did give her good advice and *baiser la, elle* weeping still.

June 18. Up betimes and to the office. At noon home to dinner, where my wife still in a melancholy, fusty humour, and crying, and do not tell me plainly what it is; but I by little words find that she hath heard of my going to plays, and carrying people abroad every day, in her absence; and that I cannot help but the storm will break out, I think, in a little time. After dinner carried her by coach to St. James's.

June 19. I home, and there we to bed again, and slept pretty well, and about nine rose, and then my wife fell into her blubbering again, and at length had a request to make of me, which was, that she might go into France, and live there, out of trouble; and then all come out, that I loved pleasure and denied her any, and a deal of do; and I find that there have been great fallings out between my father and her, whom, for ever hereafter, I must keep asunder, for they cannot possibly agree. And I said nothing, but, with very mild words and few, suffered her humour to spend, till we begun to be very quiet, and I think all will be over, and friends, and so I to the office where all the morning doing business.

July 18. Creed told me this day how when the King was at my Lord Cornwallis's, when he went last to Newmarket, that being there on a Sunday, the Duke of Buckingham did in the afternoon to please the King make a bawdy sermon to him out of Canticles, and that my Lord Cornwallis did endeavour to get the King a whore, and that must be a pretty girl the daughter of the parson of the place, but that she did get away, and leaped off of some place and killed herself, which if true is very sad.

October 25 (Lord's day). So home and to dinner, and after dinner all the afternoon got my wife and boy to read to me, and at night W. Batelier comes and sups with us; and, after supper, to have my head combed by Deb., which occasioned the greatest sorrow to me that ever I knew in this world, for my wife, coming up suddenly, did find me embracing the girl. . . . I was at a wonderful loss upon it, and the girle also, and I endeavoured to put it off, but my wife was struck mute and grew angry, and so her voice come to her, grew quite out of order, and I to say little, but to bed, and my wife said little also, but could not sleep all night, but about two in the morning waked me and cried, and fell to tell me as a great secret that she was a Roman Catholique and had received the Holy Sacrament, which troubled me, but I took no notice of it, but she went on from one thing to another till at last it appeared plainly her trouble was at what she saw, but yet I did not know how much she saw, and therefore said nothing to her. But after her much crying and reproaching me with inconstancy and preferring a sorry girl before her, I did give her no provocation, but did promise all fair usage to her and love, and foreswore any hurt that I did with her, till at last she seemed to be at ease again, and so toward morning a little sleep, and so I with some little repose and rest.

November 11. To the office, and there having done, I home and to supper and to bed, where, after lying a little while, my wife starts up, and with expressions of affright and madness, as one frantick, would rise, and I would not let her, but burst out in tears myself, and so continued almost half the night, the moon shining so that it was light, and after much sorrow and reproaches and little ravings (though I am apt to think they were counterfeit) from her, and my promise again to discharge the girle myself, all was quiet again, and so to sleep.

November 12. I to my wife and to sit with her a little and then called her and Willet to my chamber, and there did, with tears in my eyes, which I could not help, discharge her and advise her to be gone as soon as she could, and never to see me, or let me see her more while she was in the house, which she took with tears too, but I believe understands me to be her friend, and I am apt to believe by what my wife hath of late told me is a cunning girle, if not a slut. Thence, parting kindly with my wife, I away by coach to my cozen Roger.

November 13. Thence I home, and there to talk, with great pleasure all the evening, with my wife, who tells me that Deb. has been abroad to-day, and is come home and says she has got a place to go to, so as she will be gone to-morrow morning. This troubled me. But she will be gone and I not know whither. Before we went to bed my wife told me she would not have me to see her or give her her wages, and so I did give my wife £10 for her year, and half a quarter's wages, which she went into her chamber and paid her, and so to bed, and there, blessed be God! we did sleep well and with peace, which I had not done in now almost twenty nights together.

November 16. Up, and by water to White Hall. This being done I away to Holborne, about Whetstone's Park, where I never was in my life before, where I understand by my wife's discourse that Deb. is gone, which do trouble me mightily that the poor girle should be

in a desperate condition forced to go thereabouts, and there not
hearing of any such man as Allbon, with whom my wife said she
now was.

November 18. Lay long in bed talking with my wife, she being
unwilling to have me go abroad, saying and declaring herself jealous
of my going out for fear of my going to Deb., which I do deny, for
which God forgive me, for I was no sooner out about noon but I did
go by coach directly to Somerset House, and there enquired among
the porters there for Dr. Allbon, and the first I spoke with told me
he knew him, and that he was newly gone to Lincoln's Inn Fields,
but whither he could not tell me. At last he comes back and tells
me she is well, and that I may see her if I will, but no more. So I
could not be commanded by my reason, but I must go this very
night, and so by coach, it being now dark, I to her, close by my
tailor's, and she come into the coach to me, and *je* did *baiser* her.
. . . I did nevertheless give her the best council I could, to have a
care of her honour, and to fear God, and suffer no man *para avoir*
to do *con* her as *je* have done, which she promised. *Je* did give her
20s. and directions *para laisser* sealed in paper at any time the name
of the place of her being at Herringman's, my bookseller in the
'Change, by which I might go *para* her, and so bid her good night
with much content to my mind, and resolution to look after her
no more till I heard from her. And so home, and there told my wife
a fair tale, God knows, how I spent the whole day, with which the
poor wretch was satisfied, or at least seemed so, she having been
mighty busy all day in getting of her house in order against to-morrow
to hang up our new hangings and furnishing our best chamber.

November 19. Up, and at the Office all the morning, with my heart
full of joy to think in what a safe condition all my matters now
stand between my wife and Deb. and me, and at noon running
up stairs to see the upholsters, who are at work upon hanging my
best room, and setting up my new bed, I find my wife sitting sad in
the dining room; which enquiring into the reason of, she begun to
call me all the false, rotten-hearted rogues in the world, letting me
understand that I was with Deb. yesterday, which, thinking it impossible for her ever to understand, I did a while deny, but at last
did, for the ease of my mind and hers, and for ever to discharge my
heart of this wicked business, I did confess all, and above stairs in
our bed chamber there I did endure the sorrow of her threats and
vows and curses all the afternoon, and, what was worse, she swore
by all that was good that she would slit the nose of this girle, and

be gone herself this very night from me, and did there demand 3 or
£400 of me to buy my peace, that she might be gone without making
any noise, or else protested that she would make all the world know
of it. So with most perfect confusion of face and heart, and sorrow
and shame, in the greatest agony in the world I did pass this afternoon, fearing that it will never have an end; but at last I did call for
W. Hewer, who I was forced to make privy now to all, and the poor
fellow did cry like a child, [and] obtained what I could not, that she
would be pacified upon condition that I would give it under my
hand never to see or speak with Deb. while I live. So, before it was
late, there was, beyond my hopes as well as desert, a durable peace;
and so to supper, and pretty kind words, and to bed, and did this
night begin to pray to God upon my knees alone in my chamber,
which God knows I cannot yet do heartily; but I hope God will give
me the grace more and more every day to fear Him, and to be true
to my poor wife.

March 12, 1669. In my coach with W. Hewer towards Westminster; and there to Nott's, the famous bookbinder, that bound for my
Lord Chancellor's library; and here I did take occasion for curiosity
to bespeak a book to be bound, only that I might have one of his
binding. And so home, where, thinking to meet my wife with content, after my pains all this day, I find her in her closet, alone, in the
dark, in a hot fit of railing against me, upon some news she has this
day heard of Deb.'s living very fine, and with black spots, and
speaking ill words of her mistress, which with good reason might
vex her; and the baggage is to blame, but, God knows, I know nothing of her, nor what she do, nor what becomes of her, though God
knows that my devil that is within me do wish that I could. But in
her fit she did tell me what vexed me all the night, that this had
put her upon putting off her handsome maid and hiring another
that was full of the small pox, which did mightily vex me, though I
said nothing, and do still.

April 13. I away home, and there sent for W. Hewer, and he and
I by water to White Hall to look, among other things, for Mr. May,
to unbespeak his dining with me to-morrow. But here being in the
court-yard, as God would have it, I spied Deb., which made my heart
and head to work, and I presently could not refrain, but sent W.
Hewer away to look for Mr. Wren (W. Hewer, I perceive, did see
her, but whether he did see me see her I know not, or suspect my
sending him away I know not, but my heart could not hinder me),
and I run after her and two women and a man, more ordinary

people, and she in her old clothes, and after hunting a little, find them in the lobby of the chapel below stairs, and there I observed she endeavoured to avoid me, but I did speak to her and she to me, and did get her *pour dire me où* she *demeurs* now, and did charge her *para* say nothing of me that I had *vu elle*, which she did promise, and so with my heart full of surprize and disorder I away. And so back to White Hall, and then back to the Park with Mr. May, but could see her no more, and so with W. Hewer, who I doubt by my countenance might see some disorder in me, we home by water, to my wife, who is come home from Deptford. But, God forgive me I hardly know how to put on confidence enough to speak as innocent, having had this passage to-day with Deb., though only, God knows, by accident. But my great pain is lest God Almighty shall suffer me to find out this girl, whom indeed I love, and with a bad *amour*, but I will pray to God to give me grace to forbear it.

April 15. Up, and to the office, and thence before the office sat to the Excise Office with W. Hewer, but found some occasion to go another way to the Temple upon business, and I by Deb.'s direction did know whither in Jewen Street to direct my hackney coachman. Thence I away, and through Jewen Street, my mind, God knows, running that way, but stopped not, but going down Holborne hill, by the Conduit, I did see Deb. on foot going up the hill. I saw her, and she me, but she made no stop, but seemed unwilling to speak to me; so I away on, but then stopped and 'light, and after her and overtook her at the end of Hosier lane in Smithfield, and without standing in the street desired her to follow me, and I led her into a little blind alehouse within the walls, and there she and I alone fell to talk and *baiser la* and *toker su mammailles*, but she mighty coy, and I hope modest. . . . I did give her in a paper 20s., and we did agree *para* meet again in the Hall at Westminster on Monday next; and so giving me great hopes by her carriage that she continues modest and honest, we did there part, she going home and I to Mrs. Turner's.

April 26. Creed, coming just now to see me, my wife, and he, and I out, and I set him down at Temple Bar, and myself and wife went down the Temple upon seeming business, only to put him off, and just at the Temple gate I spied Deb. with another gentlewoman, and Deb. winked on me and smiled, but undiscovered, and I was glad to see her.

May 16 (Lord's day). I all the afternoon drawing up a foul draught of my petition to the Duke of York, about my eyes, for leave to spend three or four months out of the Office, drawing it so as to give occasion to a voyage abroad, which I did, to my pretty good liking.

May 31. Up very betimes, and so continued all the morning with W. Hewer, upon examining and stating my accounts, in order to the fitting myself to go abroad beyond sea, which the ill condition of my eyes, and my neglect for a year or two, hath kept me behindhand in, and so as to render it very difficult now, and troublesome to my mind to do it; but I this day made a satisfactory entrance therein. Dined at home, and in the afternoon by water to White Hall, calling by the way at Michell's, where I have not been many a day till just the other day, and now I met her mother there and knew her husband to be out of town. And there *je* did *baiser elle*. And thence had another meeting with the Duke of York, at White Hall, on yesterday's work, and made a good advance: and so, being called by my wife, we to the Park, Mary Batelier, and a Dutch gentleman, a friend of hers, being with us. Thence to "The World's End," a drinking-house by the Park; and there merry, and so home late.

And thus ends all that I doubt I shall ever be able to do with my own eyes in the keeping of my Journal, I being not able to do it any longer, having done now so long as to undo my eyes almost every time that I take a pen in my hand; and, therefore, whatever comes of it, I must forbear: and, therefore, resolve, from this time forward, to have it kept by my people in long-hand, and must therefore be contented to set down no more than is fit for them and all the world to know; or, if there be anything, which cannot be much, now my *amours* to Deb. are past, and my eyes hindering me in almost all other pleasures, I must endeavour to keep a margin in my book open, to add, here and there, a note in short-hand with my own hand.

And so I betake myself to that course, which is almost as much as to see myself go into my grave: for which, and all the discomforts that will accompany my being blind, the good God prepare me!

JOHN MILTON

It is necessary to remind oneself that the great Puritan epic, Paradise Lost, was written, in part at least, during the early years of the Restoration, and that its audience, though small compared with Dryden's, was not inconsiderable. Some 1,800 copies were sold

*before 1674, when a new edition was called for. Nor did its author
belong entirely to the past. Blind, old and lonely, he nevertheless
remained a symbol of what the best men of England had worked
for, and it is not to be supposed that he was unaware of what was
going on or silent about it to his friends. The theme of "love which
is truly so" and of the dangers to human happiness which lie in its
violation is central in the poem. Milton had conceived it in his youth
and matured it through a lifetime by observation and experience. He
must have felt when the finished masterpiece lay before him that
never in history had the lessons it contained been more desperately
needed. The passage quoted was perhaps written before 1660. It is
appropriate here as an introduction to the examples we have to give
of conjugal loyalty in contrast to better-publicized and more amusing
records of illicit love.*

Hail Wedded Love

Thus at their shady lodge arrived, both stood,
Both turned, and under open sky adored
The God that made both Sky, Air, Earth, and Heaven,
Which they beheld, the Moon's resplendent globe,
And starry Pole:—"Thou also madest the Night,
Maker Omnipotent; and thou the Day,
Which we, in our appointed work employed,
Have finished, happy in our mutual help
And mutual love, the crown of all our bliss
Ordained by thee; and this delicious place,
For us too large, where thy abundance wants
Partakers, and uncropt falls to the ground.
But thou hast promised from us two a race
To fill the Earth, who shall with us extol
Thy goodness infinite, both when we wake,
And when we seek, as now, thy gift of sleep."
This said unanimous, and other rites
Observing none, but adoration pure,
Which God likes best, into their inmost bower
Handed they went; and, eased the putting-off
These troublesome disguises which we wear,
Straight side by side were laid; nor turned, I ween,
Adam from his fair spouse, nor Eve the rites
Mysterious of connubial love refused:

Whatever hypocrites austerely talk
Of purity, and place, and innocence,
Defaming as impure what God declares
Pure, and commands to some, leaves free to all.
Our Maker bids increase; who bids abstain
But our destroyer, foe to God and Man?
Hail wedded Love, mysterious law, true source
Of human offspring, sole propriety
In Paradise of all things common else.
By thee adulterous lust was driven from men
Among the bestial herds to range; by thee,
Founded in reason, loyal, just, and pure,
Relations dear, and all the charities
Of father, son, and brother first were known.
Far be it that I should write thee sin or blame,
Or think thee unbefitting holiest place,
Perpetual fountain of domestic sweets,
Whose bed is undefiled and chaste pronounced,
Present or past, as saints and patriarchs used.
Here Love his golden shafts employs, here lights
His constant lamp, and waves his purple wings,
Reigns here and revels; not in the bought smile
Of harlots, loveless, joyless, unendeared,
Casual fruition; nor in court-amours,
Mixed dance, or wanton mask, or midnight ball,
Or serenate, which the starved lover sings
To his proud fair, best quitted with disdain.
These lulled by nightingales, embracing slept,
And on their naked limbs the flowery roof
Showered roses, which the morn repaired. Sleep on
Blest pair; and O yet happiest if ye seek
No happier state, and know to know no more.

LADY ANNE FANSHAWE

*Sir Richard Fanshawe, diplomat and man of letters, wore the
badge of loyalty to Charles in exile and was duly honored by positions of trust, if not of profit, after the Restoration. His wife's
memoir, addressed to her "dear and only son" in the hope that he
might imitate his father's virtues, is an engaging record of their ad-*

*venturous life together and a monument of womanly devotion in
the highest tradition of the cavalier. The selections are from the
earlier portion of the narrative, before 1660, when the Fanshawes
were often separated, moving hither and yon on dangerous missions.
The last half of the memoir contains an account of Sir Richard's
ambassadorship to Spain, of his untimely death in 1666, of her long
journey back to England with his body and of her hard usage by
Lord Shaftesbury in the settlement of his accounts. "So maliciously
did he oppress me," she writes, outdoing even Dryden in the energy
of her denunciation, "as if he hoped in me to destroy the whole
stock of honesty and innocence, which he mortally hates. I have
been told he did this to have a bribe. Only I wish I had given him
one, though I had poured it down his throat, for the good of
mankind."*

A Hoyting Girl

Now it is necessary to say something of my mother's education of
me, which was with all the advantages that time afforded, both
for working all sorts of fine work with my needle, and learning
French, singing, lute, virginals, and dancing; and, notwithstanding
I learned as well as most did, yet I was wild to that degree, that
the hours of my beloved recreation took up too much of my time;
for I loved riding in the first place, and running, and all active
pastimes; and in fine I was that which we graver people call a
hoyting girl. But to be just to myself, I never did mischief to myself
or people, nor one immodest action or word in my life; but skipping
and activity was my delight. But upon my mother's death I then
began to reflect, and as an offering to her memory I flung away those
little childishnesses that had formerly possessed me, and by my
father's command took upon me the charge of his house and family,
which I so ordered by my excellent mother's example, as found acceptance in his sight.

What News?

My Lady Rivers, a brave woman, and one that had suffered many
thousand pounds' loss for the King, and that I had great reverence
for, and she had a kindness for me as a kinswoman, in discourse she

tacitly commended the knowledge of state affairs, and that some
women were very happy in a good understanding thereof, as my
Lady Aubigny, Lady Isabella Thynne and divers others, and yet none
was at first more capable than I; that in the night she knew there
came a post from Paris from the Queen, and she would be extremely
glad to hear what the Queen commanded the King in order to his
affairs; saying if I would ask my husband privately, he would tell me
what he found in the packet, and I might tell her. I that was young,
innocent, and to that day had never in my mouth "What news?"
begun to think there was more in inquiring into business of public
affairs than I thought of, and that it being a fashionable thing would
make me more beloved of my husband (if that had been possible)
than I was. When my husband returned from Council, after welcoming him home, as his custom ever was, he went with his handful
of papers into his study for an hour or more. I followed him. He
turning hastily said, "What wouldst thou, my Life?" I told him I
heard the Prince had received a packet from the Queen, and I
guessed it that in his hand, and I desired to know what was in it. He
smilingly replied, "My Love, I will immediately come to thee. Pray
thee go, for I am very busy." When he came out of his closet I
revived my suit. He kissed me and talked of other things. At supper
I would eat nothing; he as usually sat by me and drank often to me,
which was his custom, and was full of discourse to company that was
at table. Going to bed I asked him again, and said I could not believe
he loved me, if he refused to tell me all he knew; but he answered
nothing but stopped my mouth with kisses. So we went to bed; I
cried, and he went to sleep. Next morning very early, as his custom
was, he called to rise, but begun to discourse with me first, to which
I made no reply. He rose, came on the other side of the bed and
kissed me, and drew the curtain softly and went to Court. When he
came home to dinner, he presently came to me, as was usual, and
when I had him by the hand I said, "Thou dost not care to see
me troubled." To which he, taking me in his arms, answered, "My
dearest soul, nothing on earth can afflict me like that; and when you
asked me of my business, it was wholly out of my power to satisfy
thee; for my life and fortune shall be thine, and every thought of my
heart, in which the trust I am in may not be revealed. But my honor
is my own, which I cannot preserve if I communicate the Prince's
affairs; and pray thee with this answer rest satisfied." So great was his
reason and goodness, that upon consideration it made my folly appear

to me so vile that from that day until the day of his death I never thought fit to ask him any business, but that he communicated freely to me, in order to his estate or family.

That Passion

We pursued our voyage with prosperous winds, but with a most tempestuous master, a Dutchman (which is enough to say), but truly, I think, the greatest beast I ever saw of his kind. When we had just passed the Straits, we saw coming towards us with full sail a Turkish galley, well manned, and we believed we should all be carried away slaves. For this man had so loaded his goods for Spain that his guns were useless, though the ship carried sixty guns. He called for brandy, and after he had well drunken and all his men (which were near two hundred), he called for arms and cleared the deck as well as he could, resolving to fight rather than lose his ship, that was worth thirty thousand pounds. This was sad for us passengers; but my husband bid us be sure to keep in the cabin and no woman appear, which would make the Turk think we were a man-of-war; but if they saw women they would take us for merchants and board us. He went upon the decks and took a gun and bandoliers and sword, and with the rest of the ship's company stood on the deck expecting the arrival of the Turkish man-of-war. This beast captain had locked me up in the cabin. I knocked and called long to no purpose, until at length a cabin-boy came and opened the door. I all in tears desired him to be so good as to give me his blue thrum-cap he wore, and his tarred coat; which he did, and I gave him half a crown; and putting them on, and flinging away my night's clothes, I crept up softly and stood upon the deck by my husband's side as free from sickness and fear as, I confess, from discretion; but it was the effect of that passion which I could never master. By this time the two vessels were engaged in parley, and so well satisfied with speech and sight of each other's forces, that the Turkish man-of-war tacked about, and we continued our course. But when your father saw it convenient to retreat, looking upon me as he blessed himself, and snatched me up in his arms, saying, "Good God, that love can make this change!"; and though he seemingly chid me, he would laugh at it as often as he remembered that voyage.

LADY RACHAEL RUSSELL

The life and death of Lord Russell have been made more memorable by the devotion of his wife, as we read it in her preserved letters written both before and after his involvement in the conspiracy which brought about his downfall. Though of a less romantic temperament, perhaps, than Lady Fanshawe, Lady Russell affords an even finer example of domestic virtue in high life to offset the prevailing record of infidelity. Lady Russell lived a widow till her death in 1723 at the age of eighty-seven. Her long religious correspondence with Dr. Fitzwilliam came to concern itself less with her own sorrows and more with the welfare of her children and with public matters. It was the intention that it should be published.

Letters

TO LORD RUSSELL

1.

September 23, 1672

If I were more fortunate in my expression I could do myself more right when I would own to my dearest Mr. Russell what real and perfect happiness I enjoy from that kindness he allows me every day to receive new marks of, such as, in spite of the knowledge I have of my own wants, will not suffer me to mistrust I want his love, though I do not merit to so desireable a blessing. But, my best life, you that know so well how to love and to oblige, make my felicity entire by believing my heart possessed with all the gratitude, honor, and passionate affection to your person, any creature is capable of, or can be obliged to; and this granted, what have I to ask but a continuance (if God see fit) of these present enjoyments? If not, a submission without murmur to his most wise dispensations and unerring providence, having a thankful heart for the years I have been so perfectly contented in. He knows best when we have had enough here. What I most earnestly beg from his mercy is that we both live so as, which ever goes first, the other may not sorrow as for one of whom they have no hope. Then let us cheerfully expect to be together to a good old age; if not, let us not doubt but he will support us under what trial he will inflict upon us. These are necessary meditations sometimes that we may not be surprised above our strength by a sudden accident, being unprepared. Excuse me if I dwell too long upon it. It is from my opinion that if we can be prepared for all conditions, we can with the greater tranquillity enjoy the present, which I hope will be long; though when we change, it will be for the better, I trust, through the merits of Christ. . . .

R. RUSSELL

2.

March 1678

My sister being here tells me she overheard you tell her Lord last night that you would take notice of the business (you know what I mean) in the House. This alarms me, and I do earnestly beg of you to tell me truly if you have or mean to do it. If you do, I am most assured you will repent it. I beg once more to know the truth. It is more pain to be in doubt, and to your sister, too. And if I have any interest, I use it to beg your silence, at least today.

R. RUSSELL

3.

June 12, 1680

My dearest heart, flesh and blood cannot have a truer and greater sense of their own happiness than your poor but honest wife has. I am glad you find Stratton so sweet. May you live to do so one fifty years more; and, if God pleases, I shall be glad I may keep your company most of those years unless you wish other at any time. Then I think I could willingly leave all in the world, knowing you would take care of our brats. They are both well, and your great one's letter she hopes came to you. . . .

R. RUSSELL

4.

September 20, 1681

To see anybody preparing and taking their way to see what I long to do a thousand times more than they, makes me not endure to suffer their going without saying something to my best life, though it is a kind of anticipating my joy when we shall meet to allow myself so much before the time. But I confess I feel a great deal that, though I left London with great reluctance (as it is easy to persuade men a woman does), yet I am not like to leave Stratton with greater. They will tell you how well I got hither and how well I found our dear treasure here. Your boy will please you. You will, I think, find him improved, though I tell you so beforehand. They fancy he wanted you, for, as soon as I alighted, he followed, calling Papa, but I suppose it is the word he has most command of so was not disobliged by the little fellow. The girls were fine, in remembrance of the happy 29th of September, and we drank your health, after a red-deer pie, and at night your girls and I supped on a sack posset. Nay, Master would have his room, and for haste burnt his fingers in the posset, but he does but rub his hands for it. It is the most glorious weather here that ever was seen. The coach shall meet you at the cabbage garden. Be there by eight o'clock or a little after, though I guess you can hardly be there so soon, day breaks so late; and indeed the mornings are so misty it is not wholesome to be in the air so early. I do propose going to my neighbour Worsley today. I would fain be telling my heart more things—anything to be in a kind of talk with him. But I believe Spencer stays for my dispatch. He was willing to go early but this was to be the delight of this morning and the support of the day. It is performed in bed, thy pillow at my back; where thy dear head shall lie, I hope, tomorrow night and many more, I trust in His mercy notwithstanding all our enemies or ill-wishers. Love, and be willing to be loved, by

R. RUSSELL

5.

September 25, 1682

I stayed till I came from church, that I might, as late as I could, tell you all your concerns here are just as you left them. The young man as mad, winking at me, and striking with his drumstick whatever comes to his reach. If I had written before church whilst my morning draught was in my head, this might have entertained you better. But, now those fumes are laid, I find my spirits more dull than usual, as I have more cause: the much dearer and pleasanter part of my life being absent from me. I leave my Lord Russell to guess who that is. I had a letter last post from Mrs. Lacon. Pray tell her so, and that you had the paper about the King of Poland for she is very inquisitive to know, it being so new she says Charlton had not seen it. I know nothing new since you went but I know, as certainly as I live, that I have been for twelve years as passionate a lover as ever woman was, and hope to be so one twelve years more. Happy still, and entirely yours,

R. RUSSELL

TO DR. FITZWILLIAM

Woburn Abbey, September 30, 1683
I need not tell you, Good Doctor, how little capable I have been
of such an exercise as this. You will soon find how unfit I am still
for it, since my yet disordered thoughts can offer me no other than
such words as express the deepest sorrows, and confused as my yet
amazed mind is. But such men as you, and particularly one so much
my friend, will, I know, bear with my weakness and compassionate
my distress, as you have already done by your good letter and excellent prayer. I endeavor to make the best use I can of both, but I am
so evil and unworthy a creature that, though I have desires, yet I
have no dispositions or worthiness toward receiving comfort. I know
it is common with others to lose a friend, but to have lived with such
a one, it may be questioned how few can glory in the like happiness,
so consequently lament the like loss. . . . Lord let me understand
the reason of these dark and wounding providences, that I sink not
under the discouragements of my own thoughts. I know I have deserved my punishment and will be silent under it; but yet secretly my
heart mourns, too sadly, I fear, and cannot be comforted, because
I have not the dear companion and sharer of all my joys and sorrows.
I want him to talk with, to walk with, to eat and sleep with. . . .
Good Doctor, you will think, as you have reason, that I set no
bounds when I let myself loose to my complaints; but I will release
you, first fervently asking the continuance of your prayers for
Your infinitely afflicted
But very faithful servant,
R. RUSSELL

THE DUCHESS OF NEWCASTLE

*The legend of good (and pitiable) women in Restoration times is
further enhanced by the story of Margaret, First Duchess of Newcastle, and her husband, William Cavendish. This story she herself
tells, too voluminously, perhaps, but with an appealing earnestness.
The Duke had married her in Paris after the death of his first wife,
he being a veteran Cavalier of fifty, she a twenty-year-old maid of
honor to the exiled Queen. Recovering only a part of his vast estate*

he retired from court after the Restoration to pursue his old avo-
cations of horse training and belles-lettres, while she in the absence
of children wrote furiously and lavished an immense affection on her
lord. Like those other rarae aves of the pen, the Matchless Orinda
and the Incomparable Astraea, she dearly loved the headlines, and
she soon became fabulous both for her intellectual pretensions and
for her eccentricities. "The whole story of this lady is romance,"
writes Pepys, "and all she dos is romantic." He describes her as
going, on one of her London visits, in a large black coach, adorned
with silver instead of gold, her footmen all in velvet, herself ex-
travagantly dressed, "with her velvet cap, her hair about her ears,
many black patches because of pimples about her mouth, naked-
necked without a thing about it, and a black just-au-corps." Small
wonder that she was so followed and crowded by coaches that
nobody could come near her and that a hundred boys and girls ran
looking at her equipage. Space forbids recounting how she invited
herself to a meeting of the Royal Society, the first woman ever to
pass its doors, and was received only after much debating pro and
con and the fear of members that ballads would be made of it. But
indeed the true and serious portrait of this remarkable woman is
already enough distorted. We shall do better to let her speak for
herself in characteristic passages from The Life of Newcastle.

Of My Lord's Natural Wit and Understanding

Although my Lord has not so much of scholarship and learning as
had his brother Sir Charles Cavendish, yet he hath an excellent natural wit and judgment, and dives into the bottom of everything; as
is evidently apparent in the fore-mentioned art of horsemanship
and weapons, which by his own ingenuity he has reformed and
brought to such perfection as never anyone has done heretofore.
And though he is no mathematician by art, yet he hath a very good
mathematical brain, to demonstrate truth by natural reason, and is
both a good natural and moral philosopher, not by reading philosophical books but by his own natural understanding and observation,
by which he hath found out many truths.

To pass by other instances I'll but mention that when my Lord
was at Paris in his exile it happened one time that he, discoursing
with some of his friends, amongst whom was also that learned philosopher Hobbes, they began among the rest to argue upon this subject, namely, whether it were possible to make man fly as birds do;

and when some of the company had delivered their opinion, viz. that they thought it probable to be done by the help of artificial wings, my Lord declared that he deemed it altogether impossible, and demonstrated it by this following reason. "Man's arms," said he, "are not set on his shoulders in the same manner as bird's wings are; for that part of the arm which joins to the shoulder is in man placed inward, as towards the breast, which difference and contrary position or shape hinders that man cannot have the same flying action as birds have with their wings. Which argument Mr. Hobbes liked so well that he was pleased to make use of it in one of his books called Leviathan, if I remember well.

Of His Natural Humor and Disposition

My Lord may justly be compared to Titus, the deliciae of mankind, by reason of his sweet, gentle, and obliging nature; for though his wisdom and experience found it impossible to please all men because of their different humors and dispositions, yet his nature is such that he will be sorry when he seeth that men are displeased with him out of their own ill natures without any cause, for he loves all that are his friends and hates none that are his enemies. He is a loyal subject, a kind husband, a loving father, a generous master, and a constant friend.

He is true and just both in his words and actions and has no mean or petty designs, but they are all just and honest.

He is full of charity and compassion to persons that are in misery and full of clemency and mercy; insomuch that when he was general of a great army he would never sit in council himself upon cause of life and death, but granted pardon to many delinquents that were condemned by his council of war; so that some were forced to petition him not to do it by reason it was an ill precedent for others. To which my Lord merrily answered that if they did hang all they would leave him none to fight.

His noble bounty is so manifest to all the world that should I light a candle to the sun if I should strive to illustrate it.

In short I know him not addicted to any manner of vice, except that he hath been a great lover and admirer of the female sex, which whether it be so great a crime as to condemn him for it, I'll leave to the judgment of young gallants and beautiful ladies.

Of His Outward Shape and Behavior

His shape is neat and exactly proportioned; his stature of a middle-size, and his complexion sanguine. His behavior is such that it might be a pattern for all gentlemen, for it is courtly, civil, easy, and free, and yet hath something in it of grandeur that causes an awful respect towards him.

Of His Diet

In his diet he is so sparing and temperate that he never drinks beyond his set proportion, so as to satisfy only his natural appetite. He makes but one meal a day, at which he drinks two good glasses of small beer, one at the beginning, the other at the end thereof, and a little glass of sack in the middle of his dinner, which glass of sack he also uses in the morning for his breakfast, with a morsel of bread. His supper consists of an egg and a glass of small beer. And by this temperance he finds himself very healthful and may yet live many years, he being now of the age of seventy-three, which I pray God from my soul to grant him.

III Wits' Recreations

1 *The Stage*

The stage was the center of Restoration high jinks. It held up the mirror, not to nature, but to the glittering surface of society represented by the beau monde. It embodied the great jest of sexual misbehavior, with its concomitants of dicing, drunkenness, practical joking and miscellaneous intrigue. It did this without abashment in language or idea but somehow managed to avoid the kind of suggestiveness now permitted in fiction and on the screen. Sometimes it proceeded in the manner of gross caricature, sometimes with a subtlety unmatched save in the contemporary comedies of Molière. The performances were probably more bawdy than the texts. The actresses, however, were apparently fully clothed. Off the stage these actresses supplied Charles and a few other privileged characters with some of the objects of their lusts, the rest of the audience with their pin-up girls, their models of fashionable dress and manners and their topics of drawing-room conversation. To the people generally it was part and parcel of the new regime inaugurated by the Merry Monarch and the ministers of his amusements, a penny peep show to some but to others a moral horror. Better than this, it was a vehicle of talent. The serious plays, to be sure, were for the most part spectacular and pretentious eyewash, but the comic writers, in spite of their moral irresponsibility, were genuine artists who had discovered for the moment a fitting medium and a fitting audience. Obviously, this was something which, in sober England, could not last. And even before the Revolution there were the beginnings of a change. Dryden came to repent his part in pandering to the corruption of the times. Jeremy Collier voiced the rising sentiment of decency in his *Short View of the Immorality and Profaneness of the English Stage*. But when decency had been achieved, the last great epoch of the English drama was at an end.

CHARLES II

The public theaters, which had flourished under Elizabeth and James, were officially closed in 1642, though various sorts of dramatic entertainment existed throughout the Puritan period and became

*elaborate toward its end. Sir William Davenant, a playwright under
the old regime, had produced an approximation of opera and a
heroic play and had opened the Drury Lane Theatre before 1660.
At the Restoration he and Thomas Killigrew received patents
which gave their playhouses and companies a monopoly of show
business under the protection respectively of the Duke of York and
the King himself. The theater became thereby an affair of class. The
following extract from the patent to Davenant is suggestive of the
royal hand and temper. It was a touch of policy, if not of humor, to
forbid profaneness and at the same time to permit women to act
on the ground that female impersonation had given offense. As a
matter of fact, boys continued to act women's parts while there was
still a dearth of actresses.*

Letters Patent for Erecting a New Theatre

Know ye that we of our especial grace, certain knowledge, and meer
motion, and upon the humble petition of the said Sir William
D'Avenant, and in consideration of the good and faithful service
which he the said Sir William D'Avenant hath done unto us, and doth
intend to do for the future; and in consideration of the said sur-
render, have given and granted, and by these presents, for us, our
heirs and successors, do give and grant, unto the said Sir William
D'Avenant, his heirs, executors, administrators, and assigns, full
power, licence, and authority, that he, they, and every one of them,
by him and themselves, and by all and every such person and persons
as he or they should depute or appoint, and his or their labourers,
servants, and workmen, shall and may lawfully, peaceably, and
quietly, frame, erect, new build, and set up, in any place within our
cities of London and Westminster, or the suburbs thereof, where he
or they shall find best accomodations for that purpose, to be assigned
and allotted out by the surveyor of our works, one theatre or play
house, with necessary tiring and retiring rooms and other places convenient, of such extent and dimension as the said Sir William D'Avenant, his heirs or assigns shall think fitting: wherein tragedies, comedies, plays, operas, music, scenes, and all other entertainments of the
stage whatsoever may be shown and presented.

And we do hereby, for us, our heirs and successors, grant unto the
said Sir William D'Avenant, his heirs and assigns, full power, licence,
and authority, from time to time to gather together, entertain, govern, privilege and keep such and so many players and persons to

exercise and act tragedies, comedies, plays, operas, and other performances of the stage, within the house to be built as aforesaid, or within
the house in Lincoln's Inn Fields, wherein the said Sir William
D'Avenant doth now exercise the premises; or within any other house,
where he or they can best be fitted for that purpose, within our
cities of London and Westminster or the suburbs thereof; which
said company shall be the servants of our dearly beloved brother,
James Duke of York, and shall consist of such number as the said
Sir William D'Avenant, his heirs or assigns, shall from time to time
think meet. . . .

And for that we are informed that divers companies of players
have taken upon them to act plays publicly in our said cities of London and Westminster, or the suburbs thereof, without any authority
for that purpose; we do hereby declare our dislike of the same, and
will and grant that only the said company erected and set up or to
be erected and set up by the said Sir William D'Avenant, his heirs
and assigns, by virtue of these presents, and one other company
erected and set up or to be erected and set up by Thomas Killigrew,
Esq., his heirs or assigns, and none other, shall from henceforth act
or represent comedies, tragedies, plays, or entertainments of the
stage within our said cities of London and Westminster or the
suburbs thereof. Which said company to be erected by the said
Thomas Killigrew, his heirs or assigns, shall be subject to his and their
government and authority, and shall be styled the Company of Us
and our Royal Consort.

And the better to preserve amity and correspondence betwixt the
said companies and that the one may not incroach upon the other by
any indirect means, we will and ordain that no actor or other person
employed about either of the said theatres, erected by the said Sir
William D'Avenant and Thomas Killigrew or either of them, or
deserting his company, shall be received by the governor or any of
the said other company, or any other person or persons to be employed in acting or in any matter relating to the stage without the
consent and approbation of the governor of the company whereof
the said person so ejected or deserting was a member, signified under
his hand and seal. And we do by these presents declare all other company and companies saving the two companies before mentioned, to
be silenced and suppressed.

And forasmuch as many plays formerly acted do contain several
profane, obscene, and scurrilous passages; and the woman's parts
therein have been acted by men in the habits of women, at which

some have taken offence: for the preventing of these abuses for the
future, we do hereby straightly charge and command and enjoin that
from henceforth no new play shall be acted by either of the said
companies containing any passages offensive to piety and good manners, nor any old or revived play containing any such offensive passages as aforesaid, until the same shall be corrected and purged by the
said masters or governors of the said respective companies from all
such offensive and scandalous passages, as aforesaid. And we do
likewise permit and give leave that all the women's parts to be acted
in either of the said two companies for the time to come may be
performed by women, so long as these recreations, which by reason
of the abuses aforesaid were scandalous and offensive, may by such
reformation be esteemed not only harmless delights but useful and
constructive representations of humane life to such of our good
subjects as shall resort to see the same. . . .

SAMUEL PEPYS

*Gossip of the theater is a perennial source of interest in the
literature of the period. We can best attend the plays with Samuel
Pepys, who loved them dearly and whose roving eye missed little
of the goings on, whether of the pit, the gallery, the tiring room
or the stage itself. He reports literally dozens of performances, in
spite of his repeated resolutions against overindulgence in this
pleasure. Pepys's interest in stage folk centered in the person of Mrs.
Knipp or Knep, who responded warmly to his patronage and in whose
society he spent some of his happiest hours. Their relationship well
illustrates Pepys's delight in music and his amateur aspirations as
performer, composer and impresario.*

Diary of a Playgoer

September 7, 1661. At the office all the morning. At noon Mr.
Moore dined with me, and then in comes Wm. Joyce to answer a
letter of mine I wrote this morning to him about a maid of his that
my wife had hired, and she sent us word that she was hired to stay
longer with her master, which mistake he came to clear himself of,
and I took it very kindly. So I having appointed the young ladies at
the Wardrobe to go with them to a play to-day, I left him and my
brother Tom who came along with him to dine, and my wife and I

took them to the Theatre, where we seated ourselves close by the King, and Duke of York, and Madame Palmer, which was great content; and, indeed, I can never enough admire her beauty. And here was "Bartholomew Fayre," with the puppet-show, acted to-day, which had not been these forty years (it being so satyricall against Puritanism, they durst not till now, which is strange they should already dare to do it, and the King do countenance it), but I do never a whit like it the better for the puppets, but rather the worse. Thence home with the ladies, it being by reason of our staying a great while for the King's coming, and the length of the play, near nine o'clock before it was done, and so in their coach home, and still in discontent with my wife, to bed, and rose so this morning also.

September 29, 1662. (Michaelmas day). This day my oaths for drinking of wine and going to plays are out, and so I do resolve to take a liberty to-day, and then to fall to them again. Up and by coach to White Hall, in my way taking up Mr. Moore, and walked with him, talking a good while about business, in St. James's Park, and there left him, and to Mr. Coventry's, and so with him and Sir W. Pen up to the Duke where the King came also and staid till the Duke was ready. It being Collar-day we had no time to talk with him about any business. They went out together. So we parted, and in the park Mr. Cooke by appointment met me, to whom I did give my thoughts concerning Tom's match and their journey to-morrow, and did carry him by water to Tom's, and there taking up my wife, maid, dog, and him, did carry them home, where my wife is much pleased with my house, and so am I fully. I sent for some dinner and there dined, Mrs. Margaret Pen being by, to whom I had spoke to go along with us to a play this afternoon, and then to the King's Theatre, where we saw "Midsummer's Night's Dream," which I had never seen before, nor shall ever again, for it is the most insipid ridiculous play that ever I saw in my life. I saw, I confess, some good dancing and some handsome women, which was all my pleasure.

June 1, 1664. Thence to W. Joyce's where by appointment I met my wife (but neither of them at home), and she and I to the King's house, and saw "The Silent Woman"; but methought not so well done or so good a play as I formerly thought it to be, or else I am now-a-days out of humour. Before the play was done, it fell such a storm of hayle, that we in the middle of the pit were fain to rise; and all the house in a disorder, and so my wife and I out and got into a little alehouse, and staid there an hour after the play was done before we could get a coach, which at last we did (and by chance took up Joyce Norton and Mrs. Bowles and set them at home), and so home ourselves, and I, after a little to my office, so home to supper and to bed.

December 8, 1665. Thence by water down to Greenwich, and there found all my company come; that is, Mrs. Knipp, and an ill, melancholy, jealous-looking fellow, her husband, that spoke not a word to us all the night, Pierce and his wife, and Rolt, Mrs. Worshipp and her daughter, Coleman and his wife, and Laneare, and, to make us perfectly happy, there comes by chance to towne Mr. Hill to see us. Most excellent musique we had in abundance, and a good supper, dancing, and a pleasant scene of Mrs. Knipp's rising sicke from table, but whispered me it was for some hard word or other her husband gave her just now when she laughed and was more merry than ordinary. But we got her in humour again, and mighty merry; spending the night, till two in the morning, with most complete content as ever in my life, it being increased by my day's work with Gawden. Then broke up, and we to bed, Mr. Hill and I, whom I love more and more, and he us.

February 23, 1666. Anon comes Mrs. Knipp to see my wife, who is gone out, so I fain to entertain her, and took her out by coach to look my wife at Mrs. Pierce's and Unthanke's, but find her not. So back again, and then my wife comes home, having been buying of things, and at home I spent all the night talking with this baggage, and teaching her my song of "Beauty retire," which she sings and makes go most rarely, and a very fine song it seems to be. She also entertained me with repeating many of her own and others' parts of the play-house, which she do most excellently; and tells me the whole practices of the play-house and players, and is in every respect most excellent company. So I supped, and was merry at home all the evening, and the rather it being my birthday, 33 years, for which God be praised that I am in so good a condition of healthe and estate, and every thing else as I am, beyond expectation, in all. So she to Mrs. Turner's to lie, and we to bed. Mightily pleased to find myself in condition to have these people come about me and to be able to entertain them, and have the pleasure of their qualities, than which no man can have more in the world.

November 14, 1666. Up, and by water to White Hall, and thence to Westminster, where I bought several things, as a hone, ribbon, gloves, books and then took coach and to Knipp's lodging, whom I find not ready to go home with me. So I away to do a little business, among others to call upon Mr. Osborne for my Tangier warrant for the last quarter, and so to the Exchange for some things for my wife, and then to Knipp's again, and there staid reading of Waller's verses, while she finished dressing, her husband being by. I had no other pastime. Her lodging very mean, and the condition she lives in; yet makes a shew without doors, God bless us! I carried him along with us into the City, and set him down in Bishopsgate Street, and then home with her. She tells me how Smith, of the Duke's house, hath killed a man upon a quarrel in play; which makes every body sorry, he being a good actor, and they say, a good man, however this happens. The ladies of the Court do much bemoan him, she says. Here she and we alone at dinner to some good victuals, that we could not put off, that was intended for the great dinner of my Lord Hinchingbroke's, if he had come. After dinner I to teach her my new recitative of "It is decreed," of which she learnt a good part, and I do well like it and believe shall be well pleased when she hath it all, and that it will be found an agreeable thing.

February 18, 1667. Thence away, and with my wife by coach to the Duke of York's play-house, expecting a new play, and so stayed not no more than other people, but to the King's house, to "The Mayd's Tragedy;" but vexed all the while with two talking ladies and Sir Charles Sedley; yet pleased to hear their discourse, he being a stranger. And one of the ladies would, and did sit with her mask on, all the play, and, being exceeding witty as ever I heard woman, did talk most pleasantly with him; but was, I believe, a virtuous woman, and of quality. He would fain know who she was, but she would not tell; yet did give him many pleasant hints of her knowledge of him, by that means setting his brains at work to find out who she was, and did give him leave to use all means to find out who she was, but pulling off her mask. He was mighty witty, and she also making sport with him very inoffensively, that a more pleasant rencontre I never heard. But by that means lost the pleasure of the play wholly, to which now and then Sir Charles Sedley's exceptions against both words and pronouncing were very pretty. So home and to the office, did much business, then home, to supper, and to bed.

March 2, 1667. After dinner, with my wife, to the King's house to see "The Mayden Queene," a new play of Dryden's, mightily commended for the regularity of it, and the strain and wit; and, the truth is, there is a comical part done by Nell, which is Florimell, that I never can hope ever to see the like done again, by man or woman. The King and Duke of York were at the play. But so great performance of a comical part was never, I believe, in the world before as

Nell do this, both as a mad girle, then most and best of all when she comes in like a young gallant; and hath the motions and carriage of a spark the most that ever I saw any man have. It makes me, I confess, admire her.

February 6, 1668. I to the Duke of York's playhouse; where a new play of Etherige's, called "She Would if she Could;" and though I was there by two o'clock, there was 1000 people put back that could not have room in the pit: and I at last, because my wife was there, made shift to get into the 18d. box, and there saw; but, Lord! how full was the house, and how silly the play, there being nothing in the world good in it, and few people pleased in it. The King was there; but I sat mightily behind, and could see but little, and hear not all. The play being done, I into the pit to look [for] my wife, and it being dark and raining, I to look my wife out, but could not find her; and so staid going between the two doors and through the pit an hour and half, I think, after the play was done; the people staying there till the rain was over, and to talk with one another. And, among the rest, here was the Duke of Buckingham to-day openly sat in the pit; and there I found him with my Lord Buckhurst, and Sidly, and Etherige, the poet; the last of whom I did hear mightily find fault with the actors, that they were out of humour, and had not their parts perfect, and that Harris did do nothing, nor could so much as sing a ketch in it; and so was mightily concerned: while all the rest did, through the whole pit, blame the play as a silly, dull thing, though there was something very roguish and witty; but the design of the play, and end, mighty insipid. At last I did find my wife staying for me in the entry, and with her was Betty Turner, Mercer, and Deb. So I got a coach, and a humour took us, and I carried them to Hercules Pillars, and there did give them a kind of a supper of about 7s.

February 27, 1668. All the morning at the office, and at noon home to dinner, and thence with my wife and Deb. to the King's House, to see "The Virgin Martyr," the first time it hath been acted a great while: and it is mighty pleasant; not that the play is worth much, but it is finely acted by Becke Marshal. But that which did please me beyond any thing in the whole world was the wind-musique when the angel comes down, which is so sweet that it ravished me, and indeed, in a word, did wrap up my soul so that it made me really sick, just as I have formerly been when in love with my wife; that neither then, nor all the evening going home, and at home, I was able to think of any thing, but remained all night transported, so as I could not believe that ever any musick hath real command over the soul of a man as this did upon me: and makes me resolve to practice wind-musique, and to make my wife do the like.

April 7, 1668. Then I by coach to the King's playhouse, and there saw "The English Monsieur;" sitting for privacy sake in an upper box: the play hath much mirth in it as to that particular humour. After the play done, I down to Knipp, and did stay her undressing herself; and there saw the several players, men and women go by; and pretty to see how strange they are all, one to another, after the play is done. Here I saw a wonderful pretty maid of her own, that come to undress her, and one so pretty that she says she intends not to keep her, for fear of her being undone in her service, by coming to the playhouse. Here I hear Sir W. Davenant is just now dead; and so who will succeed him in the mastership of the house is not yet known. The eldest Davenport is, it seems, gone from this house to be kept by somebody; which I am glad of, she being a very bad actor. I took her then up into a coach and away to the Park, which is now very fine after some rain, but the company was going away most, and so I took her to the Lodge, and there treated her and had a deal of good talk, and now and then did *baiser la*, and that was all, and that as much or more than I had much mind to because of her paint. She tells me mighty news, that my Lady Castlemayne is mightily in love with Hart of their house: and he is much with her in private, and she goes to him, and do give him many presents; and that the thing is most certain, and Becke Marshall only privy to it, and the means of bringing them together, which is a very odd thing; and by this means she is even with the King's love to Mrs. Davis. This done, I carried her and set her down at Mrs. Manuel's, but stayed not there myself, nor went in; but straight home, and there to my letters, and so home to bed.

May 7, 1668. Up, and to the office, where all the morning. At noon home to dinner, and thither I sent for Mercer to dine with me, and after dinner she and I called Mrs. Turner, and I carried them to the Duke of York's house, and there saw "The Man's the Master," which proves, upon my seeing it again, a very good play. Thence called Knepp from the King's house, where going in for her, the play being done, I did see Beck Marshall come dressed, off of the stage, and looks mighty fine, and pretty, and noble: and also Nell, in her boy's clothes, mighty pretty. But, Lord! their confidence! and how many men do hover about them as soon as they come off the stage, and how confident they are in their talk! Here I did kiss the pretty woman newly come, called Pegg, that was Sir Charles Sidly's mistress, a mighty pretty woman, and seems, but is not, modest. Here took up Knepp into our coach, and all of us with her to her lodgings, and thither comes Bannister with a song of her's, that he hath set in Sir Charles Sidly's play for her, which is, I think, but very meanly set; but this he did, before us, teach her, and it being but a slight, silly, short ayre, she learnt it presently. But I did get him to prick me down the notes of the Echo in "The Tempest," which pleases me mightily. Here was also Haynes, the incomparable dancer of the King's house, and a seeming civil man, and sings pretty well, and they gone, we abroad to Marrowbone, and there walked in the garden, the first time I ever was there; and a pretty place it is, and here we eat and drank and stayed till 9 at night, and so home by moonshine. . . . And so set Mrs. Knepp at her lodgings, and so the rest, and I home talking with a great deal of pleasure, and so home to bed.

September 4, 1668. Up, and met at the Office all the morning; and at noon my wife, and Deb., and Mercer, and W. Hewer and I to the Fair, and there, at the old house, did eat a pig, and was pretty merry, but saw no sights, my wife having a mind to see the play "Bartholomew-Fayre," with puppets. Which we did, and it is an excellent play; the more I see it, the more I love the wit of it; only the business of abusing the Puritans begins to grow stale, and of no use, they being the people that, at last, will be found the wisest. And here Knepp come to us, and sat with us, and thence took coach in two coaches, and losing one another, my wife and Knepp and I to Hercules Pillars, and there supped, and I did take from her mouth the words and notes of her song of "the Larke," which pleases me mightily. And so set her at home, and away we home, where our company come home before us. This night Knepp tells us that there is a Spanish woman lately come over, that pretends to sing as well as Mrs. Knight; both of which I must endeavor to hear. So, after supper, to bed.

WILLIAM WYCHERLEY

"Manly Wycherley," Dryden dubbed him, and certainly no one would be tempted to call his plays effeminate. The Country Wife is by all odds the lustiest, bawdiest, most blatantly antimoral of all Restoration comedies. It is also one of the very cleverest. And when one has recovered from the shock of its ideas and language one sees

that it has a certain greatness. Congreve refined the rawness of this unabashed contemporary but he did not improve on his wit nor provoke a deeper reflection from the modern reader who stands aside and tries to appraise the validity and profitableness of this brief moment of untrammeled freedom on the English stage. Wycherley, like the others, was a member of the irresponsible society which he portrays. He saw its evils as clearly as we do, but he accepted them as part of the character of an intelligible world for which a case can be made out. "By what I've heard," says Hippolita in The Gentleman Dancing-Master, " 'tis a pleasant, well bred, complaisant, free, frolic, good-natured, pretty age; and if you do not like it leave it to us that do."

The Restoration writers sometimes lulled their consciences by calling their ebullitions satire and pretending that they were reformers of society. It is the fashion of critics to declaim against their hypocrisy, but who can doubt that Pinchwife once and for all discredits lock and key as a method of keeping marriage chaste, and that Mrs. Pinchwife proves the fallacy of innocence as a prophylactic against sin?

The Country Wife is more complexly organized than these selections show, since one strand in the plot is here largely omitted. Sparkish, who is too vain for jealousy and almost forces his lady into another's arms, is a foil for Pinchwife, but the two are bracketed impartially together as social incompetents. Horner is a Rabelaisian figure, titular hero in the monstrous farce of cuckoldry. Harcourt and Alithea somewhat resemble Mirabell and Millamant of The Way of the World. It is necessary, even in Wycherley, that there should be a standard against which the comic abnormalities can be measured.

The Country Wife

ACT I, SCENE I—HORNER's Lodging

Enter HORNER, *and* QUACK *following him at a distance.*

Horn. [*Aside.*] A quack is as fit for a pimp, as a midwife for a bawd; they are still but in their way, both helpers of nature.—[*Aloud.*] Well, my dear doctor, hast thou done what I desired?

Quack. I have undone you for ever with the women, and reported you throughout the whole town as bad as an eunuch, with as much trouble as if I had made you one in earnest.

Horn. But have you told all the midwives you know, the orange wenches at the playhouses, the city husbands, and old fumbling keepers of this end of the town? for they'll be the readiest to report it.

Quack. I have told all the chambermaids, waiting-women, tire-women, and old women of my acquaintance; nay, and whispered it as a secret to 'em, and to the whisperers of Whitehall; so that you need not doubt 'twill spread, and you will be as odious to the handsome young women as——

Horn. As the small-pox. Well——

Quack. And to the married women of this end of the town, as——

Horn. As the great one; nay, as their own husbands.

Quack. And to the city dames, as aniseed Robin, of filthy and contemptible memory; and they will frighten their children with your name, especially their females.

Horn. And cry, Horner's coming to carry you away. I am only afraid 'twill not be believed. You told 'em it was by an English-French disaster, and an English-French chirurgeon, who has given me at once not only a cure, but an antidote for the future against that damned malady, and that worse distemper, love, and all other women's evils?

Quack. Your late journey into France has made it the more credible, and your being here a fortnight before you appeared in public, looks as if you apprehended the shame, which I wonder you do not. Well, I have been hired by young gallants to belie 'em t'other way; but you are the first would be thought a man unfit for women.

Horn. Dear Mr. Doctor, let vain rogues be contented only to be thought abler men than they are, generally 'tis all the pleasure they have; but mine lies another way.

Quack. You take, methinks, a very preposterous way to it, and as ridiculous as if we operators in physic should put forth bills to disparage our medicaments, with hopes to gain customers.

Horn. Doctor, there are quacks in love as well as physic, who get but the fewer and worse patients for their boasting; a good name is seldom got by giving it one's self; and women, no more than honour, are compassed by bragging. Come, come, Doctor, the wisest lawyer never discovers the merits of his cause till the trial; the wealthiest man conceals his riches, and the cunning gamester his play. Shy husbands and keepers, like old rooks, are not to be cheated but by a new unpractised trick: false friendship will pass now no more than false dice upon 'em; no, not in the city.

NELL GWYN

From a portrait by Sir Peter Lely. Reproduced by permission of The Metropolitan Museum of Art.

JAMES II

From a portrait by an unknown artist. Reproduced by permission of The
National Portrait Gallery

Enter Boy.

Boy. There are two ladies and a gentleman coming up. [*Exit.*

Horn. A pox! some unbelieving sisters of my former acquaintance, who, I am afraid, except their sense should be satisfied of the falsity of the report. No—this formal fool and women!

Enter Sir JASPER FIDGET, Lady FIDGET, *and* Mrs. DAINTY
FIDGET.

Quack. His wife and sister.

Sir Jasp. My coach breaking just now before your door, sir, I look upon as an occasional reprimand to me, sir, for not kissing your hands, sir, since your coming out of France, sir; and so my disaster, sir, has been my good fortune, sir; and this is my wife and sister, sir.

Horn. What then, sir?

Sir Jasp. My lady, and sister, sir.—Wife, this is Master Horner.

Lady Fid. Master Horner, husband!

Sir Jasp. My lady, my Lady Fidget, sir.

Horn. So, sir.

Sir Jasp. Won't you be acquainted with her, sir?—[*Aside.*] So, the report is true, I find, by his coldness or aversion to the sex, but I'll play the wag with him.—[*Aloud.*] Pray salute my wife, my lady, sir.

Horn. I will kiss no man's wife, sir, for him, sir; I have taken my eternal leave, sir, of the sex already, sir.

Sir Jasp. [*Aside.*] Ha! ha! ha! I'll plague him yet.—[*Aloud.*] Not know my wife, sir?

Horn. I do know your wife, sir; she's a woman, sir, and consequently a monster, sir, a greater monster than a husband, sir.

Sir Jasp. A husband! how, sir?

Horn. So, sir; but I make no more cuckolds, sir.   [*Makes horns.*

Sir Jasp. Ha! ha! ha! Mercury! Mercury!

Lady Fid. Pray, Sir Jasper, let us be gone from this rude fellow.

Mrs. Dain. Who, by his breeding, would think he had ever been in France?

Lady Fid. Foh! he's but too much a French fellow, such as hate women of quality and virtue for their love to their husbands. Sir Jasper, a woman is hated by 'em as much for loving her husband as for loving their money. But pray let's be gone.

Horn. You do well, madam; for I have nothing that you came for. I have brought over not so much as a bawdy picture, no new postures, nor the second part of the *Ecole des Filles*; nor——

Quack. Hold, for shame, sir! what d'ye mean? you'll ruin yourself for ever with the sex——   [*Apart to* HORNER.

Sir Jasp. Ha! ha! ha! he hates women perfectly, I find.

Mrs. Dain. What pity 'tis he should!

Lady Fid. Ay, he's a base fellow for't. But affectation makes not a woman more odious to them than virtue.

Horn. Because your virtue is your greatest affectation, madam.

Lady Fid. How, you saucy fellow! would you wrong my honour?

Horn. If I could.

Lady Fid. How d'ye mean, sir?

Sir Jasp. Ha! ha! ha! no, he can't wrong your ladyship's honour, upon my honour. He, poor man—hark you in your ear—a mere eunuch.   [*Whispers.*

Lady Fid. O filthy French beast! foh! foh! why do we stay? let's be gone: I can't endure the sight of him.

Sir Jasp. Stay but till the chairs come; they'll be here presently.

Lady Fid. No.

Sir Jasp. Nor can I stay longer. 'Tis, let me see, a quarter and half quarter of a minute past eleven. The council will be sat; I must away. Business must be preferred always before love and ceremony with the wise, Mr. Horner.

Horn. And the impotent, Sir Jasper.

Sir Jasp. Ay, ay, the impotent, Master Horner; hah! hah! hah!

Lady Fid. What, leave us with a filthy man alone in his lodgings?

Sir Jasp. He's an innocent man now, you know. Pray stay, I'll hasten the chairs to you.—Mr. Horner, your servant; I should be glad to see you at my house. Pray come and dine with me, and play at cards with my wife after dinner; you are fit for women at that game yet, ha! ha!—[*Aside.*] 'Tis as much a husband's prudence to provide innocent diversion for a wife as to hinder her unlawful pleasures; and he had better employ her than let her employ herself.—[*Aloud.*] Farewell.

Horn. Your servant, Sir Jasper.   [*Exit* Sir JASPER.

Lady Fid. I will not stay with him, foh!——

Horn. Nay, madam, I beseech you stay, if it be but to see I can be as civil to ladies yet as they would desire.

Lady Fid. No, no, foh! you cannot be civil to ladies.

Mrs. Dain. You as civil as ladies would desire?

Lady Fid. No, no, no, foh! foh! foh!

         Exeunt Lady FIDGET *and* Mrs. DAINTY FIDGET.

Quack. Now, I think, I, or you yourself, rather, have done your business with the women.

Horn. Thou art an ass. Don't you see already, upon the report, and my carriage, this grave man of business leaves his wife in my lodgings, invites me to his house and wife, who before would not be acquainted with me out of jealousy?

Quack. Nay, by this means you may be the more acquainted with the husbands, but the less with the wives.

Horn. Let me alone; if I can but abuse the husbands, I'll soon disabuse the wives. Stay—I'll reckon you up the advantages I am like to have by my stratagem. First, I shall be rid of all my old acquaintances, the most insatiable sort of duns, that invade our lodgings in a morning; and next to the pleasure of making a new mistress is that of being rid of an old one, and of all old debts. Love, when it comes to be so, is paid the most unwillingly.

Quack. Well, you may be so rid of your old acquaintances; but how will you get any new ones?

Horn. Doctor, thou wilt never make a good chemist, thou art so incredulous and impatient. Ask but all the young fellows of the town if they do not lose more time, like huntsmen, in starting the game, than in running it down. One knows not where to find 'em; who will or will not. Women of quality are so civil, you can hardly distinguish love from good breeding, and a man is often mistaken: but now I can be sure she that shows an aversion to me loves the sport, as those women that are gone, whom I warrant to be right. And then the next thing is, your women of honour, as you call 'em, are only chary of their reputations, not their persons; and 'tis scandal they would avoid, not men. Now may I have, by the reputation of an eunuch, the privileges of one, and be seen in a lady's chamber in a morning as early as her husband; kiss virgins before their parents or lovers; and may be, in short, the *passe-partout* of the town. Now, doctor.

Quack. Nay, now you shall be the doctor; and your process is so new that we do not know but it may succeed.

Horn. Not so new either; *probatum est*, doctor.

Quack. Well, I wish you luck, and many patients, whilst I go to mine.   [*Exit.*

Enter HARCOURT *and* DORILANT. HORNER *argues against love and declares for the "glorious manly pleasures of being very drunk and very slovenly." Then enter* SPARKISH, *butt of the other gallants' wit.*

The four plan to go to dinner and the play. Sparkish *goes to fetch his mistress,* Alithea, *to whom he is engaged. Enter* Pinchwife.

Horn. Who have we here? Pinchwife?

Pinch. Gentlemen, your humble servant.

Horn. Well, Jack, by thy long absence from the town, the grumness of thy countenance, and the slovenliness of thy habit, I should give thee joy, should I not, of marriage?

Pinch. [*Aside.*] Death! does he know I'm married too? I thought to have concealed it from him at least.—[*Aloud.*] My long stay in the country will excuse my dress; and I have a suit of law that brings me up to town, that puts me out of humour. Besides, I must give Sparkish to-morrow five thousand pounds to lie with my sister.

Horn. Nay, you country gentlemen, rather than not purchase, will buy anything; and he is a cracked title, if we may quibble. Well, but am I to give thee joy? I heard thou wert married.

Pinch. What then?

Horn. Why, the next thing that is to be heard, is thou'rt a cuckold.

Pinch. Insupportable name! [*Aside.*

Horn. But I did not expect marriage from such a whoremaster as you; one that knew the town so much, and women so well.

Pinch. Why, I have married no London wife.

Horn. Pshaw! that's all one. That grave circumspection in marrying a country wife, is like refusing a deceitful pampered Smithfield jade, to go and be cheated by a friend in the country.

Pinch. [*Aside.*] A pox on him and his simile!—[*Aloud.*] At least we are a little surer of the breed there, know what her keeping has been, whether foiled or unsound.

Horn. Come, come, I have known a clap gotten in Wales; and there are cousins, justices' clerks, and chaplains in the country, I won't say coachmen. But she's handsome and young?

Pinch. [*Aside.*] I'll answer as I should do.—[*Aloud.*] No, no; she has no beauty but her youth, no attraction but her modesty: wholesome, homely, and huswifely; that's all.

Dor. He talks as like a grazier as he looks.

Pinch. She's too awkward, ill-favoured, and silly to bring to town.

Har. Then methinks you should bring her to be taught breeding.

Pinch. To be taught! no, sir, I thank you. Good wives and private soldiers should be ignorant—I'll keep her from your instructions, I warrant you.

Har. The rogue is as jealous as if his wife were not ignorant.

[*Aside.*

Horn. Why, if she be ill-favoured, there will be less danger here for you than by leaving her in the country. We have such variety of dainties that we are seldom hungry.

Dor. But they have always coarse, constant, swingeing stomachs in the country.

Har. Foul feeders indeed!

Dor. And your hospitality is great there.

Har. Open house; every man's welcome.

Pinch. So, so, gentlemen.

Horn. But prithee, why shouldst thou marry her? If she be ugly, ill-bred, and silly, she must be rich then.

Pinch. As rich as if she brought me twenty thousand pound out of this town; for she'll be as sure not to spend her moderate portion, as a London baggage would be to spend hers, let it be what it would: so 'tis all one. Then, because she's ugly, she's the likelier to be my own; and being ill-bred, she'll hate conversation; and since silly and innocent, will not know the difference betwixt a man of one-and-twenty and one of forty.

Horn. Nine—to my knowledge. But if she be silly, she'll expect as much from a man of forty-nine, as from him of one-and-twenty. But methinks wit is more necessary than beauty; and I think no young woman ugly that has it, and no handsome woman agreeable without it.

Pinch. 'Tis my maxim, he's a fool that marries; but he's a greater that does not marry a fool. What is wit in a wife good for, but to make a man a cuckold?

Horn. Yes, to keep it from his knowledge.

Pinch. A fool cannot contrive to make her husband a cuckold.

Horn. No; but she'll club with a man that can: and what is worse, if she cannot make her husband a cuckold, she'll make him jealous, and pass for one: and then 'tis all one.

Pinch. Well, well, I'll take care for one. My wife shall make me no cuckold, though she had your help, Mr. Horner. I understand the town, sir.

Dor. His help! [*Aside.*

Har. He's come newly to town, it seems, and has not heard how things are with him. [*Aside.*

Horn. But tell me, has marriage cured thee of whoring, which it seldom does?

Har. 'Tis more than age can do.

Horn. No, the word is, I'll marry and live honest: but a marriage

vow is like a penitent gamester's oath, and entering into bonds and
penalties to stint himself to such a particular small sum at play for
the future, which makes him but the more eager; and not being able
to hold out, loses his money again, and his forfeit to boot.

Dor. Ay, ay, a gamester will be a gamester whilst his money lasts,
and a whoremaster whilst his vigour.

Har. Nay, I have known 'em, when they are broke, and can lose
no more, keep a fumbling with the box in their hands to fool with
only, and hinder other gamesters.

Dor. That had wherewithal to make lusty stakes.

Pinch. Well, gentlemen, you may laugh at me; but you shall never
lie with my wife: I know the town.

Horn. But prithee, was not the way you were in better? is not keeping better than marriage?

Pinch. A pox on't! the jades would jilt me, I could never keep a
whore to myself.

Horn. So, then you only married to keep a whore to yourself. Well,
but let me tell you, women, as you say, are like soldiers, made constant and loyal by good pay, rather than by oaths and covenants.
Therefore I'd advise my friends to keep rather than marry, since too
I find, by your example, it does not serve one's turn; for I saw you
yesterday in the eighteenpenny place with a pretty country-wench.

Pinch. How the devil! did he see my wife then? I sat there that
she might not be seen. But she shall never go to a play again.
                                                         [*Aside.*

Horn. What! dost thou blush, at nine-and-forty, for having been
seen with a wench?

Dor. No, faith, I warrant 'twas his wife, which he seated there out
of sight; for he's a cunning rogue, and understands the town.

Har. He blushes. Then 'twas his wife; for men are now more
ashamed to be seen with them in public than with a wench.

Pinch. Hell and damnation! I'm undone, since Horner has seen
her, and they know 'twas she.   [*Aside.*

Horn. But prithee, was it thy wife? She was exceeding pretty: I
was in love with her at that distance.

Pinch. You are like never to be nearer to her. Your servant, gentlemen.   [*Offers to go.*

Horn. Nay, prithee stay.

Pinch. I cannot; I will not.

Horn. Come, you shall dine with us.

Pinch. I have dined already.

Horn. Come, I know thou hast not: I'll treat thee, dear rogue; thou sha't spend none of thy Hampshire money to-day.

Pinch. Treat me! So, he uses me already like his cuckold.   [*Aside.*

Horn. Nay, you shall not go.

Pinch. I must; I have business at home.

Har. To beat his wife. He's as jealous of her as a Cheapside husband of a Covent Garden wife.

Horn. Why, 'tis as hard to find an old whoremaster without jealousy and the gout, as a young one without fear, or the pox:—

> As gout in age from pox in youth proceeds,
> So wenching past, then jealousy succeeds;
> The worst disease that love and wenching breeds.

                                             [*Exeunt.*

ACT II, Scene I—*A Room in* Pinchwife's *House*

Mrs. Margery Pinchwife *and* Alithea. Pinchwife *peeping behind at the door.*

Mrs. Pinch. Pray, sister, where are the best fields and woods to walk in, in London?

Alith. [*Aside.*] A pretty question!—[*Aloud.*] Why, sister, Mulberry Garden and St. James's Park; and, for close walks, the New Exchange.

Mrs. Pinch. Pray, sister, tell me why my husband looks so grum here in town, and keeps me up so close, and will not let me go a-walking, nor let me wear my best gown yesterday.

Alith. O, he's jealous, sister.

Mrs. Pinch. Jealous! what's that?

Alith. He's afraid you should love another man.

Mrs. Pinch. How should he be afraid of my loving another man, when he will not let me see any but himself?

Alith. Did he not carry you yesterday to a play?

Mrs. Pinch. Ay; but we sat amongst ugly people. He would not let me come near the gentry, who sat under us, so that I could not see 'em. He told me, none but naughty women sat there, whom they toused and moused. But I would have ventured, for all that.

Alith. But how did you like the play?

Mrs. Pinch. Indeed I was weary of the play; but I liked hugeously the actors. They are the goodliest, properest men, sister!

Alith. O, but you must not like the actors, sister.

Mrs. Pinch. Ay, how should I help it, sister? Pray, sister, when my husband comes in, will you ask leave for me to go a-walking?

Alith. [*Aside.*] A-walking! ha! ha! Lord, a country-gentlewoman's pleasure is the drudgery of a footpost; and she requires as much airing as her husband's horses.—[*Aloud.*] But here comes your husband: I'll ask, though I'm sure he'll not grant it.

Mrs. Pinch. He says he won't let me go abroad for fear of catching the pox.

Alith. Fy! the small-pox you should say.

Enter PINCHWIFE.

Mrs. Pinch. O my dear, dear bud, welcome home! Why dost thou look so fropish? who has nangered thee?

Pinch. You're a fool.   [Mrs. PINCHWIFE *goes aside, and cries.*

Alith. Faith, so she is, for crying for no fault, poor tender creature!

Pinch. What, you would have her as impudent as yourself, as arrant a jilflirt, a gadder, a magpie; and to say all, a mere notorious townwoman?

Alith. Brother, you are my only censurer; and the honour of your family will sooner suffer in your wife there than in me, though I take the innocent liberty of the town.

Pinch. Hark you, mistress, do not talk so before my wife.—The innocent liberty of the town!

Alith. Why, pray, who boasts of any intrigue with me? what lampoon has made my name notorious? what ill women frequent my lodgings? I keep no company with any women of scandalous reputations.

Pinch. No, you keep the men of scandalous reputations company.

Alith. Where? would you not have me civil? answer 'em in a box at the plays, in the drawing-room at Whitehall, in St. James's Park, Mulberry Garden, or——

Pinch. Hold, hold! Do not teach my wife where the men are to be found: I believe she's the worse for your town-documents already. I bid you keep her in ignorance, as I do.

Mrs. Pinch. Indeed, be not angry with her, bud, she will tell me nothing of the town, though I ask her a thousand times a day.

Pinch. Then you are very inquisitive to know, I find?

Mrs. Pinch. Not I indeed, dear; I hate London. Our place-house in the country is worth a thousand of't: would I were there again!

Pinch. So you shall, I warrant. But were you not talking of plays and players when I came in?—[*To* ALITHEA.] You are her encourager in such discourses.

Mrs. Pinch. No, indeed, dear; she chid me just now for liking the playermen.

Pinch. [*Aside.*] Nay, if she be so innocent as to own to me her liking them, there is no hurt in't.—[*Aloud.*] Come, my poor rogue, but thou likest none better than me?

Mrs. Pinch. Yes, indeed, but I do. The playermen are finer folks.

Pinch. But you love none better than me?

Mrs. Pinch. You are my own dear bud, and I know you. I hate a stranger.

Pinch. Ay, my dear, you must love me only; and not be like the naughty town-women, who only hate their husbands, and love every man else; love plays, visits, fine coaches, fine clothes, fiddles, balls, treats, and so lead a wicked town-life.

Mrs. Pinch. Nay, if to enjoy all these things be a town-life, London is not so bad a place, dear.

Pinch. How! if you love me, you must hate London.

Alith. The fool has forbid me discovering to her the pleasures of the town, and he is now setting her agog upon them himself.

[*Aside.*

Mrs. Pinch. But, husband, do the town-women love the playermen too?

Pinch. Yes, I warrant you.

Mrs. Pinch. Ay, I warrant you.

Pinch. Why, you do not, I hope?

Mrs. Pinch. No, no, bud. But why have we no playermen in the country?

Pinch. Ha!—Mrs. Minx, ask me no more to go to a play.

Mrs. Pinch. Nay, why, love? I did not care for going: but when you forbid me, you make me, as 'twere, desire it.

Alith. So 'twill be in other things, I warrant. [*Aside.*

Mrs. Pinch. Pray let me go to a play, dear.

Pinch. Hold your peace, I wo' not.

Mrs. Pinch. Why, love?

Pinch. Why, I'll tell you.

Alith. Nay, if he tell her, she'll give him more cause to forbid her that place. [*Aside.*

Mrs. Pinch. Pray why, dear?

Pinch. First, you like the actors; and the gallants may like you.

Mrs. Pinch. What, a homely country girl! No, bud, nobody will like me.

Pinch. I tell you yes, they may.

Mrs. Pinch. No, no, you jest—I won't believe you: I will go.

Pinch. I tell you then, that one of the lewdest fellows in town, who saw you there, told me he was in love with you.

Mrs. Pinch. Indeed! who, who, pray who was't?

Pinch. I've gone too far, and slipped before I was aware; how over-joyed she is!   [*Aside.*

Mrs. Pinch. Was it any Hampshire gallant, any of our neighbours? I promise you, I am beholden to him.

Pinch. I promise you, you lie; for he would but ruin you, as he has done hundreds. He has no other love for women but that; such as he look upon women, like basilisks, but to destroy 'em.

Mrs. Pinch. Ay, but if he loves me, why should he ruin me? answer me to that. Methinks he should not, I would do him no harm.

Alith. Ha! ha! ha!

Pinch. 'Tis very well; but I'll keep him from doing you any harm, or me either. But here comes company; get you in, get you in.

Mrs. Pinch. But, pray, husband, is he a pretty gentleman that loves me?

Pinch. In, baggage, in.   [*Thrusts her in, and shuts the door.*

ACT III, Scene I—A *Room in* Pinchwife's *House*

Enter Alithea *and* Mrs. Pinchwife.

Alith. Sister, what ails you? you are grown melancholy.

Mrs. Pinch. Would it not make any one melancholy to see you go every day fluttering about abroad, whilst I must stay at home like a poor lonely sullen bird in a cage?

Alith. Ay, sister; but you came young, and just from the nest to your cage: so that I thought you liked it, and could be as cheerful in't as others that took their flight themselves early, and are hopping abroad in the open air.

Mrs. Pinch. Nay, I confess I was quiet enough till my husband told me what pure lives the London ladies live abroad, with their dancing, meetings, and junketings, and dressed every day in their best gowns; and I warrant you, play at nine-pins every day of the week, so they do.

Enter Pinchwife.

Pinch. Come, what's here to do? you are putting the town-pleasures in her head, and setting her a-longing.

Alith. Yes, after nine-pins. You suffer none to give her those longings you mean but yourself.

Pinch. I tell her of the vanities of the town like a confessor.

Alith. A confessor! just such a confessor as he that, by forbidding a silly ostler to grease the horse's teeth, taught him to do't.

Pinch. Come, Mrs. Flippant, good precepts are lost when bad examples are still before us: the liberty you take abroad makes her hanker after it, and out of humour at home. Poor wretch! she desired not to come to London; I would bring her.

Alith. Very well.

Pinch. She has been this week in town, and never desired till this afternoon to go abroad.

Alith. Was she not at a play yesterday?

Pinch. Yes; but she ne'er asked me; I was myself the cause of her going.

Alith. Then if she ask you again, you are the cause of her asking, and not my example.

Pinch. Well, to-morrow night I shall be rid of you; and the next day, before 'tis light, she and I'll be rid of the town, and my dreadful apprehensions.—Come, be not melancholy; for thou sha't go into the country after to-morrow, dearest.

Alith. Great comfort!

Mrs. Pinch. Pish! what d'ye tell me of the country for?

Pinch. How's this! what, pish at the country?

Mrs. Pinch. Let me alone; I am not well.

Pinch. O, if that be all—what ails my dearest?

Mrs. Pinch. Truly, I don't know: but I have not been well since you told me there was a gallant at the play in love with me.

Pinch. Ha!——

Alith. That's by my example too!

Pinch. Nay, if you are not well, but are so concerned, because a lewd fellow chanced to lie, and say he liked you, you'll make me sick too.

Mrs. Pinch. Of what sickness?

Pinch. O, of that which is worse than the plague, jealousy.

Mrs. Pinch. Pish, you jeer! I'm sure there's no such disease in our receipt-book at home.

Pinch. No, thou never met'st with it, poor innocent.—Well, if thou cuckold me, 'twill be my own fault—for cuckolds and bastards are generally makers of their own fortune. [*Aside.*

Mrs. Pinch. Well, but pray, bud, let's go to a play to-night.

Pinch. 'Tis just done, she comes from it. But why are you so eager to see a play?

Mrs. Pinch. Faith, dear, not that I care one pin for their talk there; but I like to look upon the player-men, and would see, if I could, the gallant you say loves me: that's all, dear bud.

Pinch. Is that all, dear bud?

Alith. This proceeds from my example!

Mrs. Pinch. But if the play be done, let's go abroad, however, dear bud.

Pinch. Come, have a little patience and thou shalt go into the country on Friday.

Mrs. Pinch. Therefore I would see first some sights to tell my neighbours of. Nay, I will go abroad, that's once.

Alith. I'm the cause of this desire too!

Pinch. But now I think on't, who, who was the cause of Horner's coming to my lodgings to-day? That was you.

Alith. No, you, because you would not let him see your handsome wife out of your lodging.

Mrs. Pinch. Why, O Lord! did the gentleman come hither to see me indeed?

Pinch. No, no.—You are not the cause of that damned question too, Mistress Alithea?—[*Aside.*] Well, she's in the right of it. He is in love with my wife—and comes after her—'tis so—but I'll nip his love in the bud; lest he should follow us into the country, and break his chariot-wheel near our house, on purpose for an excuse to come to't. But I think I know the town.

Mrs. Pinch. Come, pray, bud, let's go abroad before 'tis late; for I will go, that's flat and plain.

Pinch. [*Aside.*] So! the obstinacy already of the town-wife; and I must, whilst she's here, humour her like one.—[*Aloud.*] Sister, how shall we do, that she may not be seen or known?

Alith. Let her put on her mask.

Pinch. Pshaw! a mask makes people but the more inquisitive, and is as ridiculous a disguise as a stage-beard: her shape, stature, habit will be known. And if we should meet with Horner, he would be sure to take acquaintance with us, must wish her joy, kiss her, talk to her, leer upon her, and the devil and all. No, I'll not use her to a mask, 'tis dangerous; for masks have made more cuckolds than the best faces that ever were known.

Alith. How will you do then?

Mrs. Pinch. Nay, shall we go? The Exchange will be shut, and I have a mind to see that.

Pinch. So—I have it—I'll dress her up in the suit we are to carry down to her brother, little Sir James; nay, I understand the town-tricks. Come, let's go dress her. A mask! no—a woman masked, like a covered dish, gives a man curiosity and appetite; when, it may be, uncovered, 'twould turn his stomach: no, no.

Alith. Indeed your comparison is something a greasy one: but I had a gentle gallant used to say, A beauty masked, like the sun in eclipse, gathers together more gazers than if it shined out.   [*Exeunt.*

ACT IV, SCENE II—*A Bedchamber in* PINCHWIFE'S *House*

PINCHWIFE *and* Mrs. PINCHWIFE *discovered. She has met the gallants at the play.* HORNER *has made love to her both in* PINCHWIFE'S *presence and aside, pretending not to have penetrated her boy's disguise.*

Pinch. Come, tell me, I say.

Mrs. Pinch. Lord! han't I told it a hundred times over?

Pinch. [*Aside.*] I would try, if in the repetition of the ungrateful tale, I could find her altering it in the least circumstance; for if her story be false, she is so too.—[*Aloud.*] Come, how was't, baggage?

Mrs. Pinch. Lord, what pleasure you take to hear it sure!

Pinch. No, you take more in telling it I find; but speak, how was't?

Mrs. Pinch. He carried me up into the house next to the Exchange.

Pinch. So, and you two were only in the room!

Mrs. Pinch. Yes, for he sent away a youth that was there, for some dried fruit, and China oranges.

Pinch. Did he so? Damn him for it—and for——

Mrs. Pinch. But presently came up the gentlewoman of the house.

Pinch. O, 'twas well she did; but what did he do whilst the fruit came?

Mrs. Pinch. He kissed me a hundred times, and told me he fancied he kissed my fine sister, meaning me, you know, whom he said he loved with all his soul, and bid me to be sure to tell her so, and to desire her to be at her window, by eleven of the clock this morning, and he would walk under it at that time.

Pinch. And he was as good as his word, very punctual; a pox reward him for't.   [*Aside.*

Mrs. Pinch. Well, and he said if you were not within, he would come up to her, meaning me, you know, bud, still.

Pinch. [*Aside.*] So—he knew her certainly; but for this confession, I am obliged to her simplicity.—[*Aloud.*] But what, you stood very still when he kissed you?

Mrs. Pinch. Yes, I warrant you; would you have had me discovered myself?

Pinch. But you told me he did some beastliness to you, as you call it; what was't?

Mrs. Pinch. Why, he put——

Pinch. What?

Mrs. Pinch. Why, he put the tip of his tongue between my lips, and so mousled me—and I said, I'd bite it.

Pinch. An eternal canker seize it, for a dog!

Mrs. Pinch. Nay, you need not be so angry with him neither, for to say truth, he has the sweetest breath I ever knew.

Pinch. The devil! you were satisfied with it then, and would do it again?

Mrs. Pinch. Not unless he should force me.

Pinch. Force you, changeling! I tell you, no woman can be forced.

Mrs. Pinch. Yes, but she may sure, by such a one as he, for he's a proper, goodly, strong man; 'tis hard, let me tell you, to resist him.

Pinch. [*Aside.*] So, 'tis plain she loves him, yet she has not love enough to make her conceal it from me; but the sight of him will increase her aversion for me and love for him; and that love instruct her how to deceive me and satisfy him, all idiot as she is. Love! 'twas he gave women first their craft, their art of deluding. Out of Nature's hands they came plain, open, silly, and fit for slaves, as she and Heaven intended 'em; but damned Love—well—I must strangle that little monster whilst I can deal with him.—[*Aloud.*] Go fetch pen, ink, and paper out of the next room.

Mrs. Pinch. Yes, bud.   [*Exit.*

Pinch. Why should women have more invention in love than men? It can only be, because they have more desires, more soliciting passions, more lust, and more of the devil.

Re-enter Mrs. PINCHWIFE.

Come, minx, sit down and write.

Mrs. Pinch. Ay, dear bud, but I can't do't very well.

Pinch. I wish you could not at all.

Mrs. Pinch. But what should I write for?

Pinch. I'll have you write a letter to your lover.

Mrs. Pinch. O Lord, to the fine gentleman a letter!

Pinch. Yes, to the fine gentleman.

Mrs. Pinch. Lord, you do but jeer: sure you jest.

Pinch. I am not so merry: come, write as I bid you.

Mrs. Pinch. What, do you think I am a fool?

Pinch. [*Aside.*] She's afraid I would not dictate any love to him, therefore she's unwilling.—[*Aloud.*] But you had best begin.

Mrs. Pinch. Indeed, and indeed, but I won't, so I won't.

Pinch. Why?

Mrs. Pinch. Because he's in town; you may send for him if you will.

Pinch. Very well, you would have him brought to you; is it come to this? I say, take the pen and write, or you'll provoke me.

Mrs. Pinch. Lord, what d'ye make a fool of me for? Don't I know that letters are never writ but from the country to London, and from London into the country? Now he's in town, and I am in town too; therefore I can't write to him, you know.

Pinch. [*Aside.*] So, I am glad it is no worse; she is innocent enough yet.—[*Aloud.*] Yes, you may, when your husband bids you, write letters to people that are in town.

Mrs. Pinch. O, may I so? then I'm satisfied.

Pinch. Come, begin:—"Sir"—— [*Dictates.*

Mrs. Pinch. Shan't I say, "Dear Sir?"—You know one says always something more than bare "Sir."

Pinch. Write as I bid you, or I will write whore with this penknife in your face.

Mrs. Pinch. Nay, good bud—"Sir—— [*Writes.*

Pinch. "Though I suffered last night your nauseous, loathed kisses and embraces"—Write!

Mrs. Pinch. Nay, why should I say so? You know I told you he had a sweet breath.

Pinch. Write!

Mrs. Pinch. Let me but put out "loathed."

Pinch. Write, I say!

Mrs. Pinch. Well then. [*Writes.*

Pinch. Let's see, what have you writ?—[*Takes the paper and reads.*] "Though I suffered last night your kisses and embraces"— Thou impudent creature! where is "nauseous" and "loathed?"

Mrs. Pinch. I can't abide to write such filthy words.

Pinch. Once more write as I'd have you, and question it not, or I will spoil thy writing with this. I will stab out those eyes that cause my mischief. [*Holds up the penknife.*

Mrs. Pinch. O Lord! I will.

Pinch. So—so—let's see now.—[*Reads.*] "Though I suffered last night your nauseous, loathed kisses and embraces"—go on—"yet I would not have you presume that you shall ever repeat them"—so——　　　　　　　　　　　　　　　　　　　　　[*She writes.*

Mrs. Pinch. I have writ it.

Pinch. Oh, then—"I then concealed myself from your knowledge, to avoid your insolencies."——　　　　　　　　[*She writes.*

Mrs. Pinch. So——

Pinch. "The same reason, now I am out of your hands"——

　　　　　　　　　　　　　　　　　　　　　　　　[*She writes.*

Mrs. Pinch. So——

Pinch. "Makes me own to you my unfortunate, though innocent frolic, of being in man's clothes"——　　　　　　[*She writes.*

Mrs. Pinch. So——

Pinch. "That you may for evermore cease to pursue her, who hates and detests you"——　　　　　　　　　[*She writes on.*

Mrs. Pinch. So—heigh!　　　　　　　　　　　　　[*Sighs.*

Pinch. What, do you sigh?—"detests you—as much as she loves her husband and her honour."

Mrs. Pinch. I vow, husband, he'll ne'er believe I should write such a letter.

Pinch. What, he'd expect a kinder from you? Come, now your name only.

Mrs. Pinch. What, shan't I say "Your most faithful humble servant till death?"

Pinch. No, tormenting fiend!—[*Aside.*] Her style, I find, would be very soft.—[*Aloud.*] Come, wrap it up now, whilst I go fetch wax and a candle; and write on the backside, "For Mr. Horner."　[*Exit.*

Mrs. Pinch. "For Mr. Horner."—So, I am glad he has told me his name. Dear Mr. Horner! but why should I send thee such a letter that will vex thee, and make thee angry with me?—Well, I will not send it.—Ay, but then my husband will kill me—for I see plainly he won't let me love Mr. Horner—but what care I for my husband?—I won't, so I won't, send poor Mr. Horner such a letter—But then my husband—but oh, what if I writ at bottom my husband made me write it?—Ay, but then my husband would see't—Can one have no shift? ah, a London woman would have had a hundred presently. Stay—what if I should write a letter, and wrap it up like this, and write upon't too? Ay, but then my husband would see't—I don't know what to do.—But yet evads I'll try, so I will—for I will not send this letter to poor Mr. Horner, come what will on't.

"Dear, sweet Mr. Horner"—[*Writes and repeats what she writes.*] —so—"my husband would have me send you a base, rude, unmannerly letter; but I won't"—so—"and would have me forbid you loving me; but I won't"—so—"and would have me say to you, I hate you, poor Mr. Horner; but I won't tell a lie for him"—there—"for I'm sure if you and I were in the country at cards together"—so—"I could not help treading on your toe under the table"—so—"or rubbing knees with you, and staring in your face, till you saw me" —very well—"and then looking down, and blushing for an hour together"—so—"but I must make haste before my husband comes: and now he has taught me to write letters, you shall have longer ones from me, who am, dear, dear, poor, dear Mr. Horner, your most humble friend, and servant to command till death,—Margery Pinchwife."

Stay, I must give him a hint at bottom—so—now wrap it up just like t'other—so—now write "For Mr. Horner"—But oh now, what shall I do with it? for here comes my husband.

Re-enter PINCHWIFE.

Pinch. [*Aside.*] I have been detained by a sparkish coxcomb, who pretended a visit to me; but I fear 'twas to my wife.—[*Aloud.*] What, have you done?

Mrs. Pinch. Ay, ay, bud, just now.

Pinch. Let's see't: what d'ye tremble for? what, you would not have it go?

Mrs. Pinch. Here.—[*Aside.*] No, I must not give him that: so I had been served if I had given him this.

[*He opens and reads the first letter.*

Pinch. Come, where's the wax and seal?

Mrs. Pinch. [*Aside.*] Lord, what shall I do now? Nay, then I have it.—[*Aloud.*] Pray let me see't. Lord, you will think me so arrant a fool, I cannot seal a letter; I will do't, so I will.

[*Snatches the letter from him, changes it for the other, seals it, and delivers it to him.*

Pinch. Nay, I believe you will learn that, and other things too, which I would not have you.

Mrs. Pinch. So, han't I done it curiously?—[*Aside.*] I think I have; there's my letter going to Mr. Horner, since he'll needs have me send letters to folks.

Pinch. 'Tis very well; but I warrant, you would not have it go now?

Mrs. Pinch. Yes, indeed, but I would, bud, now.

Pinch. Well, you are a good girl then. Come, let me lock you up in your chamber, till I come back; and be sure you come not within three strides of the window when I am gone, for I have a spy in the street.—[*Exit Mrs.* PINCHWIFE, PINCHWIFE *locks the door.*] At least, 'tis fit she think so. If we do not cheat women, they'll cheat us, and fraud may be justly used with secret enemies, of which a wife is the most dangerous; and he that has a handsome one to keep, and a frontier town, must provide against treachery, rather than open force. Now I have secured all within, I'll deal with the foe without, with false intelligence. [*Holds up the letter. Exit.*

Scene III—Horner's *Lodging*

Enter HORNER *and* QUACK. HORNER *has by this time successfully unmasked himself to* Lady FIDGET *and to her sister,* Mrs. SQUEAMISH.

Quack. Well, sir, how fadges the new design? have you not the luck of all your brother projectors, to deceive only yourself at last?

Horn. No, good domine doctor, I deceive you, it seems, and others too; for the grave matrons, and old, rigid husbands think me as unfit for love, as they are; but their wives, sisters, and daughters know, some of 'em, better things already.

Quack. Already!

Horn. Already, I say. Last night I was drunk with half-a-dozen of your civil persons, as you call 'em, and people of honour, and so was made free of their society and dressing-rooms for ever hereafter; and am already come to the privileges of sleeping upon their pallets, warming smocks, tying shoes and garters, and the like, doctor, already, already, doctor.

Quack. You have made good use of your time, sir.

Horn. I tell thee, I am now no more interruption to 'em, when they sing, or talk bawdy, than a little squab French page who speaks no English.

Quack. But do civil persons and women of honour drink, and sing bawdy songs?

Horn. O, amongst friends, amongst friends. For your bigots in honour are just like those in religion; they fear the eye of the world more than the eye of Heaven; and think there is no virtue, but railing at vice, and no sin, but giving scandal. They rail at a poor, little, kept player, and keep themselves some young, modest pulpit comedian to be privy to their sins in their closets, not to tell 'em of them in their chapels.

Quack. Nay, the truth on't is, priests, amongst the women now, have quite got the better of us lay-confessors, physicians.

Horn. And they are rather their patients; but——

Enter Lady FIDGET, *looking about her.*

Now we talk of women of honour, here comes one. Step behind the screen there, and but observe, if I have not particular privileges with the women of reputation already, doctor, already.

[QUACK *retires.*

Lady Fid. Well, Horner, am not I a woman of honour? you see, I'm as good as my word.

Horn. And you shall see, madam, I'll not be behind-hand with you in honour; and I'll be as good as my word too, if you please but to withdraw into the next room.

Lady Fid. But first, my dear sir, you must promise to have a care of my dear honour.

Horn. If you talk a word more of your honour, you'll make me incapable to wrong it. To talk of honour in the mysteries of love, is like talking of Heaven or the Deity, in an operation of witchcraft, just when you are employing the devil: it makes the charm impotent.

Lady Fid. Nay, fy! let us not be smutty. But you talk of mysteries and bewitching to me; I don't understand you.

Horn. I tell you, madam, the word money in a mistress's mouth, at such a nick of time, is not a more disheartening sound to a younger brother, than that of honour to an eager lover like myself.

Lady Fid. But you can't blame a lady of my reputation to be chary.

Horn. Chary! I have been chary of it already, by the report I have caused of myself.

Lady Fid. Ay, but if you should ever let other women know that dear secret, it would come out. Nay, you must have a great care of your conduct; for my acquaintance are so censorious (oh, 'tis a wicked, censorious world, Mr. Horner!), I say, are so censorious, and detracting, that perhaps they'll talk to the prejudice of my honour, though you should not let them know the dear secret.

Horn. Nay, madam, rather than they shall prejudice your honour, I'll prejudice theirs; and, to serve you, I'll lie with 'em all, make the secret their own, and then they'll keep it. I am a Machiavel in love, madam.

Lady Fid. Oh, no, sir, not that way.

Horn. Nay, the devil take me, if censorious women are to be silenced any other way.

Lady Fid. A secret is better kept, I hope, by a single person than a multitude; therefore pray do not trust anybody else with it, dear, dear Mr. Horner. [*Embracing him.*

Enter Sir JASPER FIDGET

Sir Jasp. How now!

Lady Fid. [*Aside.*] O my husband!—prevented—and what's almost as bad, found with my arms about another man—that will appear too much—what shall I say?—[*Aloud.*] Sir Jasper, come hither: I am trying if Mr. Horner were ticklish, and he's as ticklish as can be. I love to torment the confounded toad; let you and I tickle him.

Sir Jasp. No, your ladyship will tickle him better without me, I suppose. But is this your buying china? I thought you had been at the china-house.

Horn. [*Aside.*] China-house! that's my cue, I must take it.— [*Aloud.*] A pox! can't you keep your impertinent wives at home? Some men are troubled with the husbands, but I with the wives; but I'd have you to know, since I cannot be your journeyman by night, I will not be your drudge by day, to squire your wife about, and be your man of straw, or scarecrow only to pies and jays, that would be nibbling at your forbidden fruit; I shall be shortly the hackney gentleman-usher of the town.

Sir Jasp. [*Aside.*] He! he! he! poor fellow, he's in the right on't, faith. To squire women about for other folks is as ungrateful an employment, as to tell money for other folks.—[*Aloud.*] He! he! he! be'n't angry, Horner.

Lady Fid. No, 'tis I have more reason to be angry, who am left by you, to go abroad indecently alone; or, what is more indecent, to pin myself upon such ill-bred people of your acquaintance as this is.

Sir Jasp. Nay, prithee, what has he done?

Lady Fid. Nay, he has done nothing.

Sir Jasp. But what d'ye take ill, if he has done nothing?

Lady Fid. Ha! ha! ha! faith, I can't but laugh however; why d'ye think the unmannerly toad would come down to me to the coach? I was fain to come up to fetch him, or go without him, which I was resolved not to do; for he knows china very well, and has himself very good, but will not let me see it, lest I should beg some; but I will find it out, and have what I came for yet.

Horn. [*Apart to* Lady FIDGET, *as he follows her to the door.*] Lock the door, madam.—[*Exit* Lady FIDGET, *and locks the door.*]— [*Aloud.*] So, she has got into my chamber and locked me out. Oh the impertinency of woman-kind! Well, Sir Jasper, plain-dealing is a jewel; if ever you suffer your wife to trouble me again here, she shall carry you home a pair of horns; by my lord mayor she shall; though I cannot furnish you myself, you are sure, yet I'll find a way.

Sir Jasp. Ha! ha! he!—[*Aside.*] At my first coming in, and finding her arms about him, tickling him it seems, I was half jealous, but now I see my folly.—[*Aloud.*] He! he! he! poor Horner.

Horn. Nay, though you laugh now, 'twill be my turn ere long. Oh women, more impertinent, more cunning, and more mischievous than their monkeys, and to me almost as ugly!—Now is she throwing my things about and rifling all I have; but I'll get in to her the back way, and so rifle her for it.

Sir Jasp. Ha! ha! ha! poor angry Horner.

Horn. Stay here a little, I'll ferret her out to you presently, I warrant.   [*Exit at the other door.*

    [Sir JASPER *talks through the door to his* Wife, *she answers from within.*

Sir Jasp. Wife! my Lady Fidget! wife! he is coming into you the back way.

Lady Fid. Let him come, and welcome, which way he will.

Sir Jasp. He'll catch you, and use you roughly, and be too strong for you.

Lady Fid. Don't you trouble yourself, let him if he can.

Quack. [*Aside.*] This indeed I could not have believed from him, nor any but my own eyes.

Enter Mrs. SQUEAMISH.

Mrs. Squeam. Where's this woman-hater, this toad, this ugly, greasy, dirty sloven?

Sir Jasp. [*Aside.*] So, the women all will have him ugly: methinks he is a comely person, but his wants make his form contemptible to 'em; and 'tis e'en as my wife said yesterday, talking of him, that a proper handsome eunuch was as ridiculous a thing as a gigantic coward.

Mrs. Squeam. Sir Jasper, your servant: where is the odious beast?

Sir Jasp. He's within in his chamber, with my wife; she's playing the wag with him.

Mrs. Squeam. Is she so? and he's a clownish beast, he'll give her no quarter, he'll play the wag with her again, let me tell you: come, let's go help her.—What, the door's locked?

Sir Jasp. Ay, my wife locked it.

Mrs. Squeam. Did she so? let's break it open then.

Sir Jasp. No, no, he'll do her no hurt.

Mrs. Squeam. [*Aside.*] But is there no other way to get in to 'em? whither goes this? I will disturb 'em.   [*Exit at another door.*

Enter Old Lady SQUEAMISH.

Lady Squeam. Where is this harlotry, this impudent baggage, this rambling tomrigg? O Sir Jasper, I'm glad to see you here; did you not see my vile grandchild come in hither just now?

Sir Jasp. Yes.

Lady Squeam. Ay, but where is she then? where is she? Lord, Sir Jasper, I have e'en rattled myself to pieces in pursuit of her: but can you tell what she makes here? they say below, no woman lodges here.

Sir Jasp. No.

Lady Squeam. No! what does she here then? say, if it be not a woman's lodging, what makes she here? But are you sure no woman lodges here?

Sir Jasp. No, nor no man neither, this is Mr. Horner's lodging.

Lady Squeam. Is it so, are you sure?

Sir Jasp. Yes, yes.

Lady Squeam. So; then there's no hurt in't, I hope. But where is he?

Sir Jasp. He's in the next room with my wife.

Lady Squeam. Nay, if you trust him with your wife, I may with my Biddy. They say, he's a merry harmless man now, e'en as harmless a man as ever came out of Italy with a good voice, and as pretty, harmless company for a lady, as a snake without his teeth.

Sir Jasp. Ay, ay, poor man.

Re-enter Mrs. SQUEAMISH.

Mrs. Squeam. I can't find 'em.—Oh, are you here, grandmother? I followed, you must know, my Lady Fidget hither; 'tis the prettiest lodging, and I have been staring on the prettiest pictures——

Re-enter Lady FIDGET *with a piece of china in her hand, and* HORNER *following.*

Lady Fid. And I have been toiling and moiling for the prettiest piece of china, my dear.

Horn. Nay, she has been too hard for me, do what I could.

Mrs. Squeam. Oh, lord, I'll have some china too. Good Mr. Horner, don't think to give other people china, and me none; come in with me too.

Horn. Upon my honour, I have none left now.

Mrs. Squeam. Nay, nay, I have known you deny your china before now, but you shan't put me off so. Come.

Horn. This lady had the last there.

Lady Fid. Yes indeed, madam, to my certain knowledge, he has no more left.

Mrs. Squeam. O, but it may be he may have some you could not find.

Lady Fid. What, d'ye think if he had had any left, I would not have had it too? for we women of quality never think we have china enough.

Horn. Do not take it ill, I cannot make china for you all, but I will have a roll-waggon for you too, another time.

Mrs. Squeam. Thank you, dear toad.

Lady Fid. What do you mean by that promise?

[*Aside to* HORNER.

Horn. Alas, she has an innocent, literal understanding.

[*Aside to* Lady FIDGET.

Lady Squeam. Poor Mr. Horner! he has enough to do to please you all, I see.

Horn. Ay, madam, you see how they use me.

Lady Squeam. Poor gentleman, I pity you.

Horn. I thank you, madam: I could never find pity, but from such reverend ladies as you are; the young ones will never spare a man.

Mrs. Squeam. Come, come, beast, and go dine with us; for we shall want a man at ombre after dinner.

Horn. That's all their use of me, madam, you see.

Mrs. Squeam. Come, sloven, I'll lead you, to be sure of you.

[*Pulls him by the cravat.*

Lady Squeam. Alas, poor man, how she tugs him! Kiss, kiss her; that's the way to make such nice women quiet.

Horn. No, madam, that remedy is worse than the torment; they know I dare suffer anything rather than do it.

Lady Squeam. Prithee kiss her, and I'll give you her picture in little, that you admired so last night; prithee do.

Horn. Well, nothing but that could bribe me: I love a woman only in effigy, and good painting as much as I hate them.—I'll do't, for I could adore the devil well painted.   [*Kisses* Mrs. SQUEAMISH.

Mrs. Squeam. Foh, you filthy toad! nay, now I've done jesting.

Lady Squeam. Ha! ha! ha! I told you so.

Mrs. Squeam. Foh! a kiss of his——

Sir Jasp. Has no more hurt in't than one of my spaniel's.

Mrs. Squeam. Nor no more good neither.

Quack. I will now believe anything he tells me.   [*Aside.*

ACT V, SCENE IV—HORNER'S *Lodging. A table, banquet,
and bottles*

Enter HORNER, Lady FIDGET, Mrs. DAINTY FIDGET, *and* Mrs.
SQUEAMISH. HORNER *is expecting a visit from* Mrs. PINCHWIFE, *who
with the help of* ALITHEA's *maid has disguised herself in* ALITHEA's
clothing in order to elude the vigilance of her husband. PINCHWIFE,
thinking her with his sister and wishing to divert HORNER's *attentions
away from his wife, is now promoting their acquaintance. It is to be
remembered that* PINCHWIFE, *alone of the men, is uninstructed as
to* HORNER's *supposed impotence.*

Horn. A pox! they are come too soon—before I have sent back my
new mistress. All that I have now to do is to lock her in, that they
may not see her.   [*Aside.*

Lady Fid. That we may be sure of our welcome, we have brought
our entertainment with us, and are resolved to treat thee, dear toad.

Mrs. Dain. And that we may be merry to purpose, have left Sir
Jasper and my old Lady Squeamish quarrelling at home at back-
gammon.

Mrs. Squeam. Therefore let us make use of our time, lest they
should chance to interrupt us.

Lady Fid. Let us sit then.

Horn. First, that you may be private, let me lock this door and
that, and I'll wait upon you presently.

Lady Fid. No, sir, shut 'em only, and your lips for ever; for we
must trust you as much as our women.

Horn. You know all vanity's killed in me; I have no occasion for
talking.

Lady Fid. Now, ladies, supposing we had drank each of us two
bottles, let us speak the truth of our hearts.

Mrs. Dain. and Mrs. Squeam. Agreed.

Lady Fid. By this brimmer, for truth is nowhere else to be found
—[*aside to* HORNER] not in thy heart, false man!

Horn. You have found me a true man, I'm sure.

[*Aside to* Lady FIDGET.

Lady Fid. [*Aside to* HORNER.] Not every way.—But let us sit and be merry. [*Sings.*

> Why should our damned tyrants oblige us to live
> On the pittance of pleasure which they only give?
>   We must not rejoice
>   With wine and with noise:
> In vain we must wake in a dull bed alone,
> Whilst to our warm rival the bottle they're gone.
>   Then lay aside charms,
>   And take up these arms.
> 'Tis wine only gives 'em their courage and wit;
> Because we live sober, to men we submit.
>   If for beauties you'd pass,
>   Take a lick of the glass,
> 'Twill mend your complexions, and when they are gone,
>   The best red we have is the red of the grape:
> Then, sisters, lay't on,
>   And damn a good shape.

Mrs. Dain. Dear brimmer! Well, in token of our openness and plain-dealing, let us throw our masks over our heads.

Horn. So, 'twill come to the glasses anon. [*Aside.*

Mrs. Squeam. Lovely brimmer! let me enjoy him first.

Lady Fid. No, I never part with a gallant till I've tried him. Dear brimmer! that makest our husbands short-sighted.

Mrs. Dain. And our bashful gallants bold.

Mrs Squeam. And, for want of a gallant, the butler lovely in our eyes.—Drink, eunuch.

Lady Fid. Drink, thou representative of a husband. Damn a husband!

Mrs. Dain. And, as it were a husband, an old keeper.

Mrs. Squeam. And an old grandmother.

Horn. And an English bawd, and a French surgeon.

Lady Fid. Ay, we have all reason to curse 'em.

Horn. For my sake, ladies?

Lady Fid. No, for our own; for the first spoils all young gallants' industry.

Mrs. Dain. And the other's art makes 'em bold only with common women.

Mrs. Squeam. And rather run the hazard of the vile distemper amongst them, than of a denial amongst us.

Mrs. Dain. The filthy toads choose mistresses now as they do stuffs, for having been fancied and worn by others.

Mrs. Squeam. For being common and cheap.

Lady Fid. Whilst women of quality, like the richest stuffs, lie untumbled, and unasked for.

Horn. Ay, neat, and cheap, and new, often they think best.

Mrs. Dain. No, sir, the beasts will be known by a mistress longer than by a suit.

Mrs. Squeam. And 'tis not for cheapness neither.

Lady Fid. No; for the vain fops will take up druggets and embroider 'em. But I wonder at the depraved appetites of witty men; they used to be out of the common road, and hate imitation. Pray tell me, beast, when you were a man, why you rather chose to club with a multitude in a common house for an entertainment, than to be the only guest at a good table.

Horn. Why, faith, ceremony and expectation are unsufferable to those that are sharp bent. People always eat with the best stomach at an ordinary, where every man is snatching for the best bit.

Lady Fid. Though he get a cut over the fingers.—But I have heard, that people eat most heartily of another man's meat, that is, what they do not pay for.

Horn. When they are sure of their welcome and freedom; for ceremony in love and eating is as ridiculous as in fighting: falling on briskly is all should be done on those occasions.

Lady Fid. Well, then, let me tell you, sir, there is nowhere more freedom than in our houses; and we take freedom from a young person as a sign of good breeding; and a person may be as free as he pleases with us, as frolic, as gamesome, as wild as he will.

Horn. Han't I heard you all declaim against wild men?

Lady Fid. Yes, but for all that, we think wildness in a man as desirable a quality as in a duck or rabbit: a tame man! foh!

Horn. I know not, but your reputations frightened me as much as your faces invited me.

Lady Fid. Our reputation! Lord, why should you not think that we women make use of our reputation, as you men of yours, only to deceive the world with less suspicion? Our virtue is like the statesman's religion, the quaker's word, the gamester's oath, and the great man's honour; but to cheat those that trust us.

Mrs. Squeam. And that demureness, coyness, and modesty, that you see in our faces in the boxes at plays, is as much a sign of a kind woman as a vizard-mask in the pit.

Mrs. Dain. For, I assure you, women are least masked when they have the velvet vizard on.

Lady Fid. You would have found us modest women in our denials only.

Mrs. Squeam. Our bashfulness is only the reflection of the men's.

Mrs. Dain. We blush when they are shamefaced.

Horn. I beg your pardon, ladies, I was deceived in you devilishly. But why that mighty pretence to honour?

Lady Fid. We have told you; but sometimes 'twas for the same reason you men pretend business often, to avoid ill company, to enjoy the better and more privately those you love.

Horn. But why would you ne'er give a friend a wink then?

Lady Fid. Faith, your reputation frightened us, as much as ours did you, you were so notoriously lewd.

Horn. And you so seemingly honest.

Lady Fid. Was that all that deterred you?

Horn. And so expensive—you allow freedom, you say.

Lady Fid. Ay, ay.

Horn. That I was afraid of losing my little money, as well as my little time, both which my other pleasures required.

Lady Fid. Money! foh! you talk like a little fellow now: do such as we expect money?

Horn. I beg your pardon, madam, I must confess, I have heard that great ladies, like great merchants, set but the higher prices upon what they have, because they are not in necessity of taking the first offer.

Mrs. Dain. Such as we make sale of our hearts?

Mrs. Squeam. We bribed for our love? foh!

Horn. With your pardon, ladies, I know, like great men in offices, you seem to exact flattery and attendance only from your followers; but you have receivers about you, and such fees to pay, a man is afraid to pass your grants. Besides, we must let you win at cards, or we lose your hearts; and if you make an assignation, 'tis at a goldsmith's, jeweller's, or china-house; where for your honour you deposit to him, he must pawn his to the punctual cit, and so paying for what you take up, pays for what he takes up.

Mrs. Dain. Would you not have us assured of our gallants' love?

Mrs. Squeam. For love is better known by liberality than by jealousy.

Lady Fid. For one may be dissembled, the other not.—[*Aside.*] But my jealousy can be no longer dissembled, and they are telling ripe.—[*Aloud.*]—Come, here's to our gallants in waiting, whom we must name, and I'll begin. This is my false rogue.

[*Claps him on the back.*

Mrs. Squeam. How!

Horn. So, all will out now. [*Aside.*

Mrs. Squeam. Did you not tell me, 'twas for my sake only you reported yourself no man? [*Aside to* HORNER.

Mrs. Dain. Oh, wretch! did you not swear to me, 'twas for my love and honour you passed for that thing you do?

[*Aside to* HORNER.

Horn. So, so.

Lady Fid. Come, speak, ladies: this is my false villain.

Mrs. Squeam. And mine too.

Mrs. Dain. And mine.

Horn. Well then, you are all three my false rogues too, and there's an end on't.

Lady Fid. Well then, there's no remedy; sister sharers, let us not fall out, but have a care of our honour. Though we get no presents, no jewels of him, we are savers of our honour, the jewel of most value and use, which shines yet to the world unsuspected, though it be counterfeit.

Horn. Nay, and is e'en as good as if it were true, provided the world think so; for honour, like beauty now, only depends on the opinion of others.

Lady Fid. Well, Harry Common, I hope you can be true to three. Swear; but 'tis to no purpose to require your oath, for you are as often forsworn as you swear to new women.

Horn. Come, faith, madam, let us e'en pardon one another; for all the difference I find betwixt we men and you women, we forswear ourselves at the beginning of an amour, you as long as it lasts.

Enter Sir JASPER FIDGET, *and* Old Lady SQUEAMISH.

Sir Jasp. Oh, my Lady Fidget, was this your cunning, to come to Mr. Horner without me? but you have been nowhere else, I hope.

Lady Fid. No, Sir Jasper.

Lady Squeam. And you came straight hither, Biddy?

Mrs. Squeam. Yes, indeed, lady grandmother.

Sir Jasp. 'Tis well, 'tis well; I knew when once they were thoroughly acquainted with poor Horner, they'd ne'er be from him: you may let her masquerade it with my wife and Horner, and I warrant her reputation safe.

Enter Boy.

Boy. O, sir, here's the gentleman come, whom you bid me not suffer to come up, without giving you notice, with a lady too, and other gentlemen.

Horn. Do you all go in there, whilst I send 'em away; and, boy, do you desire 'em to stay below till I come, which shall be immediately.

[*Exeunt* Sir JASPER FIDGET, Lady FIDGET, Lady SQUEAMISH, Mrs. SQUEAMISH, *and* Mrs. DAINTY FIDGET.

Boy. Yes, sir.   [*Exit.*

[*Exit* HORNER *at the other door, and returns with* Mrs. PINCHWIFE.

Horn. You would not take my advice, to be gone home before your husband came back, he'll now discover all; yet pray, my dearest, be persuaded to go home, and leave the rest to my management; I'll let you down the back way.

Mrs. Pinch. I don't know the way home, so I don't.

Horn. My man shall wait upon you.

Mrs. Pinch. No, don't you believe that I'll go at all; what, are you weary of me already?

Horn. No, my life, 'tis that I may love you long, 'tis to secure my love, and your reputation with your husband; he'll never receive you again else.

Mrs. Pinch. What care I? d'ye think to frighten me with that? I don't intend to go to him again; you shall be my husband now.

Horn. I cannot be your husband, dearest, since you are married to him.

Mrs. Pinch. O, would you make me believe that? Don't I see every day at London here, women leave their first husbands, and go and live with other men as their wives? pish, pshaw! you'd make me angry, but that I love you so mainly.

Horn. So, they are coming up—In again, in, I hear 'em.—[*Exit* Mrs. PINCHWIFE.] Well, a silly mistress is like a weak place, soon got, soon lost, a man has scarce time for plunder; she betrays her husband first to her gallant, and then her gallant to her husband.

Enter PINCHWIFE, ALITHEA, HARCOURT, SPARKISH, LUCY, *and a* Parson. ALITHEA *has been engaged to* SPARKISH, *but is heavily besieged by* HARCOURT, *aided by* LUCY, ALITHEA's *maid. A part of their plan is to compromise* ALITHEA *with* HORNER. *The* Parson *is present*

by arrangement of PINCHWIFE *to officiate at a shotgun marriage be-*
tween HORNER *and* ALITHEA. ALITHEA *by this time is disgusted with*
SPARKISH *and prefers* HARCOURT, *though, being the one honorable*
woman in the play, she still intends to go through with her agree-
ment. The tangle is now unraveled in this uproarious finale, which
leaves HORNER *sitting pretty amid his rapidly expanding harem.*

Pinch. Come, madam, 'tis not the sudden change of your dress,
the confidence of your asseverations, and your false witness there,
shall persuade me I did not bring you hither just now; here's my
witness, who cannot deny it, since you must be confronted.—Mr.
Horner, did not I bring this lady to you just now?

Horn. Now must I wrong one woman for another's sake,—but
that's no new thing with me, for in these cases I am still on the
criminal's side against the innocent.   [*Aside.*

Alith. Pray speak, sir.

Horn. It must be so. I must be impudent, and try my luck; impudence uses to be too hard for truth.   [*Aside.*

Pinch. What, you are studying an evasion or excuse for her!
Speak, sir.

Horn. No, faith, I am something backward only to speak in
women's affairs or disputes.

Pinch. She bids you speak.

Alith. Ah, pray, sir, do, pray satisfy him.

Horn. Then truly, you did bring that lady to me just now.

Pinch. O ho!

Alith. How, sir?

Har. How, Horner?

Alith. What mean you, sir? I always took you for a man of honour.

Horn. Ay, so much a man of honour, that I must save my mistress,
I thank you, come what will on't.   [*Aside.*

Spark. So, if I had had her, she'd have made me believe the moon
had been made of a Christmas pie.

Lucy. Now could I speak, if I durst, and solve the riddle, who am
the author of it.   [*Aside.*

Alith. O unfortunate woman! A combination against my honour!
which most concerns me now, because you share in my disgrace, sir,
and it is your censure, which I must now suffer, that troubles me,
not theirs.

Har. Madam, then have no trouble, you shall now see 'tis possible
for me to love too, without being jealous; I will not only believe your

innocence myself, but make all the world believe it.—[*Aside to* HORNER.] Horner, I must now be concerned for this lady's honour.

Horn. And I must be concerned for a lady's honour too.

Har. This lady has her honour, and I will protect it.

Horn. My lady has not her honour, but has given it me to keep, and I will preserve it.

Har. I understand you not.

Horn. I would not have you.

Mrs. Pinch. What's the matter with 'em all? [*Peeping in behind.*

Pinch. Come, come, Mr. Horner, no more disputing; here's the parson, I brought him not in vain.

Har. No, sir, I'll employ him, if this lady please.

Pinch. How! what d'ye mean?

Spark. Ay, what does he mean?

Horn. Why, I have resigned your sister to him, he has my consent.

Pinch. But he has not mine, sir; a woman's injured honour, no more than a man's, can be repaired or satisfied by any but him that first wronged it; and you shall marry her presently, or——

[*Lays his hand on his sword.*

Re-enter Mrs. PINCHWIFE.

Mrs. Pinch. O Lord, they'll kill poor Mr. Horner! besides, he shan't marry her whilst I stand by, and look on; I'll not lose my second husband so.

Pinch. What do I see?

Alith. My sister in my clothes!

Spark. Ha!

Mrs. Pinch. Nay, pray now don't quarrel about finding work for the parson, he shall marry me to Mr. Horner; or now, I believe, you have enough of me.   [*To* PINCHWIFE.

Horn. Damned, damned loving changeling!   [*Aside.*

Mrs. Pinch. Pray, sister, pardon me for telling so many lies of you.

Horn. I suppose the riddle is plain now.

Lucy. No, that must be my work.—Good sir, hear me.

[*Kneels to* PINCHWIFE, *who stands doggedly with his hat over his eyes.*

Pinch. I will never hear woman again, but make 'em all silent thus——   [*Offers to draw upon his* Wife.

Horn. No, that must not be.

Pinch. You then shall go first, 'tis all one to me.

[Offers to draw on HORNER, *but is stopped by* HARCOURT.
Har. Hold!

Re-enter Sir JASPER FIDGET, Lady FIDGET, Lady SQUEAMISH,
Mrs. DAINTY FIDGET, *and* Mrs. SQUEAMISH.

Sir Jasp. What's the matter? what's the matter? pray, what's the
matter, sir? I beseech you communicate, sir.
Pinch. Why, my wife has communicated, sir, as your wife may have
done too, sir, if she knows him, sir.
Sir Jasp. Pshaw, with him! ha! ha! he!
Pinch. D'ye mock me, sir? a cuckold is a kind of a wild beast;
have a care, sir.
Sir Jasp. No, sure, you mock me, sir. He cuckold you! It can't
be, ha! ha! he! why, I'll tell you, sir——   *[Offers to whisper.*
Pinch. I tell you again, he has whored my wife, and yours too,
if he knows her, and all the women he comes near; 'tis not his dis-
sembling, his hypocrisy, can wheedle me.
Sir Jasp. How! does he dissemble? is he a hypocrite? Nay, then—
how—wife—sister, is he a hypocrite?
Lady Squeam. A hypocrite! a dissembler! Speak, young harlotry,
speak, how?
Sir Jasp. Nay, then—O my head too!—O thou libidinous lady!
Lady Squeam. O thou harloting harlotry! hast thou done't then?
Sir Jasp. Speak, good Horner, art thou a dissembler, a rogue? hast
thou——
Horn. So!
Lucy. I'll fetch you off, and her too, if she will but hold her
tongue.   *[Apart to* HORNER.
Horn. Canst thou? I'll give thee——   *[Apart to* LUCY.
Lucy. [*To* PINCHWIFE.] Pray have but patience to hear me, sir,
who am the unfortunate cause of all this confusion. Your wife is
innocent, I only culpable; for I put her upon telling you all these
lies concerning my mistress, in order to the breaking off the match
between Mr. Sparkish and her, to make way for Mr. Harcourt.
Spark. Did you so, eternal rotten tooth? Then, it seems, my mistress was not false to me, I was only deceived by you. Brother, that
should have been, now man of conduct, who is a frank person now,
to bring your wife to her lover, ha?
Lucy. I assure you, sir, she came not to Mr. Horner out of love,
for she loves him no more——

THE DUKE OF MONMOUTH

From a mezzotint after a portrait by Sir Peter Lely. Sutherland Collection.

FRANCES STUART, DUCHESS OF RICHMOND, AS DIANA

From a painting by Sir Peter Lely.

Mrs. Pinch. Hold, I told lies for you, but you shall tell none for me, for I do love Mr. Horner with all my soul, and nobody shall say me nay; pray, don't you go to make poor Mr. Horner believe to the contrary; 'tis spitefully done of you, I'm sure.

Horn. Peace, dear idiot.   [*Aside to* Mrs. PINCHWIFE.

Mrs. Pinch. Nay, I will not peace.

Pinch. Not till I make you.

Enter DORILANT *and* QUACK.

Dor. Horner, your servant; I am the doctor's guest, he must excuse our intrusion.

Quack. But what's the matter, gentlemen? for Heaven's sake, what's the matter?

Horn. Oh, 'tis well you are come. 'Tis a censorious world we live in; you may have brought me a reprieve, or else I had died for a crime I never committed, and these innocent ladies had suffered with me; therefore, pray satisfy these worthy, honourable, jealous gentlemen—that——   [*Whispers.*

Quack. O, I understand you, is that all?—Sir Jasper, by Heavens, and upon the word of a physician, sir——

         [*Whispers to* Sir JASPER.

Sir Jasp. Nay, I do believe you truly.—Pardon me, my virtuous lady, and dear of honour.

Lady Squeam. What, then all's right again?

Sir Jasp. Ay, ay, and now let us satisfy him too.

         [*They whisper with* PINCHWIFE.

Pinch. An eunuch! Pray, no fooling with me.

Quack. I'll bring half the chirurgeons in town to swear it.

Pinch. They!—they'll swear a man that bled to death through his wounds, died of an apoplexy.

Quack. Pray, hear me, sir—why, all the town has heard the report of him.

Pinch. But does all the town believe it?

Quack. Pray, inquire a little, and first of all these.

Pinch. I'm sure when I left the town, he was the lewdest fellow in't.

Quack. I tell you, sir, he has been in France since; pray, ask but these ladies and gentlemen, your friend Mr. Dorilant. Gentlemen and ladies, han't you all heard the late sad report of poor Mr. Horner?

All the Ladies. Ay, ay, ay.

Dor. Why, thou jealous fool, dost thou doubt it? he's an arrant French capon.

Mrs. Pinch. 'Tis false, sir, you shall not disparage poor Mr. Horner, for to my certain knowledge——

Lucy. O, hold!

Mrs. Squeam. Stop her mouth!   [*Aside to* LUCY.

Lady Fid. Upon my honour, sir, 'tis as true—— [*To* PINCHWIFE.

Mrs. Dain. D'ye think we would have been seen in his company?

Mrs. Squeam. Trust our unspotted reputations with him?

Lady Fid. This you get, and we too, by trusting your secret to a fool.   [*Aside to* HORNER.

Horn. Peace, madam.—[*Aside to* QUACK.] Well, doctor, is not this a good design, that carries a man on unsuspected, and brings him off safe?

Pinch. Well, if this were true—but my wife——   [*Aside.*

[DORILANT *whispers with* MRS. PINCHWIFE.

Alith. Come, brother, your wife is yet innocent, you see; but have a care of too strong an imagination, lest, like an over-concerned timorous gamester, by fancying an unlucky cast, it should come. Women and fortune are truest still to those that trust 'em.

Lucy. And any wild thing grows but the more fierce and hungry for being kept up, and more dangerous to the keeper.

Alith. There's doctrine for all husbands, Mr. Harcourt.

Har. I edify, madam, so much, that I am impatient till I am one.

Dor. And I edify so much by example, I will never be one.

Spark. And because I will not disparage my parts, I'll ne'er be one.

Horn. And I, alas! can't be one.

Pinch. But I must be one—against my will to a country wife, with a country murrain to me!

Mrs. Pinch. And I must be a country wife still too, I find; for I can't, like a city one, be rid of my musty husband, and do what I list.   [*Aside.*

Horn. Now, sir, I must pronounce your wife innocent, though I blush whilst I do it; and I am the only man by her now exposed to shame, which I will straight drown in wine, as you shall your suspicion; and the ladies' troubles we'll divert with a ballad.—Doctor, where are your maskers?

Lucy. Indeed, she's innocent, sir, I am her witness; and her end of coming out was but to see her sister's wedding; and what she has

said to your face of her love to Mr. Horner, was but the usual innocent revenge on a husband's jealousy—was it not, madam, speak?

   Mrs. Pinch. [*Aside to* LUCY *and* HORNER.] Since you'll have me
tell more lies.—[*Aloud.*] Yes, indeed, bud.

   Pinch. For my own sake fain I would all believe;
    Cuckolds, like lovers, should themselves deceive.
    But——   [*Sighs.*
    His honour is least safe (too late I find)
    Who trusts it with a foolish wife or friend.

A Dance of Cuckolds.

   Horn. Vain fops but court and dress, and keep a pother,
    To pass for women's men with one another;
    But he who aims by women to be prized,
    First by the men, you see, must be despised.   [*Exeunt.*

WILLIAM CONGREVE

   In the following scene from Congreve's masterpiece, The Way
of the World, *we have the wits, the would-be wits, and the plain
fools of Restoration society setting one another off in a pattern as
artistically subtle as it is dramatically effective. Lady Wishfort is
preparing for a visit from a potential husband, Sir Roland, actually
a masquerading servant already married to Foible, her maid. Sir
Wilfull Witwould, her nephew, a country squire who is being ab-
surdly egged on to play the sophisticated city game, goes forth to
woo the sparkling Millamant, apparent queen of high society. Mirabell, the true gallant, takes the affair deftly out of his bungling and
drunken hands. Mrs. Fainall, Lady Wishfort's daughter, has been
Mirabell's mistress but for economic reasons is promoting his match
with Millamant.*

   *The striking thing about this play, aside from the incredible bril-
liancy of the dialogue, is that Millamant, though an uncensorious,
well-informed and eminently successful member of the gay world,
is untouched by its licentiousness or its deeper cynicism. Her desir-
ability is of the mind and spirit, even more than of the person, and
it is a wonderful thing to see her softening to love. Mirabell, too,
is something more than a man of wit and fashion. The pair is like
Beatrice and Benedict in Shakespeare's* Much Ado, *except that the
man is master of the situation. Congreve's spirited lovers, no less
than his master's, are "sound in the noble parts," and the portrayal of
their relationship is humanly significant. Knowing them we feel a*

*measure of reassurance about the worldly society to which, in spite
of their superiority, they seem so well adjusted.*

The Way of the World

ACT IV, Scene I—A *Room in* Lady Wishfort's *House*

Lady Wishfort *and* Foible.

Lady Wish. Is Sir Rowland coming, sayest thou, Foible? and are
things in order?

Foib. Yes, madam, I have put wax lights in the sconces, and
placed the footmen in a row in the hall, in their best liveries, with
the coachman and postillion to fill up the equipage.

Lady Wish. Have you pulvilled the coachman and postillion, that
they may not stink of the stable when Sir Rowland comes by?

Foib. Yes, madam.

Lady Wish. And are the dancers and the music ready, that he may
be entertained in all points with correspondence to his passion?

Foib. All is ready, madam.

Lady Wish. And—well—and how do I look, Foible?

Foib. Most killing well, madam.

Lady Wish. Well, and how shall I receive him? in what figure
shall I give his heart the first impression? there is a great deal in
the first impression. Shall I sit?—no, I won't sit—I'll walk—ay, I'll
walk from the door upon his entrance; and then turn full upon him
—no, that will be too sudden. I'll lie—ay, I'll lie down—I'll receive
him in my little dressing-room, there's a couch—yes, yes, I'll give the
first impression on a couch.—I won't lie neither, but loll and lean
upon one elbow: with one foot a little dangling off, jogging in a
thoughtful way—yes—and then as soon as he appears, start, ay, start
and be surprised, and rise to meet him in a pretty disorder—yes—O,
nothing is more alluring than a levee from a couch, in some confusion:—it shows the foot to advantage, and furnishes with blushes,
and recomposing airs beyond comparison. Hark! there's a coach.

Foib. 'Tis he, madam.

Lady Wish. O dear!—Has my nephew made his addresses to Millamant? I ordered him.

Foib. Sir Wilfull is set in to drinking, madam, in the parlour.

Lady Wish. Odds my life, I'll send him to her. Call her down,
Foible; bring her hither. I'll send him as I go—when they are to-

gether, then come to me, Foible, that I may not be too long alone
with Sir Rowland.   [*Exit.*

Enter Mrs. MILLAMANT *and* Mrs. FAINALL.

Foib. Madam, I stayed here, to tell your ladyship that Mr.
Mirabell has waited this half hour for an opportunity to talk with
you: though my lady's orders were to leave you and Sir Wilfull together. Shall I tell Mr. Mirabell that you are at leisure?

Mrs. Mil. No,—what would the dear man have? I am thoughtful,
and would amuse myself—bid him come another time.

> "There never yet was woman made
> Nor shall but to be cursed."

> [*Repeating, and walking about.*

That's hard.

Mrs. Fain. You are very fond of Sir John Suckling to-day, Millamant, and the poets.

Mrs. Mil. He? Ay, and filthy verses—so I am.

Foib. Sir Wilfull is coming, madam. Shall I send Mr. Mirabell
away?

Mrs. Mil. Ay, if you please, Foible, send him away—or send him
hither—just as you will, dear Foible.—I think I'll see him—shall I?
ay, let the wretch come.   [*Exit* FOIBLE.

> "Thyrsis, a youth of the inspirèd train."

> [*Repeating.*

Dear Fainall, entertain Sir Wilfull—thou hast philosophy to undergo
a fool, thou art married and hast patience—I would confer with my
own thoughts.

Mrs. Fain. I am obliged to you, that you would make me your
proxy in this affair; but I have business of my own.

Enter Sir WILFULL.

Mrs. Fain. O Sir Wilfull, you are come at the critical instant.
There's your mistress up to the ears in love and contemplation;
pursue your point now or never.

Sir Wil. Yes; my aunt will have it so—I would gladly have been
encouraged with a bottle or two, because I'm somewhat wary at first
before I am acquainted.—[*This while* MILLAMANT *walks about repeating to herself.*]—But I hope, after a time, I shall break my mind
—that is, upon further acquaintance—so for the present, cousin, I'll

take my leave—if so be you'll be so kind to make my excuse, I'll return to my company—

Mrs. Fain. O fy, Sir Wilfull! what, you must not be daunted.

Sir Wil. Daunted! no, that's not it, it is not so much for that—for if so be that I set on't, I'll do't. But only for the present, 'tis sufficient till further acquaintance, that's all—your servant.

Mrs. Fain. Nay, I'll swear you shall never lose so favorable an opportunity, if I can help it. I'll leave you together, and lock the door.   [*Exit.*

Sir Wil. Nay, nay, cousin—I have forgot my gloves—what d'ye do?—S'heart, a'has locked the door indeed, I think—nay, Cousin Fainall, open the door—pshaw, what vixen trick is this?—Nay, now a'has seen me too.—Cousin, I made bold to pass through as it were —I think this door's enchanted!

Mrs. Mil. [*Repeating.*]

> "I prithee spare me, gentle boy,
> Press me no more for that slight toy."

Sir Wil. Anan? Cousin, your servant.

Mrs. Mil. [*Repeating.*]

> "That foolish trifle of a heart."

Sir Wilfull!

Sir Wil. Yes—your servant. No offence, I hope, cousin.

Mrs. Mil. [*Repeating.*]

> "I swear it will not do its part,
> Though thou dost thine, employest thy power and art."

Natural, easy Suckling!

Sir Wil. Anan? Suckling! no such suckling neither, cousin, nor stripling: I thank Heaven, I'm no minor.

Mrs. Mil. Ah, rustic, ruder than Gothic!

Sir Wil. Well, well I shall understand your lingo one of these days, cousin; in the meanwhile I must answer in plain English.

Mrs. Mil. Have you any business with me, Sir Wilfull?

Sir Wil. Not at present, cousin—yes I make bold to see, to come and know if that how you were disposed to fetch a walk this evening, if so be that I might not be troublesome, I would have sought a walk with you.

Mrs. Mil. A walk! what then?

Sir Wil. Nay, nothing—only for the walk's sake, that's all.

Mrs. Mil. I nauseate walking; 'tis a country diversion; I loathe the country, and everything that relates to it.

Sir Wil. Indeed! ha! look ye, look ye, you do? Nay, 'tis like you may—here are choice of pastimes here in town, as plays and the like; that must be confessed indeed.

Mrs. Mil. Ah l'étourdi! I hate the town too.

Sir Wil. Dear heart, that's much—ha! that you should hate 'em both! ha! 'tis like you may; there are some can't relish the town, and others can't away with the country—'tis you may be one of those, cousin.

Mrs. Mil. Ha! ha! ha! yes, 'tis like I may.—You have nothing further to say to me?

Sir Wil. Not at present, cousin.—'Tis like when I have an opportunity to be more private—I may break my mind in some measure—I conjecture you partly guess—however, that's as time shall try—but spare to speak and spare to speed, as they say.

Mrs. Mil. If it is of no great importance, Sir Wilfull, you will oblige me to leave me; I have just now a little business—

Sir Wil. Enough, enough, cousin: yes, yes, all a case—when you're disposed: now's as well as another time; and another time as well as now. All's one for that—yes, yes, if your concerns call you, there's no haste; it will keep cold, as they say.—Cousin, your servant—I think this door's locked.

Mrs. Mil. You may go this way, sir.

Sir Wil. Your servant; then with your leave I'll return to my company.   [*Exit.*

Mrs. Mil. Ay, ay; ha! ha! ha!

"Like Phœbus sung the no less amorous boy."

Enter MIRABELL.

Mir.   "Like Daphne she, as lovely and as coy."

Do you lock yourself up from me, to make my search more curious? or is this pretty artifice contrived to signify that here the chase must end, and my pursuits be crowned? For you can fly no further.

Mrs. Mil. Vanity! no—I'll fly, and be followed to the last moment. Though I am upon the very verge of matrimony, I expect you should solicit me as much as if I were wavering at the grate of a monastery, with one foot over the threshold. I'll be solicited to the very last, nay, and afterwards.

Mir. What, after the last?

Mrs. Mil. Oh, I should think I was poor and had nothing to bestow, if I were reduced to an inglorious ease, and freed from the agreeable fatigues of solicitation.

Mir. But do not you know, that when favours are conferred upon instant and tedious solicitation, that they diminish in their value, and that both the giver loses the grace, and the receiver lessens his pleasure?

Mrs. Mil. I may be in things of common application; but never sure in love. Oh, I hate a lover that can dare to think he draws a moment's air, independent of the bounty of his mistress. There is not so impudent a thing in nature, as the saucy look of an assured man, confident of success. The pedantic arrogance of a very husband has not so pragmatical an air. Ah! I'll never marry, unless I am first made sure of my will and pleasure.

Mir. Would you have 'em both before marriage? or will you be contented with the first now, and stay for the other till after grace?

Mrs. Mil. Ah! don't be impertinent.—My dear liberty, shall I leave thee? my faithful solitude, my darling contemplation, must I bid you then adieu? Ay-h adieu—my morning thoughts, agreeable wakings, indolent slumbers, all ye *douceurs*, ye *sommeils du matin*, *adieu?*—I can't do't, 'tis more than impossible—positively, Mirabell, I'll lie abed in a morning as long as I please.

Mir. Then I'll get up in a morning as early as I please.

Mrs. Mil. Ah! idle creature, get up when you will—and d'ye hear, I won't be called names after I'm married; positively I won't be called names.

Mir. Names!

Mrs. Mil. Ay, as wife, spouse, my dear, joy, jewel, love, sweetheart, and the rest of that nauseous can't, in which men and their wives are so fulsomely familiar—I shall never bear that—good Mirabell, don't let us be familiar or fond, nor kiss before folks, like my Lady Fadler and Sir Francis: nor go to Hyde-park together the first Sunday in a new chariot, to provoke eyes and whispers, and then never to be seen there together again; as if we were proud of one another the first week, and ashamed of one another ever after. Let us never visit together, nor go to a play together; but let us be very strange and well-bred: let us be as strange as if we had been married a great while; and as well-bred as if we were not married at all.

Mir. Have you any more conditions to offer? Hitherto your demands are pretty reasonable.

Mrs. Mil. Trifles!—As, liberty to pay and receive visits to and from whom I please; to write and receive letters, without interrogatories or wry faces on your part; to wear what I please; and choose conversation with regard only to my own taste; to have no obligation upon me to converse with wits that I don't like, because they are your acquaintance: or to be intimate with fools, because they may be your relations. Come to dinner when I please; dine in my dressing-room when I'm out of humour, without giving a reason. To have my closet inviolate; to be sole empress of my tea-table, which you must never presume to approach without first asking leave. And lastly, wherever I am, you shall always knock at the door before you come in. These articles subscribed, if I continue to endure you a little longer, I may by degrees dwindle into a wife.

Mir. Your bill of fare is something advanced in this latter account. —Well, have I liberty to offer conditions—that when you are dwindled into a wife, I may not be beyond measure enlarged into a husband?

Mrs. Mil. You have free leave; propose your utmost, speak and spare not.

Mir. I thank you.—*Imprimis* then, I covenant, that your acquaintance be general; that you admit no sworn confidant, or intimate of your own sex; no she friend to screen her affairs under your countenance, and tempt you to make trial of a mutual secrecy. No decoy duck to wheedle you a fop-scrambling to the play in a mask—then bring you home in a pretended fright, when you think you shall be found out—and rail at me for missing the play, and disappointing the frolic which you had to pick me up, and prove my constancy.

Mrs. Mil. Detestable *imprimis!* I go to the play in a mask!

Mir. *Item,* I article, that you continue to like your own face, as long as I shall: and while it passes current with me, that you endeavour not to new-coin it. To which end, together with all vizards for the day, I prohibit all masks for the night, made of oiled-skins, and I know not what—hogs' bones, hares' gall, pig-water, and the marrow of a roasted cat. In short, I forbid all commerce with the gentlewoman in what d'ye call it court. *Item,* I shut my doors against all bawds with baskets, and pennyworths of muslin, china, fans, atlasses, etc.—*Item,* when you shall be breeding—

Mrs. Mil. Ah! name it not.

Mir. Which may be presumed with a blessing on our endeavours.

Mrs. Mil. Odious endeavours!

Mir. I denounce against all strait lacing, squeezing for a shape, till you mould my boy's head like a sugar-loaf, and instead of a man

child, make me father to a crooked billet. Lastly, to the dominion of
the tea-table I submit—but with proviso, that you exceed not in your
province; but restrain yourself to native and simple tea-table drinks,
as tea, chocolate, and coffee: as likewise to genuine and authorised
tea-table talk—such as mending fashions, spoiling reputations, railing at absent friends, and so forth—but that on no account you
encroach upon the men's prerogative, and presume to drink healths,
or toast fellows; for prevention of which I banish all foreign forces,
all auxiliaries to the tea-table, as orange-brandy, all aniseed, cin-
namon, citron, and Barbadoes waters, together with ratafia, and the
most noble spirit of clary—but for cowslip wine, poppy water, and
all dormitives, those I allow.—These provisos admitted, in other
things I may prove a tractable and complying husband.

Mrs. Mil. O horrid provisos! filthy strong-waters! I toast fellows!
odious men! I hate your odious provisos.

Mir. Then we are agreed! shall I kiss your hand upon the contract?
And here comes one to be a witness to the sealing of the deed.

Enter Mrs. FAINALL.

Mrs. Mil. Fainall, what shall I do? shall I have him? I think I
must have him.

Mrs. Fain. Ay, ay, take him, take him, what should you do?

Mrs. Mil. Well then—I'll take my death I'm in a horrid fright—
Fainall, I shall never say it—well—I think—I'll endure you.

Mrs. Fain. Fy! fy! have him, have him, and tell him so in plain
terms: for I am sure you have a mind to him.

Mrs. Mil. Are you? I think I have—and the horrid man looks as
if he thought so too—well, you ridiculous thing you, I'll have you—
I won't be kissed, nor I won't be thanked—here kiss my hand though.
—So, hold your tongue now, don't say a word.

Mrs. Fain. Mirabell, there's a necessity for your obedience;—you
have neither time to talk nor stay. My mother is coming; and in my
conscience if she should see you, would fall into fits, and maybe not
recover time enough to return to Sir Rowland, who, as Foible tells
me, is in a fair way to succeed. Therefore spare your ecstacies for
another occasion, and slip down the back-stairs, where Foible waits
to consult you.

Mrs. Mil. Ay, go, go. In the mean time I suppose you have said
something to please me.

Mir. I am all obedience. [*Exit.*

Mrs. Fain. Yonder Sir Wilfull's drunk, and so noisy that my mother has been forced to leave Sir Rowland to appease him; but he answers her only with singing and drinking—what they may have done by this time I know not; but Petulant and he were upon quarrelling as I came by.

Mrs. Mil. Well, if Mirabell should not make a good husband, I am a lost thing,—for I find I love him violently.

Mrs. Fain. So it seems; for you mind not what's said to you.—If you doubt him, you had best take up with Sir Wilfull.

Mrs. Mil. How can you name that superannuated lubber? foh!

The two wooing scenes from Love for Love *which follow invite comparison not only with each other but with the matched pair we have just given from* The Way of the World. *Tattle is a half-witted beau, vain of his amours, Prue a silly awkward girl, step-daughter to Mrs. Foresight. The latter for reasons of her own wishes to prevent Prue's supposed marriage to Sailor Ben, half home-bred and half sea-bred son of Sir Samson Legend. She, therefore, is more than willing that the girl should be seduced by Tattle, who is more than willing to accommodate. Later she and Tattle, the male and female rounders, are tricked into marrying each other. In the second scene Ben follows his father's orders like a good seaman, but Prue is already conditioned against his salty love-making.*

Love for Love

ACT II, Scene II

Enter Tattle *and* Miss Prue *to* Mrs. Foresight *and* Mrs. Frail.

Prue. Mother, mother, mother, look you here!

Mrs. Fore. Fy, fy, miss! how you bawl.—Besides, I have told you, you must not call me mother.

Prue. What must I call you then? are you not my father's wife?

Mrs. Fore. Madam; you must say madam.—By my soul, I shall fancy myself old indeed, to have this great girl call me mother!— Well, but, miss, what are you so overjoyed at?

Prue. Look you here, madam, then, what Mr. Tattle has given me. —Look you here, cousin, here's a snuff-box; nay, there's snuff in't; —here, will you have any?—Oh good! how sweet it is.—Mr. Tattle is all over sweet, his peruke is sweet, and his gloves are sweet, and his handkerchief is sweet, pure sweet, sweeter than roses.—Smell him, mother, madam, I mean.—He gave me this ring for a kiss.

Tat. O fy, miss! you must not kiss and tell.

Prue. Yes; I may tell my mother.—And he says he'll give me something to make me smell so.—[*To* TATTLE.] Oh pray lend me your handkerchief.—Smell, cousin; he says, he'll give me something that will make my smocks smell this way.—Is not it pure?—It's better than lavender, mun—I'm resolved I won't let nurse put any more lavender among my smocks—ha, cousin?

Mrs. Frail. Fy, miss! amongst your linen, you must say;—you must never say smock.

Prue. Why, it is not bawdy, is it, cousin?

Tat. Oh, madam, you are too severe upon miss; you must not find fault with her pretty simplicity, it becomes her strangely.—Pretty miss, don't let 'em persuade you out of your innocency.

Mrs. Fore. Oh, demn you, toad!—I wish you don't persuade her out of her innocency.

Tat. Who I, madam?—Oh Lord, how can your ladyship have such a thought—sure you don't know me?

Mrs. Frail. Ah, devil! sly devil!—He's as close, sister, as a confessor. —He thinks we don't observe him.

Mrs. Fore. A cunning cur! how soon he could find out a fresh harmless creature! and left us, sister, presently.

Tat. Upon reputation—

Mrs. Fore. They're all so, sister, these men:—they love to have the spoiling of a young thing, they are as fond of it, as of being first in the fashion, or of seeing a new play the first day.—I warrant it would break Mr. Tattle's heart, to think that anybody else should be beforehand with him.

Tat. Oh Lord, I swear I would not for the world—

Mrs. Frail. O hang you! who'll believe you?—You'd be hanged before you'd confess—we know you—she's very pretty!—Lord, what pure red and white!—she looks so wholesome;—ne'er stir, I don't know, but I fancy, if I were a man—

Prue. How you love to jeer one, cousin!

Mrs. Fore. Hark ye, sister.—By my soul the girl is spoiled already —d'ye think she'll ever endure a great lubberly tarpaulin!—gad, I warrant you, she won't let him come near her, after Mr. Tattle.

Mrs. Frail. O' my soul, I'm afraid not—eh!—filthy creature, that smells of all pitch and tar.—[*To* TATTLE.] Devil take you, you confounded toad!—why did you see her before she was married?

Mrs. Fore. Nay, why did we let him?—My husband will hang us; —he'll think we brought 'em acquainted.

Mrs. Frail. Come, faith, let us begone.—If my brother Foresight should find us with them, he'd think so, sure enough.

Mrs. Fore. So he would—but then leaving 'em together is as bad. —And he's such a sly devil, he'll never miss an opportunity.

Mrs. Frail. I don't care; I won't be seen in't.

Mrs. Fore. Well, if you should, Mr. Tattle, you'll have a world to answer for;—remember I wash my hands of it.—I'm thoroughly innocent.   [*Exeunt* Mrs. FORESIGHT *and* Mrs. FRAIL.

Prue. What makes 'em go away, Mr. Tattle? what do they mean, do you know?

Tat. Yes, my dear,—I think I can guess;—but hang me if I know the reason of it.

Prue. Come, must not we go too?

Tat. No, no, they don't mean that.

Prue. No! what then? what shall you and I do together?

Tat. I must make love to you, pretty miss; will you let me make love to you?

Prue. Yes, if you please.

Tat. [*Aside.*] Frank, egad, at least. What a pox does Mrs. Foresight mean by this civility? Is it to make a fool of me? or does she leave us together out of good morality, and do as she would be done by?—Gad, I'll understand it so.

Prue. Well; and how will you make love to me? come, I long to have you begin. Must I make love too? you must tell me how.

Tat. You must let me speak, miss, you must not speak first; I must ask you questions, and you must answer.

Prue. What, is it like the catechism?—come then, ask me.

Tat. D'ye think you can love me?

Prue. Yes.

Tat. Pooh! pox! you must not say yes already; I shan't care a farthing for you then in a twinkling.

Prue. What must I say then?

Tat. Why, you must say no, or you believe not, or you can't tell.

Prue. Why, must I tell a lie then?

Tat. Yes, if you'd be well-bred;—all well-bred persons lie.—Besides, you are a woman, you must never speak what you think: your words must contradict your thoughts; but your actions may contradict your words. So, when I ask you, if you can love me, you must say no, but you must love me too. If I tell you you are handsome, you must deny it, and say I flatter you. But you must think yourself more charming than I speak you: and like me, for the beauty which I say you have, as much as if I had it myself. If I ask you to kiss me, you must be angry, but you must not refuse me. If I ask you for more, you must be more angry,—but more complying; and as soon as ever I make you say you'll cry out, you must be sure to hold your tongue.

Prue. O Lord, I swear this is pure!—I like it better than our old-fashioned country way of speaking one's mind; and must not you lie too?

Tat. Hum!—Yes; but you must believe I speak truth.

Prue. O Gemini! well, I always had a great mind to tell lies: but they frighted me, and said it was a sin.

Tat. Well, my pretty creature; will you make me happy by giving me a kiss?

Prue. No, indeed; I'm angry at you.   [*Runs and kisses him.*

Tat. Hold, hold, that's pretty well;—but you should not have given it me, but have suffered me to have taken it.

Prue. Well, we'll do't again.

Tat. With all my heart. Now then, my little angel!   [*Kisses her.*

Prue. Pish!

Tat. That's right—again, my charmer.   [*Kisses her again.*

Prue. O fy! nay, now I can't abide you.

Tat. Admirable! that was as well as if you had been born and bred in Covent Garden. And won't you show me, pretty miss, where your bedchamber is?

Prue. No, indeed, won't I; but I'll run there and hide myself from you behind the curtains.

Tat. I'll follow you.

Prue. Ah, but I'll hold the door with both hands, and be angry; and you shall push me down before you come in.

Tat. No, I'll come in first, and push you down afterwards.

Prue. Will you? then I'll be more angry, and more complying.

Tat. Then I'll make you cry out.

Prue. Oh, but you shan't; for I'll hold my tongue.

Tat. Oh, my dear apt scholar!

Prue. Well, now I'll run, and make more haste than you.

Tat You shall not fly so fast as I'll pursue.   [*Exeunt.*

ACT III, Scene II

Ben *and* Prue.

Ben. Come, mistress, will you please to sit down? for an you stand astern a that'n, we shall never grapple together.—Come, I'll haul a chair; there, an you please to sit I'll sit by you.

Prue. You need not sit so near one; if you have anything to say I can hear you farther off, I an't deaf.

Ben. Why, that's true, as you say; nor I an't dumb; I can be heard as far as another;—I'll heave off to please you.—[*Sits farther off.*] An we were a league asunder, I'd undertake to hold discourse with you, an 'twere not a main high wind indeed, and full in my teeth. Look you, forsooth, I am, as it were, bound for that land of matrimony; 'tis a voyage, d'ye see, that was none of my seeking, I was commanded by father, and if you like of it mayhap I may steer into your harbour. How say you, mistress? The short of the thing is, that if you like me, and I like you, we may chance to swing in a hammock together.

Prue. I don't know what to say to you, nor I don't care to speak with you at all.

Ben. No? I'm sorry for that.—But pray, why are you so scornful?

Prue. As long as one must not speak one's mind, one had better not speak at all, I think, and truly I won't tell a lie for the matter.

Ben. Nay, you say true in that, 'tis but a folly to lie: for to speak one thing, and to think just the contrary way, is, as it were, to look one way and row another. Now, for my part, d'ye see, I'm for carrying things above board, I'm not for keeping anything under hatches, —so that if you ben't as willing as I, say so a' God's name, there's no harm done. Mayhap you may be shamefaced? some maidens, tho'f they love a man well enough, yet they don't care to tell'n so to's face: if that's the case, why silence gives consent.

Prue. But I'm sure it is not so, for I'll speak sooner than you should believe that; and I'll speak truth, though one should always tell a lie to a man; and I don't care, let my father do what he will; I'm too big to be whipped so I'll tell you plainly I don't like you, nor love you at all, nor never will, that's more: so, there's your answer for you; and don't trouble me no more, you ugly thing!

Ben. Look you, young woman, you may learn to give good words however. I spoke you fair, d'ye see, and civil.—As for your love or your liking, I don't value it of a rope's end;—and mayhap I like you as little as you do me.—What I said was in obedience to father; gad, I fear a whipping no more than you do. But I tell you one thing, if you should give such language at sea you'd have a cat o' nine-tails laid across your shoulders. Flesh! who are you? You heard t'other handsome young woman speak civilly to me, of her own accord: whatever you think of yourself, gad, I don't think you are any more to compare to her than a can of small beer to a bowl of punch.

Prue. Well, and there's a handsome gentleman, and a fine gentleman, and a sweet gentleman, that was here, that loves me, and I love him; and if he sees you speak to me any more he'll thrash your jacket for you, he will, you great sea-calf!

Ben. What, do you mean that fair-weather spark that was here just now? will he thrash my jacket?—let'n—let'n. But an he comes near me, mayhap I may giv'n a salt eel for's supper, for all that. What does father mean to leave me alone as soon as I come home, with such a dirty dowdy? Sea-calf! I an't calf enough to lick your chalked face, you cheese-curd you!—Marry thee! 'oons, I'll marry a Lapland witch as soon, and live upon selling contrary winds and wrecked vessels.

Prue. I won't be called names, nor I won't be abused thus, so I won't.—If I were a man [*Cries*], you durst not talk at this rate;—no, you durst not, you stinking tar-barrel!

Enter Mrs. FORESIGHT *and* Mrs. FRAIL.

Mrs. Fore. [*Aside to* Mrs. FRAIL.] They have quarreled just as we could wish.

Ben. Tar-barrel? let your sweetheart there call me so if he'll take your part, your Tom Essence, and I'll say something to him; gad, I'll lace his musk doublet for him! I'll make him stink! he shall smell more like a weasel than a civet cat afore I ha' done with 'en.

Mrs. Fore. Bless me, what's the matter, miss? What, does she cry? —Mr. Benjamin, what have you done to her?

Ben. Let her cry: the more she cries, the less she'll—she has been gathering foul weather in her mouth, and now it rains out at her eyes.

Mrs. Fore. Come, miss, come along with me, and tell me, poor child.

Mrs. Frail. Lord, what shall we do? there's my brother Foresight and Sir Sampson coming.—Sister, do you take miss down into the parlour, and I'll carry Benjamin into my chamber, for they must not know that they are fallen out.—Come, sir, will you venture yourself with me?   [*Looking kindly on him.*

Ben. Venture, mess, and that I will, though 'twere to sea in a storm.   [*Exeunt.*

SIR JOHN VANBRUGH

The following scenes from Vanbrugh's best play display the personality and behavior of a married debauchee who, in the course of the action, is properly paid off for his mistreatment of his wife. The satire is coarse but effective. We are reminded of more than one anecdote of the behavior of Restoration characters in real life and of John Milton's comment on such disgraces in Paradise Lost:

> ". . . in luxurious cities, where the noise
> Of riot ascends above their loftiest towers,
> And injury and outrage; and when night
> Darkens the streets, then wander forth the sons
> Of Belial, flown with insolence and wine."

The Provoked Wife

ACT I, Scene I—Sir John Brute's *House*

Enter Sir John, *solus.*

What cloying meat is love,—when matrimony's the sauce to it. Two years' marriage has debauched my five senses. Every thing I see, every thing I hear, every thing I feel, every thing I smell, and every thing I taste—methinks has wife in't.

No boy was ever so weary of his tutor; no girl of her bib; no nun of doing penance nor old maid of being chaste, as I am of being married.

Sure there's a secret curse entailed upon the very name of wife. My lady is a young lady, a fine lady, a witty lady, a virtuous lady—and yet I hate her. There is but one thing on earth I loath beyond her: That's fighting. Would my courage come up but to a fourth part of my ill nature, I'd stand buff to her relations, and thrust her out of doors.

But marriage has sunk me down to such an ebb of resolution, I dare not draw my sword, tho' even to get rid of my wife. But here she comes.

Enter Lady Brute.

Lady. Do you dine at home to day, Sir John?

Sir Joh. Why, do you expect I should tell you, what I don't know my self?

Lady. I thought there was no harm in asking you.

Sir Joh. If thinking wrong were an excuse for impertinence, women might be justified in most things they say or do.

Lady. I'm sorry I have said any thing to displease you.

Sir Joh. Sorrow for things past, is of as little importance to me as my dining at home or abroad ought to be to you.

Lady B. My enquiry was only that I might have provided what you liked.

Sir Joh. Six to four you had been in the wrong there again, for what I liked yesterday I don't like to day, and what I like to day, 'tis odds I mayn't like to morrow.

Lady B. But if I had ask'd you what you liked?

Sir Joh. Why then there would have been more asking about it, than the thing was worth.

Lady B. I wish I did but know how I might please you.

Sir Joh. Ay, but that sort of knowledge is not a wife's talent.

Lady B. What ever my talent is, I'm sure my will has ever been to make you easy.

Sir Joh. If women were to have their wills, the world would be finely governed.

Lady B. What reason have I given you to use me as you do of late? It once was otherwise: You married me for love.

Sir Joh. And you me for money; So you have your reward, and I have mine.

Lady B. What is it that disturbs you?

Sir Joh. A parson.

Lady B. Why, what has he done to you?

Sir Joh. He has married me.　　　　　　　　　　［*Exit* Sir JOHN.

Lady BRUTE, *sola.*

The Devil's in the fellow I think—I was told before I married him, that thus 'twould be. But I thought I had charms enough to govern him and that where there was an estate a woman must needs be happy; so my vanity has deceived me, and my ambition has made me uneasy. But some comfort still; if one would be revenged of him, these are good times; a woman may have a gallant, and a separate maintenance too—the surly puppy—yet he's a fool for't: For hitherto he has been no monster, but who knows how far he may provoke me? I never lov'd him, yet I have been ever true to him; and that, in spite of all the attacks of art and nature upon a poor weak woman's heart, in favour of a tempting lover.

Methinks so noble a defense as I have made, should be rewarded with a better usage—Or who can tell?—Perhaps a good part of what I suffer from my husband may be a judgment upon me for my cruelty to my lover.—Lord, with what pleasure could I indulge that thought, were there but a possibility of finding arguments to make it good.—And how do I know but there may?—Let me see—What opposes?—My matrimonial vow?—Why, what did I vow? I think I promised to be true to my husband.

Well; and he promised to be kind to me.

But he han't kept his word—

Why then I'm so absolved from mine—ay, that seems clear to me. The argument's good between the King and the People, why not between the husband and the wife? O, but that condition was not expressed.—No matter, it was understood.

Well, by all I see, If I argue the matter a little longer with my self, I shan't find so many bug-bears in the way, as I thought I should: Lord, what fine notions of virtue do we women take up upon the credit of old foolish philosophers. Virtue's its own reward, virtue's this, virtue's that;—virtue's an ass, and a gallant's worth forty on't.

ACT III, SCENE II—Lord BRUTE's *House*

Lord RAKE, Sir JOHN, &c., *at a table drinking.*

All. Huzza.

Lord R. Come, boys, charge again.—So—confusion to all order. Here's liberty of conscience.

All. Huzza.

Lord R. I'll sing you a song I made this morning to this purpose.

Sir J. 'Tis wicked I hope.

Col. B. Don't my Lord tell you he made it?

Sir J. Well then, let's have it.

Lord R. [*Sings.*]

I

What a pother of late
Have they kept in the state
    About setting our consciences free.
A bottle has more
Dispensation in store,
    Than the King and the State can decree.

II

When my head's full of wine,
I o'er flow with design
   And know no penal laws that can curb me.
What e'er I devise,
Seems good in my eyes,
   And religion ne'er dares to disturb me.

III

No saucy remorse
Intrudes in my course,
   Nor impertinent notions of evil:
So there's claret in store,
In peace I've my whore,
   And in peace I jog on to the devil.

All. [*Sing.*] So there's claret, &c.

Lord R. Well, how do you like it, gentlemen?

All. O, admirable.

Sir J. I would not give a fig for a song that is not full of sin and impudence.

Lord R. Then my muse is to your taste. But drink away; the night steals upon us; we shall want time to be lewd in. Hey, page, sally out, sirrah, and see what's doing in the camp; we'll beat up their quarters presently.

Page. I'll bring your Lordship an exact account.   [*Exit* Page.

Lord R. Now let the spirit of clary go round. Fill me a brimmer. Here's to our forlorn-hope. Courage knight; victory attends you.

Sir J. And laurels shall crown me. Drink away and be damned.

Lord R. Again boys; t'other glass, and damn morality.

Sir J. [*Drunk.*] Ay—damn morality—and damn the watch. And let the constable be married.

All. Huzza.

Re-enter Page.

Lord R. How are the streets inhabited, sirrah?

Page. My Lord, it's Sunday night; they are full of drunken citizens.

Lord R. Along then boys, we shall have a feast.

Col. B. Along noble knight.

Sir J. Ay—along bully; and he that says Sir John Brute is not as drunk and as religious as the drunkenest citizen of 'em all—is a liar, and the son of a whore.

Col. B. Why, that was bravely spoke, and like a free-born English-man.

Sir J. What's that to you, Sir, whether I am an English man or a French man?

Col. B. Zoons, you are not angry, sir?

Sir J. Zoons, I am angry, sir,—for if I am a free-born English man, what have you to do, even to talk of my privileges?

Lord R. Why prithee knight, don't quarrel here; leave private animosities to be decided by day light; let the night be employed against the public enemy.

Sir J. My Lord, I respect you, because you are a man of quality: But I'll make that fellow know I am within a hair's breadth as absolute by my priveleges, as the King of France is by his prerogative. He by his prerogative takes money where it is not his due; I, by my privelege refuse paying it, where I owe it. Liberty and property and Old England, Huzza.

[*Exit* Sir J. *reeling, all following him.*

All. Huzza.

ACT IV, SCENE I—*Covent-Garden*

Enter Lord RAKE, Sir JOHN, *&c., with swords drawn.*

Lord R. Is the dog dead?

Bully. No, damn him, I heard him wheeze.

Lord R. How the witch his wife howled!

Bully. Ay, she'll alarm the watch presently.

Lord R. Appear, Knight, then; come, you have a good cause to fight for, there's a man murdered.

Sir John. Is there? Then let his ghost be satisfied: for I'll sacrifice a constable to it presently; and burn his body upon his wooden chair.

Enter a Taylor, *with a Bundle under his Arm.*

Bully. How now? What have we got here? A thief?

Taylor. No an't please you; I'm no thief.

Lord R. That we'll see presently; Here, let the general examine him.

Sir John. Ay, ay, let me examine him; and I'll lay a hundred pound I find him guilty in spite of his teeth—for he looks—like a —sneaking rascal. Come sirrah, without equivocation, or mental reservation, tell me of what opinion you are, and what calling; for by them—I shall guess at your morals.

Taylor. An't please you, I'm a dissenting journeyman taylor.

Sir John. Then sirrah, you love lying by your religion, and theft by your trade. And so, that your punishment may be suitable to your crimes,—I'll have you first gagged,—and then hanged.

Taylor. Pray good worthy gentlemen, don't abuse me; indeed I'm an honest man, and a good workman, though I say it, that should not say it.

Sir John. No words, sirrah, but attend your fate.

Lord R. Let me see what's in that bundle.

Taylor. An't please you, it's the doctor of the parish's gown.

Lord R. The doctor's gown!—Hark you, Knight, you won't stick at abusing the clergy, will you?

Sir John. No, I'm drunk, and I'll abuse any thing—but my wife; and her I name—with reverence.

Lord R. Then you shall wear this gown, whilst you charge the watch. That though the blows fall upon you, the scandal may light upon the Church.

Sir John. A generous design—by all the gods—give it me.

[*Takes the gown and puts it on.*

Taylor. O dear gentlemen, I shall be quite undone, if you take the gown.

Sir John. Retire, sirrah; and since you carry off your skin—go home, and be happy.

Taylor. [*Pausing.*] I think I had even as good follow the gentleman's friendly advice. For if I dispute any longer, who knows but the whim may take him to case me. These courtiers are fuller of tricks than they are of money; they'll sooner cut a man's throat, than pay his bill. [*Exit* Taylor.

Sir John. So, how d'ye like my shapes now?

Lord R. This will do to a miracle; he looks like a bishop going to the Holy War. But to your arms, gentlemen, the enemy appears.

Enter Constable *and* Watch.

Watchman. Stand! Who goes there? Come before the constable.

Sir John. The constable's a rascal—and you are the son of a whore.

Watchman. A good civil answer for a parson, truly.

Constable. Methinks sir, a man of your coat might set a better example

Sir John. Sirrah, I'll make you know—there are men of my coat can set as bad examples—as you can do, you dog you.

[*Sir* JOHN *strikes the* Constable. *They knock him down, disarm him and seize him.* Lord R. &c., *run away.*

Constable. So, we have secured the parson however.

Sir John. Blood and blood—and blood.

Watchman. Lord have mercy upon us: how the wicked wretch raves of blood. I'll warrant he has been murdering some body tonight.

Sir John. Sirrah, there's nothing got by murder but a halter: my talent lies towards drunkenness and simony.

Watchman. Why, that now was spoke like a man of parts, neighbours: it's pity he should be so disguised.

Sir John. You lie,—I am not disguised; for I am drunk barefaced.

Watchman. Look you there again—this is a mad parson, Mr. Constable, I'll lay a pot of ale upon's head, he's a good preacher.

Constable. Come sir, out of respect to your calling, I shan't put you into the round-house; but we must secure you in our drawing-room till morning, that you may do no mischief. So, come along.

Sir John. You may put me where you will, sirrah, now you have overcome me—But if I can't do mischief, I'll think of mischief—in spite of your teeth, you dog you.   [*Exeunt.*

ACT IV, SCENE III—A Magistrate's *House*

Enter Constable, &c., *with* Sir JOHN.

Constable. Come along, sir, I thought to have let you slip this morning, because you were a minister; but you are as drunk and as abusive as ever. We'll see what the Justice of the Peace will say to you.

Sir John. And you shall see what I'll say to the Justice of the Peace, sirrah.   [*They knock at the door.*

Enter Servant.

Constab. Pray acquaint his worship, we have got an unruly parson here: we are unwilling to expose him, but don't know what to do with him.

Servant. I'll acquaint my master.   [*Exit* Servant.

Sir John. You—Constable—What damn'd Justice is this?

Constab. One that will take care of you, I warrant you.

Enter Justice.

Justice. Well, Mr. Constable; What's the disorder here?

Constab. An't please your Worship—

Sir John. Let me speak and be damn'd: I'm a divine, and can unfold mysteries better than you can do.

Justice. Sadness, sadness, a minister so overtaken. Pray sir, give the constable leave to speak, and I'll hear you very patiently; I assure you, sir, I will.

Sir John. Sir,—you are a very civil magistrate. Your most humble servant.

Constab. An't please your worship then, he has attempted to beat the watch tonight, and swore—

Sir John. You lie.

Justice. Hold, pray sir, a little.

Sir John. Sir, your very humble servant.

Constab. Indeed, sir, he came at us without any provocation, called us whores and rogues, and laid us on with a great quarter-staff. He was in my Lord Rake's company. They have been playing the devil tonight.

Justice. Hem—Hem—Pray Sir—May you be chaplain to my Lord?

Sir John. Sir—I presume—I may if I will.

Justice. My meaning, sir, is—Are you so?

Sir John. Sir,—You mean very well.

Justice. He hem—hem—Under favour, sir, pray answer me directly.

Sir John. Under favour, sir—Do you use to answer directly when you are drunk?

Justice. Good lack, good lack: Here's nothing to be got from him. Pray sir, may I crave your name?

Sir John. Sir,—My name's— [*He Hyccops.* Hyccop, sir.

Justice. Hyccop? Doctor Hyccop. I have known a great many country parsons of that name, especially down in the fens. Pray where do you live, sir?

Sir John. Here—and there, sir.

Justice. Why, what a strange man is this? Where do you preach, sir? Have you any cure?

Sir John. Sir—I have—a very good cure—for a clap, at your service.

Justice. Lord have mercy upon us.

Sir John. [*Aside.*] This fellow does ask so many impertinent questions, I believe i'gad, 'tis the justice's wife, in the justice's clothes.

Justice. Mr. Constable, I vow and protest, I don't know what to do with him.

Constab. Truly, he has been but a troublesome guest to us all night.

Justice. I think, I had even best let him go about his business, for I'm unwilling to expose him.

Constab. Even what your Worship thinks fit.

Sir John. Sir,—not to interrupt Mr. Constable, I have a small favour to ask.

Justice. Sir, I open both my ears to you.

Sir John. Sir, your very humble servant. I have a little urgent business calls upon me; And therefore I desire the favour of you, to bring matters to a conclusion.

Justice. Sir, If I were sure that business were not to commit more disorders, I would release you.

Sir John. None,—By my priesthood.

Justice. Then, Mr. Constable, you may discharge him.

Sir John. Sir, your very humble servant. If you please to accept of a bottle—

Justice. I thank you kindly, sir; but I never drink in a morning. Good-by to ye, sir, good-by to ye.

Sir John. Good-by t'ye, good sir.   [*Exit* Justice.
So—now, Mr. Constable, shall you and I go pick up a whore together.

Constab. No, thank you, sir; my wife's enough to satisfy any reasonable man.

Sir John. [*Aside.*] He, he, he, he, he,—The fool is married then. Well, you won't go?

Constab. Not I, truly.

Sir John. Then I'll go by my self; and you and your wife may be damn.   [*Exit* Sir JOHN.
          [Constable *gazing after him.*

Constab. Why God-a-mercy, Parson.   [*Exeunt.*

2 *Belles-Lettres*

JOHN DRYDEN

The essay of Dramatic Poesy, from which the following selections are taken, represents Dryden at his best as critic and prose writer. The subject is the principles of the dramatic art, not dogmatically laid down but debated from varying points of view. There is the question of the appropriateness of rhyme in tragedy, of the need of strict adherence to the classical unities, of the relative merits of the ancients and the moderns and of the English plays of the last age and those of the present. Although the models for the discussion are French, Dryden handles the ideas with English freedom and makes the first great contribution in the language to the art of literary criticism. His style is clear and vigorous, breaking entirely with the involved rhetoric of the earlier seventeenth century. The dialogue form goes back to Plato, and though it is a far cry from these easy Englishmen to barefoot Socrates and the Greek gentlemen who walked with him from the Piraeus, there is something in Dryden's attitude and manner which makes them kin.

Of War and Poetry

It was that memorable day, in the first summer of the late war, when our navy engaged the Dutch; a day wherein the two most mighty and best appointed fleets which any age had ever seen disputed the command of the greater half of the globe, the commerce of nations, and the riches of the universe: while these vast floating bodies, on either side, moved against each other in parallel lines, and our countrymen, under the happy conduct of his royal highness, went breaking, by little and little, into the line of the enemies; the noise of the cannon from both navies reached our ears about the city, so that all men being alarmed with it, and in a dreadful suspense of the event, which they knew was then deciding, everyone went following the sound as his fancy led him; and leaving the town almost

232

empty, some took towards the park, some cross the river, others down it; all seeking the noise in the depth of silence.

Among the rest, it was the fortune of Eugenius, Crites, Lisideius, and Neander, to be in company together; three of them persons whom their wit and quality have made known to all the town; and whom I have chose to hide under these borrowed names, that they may not suffer by so ill a relation as I am going to make of their discourse.

Taking then a barge, which a servant of Lisideius had provided for them, they made haste to shoot the bridge, and left behind them that great fall of waters which hindered them from hearing what they desired: after which, having disengaged themselves from many vessels which rode at anchor in the Thames, and almost blocked up the passage towards Greenwich, they ordered the watermen to let fall their oars more gently; and then, everyone favoring his own curiosity with a strict silence, it was not long ere they perceived the air to break about them like the noise of distant thunder, or of swallows in a chimney: those little undulations of sound, though almost vanishing before they reached them, yet still seeming to retain somewhat of their first horror, which they had betwixt the fleets. After they had attentively listened till such time as the sound by little and little went from them, Eugenius, lifting up his head, and taking notice of it, was the first who congratulated to the rest that happy omen of our nation's victory: adding, that we had but this to desire in confirmation of it, that we might hear no more of that noise, which was now leaving the English coast. When the rest had concurred in the same opinion, Crites, a person of a sharp judgment, and somewhat too delicate a taste in wit, which the world have mistaken in him for ill-nature, said, smiling to us, that if the concernment of this battle had not been so exceeding great, he could scarce have wished the victory at the price he knew he must pay for it, in being subject to the reading and hearing of so many ill verses as he was sure would be made on that subject. Adding, that no argument could scape some of those eternal rhymers, who watch a battle with more diligence than the ravens and birds of prey; and the worst of them surest to be first upon the quarry: while the better able, either out of modesty writ not at all, or set that due value upon their poems, as to let them be often desired and long expected. "There are some of those impertinent people of whom you speak," answered Lisideius, "who to my knowledge are already so provided, either way, that they can produce not only a panegyric upon the victory, but, if need be, a funeral elegy on the duke; wherein, after they have crowned his valor with many laurels, they will at last deplore the odds under which he fell, concluding that his courage deserved a better destiny." All the company smiled at the conceit of Lisideius; but Crites, more eager than before, began to make particular exceptions against some writers, and said the public magistrate ought to send betimes to forbid them; and that it concerned the peace and quiet of all honest people, that ill poets should be as well silenced as seditious preachers.

Of Modern Wit

I should now speak of the refinement of Wit; but I have been so large on the former subject that I am forced to contract myself in this. I will therefore only observe to you that the wit of the last age was yet more incorrect than their language. Shakespeare, who many times has written better than any poet, in any language, is yet so far from writing wit always, or expressing that wit according to the dignity of the subject, that he writes, in many places, below the dullest writer of ours, or any precedent age. Never did any author precipitate himself from such height of thought to so low expressions as he often does. He is the very Janus of poets; he wears almost everywhere two faces; and you have scarce begun to admire the one ere you despise the other. Neither is the luxuriance of Fletcher (which his friends have taxed in him) a less fault than the carelessness of Shakespeare. He does not well always; and, when he does, he is a true Englishman; he knows not when to give over. If he wakes in one scene, he commonly slumbers in another; and, if he pleases you in the first three acts, he is frequently so tired with his labor that he goes heavily in the fourth, and sinks under his burden in the fifth.

For Ben Jonson, the most judicious of poets, he always writ properly, and as the character required; and I will not contest farther with my friends who call that wit: it being very certain that even folly itself, well represented, is wit in a larger signification; and that there is fancy, as well as judgment, in it, though not so much or noble: because all poetry being imitation, that of folly is a lower exercise of fancy, though perhaps as difficult as the other; for 'tis a kind of looking downward in the poet, and representing that part of mankind which is below him.

In these low characters of vice and folly lay the excellency of that inimitable writer; who, when at any time he aimed at wit in the

stricter sense, that is, sharpness of conceit, was forced either to borrow from the ancients, as to my knowledge he did very much from
Plautus; or, when he trusted himself alone, often fell into meanness
of expression. Nay, he was not free from the lowest and most grovel-
ing kind of wit, which we call clenches, of which *Every Man in his
Humor* is infinitely full; and, which is worse, the wittiest persons in
the drama speak them. His other comedies are not exempt from
them. Will you give me leave to name some few? Asper, in which
character he personates himself (and he neither was nor thought himself a fool), exclaiming against the ignorant judges of the age, speaks
thus:

> How monstrous and detested is't, to see
> A fellow, that has neither art nor brain,
> Sit like an *Aristarchus*, or *stark-ass*,
> Taking men's lines, with a *tobacco face*,
> In *snuff*, etc.

And presently after: *I mar'le whose wit 'twas to put a prologue in
yond Sackbut's mouth. They might well think he would be out of
tune, and yet you'd play upon him too.*—Will you have another of
the same stamp? *O, I cannot abide these limbs of* satin, *or rather*
Satan.

But, it may be, you will object that this was Asper, Macilente, or
Carlo Buffone: you shall, therefore, hear him speak in his own
person, and that in the two last lines or sting of an epigram. 'Tis
inscribed to *Fine Grand*, who, he says, was indebted to him for many
things which he reckons there; and concludes thus:

> Forty things more, dear *Grand*, which you know true,
> For which, or pay me quickly, or I'll pay you.

This was then the mode of wit, the vice of the age, and not Ben
Jonson's; for you see, a little before him, that admirable wit, Sir
Philip Sidney, perpetually playing with his words. In his time, I
believe, it ascended first into the pulpit, where (if you will give me
leave to clench too) it yet finds the benefit of its clergy; for they
are commonly the first corrupters of eloquence, and the last reformed
from vicious oratory; as a famous Italian has observed before me, in
his *Treatise of the Corruption of the Italian Tongue*; which he
principally ascribes to priests and preaching friars.

But, to conclude with what brevity I can, I will only add this, in
defense of our present writers, that, if they reach not some excellencies of Ben Jonson (which no age, I am confident, ever shall), yet,

at least, they are above that meanness of thought which I have taxed, and which is frequent in him.

That the wit of this age is much more courtly may easily be proved by viewing the characters of gentlemen which were written in the last. First, for Jonson:—Truewit, in *The Silent Woman*, was his masterpiece; and Truewit was a scholarlike kind of man, a gentleman with an alloy of pedantry, a man who seems mortified to the world by much reading. The best of his discourse is drawn, not from the knowledge of the town, but books; and, in short, he would be a fine gentleman in an university. Shakespeare showed the best of his skill in his Mercutio; and he said himself that he was forced to kill him in the third act to prevent being killed by him. But, for my part, I cannot find he was so dangerous a person: I see nothing in him but what was so exceeding harmless that he might have lived to the end of the play, and died in his bed, without offense to any man.

Fletcher's Don John is our only bug-bear; and yet I may affirm, without suspicion of flattery, that he now speaks better, and that his character is maintained with much more vigor in the fourth and fifth acts, than it was by Fletcher in the three former. I have always acknowledged the wit of our predecessors, with all the veneration which becomes me; but, I am sure, their wit was not that of gentlemen; there was ever somewhat that was ill-bred and clownish in it, and which confessed the conversation of the authors.

And this leads me to the last and greatest advantage of our writing, which proceeds from *conversation*. In the age wherein those poets lived, there was less of gallantry than in ours; neither did they keep the best company of theirs. Their fortune has been much like that of Epicurus, in the retirement of his gardens; to live almost unknown, and to be celebrated after their decease. I cannot find that any of them had been conversant in courts, except Ben Jonson; and his genius lay not so much that way as to make an improvement by it. Greatness was not then so easy of access, nor conversation so free, as now it is. I cannot, therefore, conceive it any insolence to affirm that, by the knowledge and pattern of their wit who writ before us, and by the advantage of our own conversation, the discourse and raillery of our comedies excel what has been written by them. And this will be denied by none but some few old fellows who value themselves on their acquaintance with the Black Friars; who, because they saw their plays, would pretend a right to judge ours. The memory of these grave gentlemen is their only plea for being wits. They can tell a story of Ben Jonson, and, perhaps, have had fancy enough to give a supper in the Apollo, that they might be called his sons; and, because they were drawn in to be laughed at in those times, they think themselves now sufficiently entitled to laugh at ours. Learning I never saw in any of them; and wit no more than they could remember. In short, they were unlucky to have been bred in an unpolished age, and more unlucky to live to a refined one. They have lasted beyond their own, and are cast behind ours; and, not contented to have known little at the age of twenty, they boast of their ignorance at threescore.

Now, if they ask me whence it is that our conversation is so much refined, I must freely, and without flattery, ascribe it to the Court; and, in it, particularly to the King, whose example gives a law to it. His own misfortunes, and the nation's, afforded him an opportunity, which is rarely allowed to sovereign princes, I mean of traveling, and being conversant in the most polished courts of Europe; and, thereby, of cultivating a spirit which was formed by nature to receive the impressions of a gallant and generous education. At his return, he found a nation lost as much in barbarism as in rebellion; and, as the excellency of his nature forgave the one, so the excellency of his manners reformed the other. The desire of imitating so great a pattern first awakened the dull and heavy spirits of the English from their natural reservedness; loosened them from their stiff forms of conversation, and made them easy and pliant to each other in discourse. Thus, insensibly, our way of living became more free; and the fire of the English wit, which was before stifled under a constrained, melancholy way of breeding, began first to display its force, by mixing the solidity of our nation with the air and gaiety of our neighbors. This being granted to be true, it would be a wonder if the poets, whose work is imitation, should be the only persons in three kingdoms who should not receive advantage by it; or, if they should not more easily imitate the wit and conversation of the present age than of the past.

Let us therefore admire the beauties and the heights of Shakespeare, without falling after him into a carelessness and, as I may call it, a lethargy of thought, for whole scenes together. Let us imitate, as we are able, the quickness and easiness of Fletcher, without proposing him as a pattern to us, either in the redundancy of his matter or the incorrectness of his language. Let us admire his wit and sharpness of conceit; but let us at the same time acknowledge that it was seldom so fixed, and made proper to his character, as that the same things might not be spoken by any person in the play. Let us applaud his scenes of love; but let us confess that he understood not either greatness or perfect honor in the parts of any of his women. In fine, let us allow that he had so much fancy as when he pleased he could write wit; but that he wanted so much judgment as seldom to have written humor, or described a pleasant folly. Let us ascribe to Jonson the height and accuracy of judgment in the ordering of his plots, his choice of characters, and maintaining what he had chosen to the end. But let us not think him a perfect pattern of imitation, except it be in humor; for love, which is the foundation of all comedies in other languages, is scarcely mentioned in any of his plays; and for humor itself, the poets of this age will be more wary than to imitate the meanness of his persons. Gentlemen will now be entertained with the follies of each other; and, though they allow Cobb and Tib to speak properly, yet they are not much pleased with their tankard or with their rags. And surely their conversation can be no jest to them in the theater when they would avoid it in the street.

To conclude all, let us render to our predecessors what is their due, without confining ourselves to a servile imitation of all they writ; and, without assuming to ourselves the title of better poets, let us ascribe to the gallantry and civility of our age the advantage which we have above them, and to our knowledge of the customs and manner of it the happiness we have to please beyond them.

JOHN WILMOT, EARL OF ROCHESTER

The second Earl of Rochester was the pattern rake of the Restoration. Modern criticism, which has discovered in the seventeenth century some of the lineaments of our own age, makes him out a frustrated idealist, a metaphysical fallen on evil days, one who, like Donne, sought but did not find a substitute for sense. In his own time he was the pet and scandal of the court, an enfant terrible among wits. By virtue of a well-publicized eleventh-hour repentance he became a memento mori to the gay world and a legacy of edification to posterity. Next to Milton, Dryden and Marvell he wrote the best poetry of the age. There is no deeper depth than is sounded in A Satire against Mankind, *no bolder devastation of the image of a king than his verses on Charles II, no more cynical flouting of the moral law than* The Maimed Debauchee. *He was deliberately unprintable in some of his lyrics, a touch bawdy and cynical in some others. But he could also write unexceptionably and with real or well-simulated passion. If some of these good lyrics fail to register as they once did, it is to be remembered that they were written to be sung.*

Rochester's letters—to his friend, Henry Savile; to a mistress, who may have been the actress, Mrs. Barry; and even to his wife—show that he was human and suggest that his ill behavior in word and deed was but theatrical posturing before an audience whose appetite for entertainment ruled out pity and a sense of shame. In the last great act of his life drama there are two protagonists, the collapsing debauchee, and the bishop standing on a rock. Burnet was an expert in conversion and had presided over a hundred dying hours. He is impervious to any doubt as to the validity of his efforts or their result. To him the repentance of one great gentleman who had flouted God was worth a wilderness of ordinary and to-be-expected pious deeds.

The Restoration

or

The History of Insipids

Chaste, pious, prudent Charles the Second,
The miracle of thy restoration
May like to that of quails be reckoned
Rained on the Israelitish nation;
The wished for blessing from Heaven sent,
Became their curse and punishment.

The virtues in thee, Charles, inherent,
Although thy countenance be an odd piece,
Proves thee as true a God's Viceregent
As e'er was Harry with the codpiece.
For chastity and pious deeds
His grandsire Harry, Charles exceeds.

Our Romish bondage-breaker, Harry,
Espoused half a dozen wives.
Charles only one resolved to marry
And other men's he never swives.
Yet hath he sons and daughters more
Than e'er had Harry by threescore.

Never was such a faith's defender.
He, like a politic prince and pious,
Gives liberty to conscience tender
And does to no religion tie us.
Jews, Turks, Christians, Papists, he'll please us
With Moses, Mahomet, or Jesus.

In all affairs of Church or State,
He very zealous is and able.
Devout at prayers, and sits up late
At the cabal and Council table.
His very dog at Council board
Sits grave and wise as any lord.

His father's foes he does reward,
Preserving those that cut off his head.
Old Cavaliers, the Crown's best guard,
He lets them starve for want of bread.
Never was any King endowed
With so much grace and gratitude.

Blood that wears treason in his face,
Villain complete in parson's gown,
How much is he at Court in grace
For stealing Ormond and the Crown?
Since loyalty does no man good,
Let's steal the King and outdo Blood.

A Parliament of knaves and sots
(Members by name you must not mention)
He keeps in pay and buys their votes,
Here with a place, there with a pension.
When to give money he can't collogue 'um,
He does with scorn prorogue, prorogue 'um.

But they long since by too much giving
Undid, betrayed, and sold the nation,
Making their memberships a living
Better than ever was sequestration.
God give thee, Charles, a resolution
To damn the knaves by dissolution.

Then, Charles, beware of thy brother York,
Who to thy Government gives law.
If once we fall to the old sport,
You must again both to Breda,
Where, spite of all that would restore you,
Grown wise by wrongs, we shall abhor you.

Then farewell, sacred majesty,
Let's pull all British tyrants down.
Where men are born and still live free,
Here every head does wear a crown.
Mankind, like miserable frogs,
Proved wretched, kinged by storks and logs.

Song

My dear Mistress has a heart
  Soft as those kind looks she gave me;
When, with love's resistless art,
  And her eyes, she did enslave me;
But her constancy's so weak,
  She's so wild and apt to wander,
That my jealous heart would break
  Should we live one day asunder.

Melting joys about her move,
  Killing pleasures, wounding blisses,
She can dress her eyes in love,
  And her lips can arm with kisses;
Angels listen when she speaks,
  She's my delight, all mankind's wonder,
But my jealous heart would break
  Should we live one day asunder.

Constancy

I cannot change, as others do,
  Though you unjustly scorn,
Since that poor swain that sighs for you,

For you alone was born;
No, Phillis, no, your heart to move
  A surer way I'll try,—
And to revenge my slighted love,
  Will still love on, and die.

When, killed with grief, Amintas lies,
  And you to mind shall call
The sighs that now unpitied rise,
  The tears that vainly fall,
That welcome hour that ends his smart,
  Will then begin your pain,
For such a faithful tender heart
  Can never break in vain.

The Bowl

Contrive me, Vulcan, such a cup
  As Nestor used of old,
Shew all thy skill to trim it up,
  Damask it round with gold.

Make it so large, that, filled with sack
  Up to the swelling brim,
Vast toasts on that delicious lake,
  Like ships at sea, may swim.

Engrave not battle on his cheek,
  With war I've nought to do,
I'm none of those that took Maestrick,
  Nor Yarmouth leaguer knew.

Let it no name of planets tell,
  Fixed stars or constellations,
For I am no Sir Sidrophel,
  Nor none of his relations.

But carve thereon a spreading vine;
  Then add two lovely boys;

Their limbs in amorous folds entwine,
The types of future joys.

Cupid and Bacchus my saints are,
May Drink and Love still reign,
With wine I wash away my care,
And then to love again.

Song

NYMPH

Injurious charmer of my vanquished heart,
Canst thou feel love, and yet no pity know?
Since of myself from thee I cannot part,
Invent some gentle way to let me go;
For what with joy thou didst obtain,
And I with more did give,
In time will make thee false and vain,
And me unfit to live.

SHEPHERD

Frail angel, that would'st leave a heart forlorn,
With vain pretence Falsehood therein might lie,
Seek not to cast wild shadows o'er your scorn,
You cannot sooner change than I can die;
To tedious life I'll never fall,
Thrown from thy dear-lov'd breast;
He merits not to live at all,
Who cares to live unblest.

Song

When on those lovely looks I gaze,
To see a wretch pursuing,
In raptures of a blest amaze,
His pleasing happy ruin,
'Tis not for pity that I move;

His fate is too aspiring,
Whose heart, broke with a load of love,
    Dies wishing and admiring.

But if this murder you'd forego,
    Your slave from death removing,
Let me your art of charming know,
    Or you learn mine of loving;
But whether life or death betide,
    In love 'tis equal measure,
The victor lives with empty pride,
    The vanquished dies with pleasure.

Song

Absent from thee I languish still;
    Then ask me not, when I return?
The straying fool 'twill plainly kill
    To wish all day, all night to mourn.

Dear, from thine arms then let me fly,
    That my fantastic mind may prove
The torments it deserves to try,
    That tears my fixed heart from my love.

When, wearied with a world of woe,
    To thy safe bosom I retire,
Where love and peace and honour flow,
    May I contented there expire.

Lest once more wandering from that heaven,
    I fall on some base heart unblessed,
Faithless to thee, false, unforgiven,
    And lose my everlasting rest.

Song

All my past life is mine no more,
    The flying hours are gone,

Like transitory dreams given o'er,
Whose images are kept in store
By memory alone.

Whatever is to come, is not;
How can it then be mine?
The present moment's all my lot,
And that, as fast as it is got,
Phyllis, is wholly thine.

Then talk not of inconstancy,
False hearts, and broken vows;
If I, by miracle, can be
This live-long minute true to thee,
'Tis all that Heaven allows.

Letters

TO MRS. BARRY

1.

Madam:

I know not well who has the worst on't, you who love but a little, or I who dote to an extravagance. Sure, to be half kind is as bad as to be half witted, and madness, both in love and reason, bears a better character than a moderate state of either. Would I could bring you to my opinion in this point. I would then confidently pretend you had too [two?] just exceptions either against me or my passion, the flesh, and the devil. I mean all the fools of my own sex and that fat, with the other lean, one of yours, whose prudent advice is daily concerning you: how dangerous it is to be kind to the man upon earth who loves you best. I, who still persuade myself by all the arguments I can bring, that I am happy, find this none of the least, that you are too unlike these people every way to agree with them in any particular. This is writ between sleeping and waking, and I will not answer for its being sense. But I, dreaming you were at Mrs. N——'s with five or six fools and the lean lady, waked in one of your horrors, and in amaze, fright, and confusion send this to beg a kind one from you that may remove my fears and make me as happy as I am faithful.

2.

Dear Madam,

You are stark mad and therefore the fitter for me to love; and that is the reason, I think, I can never leave to be

Your Humble Servant,

3.

Madam,

There is now no minute of my life that does not afford me some new argument how much I love you. The little joy I take in everything wherein you are not concerned, the pleasing perplexity of endless thought which I fall into wherever you are brought to my remembrance, and lastly, the continual disquiet I am in during your absence, convince me sufficiently that I do you justice in loving you so as woman was never loved before.

4.

Madam,

Your safe delivery has delivered me too from fears for your sake, which were, I'll promise you, as burdensome to me as your great belly could be to you. Everything has fallen out to my wish, for you are out of danger and the child is of the soft sex I love. Shortly my hopes are to see you and in a little while after to look on you with all your beauty about you. Pray let nobody but yourself open the box I sent you. I did not know but that in lying-in you might have use of those trifles. Sick and in bed as I am, I could come at no more of them; but if you find them, or whatever is in my power of use, to your service, let me know it.

5.

Madam,

I am far from delighting in the grief I have given you by taking away the child; and you, who made it so absolutely necessary for me to do so, must take that excuse from me for all the ill nature of it. On the other side, pray be assured I love Betty so well that you need not apprehend any neglect from those I employ, and I hope very shortly to restore her to you a finer girl than ever. In the meantime, you would do well to think of the advice I gave you, for how little show soever my prudence makes in my own affairs, in yours it will prove very successful if you please to follow it, and since discretion is the thing alone you are like to want, pray study to get it.

6.

Madam,

Anger, spleen, revenge, and shame are not yet so powerful with me as to make me disown this great truth, that I love you above all things in the world. But I thank God I can distinguish, I can see every woman in you and from yourself am convinced I have never been in the wrong in my opinion of women. 'Tis impossible for me to curse you, but give me leave to pity myself, which is more than ever you will do for me. You have a character and you maintain it, but I am sorry you make me an example to prove it. It seems, as you excel in everything, you scorn to grow less in that noble quality of using your servants very hardly. You do well not to forget it, and rather practice upon me than lose the habit of being very severe. For you that choose rather to be wise than just or good natured may freely dispose of all things in your power without regard to one or the other. As I admire you, I would be glad I could imitate you. It were but manners to endeavor it, which, since I am notable to perform, I confess you are in the right to call that rude which I call kind, and to keep me in the wrong forever (which you cannot choose but take great delight in). You need but continue to make it fit for me not to love you and you can never want something to upbraid me with.

Three o'clock in the morning.

The Maimed Debauchee

1.

As some brave admiral, in former war,
   Deprived of force but pressed with courage still,
Two rival fleets appearing from afar,
   Crawls to the top of an adjacent hill,

2.

From whence (with thoughts full of concern) he views
   The wise and daring conduct of the fight:
And each bold action to his mind renews
   His present glory and his past delight.

3.

From his fierce eyes flashes of rage he throws
    As from black clouds when lightning breaks away,
Transported thinks himself amidst his foes
    And absent yet enjoys the bloody day.

4.

So when my days of impotence approach
    And I'm by love and wine's unlucky chance
Driven from the pleasing billows of debauch
    On the dull shore of lazy temperance

5.

My pains at last some respite shall afford
    While I behold the battles you maintain
When fleets of glasses sail around the board
    From whose broad sides volley of wit shall rain.

6.

Nor shall the sight of honorable scars
    Which my too forward valor did procure
Frighten new-lifted soldiers from the wars;
    Past joys have more than paid what I endure.

7.

Should some brave youth (worth being drunk) prove nice
    And from his fair inviter meanly shrink,
'Twould please the ghost of my departed vice
    If, at my counsel, he repent and drink.

8.

Or should some cold complexioned sot forbid,
    With his dull morals, our night's brisk alarms;
I'll fire his blood by telling what I did
    When I was strong and able to bear arms.

9.

I'll tell of whores attacked, their lords at home,
    Bawd's quarters beaten up, and fortress won;

Windows demolished, watches overcome,
    And handsome ills by my contrivance done.

10.

With tales like these I will such heat inspire
    As to important mischief shall incline;
I'll make him long some ancient church to fire
    And fear no lewdness they're called to by wine.

11.

Thus statesmanlike I'll saucily impose
    And, safe from danger, valiantly advise;
Sheltered in impotence urge you to blows
    And, being good for nothing else, be wise.

A Satire against Mankind

Were I, who to my cost already am
One of those strange, prodigious creatures *man*,
A spirit free, to choose for my own share,
What sort of flesh and blood I pleas'd to wear,
I'd be a dog, a monkey or a bear,
Or anything, but that vain animal,
Who is so proud of being rational.
The senses are too gross; and he'll contrive
A sixth, to contradict the other five:
And before certain instinct, will prefer
Reason, which fifty times for one does err—
Reason, an *ignis fatuus* of the mind,
Which leaves the light of Nature, sense, behind.
Pathless, and dang'rous, wand'ring ways, it takes,
Through Error's fenny bogs, and thorny brakes:
Whilst the misguided foll'wer climbs with pain
Mountains of whimseys, heap'd in his own brain,
Stumbling from thought to thought, falls headlong down
Into Doubt's boundless sea, where like to drown,
Books bear him up a while, and make him try
To swim with bladders of philosophy,
In hopes still to o'ertake the skipping light;

The vapor dances, in his dazzled sight,
Till spent, it leaves him to eternal night.
Then old age, and experience, hand in hand,
Lead him to Death, and make him understand,
After a search so painful, and so long,
That all his life he has been in the wrong.
Huddled in dirt, [the] reas'ning engine lies,
Who was so proud, so witty, and so wise:
Pride drew him in, as cheats their bubbles catch,
And made him venture to be made a wretch;
His wisdom did his happiness destroy,
Aiming to know the world he should enjoy. . . .
Those creatures are the wisest who attain
By surest means the ends at which they aim.
If therefore Jowler finds, and kills his hare
Better than Meres supplies committee chair;
Though one's a statesman, th' other but a hound,
Jowler in justice will be wiser found.
You see how far man's wisdom here extends:
Look next if human nature makes amends;
Whose principles are most generous and just;
And to whose morals you would sooner trust.
Be judge yourself, I'll bring it to the test,
Which is the basest creature, man or beast:
Birds feed on birds, beasts on each other prey;
But savage man alone does man betray.
Press'd by necessity, *they* kill for food;
Man undoes man, to do himself no good.
With teeth and claws by Nature arm'd, *they* hunt
Nature's allowance, to supply their want:
But man with smiles, embraces, friendships, praise,
Inhumanely, his fellow's life betrays,
With voluntary pains, works his distress;
Not through necessity, but wantonness.
For hunger, or for love *they* bite or tear,
Whilst wretched man is still in arms for fear:
For fear he arms, and is of arms afraid;
From fear to fear successively betray'd.
Base fear, the source whence his best passions came,
His boasted honor, and his dear-bought fame,
The lust of pow'r, to which he's such a slave,

And for the which alone he dares be brave:
To which his various projects are design'd,
Which makes him gen'rous, affable, and kind:
For which he takes such pains to be thought wise,
And screws his actions, in a forc'd disguise:
Leads a most tedious life, in misery,
Under laborious, mean hypocrisy.
Look to the bottom of his vast design,
Wherein man's wisdom, pow'r, and glory join—
The good he acts, the ill he does endure,
'Tis all from fear, to make himself secure.
Merely for safety, after fame they thirst;
For all men would be cowards if they durst:
And honesty's against all common sense—
Men must be knaves; 'tis in their own defense,
Mankind's dishonest; if they think it fair,
Amongst known cheats, to play upon the square,
You'll be undone——
Nor can weak Truth your reputation save;
The knaves will all agree to call you knave.
Wrong'd shall he live, insulted o'er, oppress'd,
Who dares be less a villain than the rest.
Thus here you see what human nature craves,
Most men are cowards, all men should be knaves.
The difference lies, as far as I can see,
Not in the thing itself, but the degree;
And all the subject matter of debate
Is only who's a knave of the first rate.

GILBERT BURNET

The Conversion of a Rake

John Wilmot, Earl of Rochester, was born in April, *anno domini*
1648. His father was Henry, Earl of Rochester, but best known by
the title of Lord Wilmot, who bore so great a part in all the late
wars that mention is often made of him in the history. When he was
at school he was an extraordinary proficient at his book; and those
shining parts which have since appeared with so much lustre began
then to show themselves. He acquired the Latin to such perfection

that to his dying day he retained a great relish for the fineness and beauty of that tongue; and was exactly versed in the incomparable authors that wrote about Augustus' time, whom he read often with that peculiar delight which the greatest wits have ever found in those studies.

When he went to the university, the general joy that overran the whole nation upon his Majesty's restoration, but was not regulated with that sobriety and temperance that became a serious gratitude to God for so great a blessing, produced some of its ill effects on him. He began to love these disorders too much.

He came from his travels in the eighteenth year of his age and appeared at court with as great advantages as most ever had. He was a graceful and well-shaped person, tall, and well made, if not a little too slender. He was exactly well bred, and what by a modest behavior natural to him, what by a civility become almost as natural, his conversation was easy and obliging. He had a strange vivacity of thought and vigor of expression. His wit had a subtility and sublimity both that were scarce imitable. His style was clear and strong. When he used figures they were very lively and yet far enough out of the common road. He had made himself master of the ancient and modern wit and of the modern French and Italian as well as the English. He loved to talk and write of speculative matters, and did it with so fine a thread that even those that hated the subjects that his fancy ran upon, yet could not but be charmed with his way of treating them. Boileau among the French and Cowley among the English wits were those he admired most. Sometimes other men's thoughts mixed with his composures, but that flowed rather from the impressions they made on him when he read them, by which they came to return upon his as his own thoughts, than that he servilely copied them from any. For few men ever had a bolder flight of fancy more steadily governed by judgment than he had. No wonder a young man so made and so improved was very acceptable in a court.

Soon after his coming thither he laid hold on the first occasion that offered, to show his readiness to hazard his life in the defense and service of his country. In the winter of 1665, he went with the Earl of Sandwich to sea, when he was sent to lie for the Dutch East India fleet, and was in the Revenge, commanded by Sir Thomas Tiddiman when the attack was made on the port of Bergen in Norway, the Dutch ships having got into that port. It was as desperate an attempt as ever was made. During the whole action, the Earl of Rochester showed as brave and as resolute courage as was possible. A person of honor told me he heard the Lord Clifford, who was in the same ship, often magnify his courage at that time very highly. Nor did the rigors of the season, the hardness of the voyage, and the extreme dangers he had been in deter him from running the like on the very next occasion. For in the summer following he went to sea again, without communicating his design to his nearest relations. He went aboard the ship commanded by Sir Edward Spragge the day before the great sea-fight of that year. Almost all the volunteers that were in the same ship were killed. Mr. Middleton (brother to Sir Hugh Middleton) was shot in his arms. During the action Sir Edward Spragge, not being satisfied with the behavior of one of the captains, could not easily find a person who would cheerfully venture through so much danger to carry his commands to that captain. This lord offered himself to the service, and went in a little boat through all the shot and delivered his message and returned back to Sir Edward, which was much commended by all that saw it. He thought it necessary to begin his life with these demonstrations of his courage in an element and way of fighting, which is acknowledged to be the greatest trial of clear and undaunted valor.

He had so entirely laid down the intemperance that was growing on him before his travels that at his return he hated nothing more. But falling into company that loved these excesses, he was, though not without difficulty and by many steps, brought back to it again. And the natural heat of his fancy being inflamed by wine made him so extravagantly pleasant that many, to be more diverted by his humor, studied to engage him in deeper and deeper intemperance; which at length did so entirely subdue him that, as he told me, for five years together he was continually drunk, not all the while under the visible effect of it, but his blood was so inflamed that it was not in all that time cool enough to be perfectly master of himself. This led him to say and do many wild and unaccountable things. By this, he said, he had broke the firm constitution of his health, that seemed so strong that nothing was too hard for it; and he had suffered so much in his reputation that he almost despaired to recover it.

There were principles in his natural temper that being heightened by that heat carried him to great excesses—a violent love of pleasure and a disposition to extravagant mirth. The one involved him in great sensuality; the other led him to many odd adventures and frolics, in which he was oft in hazard of his life. The one being the same irregular appetite in his mind, that the other was in his body, which made him think nothing diverting that was not extravagant. And though in cold blood he was a generous and good natured man, yet he would go far in his heats after any thing that might turn to a jest or matter of diversion.

He said to me he never improved his interest at court to do a premeditated mischief to other persons. Yet he laid out his wit very freely in libels and satires, in which he had a peculiar talent of mixing his wit with his malice and fitting both with such apt words that men were tempted to be pleased with them; from thence his composures came to be easily known, for few had such a way of tempering these together as he had. So that when anything extraordinary that way come out, as a child is fathered sometimes by its resemblance, so was it laid at his door as its parent and author.

These exercises in the course of his life were not always equally pleasant to him; he had often sad intervals and severe reflections on them. And though then he had not these awakened in him from any principle of religion, yet the horror that nature raised in him, especially in some sicknesses, made him too easy to receive some ill principles, which others endeavored to possess him with; so that he was soon brought to set himself to secure and fortify his mind against that, by dispossessing it of all he could of the belief or apprehensions of religion.

The licentiousness of his temper, with the briskness of his wit, disposed him to love the conversation of those who divided their time between lewd actions and irregular mirth. And so he came to bend his wit and direct his studies and endeavors to support and strengthen these ill principles both in himself and others.

An accident fell out after this which confirmed him more in these courses. When he went to sea in the year 1665 there happened to be in the same ship with him Mr. Montague and another gentleman of quality; these two, the former especially, seemed persuaded that they should never return into England. Mr. Montague said he was sure of it; the other was not so positive. The Earl of Rochester and the last of these entered into a formal engagement, not without ceremonies of religion, that if either of them died he should appear and give the other notice of the future state, if there was any. But Mr. Montague would not enter into the bond. When the day came that they thought to have taken the Dutch fleet in the port of Bergen, Mr. Montague, though he had such a strong presage in his mind of his approaching death, yet he generously stayed all the while in a place of the greatest danger. The other gentleman signalized his courage in a most undaunted manner till near the end of the action, when he fell on a sudden into such a trembling that he could scarce stand, and Mr. Montague going up to him to hold him up, as they were in each others arms, a cannon ball killed him outright, and carried away Mr. Montague's belly, so that he died within an hour after.

The Earl of Rochester told me that these presages they had in their minds made some impression on him that there were separated beings and that the soul, either by a natural sagacity, or some secret notice communicated to it, had a sort of divination. But that gentleman's never appearing was a great snare to him during the rest of his life. Though when he told me this he could not but acknowledge it was an unreasonable thing to think that beings in another state were not under such laws and limits that they could not command their own motions but as the Supreme Power should order them; and that one who had so corrupted the natural principles of truth as he had, had no reason to expect that such an extraordinary thing should be done for his conviction.

He also told me of another odd presage that one had of his approaching death in the Lady Warre, his mother-in-law's, house. The chaplain dreamed that such a day he should die, but, being by all the family put out of the belief of it, he had almost forgot it; till the evening before at supper, there being thirteen at table, according to fond conceit that one of these must soon die, one of the young ladies pointed to him that he was to die. He remembering his dream fell into some disorder, and the Lady Warre reproving him for his superstition he said he was confident he was to die before morning; but he being in perfect health it was not much minded. It was Saturday night and he was to preach the next day. He went to his chamber and sat up late, as appeared by the burning of his candle, and had been preparing his notes for his sermon, but was found dead in his bed the next morning. These things, he said, made him inclined to believe the soul was a substance distinct from matter; and this often returned into his thoughts. But that which perfected his persuasion about it was that in the sickness which brought him so near death before I first knew him, when his spirits were so low and spent that he could not move nor stir and did not expect to live an hour. He said his reason and judgment were so clear and strong that from thence he was fully persuaded that death was not the spending or dissolution of the soul but only the separation of it from matter. He had in that sickness great remorses for his past life, but he afterwards told me they were rather general and dark horrors than any convictions of sinning against God. He was sorry he lived so as to waste his strength so soon or that he had brought such an ill name upon himself; and had an agony in his mind about it which he knew not well how to express. But at such times, though he complied with his friends in suffering divines to be sent for, he said he had no great mind to it, and that it was but a piece of his breeding to desire them to pray by him, in which he joined but little himself.

As to the supreme Being, he had always some impression of one, and professed often to me that he had never known an entire atheist who fully believed there was no God. Yet when he explained his notion of that Being it amounted to no more than a vast power that had none of the attributes of goodness and justice we ascribe to the Deity. These were his thoughts about religion, as himself told me.

For morality, he freely owned to me that though he talked of it as a fine thing, yet this was only because he thought it a decent way of speaking, and that as they went always in clothes, though in their frolics they would have chosen sometimes to have gone naked if they had not feared the people; so that, though some of them found it necessary for human life to talk of morality, yet he confessed they cared not for it further than the reputation of it was necessary for their credit and affairs. Of which he gave me many instances, as their professing and swearing friendship, where they hated morality; their oaths and imprecations in their addresses to women, which they intended never to make good; the pleasure they took in defaming innocent persons and spreading false reports of some, perhaps in revenge because they could not engage them to comply with their ill designs; the delight they had in making people quarrel, their unjust usage to their creditors and putting them off by any deceitful promise they could invent that might deliver them from present importunity. So that, in detestation of these courses, he would often break forth into such hard expressions concerning himself as would be indecent for another to repeat.

Such had been his principles and practices in a course of many years, which had almost quite extinguished the natural propensities in him to justice and virtue. He would often go into the country and be for some months wholly employed in study or the sallies of his wit; which he came to direct chiefly to satire. And this he often defended to me by saying there were some people who could not be kept in order or admonished but in this way. I replied that it might be granted that a grave way of satire was sometimes no unprofitable way of reproof. Yet they who used it only out of spite and mixed lies with truth, sparing nothing that might adorn their poems or gratify their revenge, could not excuse that way of reproach, by which the innocent often suffer; since the most malicious things, if wittily expressed, might stick to and blemish the best character in the world, and the malice of a libel could hardly consist with the charity of an admonition. To this he answered, a man could not write with life unless he was heated by revenge, for to make a satire without resentment on the cold notions of philosophy was as if a man would, in cold blood, cut men's throats who had never offended him. And he said the lies in these libels came often in as ornaments that could not be spared without spoiling the beauty of the poem.

For his other studies, they were divided between the comical and witty writings of the ancients and moderns, the Roman authors, and books of physic, which the ill state of health he was fallen to made more necessary to himself and which qualified him for an odd adventure which I shall but just mention. Being under an unlucky accident which obliged him to keep out of the way, he disguised himself so that his nearest friends could not have known him and set up in Tower Street for an Italian mountebank, where he practised physic for some weeks not without success. In his latter years he read books of history more. He took pleasure to disguise himself as a porter or as a beggar; sometimes to follow some mean amours, which for the variety of them he affected. At other times, merely for diversion, he would go about in odd shapes, in which he acted his part so naturally that even those who were in the secret and saw him in these shapes could perceive nothing by which he might be discovered.

I have now made the description of his former life and principles, as fully as I thought necessary to answer my end in writing. And yet with those reserves that I hope I have given no just cause of offence to any. I have said nothing but what I had from his own mouth and have avoided the mentioning of the more particular passages of his life, of which he told me not a few. But since others were concerned in them, whose good only I design, I will say nothing that may provoke or blemish them. It is their reformation and not their disgrace I desire. This tender consideration of others has made me suppress many remarkable and useful things he told me. But finding that, though I should name none, yet I must relate such circumstances as would give great occasion for the reader to conjecture concerning the persons intended right or wrong, either of which were inconvenient enough, I have chosen to pass them quite over. But I hope those that know how much they were engaged with him in his ill courses will be somewhat touched with this tenderness I express towards them; and be thereby the rather induced to reflect on their ways, and to consider without prejudice or passion what a sense this noble lord had of their case, when he came at last seriously to reflect upon his own.

I now turn to those parts of this narrative wherein I myself bore some share and which I am to deliver upon the observations I made, after a long and free conversation with him for some months. I was not long in his company when he told me he should treat me with more freedom than he had ever used to men of my profession. He would conceal none of his principles from me but lay his thoughts open without any disguise; nor would he do it to maintain debate or show his wit, but plainly tell me what stuck with him. And he protested to me that he was not so engaged to his old maxims as to resolve not to change, but if he could be convinced he would choose rather to be of another mind. He said he would impartially weigh what I should lay before him and tell me freely when it did convince him and when it did not. He expressed this disposition of mind to me in a manner so frank that I could not but believe him and be much taken with his way of discourse. So we entered into almost all the parts of natural and revealed religion and of morality. . . .

The issue of all our discourse was this: he told me he saw vice and impiety were as contrary to human society as wild beasts let loose would be; and therefore he firmly resolved to change the whole method of his life, to become strictly just and true, to be chaste and temperate, to forbear swearing and irreligious discourse, to worship and pray to his Maker. And that, though he was not arrived at a full persuasion of Christianity, he would never employ his wit more to run it down, or to corrupt others. . . .

At this pass he was when he went from London, about the beginning of April. He had not been long in the country when he thought he was so well that, being to go to his estate in Somersetshire, he rode thither post. This heat and violent motion did so inflame an ulcer that was in his bladder that it raised a very great pain in those parts. Yet he with much difficulty came back by coach to the Lodge at Woodstock Park. He was then wounded both in body and mind. He understood physic and his own constitution and distemper so well that he concluded he could hardly recover; for the ulcer broke and vast quantities of purulent matter passed with his urine. But now the hand of God touched him, and, as he told me, it was not only a general dark melancholy over his mind such as he had formerly felt, but a most penetrating cutting sorrow. So that, though in his body he suffered extreme pain for some weeks, yet the agonies of his mind sometimes swallowed up the sense of what he felt in the body.

He told me and gave it me in charge to tell it to one for whom he was much concerned, that though there were nothing to come after this life yet all the pleasures he had ever known in sin were not worth that torture he had felt in his mind. He considered he had not only neglected and dishonored but had openly defied his Maker, and had drawn many others into the like impieties, so that he looked on himself as one that was in great danger of being damned. He then set himself wholly to turn to God unfeignedly, and to do all that was possible in that little remainder of his life which was before him to redeem those great portions of it that he had formerly so ill employed. . . .

At my coming to his house, an accident fell out not worth mentioning but that some have made a story of it. His servant, being a Frenchman, carried up my name wrong, so that he mistook it for another who had sent to him that he would undertake his cure, and he being resolved not to meddle with him, did not care to see him. This mistake lasted some hours, with which I was the better contented because he was not then in such a condition that my being about him could have been of any use to him; for that night was like to have been his last. He had a convulsion fit and raved; but opiates being given him, after some hours rest his raving left him so entirely that it never against returned to him.

I cannot easily express the transport he was in when he awoke and saw me by him. He broke out in the tenderest expressions concerning my kindness in coming so far to see such a one, using terms of great abhorrence concerning himself, which I forbear to relate. He told me, as his strength served him at several snatches, for he was then so low that he could not hold up discourse long at once, what sense he had of his past life; what sad apprehension for having so offended his Maker and dishonored his Redeemer; what horrors he had gone through and how much his mind was turned to call on God and on his crucified Saviour. So that he hoped he should obtain mercy, for he believed he had sincerely repented; and had now a calm in his mind after that storm that he had been in for some weeks. . . .

Having understood all these things from him and being pressed to give him my opinion plainly about his eternal state, I told him that though the promises of the gospel did all depend upon a real change of heart and life, as the indispensible condition upon which they were made; and that it was scarce possible to know certainly whether our hearts are changed unless it appeared in our lives; and the repentance of most dying men, being like the howlings of condemned prisoners for pardon, which flowed from no sense of their crimes but from the horror of approaching death, there was little reason to encourage any to hope much from such sorrowing; yet certainly if the mind of a sinner, even on a death-bed, be truly renewed and turned to God, so great is his mercy that he will receive him, even in that extremity.

He was sure his mind was entirely turned, and though horror had given him his first awaking, yet that was now grown up into a settled faith and conversion.

There is but one prejudice lies against all this to defeat the good ends of divine providence by it upon others as well as on himself, and that is, it was a part of his disease and that the lowness of his spirits made such an alteration in him that he was not what he had formerly been; and this some have carried so far as to say that he died mad. These reports are raised by those who are unwilling that the last thoughts or words of a person every way so extraordinary, should have any effect either on themselves or others. And it is to be feared that some may have so far seared their consciences and exceeded the common measures of sin and infidelity, that neither this testimony, nor one coming from the dead, would signify much towards their conviction.

That this lord was either mad or stupid is a thing so notoriously untrue that it is the greatest impudence for any that were about him to report it; and a very unreasonable credulity in others to believe it. All the while I was with him, after he had slept out the disorders of the fit, he was not only without ravings but had a clearness in his thoughts, in his memory, in his reflections on things and persons, far beyond what I ever saw in a person so low in his strength. He was not able to hold out long in discourse, for his spirits failed; but once for half an hour, and often for a quarter of an hour, after he awakened, he had a vivacity in his discourse that was extraordinary and in all things like himself.

He called often for his children, his son, the now Earl of Rochester, and his three daughters, and spoke to them with a sense and feeling that cannot be expressed in writing.

He called me once to look on them all and said, "See how good

God has been to me in giving me so many blessings, and I have carried myself to Him like an ungracious and unthankful dog."

He once talked a great deal to me of public affairs, and of many persons and things with the same clearness of thought and expression that he had ever done before. So that by no sign but his weakness of body and giving over discourse so soon could I perceive a difference between what his parts formerly were and what they were then.

And that wherein the presense of his mind appeared most was in the total change of an ill habit grown so much upon him that he could hardly govern himself, when he was any way heated, three minutes without falling into it; I mean swearing.

He had acknowledged to me the former winter that he abhorred it as a base and indecent thing, and had set himself much to break it off; but he confessed that he was so overpowered by that ill custom that he could not speak with any warmth without repeated oaths, which, upon any sort of provocation, came almost naturally from him. But in his last remorses this did so sensible affect him that by a resolute and constant watchfulness that habit of it was perfectly mastered; so that upon the returns of pains which were very severe and frequent upon him the last day I was with him, or upon such displeasures as people sick or in pain are apt to take of a sudden at those about them, on all these occasions he never swore an oath all the while I was there.

Once he was offended with the delay of one that he thought made not haste enough with somewhat he called for, and said in a little heat, "That d——d fellow." Soon after I told him I was glad to find his style so reformed and that he had so entirely overcome that ill habit of swearing, only that word of calling any d——d, which had returned upon him, was not decent.

His answer was, "Oh that language of fiends which was so familiar to me hangs yet about me; sure none has deserved more to be damned than I have done." And after he had humbly asked God pardon for it he desired me to call the person to him that he might ask him forgiveness; but I told him that was needless, for he had said it of one that did not hear it and so could not be offended by it. . . .

I thought to have left him on Friday, but, not without some passion, he desired me to stay that day. There appeared no symptom of present death, and a worthy physician then with him told me that, though he was so low that an accident might carry him away on a sudden, yet without that he thought he might live yet some weeks.

So on Saturday at four o'clock in the morning I left him, being the

24th of July. But I durst not take leave of him; for he had expressed so great an unwillingness to part with me the day before, that if I had not presently yielded to one day's stay it was likely to have given him some trouble; therefore I thought it better to leave him without any formality. Some hours after he asked for me, and when it was told him I was gone, he seemed to be troubled and said, "Has my friend left me? Then I shall die shortly." After that he spoke but once or twice till he died. He lay much silent; once they heard him pray very devoutly. And on Monday, about two of the clock in the morning, he died without any convulsion or so much as a groan.

SIR CHARLES SEDLEY

Sedley is a minor rake and a minor wit as compared with Roches-
ter, but he has his points in both capacities. A few of the lyrics are
as immortal as "Drink to me only," or would be if they were wedded
to immortal airs. As for rake-hellishness, the little exploit recorded
at such disproportionate length in our selection from Anthony
Wood's biography is all too well remembered. Dryden, who called
Sedley a "more elegant Tibullus," was also ready to defend his name.
Such accusations were, he said, "a fine which Fortune sets on all
extraordinary persons." Perhaps so. At any rate Sedley lived long
and became respectable in old age, Fate and change of times giving
him no occasion for a dramatic deathbed.

To Chloris

Ah, Chloris! that I now could sit
    As unconcern'd as when
Your infant beauty could beget
    No pleasure, nor no pain.

When I the dawn us'd to admire,
    And prais'd the coming day,
I little thought the growing fire
    Must take my rest away.

Your charms in harmless childhood lay
    Like metals in the mine:

Age from no face took more away
  Than youth conceal'd in thine.

But as your charms insensibly
  To their perfection press'd,
Fond Love, as unperceiv'd, did fly,
  And in my bosom rest.

My passion with your beauty grew,
  And Cupid at my heart,
Still as his mother favor'd you,
  Threw a new flaming dart.

Each gloried in their wanton part:
  To make a lover, he
Employ'd the utmost of his art;
  To make a beauty, she.

Though now I slowly bend to love,
  Uncertain of my fate,
If your fair self my chains approve,
  I shall my freedom hate.

Lovers, like dying men, may well
  At first disorder'd be,
Since none alive can truly tell
  What fortune they must see.

The Indifference

Thanks, fair Urania, to your scorn
I now am free, as I was born,
Of all the pain that I endur'd;
By your late coldness I am cur'd.

In losing me, proud nymph, you lose
The humblest slave your beauty knows;
In losing you, I but throw down
A cruel tyrant from her throne.

My ranging love did never find
Such charms of person and of mind;
Y'ave beauty, wit, and all things know,
But where you should your love bestow.

I unawares my freedom gave,
And to those tyrants grew a slave;
Would you have kept what you had won
You should have more compassion shown.

Love is a burthen, which two hearts,
When equally they bear their parts,
With pleasure carry; but no one,
Alas, can bear it long alone.

I'm not of those who court their pain,
And make an idol of disdain;
My hope in love does ne'er expire,
But it extinguishes desire.

Song

Not, Celia, that I juster am
    Or better than the rest;
For I would change each hour like them
    Were not my heart at rest.

But I am tied to very thee
    By ev'ry thought I have:
Thy face I only care to see;
    Thy heart I only crave.

All that in woman is ador'd,
    In thy dear self I find;
For the whole sex can but afford
    The handsome and the kind.

Why, then, should I seek further store,
    And still make love anew?

When change itself can give no more,
  'Tis easy to be true.

Song

Love still has something of the sea
  From whence his mother rose;
No time his slaves from doubt can free,
  Nor give their thoughts repose.

They are becalm'd in clearest days,
  And in rough weather toss'd;
They wither under cold delays,
  Or are in tempests lost.

One while they seem to touch the port,
  Then straight into the main
Some angry wind in cruel sport
  The vessel drives again.

At first disdain and pride they fear,
  Which if they chance to 'scape,
Rivals and falsehood soon appear
  In a more dreadful shape.

By such degrees to joy they come,
  And are so long withstood,
So slowly they receive the sum,
  It hardly does them good.

'Tis cruel to prolong a pain;
  And to defer a joy,
Believe me, gentle Celemene,
  Offends the winged boy.

An hundred thousand oaths your fears
  Perhaps would not remove;
And if I gaz'd a thousand years,
  I could no deeper love.

The Knotting Song

Hears not my Phyllis how the birds
    Their feather'd mates salute?
They tell their passion in their words;
    Must I alone be mute?
        Phyllis, without frown or smile,
        Sat and knotted all the while.

The god of love, in thy bright eyes,
    Does like a tyrant reign;
But in thy heart a child he lies,
    Without his dart or flame.
        Phyllis, without frown or smile,
        Sat and knotted all the while.

So many months, in silence pass'd
    And yet in raging love,
Might well deserve one word at last
    My passion should approve.
        Phyllis, without frown or smile,
        Sat and knotted all the while.

Must then your faithful swain expire,
    And not one look obtain,
Which he, to soothe his fond desire,
    Might pleasingly explain?
        Phyllis, without frown or smile,
        Sat and knotted all the while.

Song

Phyllis is my only joy,
    Faithless as the winds or seas;
Sometimes coming, sometimes coy,
    Yet she never fails to please;
        If with a frown
        I am cast down,

Phyllis smiling,
And beguiling,
Makes me happier than before.

Though, alas! too late I find
Nothing can her fancy fix,
Yet the moment she is kind,
I forgive her all her tricks;
Which though I see,
I can't get free;
She deceiving,
I believing;
What need lovers wish for more?

ANTHONY WOOD

The author of the following sketch spent the best part of his lifetime writing the history of Oxford University and the biographies of its alumni. He was not all innocence in his learned labors, as the selection shows, and the publication of his Athenae Oxonienses *in 1691-1692 resulted in his expulsion from the university.*

A Son of Belial

Charles Sedley, baronet, son of Sir John Sedley of Aylesford in Kent, baronet, by his wife, Elizabeth, daughter and heir of Sir Henry Savile, knight, sometime Warden of Merton College in Oxford, was born there or at Southfleet, or at least in the said county of Kent, became a fellow commoner of Wadham College in Lent term 1656, aged 17 years or thereabouts, but taking no degree he retired to his own country and neither went to travel or to the inns of court. Afterwards, when the nation was set at liberty and freed from the severities of the usurpers by the restoration of King Charles II, he lived mostly in the great city, became a debauchee, set up for a satirical wit, a comedian, poet and courtier of ladies, and I know not what, and therefore remembered by an eminent poet in these verses:

Sedley has that prevailing, gentle art,
That can with a resistless charm impart
The loosest wishes, to the chastest heart;

Raise such a conflict, kindle such a fire,
Betwixt declining virtue and desire;
Till the poor vanquished maid dissolves away
In dreams all night, in sighs and tears all day.

In the month of June, 1663, this our author, Sir Charles Sedley, Charles Lord Buckhurst (afterwards Earl of Middlesex), Sir Thomas Ogle, etc., were at a cook's house at the sign of the Cock in Bow Street near Covent Garden within the liberty of Westminster, and being inflamed with strong liquors they went into the balcony belonging to that house and putting down their breeches they excrementized in the street, which being done Sedley stripped himself naked and with eloquence preached blasphemy to the people; whereupon a riot being raised, the people became very clamorous and would have forced the door next to the street open, but, being hindered, the preacher and his company were pelted into their room, and the windows belonging thereunto were broken. This frolic being soon spread abroad, especially by the fanatical party, who aggravated it to the utmost by making it the most scandalous thing in nature and nothing more reproachful to religion than that, the said company were summoned to the Court of Justice in Westminster Hall, where, being indicted of a riot before Sir Robert Hyde, Lord Chief Justice of the Common Pleas, were all fined, and Sir Charles being fined £500 he made answer that he thought he was the first man that paid for shiting. Sir Robert Hyde asked him whether ever he read the book called *The Complete Gentleman*, etc., to which Sir Charles made answer that, set aside his lordship, he had read more books than himself, etc. The day for payment being appointed, Sir Charles desired Mr. Henry Killegrew and another gentleman to apply themselves to His Majesty to get it off, but instead of that they begged the said sum of His Majesty and would not abate Sir Charles two pence of the money. Afterwards, Sir Charles taking up and growing very serious, he was chosen a recruiter of that Long Parliament which began at Westminster 8 May, 1661, to serve for New Rumney in Kent as he hath been for three or more parliaments since the dissolution of that which was on the 24th of January, 1678.

APHRA BEHN

The life history of the Incomparable Astraea is sensational enough, even when shorn of all its palpably fictitious embellishments. She

*may or may not have spent her girlhood in Surinam (Dutch Guiana)
and been an eyewitness of the astonishing events recorded in* The
Royal Slave, *may or may not have married a Dutch merchant in
London and lived for a time in affluence, attracting the notice of
the King. But she was certainly employed as an English secret agent
in Holland during the war, certainly fell into dire poverty, and certainly knew the inside of a debtors' prison. Her reports and petitions
are among the state papers. Having reached the point of desperation
indicated in the letter which we quote below and finding no redress
from an impoverished and ungrateful government, she turned successfully to literature as a means of livelihood, a thing no English-
woman had ever done before.*

*She became almost overnight a successful playwright, novelist and
poet, lived a free and easy life as the toast of wits and (a Restoration
gesture!) was buried in Westminster Abbey. Her position was an exposed one and she met it with a sure instinct for survival which has
been the admiration of modern women of the pen. There is a femi-
nist touch in her reported jilting of foolish lovers. Her Love Letters
to a Gentleman, if genuine, show her to have been herself a prey to
love unsatisfied.*

*As a dramatist she competed with the best and bawdiest. She was
never without a comeback when attacked. "That day 'twas acted
first," she says of her play* The Dutch Lover, *"there comes me into
the pit a long, lither, phlegmatic, white, ill-favored, wretched fop,
an officer in masquerade newly transported with a scarf and feather
out of France, a sorry animal that has nought else to shield it from
the uttermost contempt of all mankind but that respect which we
afford to rats and toads, which, though we do not well allow to live,
yet when considered as part of God's creation we make honorable
mention of them. A thing, Reader,—but no more of such a smeltt!
This thing, I tell ye, opening that which serves it for a mouth, out
issued such a noise as this to those that sat about it: that they were
to expect a woeful play—God damn him!—for it was a woman's."*
*The language is that of a hard-bitten lady journalist who knows its
power.*

Oroonoko or The Royal Slave, *of which the concluding portion is
here given, has been valued as an early document in the protest
against slavery and as an anticipation of the realistic fiction of Defoe.
'Tis a wild tale of tender passion and heroic death. The young Negro
prince of Cromartien and his ebony love, Imoinda, have been sold
separately into slavery. They come together under the ownership of
the civilized Mr. Trefry, who, recognizing Oroonoko's royal quality,
names him appropriately Caesar and treats him rather as a brother
than as a slave. In this capacity he is admired by the whole white
population, including the Incomparable herself.*

The Royal Slave

While they sat at meat, Mr. Trefry told Cæsar that most of these young slaves were undone in love with a fine she-slave, whom they had had about six months on their land; the prince, who never heard the name of love without a sigh, nor any mention of it without the curiosity of examining further into that tale, which of all discourses was most agreeable to him, asked how they came to be so unhappy as to be all undone for one fair slave. Trefry, who was naturally amorous, and loved to talk of love as well as anybody, proceeded to tell him they had the most charming black that ever was beheld on their plantation, about fifteen or sixteen years old, as he guessed; that for his part he had done nothing but sigh for her ever since she came; and that all the white beauties he had seen never charmed him so absolutely as this fine creature had done; and that no man, of any nation, ever beheld her that did not fall in love with her; and that she had all the slaves perpetually at her feet; and the whole country resounded with the fame of Clemene. "For so," said he, "we have christened her: but she denies us all with such a noble disdain that 'tis a miracle to see that she who can give such eternal desires should herself be all ice and all unconcern. She is adorned with the most graceful modesty that ever beautified youth; the softest sigher—that, if she were capable of love, one would swear she languished for some absent happy man; and so retired as if she feared a rape even from the god of day, or that the breezes would steal kisses from her delicate mouth. Her task of work, some sighing lover every day makes it his petition to perform for her; which she accepts blushing, and with reluctancy, for fear he will ask her a look for a recompense, which he dares not presume to hope; so great an awe she strikes into the hearts of her admirers. "I do not wonder," replied the prince, "that Clemene should refuse slaves, being, as you say, so beautiful; but wonder how she escapes those that can entertain her as you can do: or why, being your slave, you do not oblige her to yield." "I confess," said Trefry, "when I have against her will entertained her with love so long as to be transported with my passion even above decency, I have been ready to make use of those advantages of strength and force nature has given me; but oh! she disarms me with that modesty and weepings, so tender and so moving that I retire, and thank my stars she overcame me." The company laughed at his civility to a slave, and Cæsar only applauded the nobleness of his passion and nature, since that slave might be noble, or, what was better, have true notions of honor and virtue in her. Thus passed they this night, after having received from the slaves all imaginable respect and obedience.

The next day, Trefry asked Cæsar to walk when the heat was allayed, and designedly carried him by the cottage of the fair slave; and told him, she whom he spoke of last night lived there retired. "But," says he, "I would not wish you to approach; for I am sure you will be in love as soon as you behold her." Cæsar assured him he was proof against all the charms of that sex; and that if he imagined his heart could be so perfidious to love again, after Imoinda, he believed he should tear it from his bosom. They had no sooner spoke but a little shock-dog, that Clemene had presented her, which she took great delight in, ran out; and she, not knowing anybody was there, ran to get it in again, and bolted out on those who were just speaking of her: when seeing them, she would have run in again, but Trefry caught her by the hand, and cried, "Clemene, however you fly a lover, you ought to pay some respect to this stranger" (pointing to Cæsar). But she, as if she had resolved never to raise her eyes to the face of a man again, bent 'em the more to the earth, when he spoke, and gave the prince the leisure to look the more at her. There needed no long gazing, or consideration, to examine who this fair creature was; he soon saw Imoinda all over her; in a minute he saw her face, her shape, her air, her modesty, and all that called forth his soul with joy at his eyes, and left his body destitute of almost life: it stood without motion, and for a minute knew not that it had a being; and, I believe, he had never come to himself, so oppressed he was with over-joy, if he had not met with this allay, that he perceived Imoinda fall dead in the hands of Trefry. This awakened him, and he ran to her aid, and caught her in his arms, where by degrees she came to herself; and 'tis needless to tell with what transports, what ecstasies of joy, they both a while beheld each other, without speaking; then snatched each other to their arms; then gazed again, as if they still doubted whether they possessed the blessing they grasped: but when they recovered their speech, 'tis not to be imagined what tender things they expressed to each other; wondering what strange fate had brought them again together. They soon informed each other of their fortunes, and equally bewailed their fate; but at the same time they mutually protested that even fetters and slavery were soft and easy, and would be supported with joy and pleasure, while they could be so happy to possess each other, and to be able to make good their vows. Cæsar swore he disdained the empire of the world, while he could behold his Imoinda; and she despised grandeur and pomp, those vanities of her sex, when she could gaze on Oroonoko. He adored the very cottage where she resided, and said, that little inch of the world would give him more happiness than all the universe could do; and she vowed, it was a palace while adorned with the presence of Oroonoko.

Trefry was infinitely pleased with this novel, and found this Clemene was the fair mistress of whom Cæsar had before spoke; and was not a little satisfied that Heaven was so kind to the prince as to sweeten his misfortunes by so lucky an accident; and leaving the lovers to themselves, was impatient to come down to Parham-House (which was on the same plantation) to give me an account of what had happened. I was as impatient to make these lovers a visit, having already made a friendship with Cæsar, and from his own mouth learned what I have related; which was confirmed by his Frenchman, who was set on shore to seek his fortune, and of whom they could not make a slave, because a Christian; and he came daily to Parham-Hill to see and pay his respects to his pupil prince. So that concerning and interesting myself in all that related to Cæsar, whom I had assured of liberty as soon as the Governor arrived, I hasted presently to the place where these lovers were, and was infinitely glad to find this beautiful young slave (who had already gained all our esteems, for her modesty and her extraordinary prettiness) to be the same I had heard Cæsar speak so much of. . . . From that happy day Cæsar took Clemene for his wife, to the general joy of all people; and there was as much magnificence as the country could afford at the celebration of this wedding: and in a very short time after she conceived with child, which made Cæsar even adore her, knowing he was . the last of his great race. This new accident made him more impatient of liberty, and he was every day treating with Trefry for his and Clemene's liberty, and offered either gold or a vast quantity of slaves, which should be paid before they let him go, provided he could have any security that he should go when his ransom was paid. They fed him from day to day with promises, and delayed him till the Lord-Governor should come; so that he began to suspect them of falsehood, and that they would delay him till the time of his wife's delivery, and make a slave of that too: for all the breed is theirs to whom the parents belong. This thought made him very uneasy, and his sullenness gave them some jealousies of him; so that I was obliged, by some persons who feared a mutiny (which is very fatal sometimes in those colonies that abound so with slaves, that they exceed the whites in vast numbers), to discourse with Cæsar, and to give him all the satisfaction I possibly could. . . .

For some time we diverted him; but now Imoinda began to show she was with child, and did nothing but sigh and weep for the captivity of her lord, herself, and the infant yet unborn; and believed if it were so hard to gain the liberty of two, 'twould be more difficult to get that for three. Her griefs were so many darts in the great heart of Cæsar, and taking his opportunity, one Sunday, when all the whites were overtaken in drink, as there were abundance of several trades, and slaves for four years, that inhabited among the negro houses; and Sunday being their day of debauch (otherwise they were a sort of spies upon Cæsar), he went, pretending out of goodness to 'em, to feast among 'em, and sent all his music, and ordered a great treat for the whole gang, about three hundred negroes, and about an hundred and fifty were able to bear arms, such as they had, which were sufficient to do execution with spirits accordingly: for the English had none but rusty swords, that no strength could draw from a scabbard; except the people of particular quality, who took care to oil 'em, and keep 'em in good order: the guns also, unless here and there one, or those newly carried from England, would do no good or harm; for 'tis the nature of that country to rust and eat up iron, or any metals but gold and silver. And they are very unexpert at the bow, which the negroes and Indians are perfect masters of.

Cæsar, having singled out these men from the women and children, made an harangue to 'em, of the miseries and ignominies of slavery; counting up all their toils and sufferings, under such loads, burdens, and drudgeries as were fitter for beasts than men; senseless brutes, than human souls. He told 'em, it was not for days, months, or years, but for eternity; there was no end to be of their misfortunes: they suffered not like men who might find a glory and fortitude in oppression; but like dogs, that loved the whip and bell, and fawned the more they were beaten: that they had lost the divine quality of men, and were become insensible asses, fit only to bear: nay, worse; an ass, or dog, or horse, having done his duty, could lie down in retreat, and rise to work again, and while he did his duty, endured no stripes; but men, villainous, senseless men, such as they, toiled on all the tedious week till *Black Friday:* and then, whether they worked or not, whether they were faulty or meriting, they, promiscuously, the innocent with the guilty, suffered the infamous whip, the sordid stripes, from their fellow-slaves, till their blood trickled from all parts of their body; blood, whose every drop ought to be revenged with a life of some of those tyrants that impose it. "And why," said he, "my dear friends and fellow-sufferers, should we be slaves to an unknown people? Have they vanquished us nobly in fight? Have they won us in honorable battle? And are we by the chance of war become their slaves? This would not anger a noble heart; this would not animate a soldier's soul: no, but we are bought and sold like apes or monkeys, to be the sport of women, fools, and cowards; and the support of rogues and runagates, that have abandoned their own countries for rapine, murders, theft, and villainies. Do you not hear every day how they upbraid each other with infamy of life, below the wildest savages? And shall we render obedience to such a degenerate race, who have no one human virtue left, to distinguish them from the vilest creatures? Will you, I say, suffer the lash from such hands?" They all replied with one accord, "No, no, no; Cæsar has spoke like a great captain, like a great king."

After this he would have proceeded, but was interrupted by a tall negro of some more quality than the rest, his name was Tuscan; who bowing at the feet of Cæsar, cried, "My Lord, we have listened with joy and attention to what you have said; and, were we only men, would follow so great a leader through the world. But oh! consider we are husbands, and parents too, and have things more dear to us than life; our wives and children, unfit for travel in those unpassable woods, mountains, and bogs. We have not only difficult lands to overcome, but rivers to wade, and mountains to encounter; ravenous beasts of prey."—To this Cæsar replied that honor was the first principle in Nature, that was to be obeyed; but as no man would pretend to that, without all the acts of virtue, compassion, charity, love, justice, and reason, he found it not inconsistent with that to take equal care of their wives and children as they would of themselves; and that he did not design, when he led them to freedom and glorious liberty, that they should leave that better part of themselves to perish by the hand of the tyrant's whip: but if there were a woman among them so degenerate from love and virtue, to choose slavery before the pursuit of her husband, and with the hazard of her life to share with him in his fortunes that such a one ought to be abandoned, and left as a prey to the common enemy. . . .

Tuscan then demanded what he would do. He said they would travel towards the sea, plant a new colony, and defend it by their valor; and when they could find a ship, either driven by stress of weather, or guided by Providence that way, they would seize it, and make it a prize, till it had transported them to their own countries: at least they should be made free in his kingdom, and be esteemed as his fellow-sufferers, and men that had the courage and the bravery to attempt, at least, for liberty; and if they died in the attempt, it would be more brave than to live in perpetual slavery.

They bowed and kissed his feet at this resolution, and with one accord vowed to follow him to death; and that night was appointed to begin their march. They made it known to their wives, and directed them to tie their hamaca about their shoulders, and under their arm, like a scarf, and to lead their children that could go, and carry those that could not. The wives, who pay an entire obedience to their husbands, obeyed, and staid for 'em where they were appointed: The men staid but to furnish themselves with what defensive arms they could get; and all met at the rendezvous, where Cæsar made a new encouraging speech to 'em, and led 'em out.

But as they could not march far that night, on Monday early, when the overseers went to call 'em all together to go to work, they were extremely surprised to find not one upon the place, but all fled with what baggage they had. You may imagine this news was not only suddenly spread all over the plantation, but soon reached the neighboring ones; and we had by noon about 600 men, they call the militia of the country, that came to assist us in the pursuit of the fugitives: but never did one see so comical an army march forth to war. The men of any fashion would not concern themselves, though it were almost the common cause; for such revoltings are very ill examples, and have very fatal consequences oftentimes, in many colonies: but they had a respect for Cæsar, and all hands were against the Parhamites (as they called those of Parham Plantation) because they did not in the first place love the Lord-Governor; and secondly, they would have it that Cæsar was ill used, and baffled with: and 'tis not impossible but some of the best in the country was of his council in this flight, and depriving us of all the slaves; so that they of the better sort would not meddle in the matter. The Deputy-Governor, of whom I have had no great occasion to speak, and who was the most fawning, fair-tongued fellow in the world, and one that pretended the most friendship to Cæsar, was now the only violent man against him; and though he had nothing, and so need fear nothing, yet talked and looked bigger than any man. He was a fellow whose character is not fit to be mentioned with the worst of the slaves. This fellow would lead his army forth to meet Cæsar, or rather to pursue him. Most of their arms were of those sort of cruel whips they call *cat with nine tails*; some had rusty useless guns for show; others old basket-hilts, whose blades had never seen the light in this age; and others had long staffs and clubs. Mr. Trefry went along, rather to be a mediator than a conqueror in such a battle; for he foresaw and knew, if by fighting they put the negroes into despair, they were a sort of sullen fellows, that would drown or kill themselves before they would yield; and he advised that fair means was best: but Byam was one that abounded in his own wit, and would take his own measures.

It was not hard to find these fugitives; for as they fled, they were forced to fire and cut the woods before 'em: so that night or day they pursued 'em by the light they made, and by the path they had cleared. But as soon as Cæsar found he was pursued, he put himself in a posture of defense, placing all the women and children in the rear; and himself, with Tuscan by his side, or next to him, all promising to die or conquer. Encouraged thus, they never stood to parley, but fell on pell-mell upon the English, and killed some, and wounded a great many they having recourse to their whips, as the best of their weapons. And as they observed no order, they perplexed the enemy so sorely, with lashing 'em in the eyes; and the women and children seeing their husbands so treated, being of fearful cowardly dispositions and hearing the English cry out, "Yield, and live! Yield, and be pardoned!" they all run in amongst their husbands and fathers, and hung about them, crying out, "Yield! Yield! and leave Cæsar to their revenge": that by degrees the slaves abandoned Cæsar, and left him only Tuscan and his heroic Imoinda, who, grown big as she was, did nevertheless press near her lord, having a bow and a quiver full of poisoned arrows, which she managed with such dexterity that she wounded several, and shot the Governor into the shoulder. . . .

In all this time you may believe we were in no little affliction for Cæsar and his wife: some were of opinion he was escaped, never to return; others thought some accident had happened to him: but however, we failed not to send out a hundred people several ways, to search for him. A party of about forty went that way he took, among whom was Tuscan, who was perfectly reconciled to Byam. They had not gone very far into the wood but they smelt an unusual smell, as of a dead body; for stinks must be very noisome that can be distinguished among such a quantity of natural sweets as every inch of that land produces: so that they concluded they should find him dead, or some body that was so; they passed on towards it, as loathsome as it was, and made such rustling among the leaves that lie thick on the ground, by continual falling, that Cæsar heard he was approached: and though he had, during the space of these eight days, endeavored to rise, but found he wanted strength, yet looking up, and seeing his pursuers, he rose, and reeled to a neighboring tree, against which he fixed his back; and being within a dozen yards of those that advanced and saw him, he called out to them, and bid them approach no nearer, if they would be safe. So that they stood still, and hardly believing their eyes, that would persuade them that it was Cæsar that spoke to 'em, so much was he altered; they asked him what he had done with his wife, for they smelt a stink that almost struck them dead. He, pointing to the dead body, sighing, cried, "Behold her there." They put off the flowers that covered her, with their sticks, and found she was killed, and cried out, "O monster! that has murdered thy wife." Then asking him why he did so cruel a deed; he replied, he had no leisure to answer impertinent questions. "You may go back," continued he, "and tell the faithless Governor he may thank Fortune that I am breathing my last; and that my arm is too feeble to obey my heart, in what it had designed him." But his tongue faltering, and trembling, he could scarce end what he was saying. The English, taking advantage of his weakness, cried, "Let us take him alive by all means." He heard 'em; and, as if he had revived from a fainting, or a dream, he cried out, "No, Gentlemen, you are deceived; you will find no more Cæsars to be whipped; no more find a faith in me: feeble as you think me, I have strength yet left to secure me from a second indignity." They swore all anew; and he only shook his head, and beheld them with scorn. Then they cried out "Who will venture on this single man? Will nobody?" They stood all silent while Cæsar replied, "Fatal will be the attempt to the first adventurer, let him assure himself" (and, at that word, held up his knife in a menacing posture). "Look ye, ye faithless crew," said he, " 'tis not life I seek, nor am I afraid of dying" (and at that word, cut a piece of flesh from his own throat, and threw it at 'em), "yet still I would live if I could, till I had perfected my revenge. But, oh! it cannot be; I feel life gliding from my eyes and heart; and if I make not haste, I shall fall a victim to the shameful whip." At that, he ripped up his own belly, and took his bowels and pulled 'em out, with what strength he could; while some, on their knees imploring, besought him to hold his hand. But when they saw him tottering, they cried out, "Will none venture on him?" A bold Englishman cried,

"Yes, if he were the Devil" (taking courage when he saw him almost dead), and swearing a horrid oath for his farewell to the world, he rushed on him. Cæsar with his armed hand met him so fairly as stuck him to the heart, and he fell dead at his feet. Tuscan, seeing that, cried out, "I love thee, O Cæsar! and therefore will not let thee die, if possible," and running to him, took him in his arms: but, at the same time, warding a blow that Cæsar made at his bosom, he received it quite through his arm; and Cæsar having not the strength to pluck the knife forth, though he attempted it, Tuscan neither pulled it out himself, nor suffered it to be pulled out, but came down with it sticking in his arm; and the reason he gave for it was, because the air should not get into the wound. They put their hands across, and carried Cæsar between six of 'em, fainting as he was, and they thought dead, or just dying; and they brought him to Parham, and laid him on a couch, and had the chirurgeon immediately to him, who dressed his wounds, and sowed up his belly, and used means to bring him to life, which they effected. We ran all to see him; and, if before we thought him so beautiful a sight, he was now so altered that his face was like a death's-head blacked over, nothing but teeth and eye-holes: for some days we suffered nobody to speak to him, but caused cordials to be poured down his throat; which sustained his life, and in six or seven days he recovered his senses: for you must know that wounds are almost to a miracle cured in the Indies; unless wounds in the legs, which they rarely ever cure.

When he was well enough to speak, we talked to him, and asked him some questions about his wife, and the reasons why he killed her; and he then told us what I have related of that resolution, and of his parting, and he besought us we would let him die, and was extremely afflicted to think it was possible he might live: He assured us, if we did not dispatch him, he would prove very fatal to a great many. We said all we could to make him live, and gave him new assurances; but he begged we would not think so poorly of him, or of his love to Imoinda, to imagine we could flatter him to life again: but the chirurgeon assured him he could not live, and therefore he need not fear. We were all (but Cæsar) afflicted at this news, and the sight was ghastly: his discourse was sad; and the earthy smell about him so strong that I was persuaded to leave the place for some time (being myself but sickly, and very apt to fall into fits of danger-ous illness upon any extraordinary melancholy). The servants, and Trefry, and the chirurgeons, promised all to take what possible care they could of the life of Cæsar; and I, taking boat, went with other company to Colonel Martin's, about three days' journey down the river. But I was no sooner gone than the Governor, taking Trefry, about some pretended earnest business, a day's journey up the river, having communicated his design to one Banister, a wild Irishman, and one of the council, a fellow of absolute barbarity, and fit to execute any villainy, but rich; he came up to Parham, and forcibly took Cæsar, and had him carried to the same post where he was whipped; and causing him to be tied to it, and a great fire made before him, he told him he should die like a dog, as he was. Cæsar replied, this was the first piece of bravery that ever Banister did, and he never spoke sense till he pronounced that word; and, if he would keep it, he would declare, in the other world, that he was the only man, of all the whites, that ever he heard speak truth. And turning to the men that had bound him, he said, "My friends, am I to die, or to be whipped?" And they cried, "Whipped! no, you shall not escape so well." And then he replied, smiling, "A blessing on thee"; and assured them they need not tie him, for he would stand fixed like a rock, and endure death so as should encourage them to die; "But if you whip me," said he, "be sure you tie me fast."

He had learned to take tobacco; and when he was assured he should die, he desired they would give him a pipe in his mouth, ready lighted; which they did. And the executioner came, and first cut off his members, and threw them into the fire; after that, with an ill-favored knife, they cut off his ears and his nose and burned them; he still smoked on, as if nothing had touched him; then they hacked off one of his arms, and still he bore up, and held his pipe; but at the cutting off the other arm, his head sunk, and his pipe dropped, and he gave up the ghost, without a groan or a reproach. My mother and sister were by him all the while, but not suffered to save him; so rude and wild were the rabble, and so inhuman were the justices who stood by to see the execution, who after paid dearly enough for their insolence. They cut Cæsar in quarters, and sent them to several of the chief plantations: one quarter was sent to Colonel Martin, who refused it, and swore he had rather see the quarters of Banister, and the Governor himself, than those of Cæsar, on his plantations; and that he could govern his negroes without terrifying and grieving them with frightful spectacles of a mangled king.

Thus died this great man, worthy of a better fate, and a more sublime wit than mine to write his praise: yet, I hope, the reputation of my pen is considerable enough to make his glorious name to survive to all ages, with that of the brave, the beautiful, and the constant Imoinda.

Letters of Aphra

TO MR. KILLIGREW

Sir,

If you could guess at the affliction of my soul, you would, I am sure, pity me. 'Tis tomorrow that I must submit myself to a prison, the time being expired, and though I endeavored all day yesterday to get a few days more, I cannot because they say they see I am dallied withal—and, so they say, I shall be forever. So I cannot revoke my doom. I have cried myself dead and could find in my heart to break through all and get to the King and never rise till he were pleased to pay this. But I am sick and weak and unfit for it or a prison. I shall go tomorrow, but I will send my mother to the King with a petition, for I see everybody are words, and I will not perish in a prison from whence he swears I shall not stir till the utmost farthing be paid. And Oh God, who considers my misery and charge too, this is my reward for all my great promises and my endeavors. Sir, if I have not the money tonight, you must send me something to keep me in prison, for I will not starve.

TO A GENTLEMAN

1.

You bid me write and I wish it were only the effect of complaisance that makes me obey you. I should be very angry with myself and you if I thought it were any other motive. I hope it is not and will not have you believe otherwise. I cannot help, however, wishing you no mirth nor any content in your dancing design, and this unwonted malice in me I do not like and would have concealed it if I could, lest you should take it for something I am not nor will believe myself guilty of. May your women be all ugly, ill-natured, ill-fashioned, and unconversable, and for your greater disappointment may every moment of your time there be taken up with thoughts of me (a sufficient curse)! . . . You know what you gave your hand upon; the date of banishment is already out and I wish you could have been so good-natured as to have disobeyed me. Pray take notice that I am better natured than you. I am profoundly melancholy since I saw you, I know not why, and should be glad to see you when your occasions will permit you to visit

ASTRAEA.

2.

You may tell me a thousand years, my dear Lycidas, of your unbounded friendship, but after so unkind a departure as that last night give me leave, when serious, to doubt it. Nay, 'tis past doubt. I know you rather hate me. What else could hurry you from me when you saw me surrounded with all the necessary impossibilities of speaking to you? I made as broad signs as one could do who durst not speak, both for your sake and my own. I acted even imprudently to make my soul be understood, that was then, if I may say so, in real agonies for your departure. 'Tis a wonder a woman so violent in all her passions as I, did not, forgetting all prudence, all considerations, fly out into absolute commands or at least entreaties that you would give me a moment's time longer. . . . Come then, I conjure you, this evening, that after it I may shut those eyes that have been too long waking. I have committed a thousand madnesses in this, but you must pardon the faults you have created. Come and do so, for I must see you tonight and that in a better humor than you were last night. No more. Obey me as you have that friendship for me you profess, and assure yourself to find a very welcome reception from, Lycidas,

Your ASTRAEA.

3.

Though it be very late I cannot go to bed but I must tell thee I have been very good ever since I saw thee, and have been writing and have seen no face of man or anybody save my own people. I am mightily pleased with your kindness to me tonight, and 'twas, I hope and believe, very innocent and undisturbing on both sides. My Lycidas says he can be soft and dear when he pleases to put off his haughty pride, which is only to see how far I dare love him ununited. Since, then, my soul's delight, you are and may ever be assured I am and ever will be yours, befall me what will, and that all the Devils of Hell shall not prevail against thee—show, then, I say, my dearest Love, all the love thou hast undissembled. Then and never till then shall I believe you love. And deserve my heart for God's sake to keep me well. And if thou hast love, as I shall never doubt if thou art always as tonight, show that love, I beseech thee. There is nothing so grateful to God and mankind as plain dealing. 'Tis too late to conjure thee further. I will be purchased with softness and dear words and kind expressions, sweet eyes and a low voice.

Farewell! I love thee dearly, passionately, and tenderly, and am resolved to be eternally, My only Dear Delight and Joy of my Life,

Thy ASTRAEA.

4.

How could anything but the man that hates me entertain me so unkindly? Witness your excellent opinion of me of loving others! Witness your passing by the end of the street where I live and squandering away your time at any coffee house rather than allow me what you know is the greatest blessing of my life, your dear dull melancholy company! I call it dull because you can never be merry where Astraea is. . . . I should be glad to see you as soon as possible. You say Thursday you can. I beg you will, and shall with impatience expect you betimes. Fail me not as you would have me think you have any value for

ASTRAEA.

TO JACOB TONSON, PUBLISHER

Dear Mr. Tonson,

I am mightily obleeged to you for the services you have done me to Mr. Dryden, in whose esteem I would choose to be rather than anybody's in the world; and I am sure I never, in thought, word, or deed, merited other from him, but if you had heard what was told me you would have excused all I said on that account. . . .

As for the verses of mine I should really have thought 'em worth thirty pound, and I hope you will find it worth £25. Not that I should dispute at any other time for five pound where I am so obleeged, but you cannot think what a preety thing the *Island* [A *Voyage to the Isle of Love*, a translation] will be and what a deal of labor I shall have yet with it. And if that pleases I will do the second *Voyage*, which will compose a little book as big as a novel by itself. But pray speak to your brother to advance the price to one £5 more. 'Twill at this time be more than given me, and I vow I would not ask it if I did not really believe it worth more. Alas, I would not lose my time in such low gettings but only, since I am about it, I am resolved to go through with it though I should give it. I pray go about it as soon as you please, for I shall finish as fast as you can go on. Methinks the *Voyage* should come last, as being the largest volume. You know Mr. Cowley's *David* is last, because a large poem, and Mrs. Phillips her plays for the same reason. I wish I had more time; I would add something to the verses that I have a mind to. But good, dear Mr. Tonson, let it be £5 more, for I may safely swear I have lost the getting of £50 by it, though that's nothing to you, or my satisfaction and humor. But I have been without getting so long that I am just on the point of breaking, especially since a body has no credit at the Playhouse for money as we used to have—50 or 60 deep, or more. I want extremely or I would not urge this.

Yours,

A. B.

Pray send me the loose papers to put to these I have, and let me know which you will go about first, the songs and verses or that. Send me an answer today.

Poems of Aphra

LOVE ARMED

Love in fantastic triumph sat
Whilst bleeding hearts around him flowed,
For whom fresh pains he did create
And strange tyrannic power he showed.

From thy bright eyes he took the fires
Which round about in sport he hurled,
But 'twas from mine he took desires
Enough t'undo the amorous world.

From me he took his sighs and tears,
From thee his pride and cruelty;
From me his languishments and fears.
And every killing dart from thee.

Thus thou and I the God have armed
And set him up a deity;

But my poor heart alone is harmed,
Whilst thine the victor is, and free.

THE WILLING MISTRESS

Amyntas led me to a grove,
Where all the trees did shade us;
The sun itself, though it had strove,
It could not have betrayed us.

The place secured from human eyes
No other fear allows
But when the winds that gently rise
Do kiss the yielding boughs.

Down there we sat upon the moss,
And did begin to play
A thousand amorous tricks, to pass
The heat of all the day.

A many kisses he did give
And I returned the same,
Which made me willing to receive
That which I dare not name.

ON MR. DRYDEN, RENEGADE

Scorning religion all thy lifetime past,
And now embracing popery at last,
Is like thyself, and what thou'st done before,
Defying wife and marrying a whore.
Alas, how leering hereticks will laugh
To see a gray old hedge-bird caught with chaff.
But this the priests will get from thee at least,
That if they mend thee miracles are not ceased;
For 'tis not more to cure the lame and blind
Than heal an impious, ulcerated mind.
This if they do, and give thee but a grain
Of common honesty or common shame,
'Twill be more credit to their cause, I grant,
Than 'twould to make another man a saint.

But thou no party ever shalt adorn,
To thy own shame and Nature's scandal born;
All shun alike thy ugly outward part.
Whilst none have right or title to thy heart.
Resolved to stand and constant to the time,
Fixed in the lewdness, settled in thy crime,
Whilst Moses with the Israelites abode
Thou seemed'est content to worship Moses' God,
But since he went away and since thy master fell
Thou found's a golden calf would do as well.
And when another Moses shall arise
Once more I know thou'lt rub and clear thy eyes
And turn to be an Israelite again;
For when the play is done and finished clean
What should a poet do but shift the scene.

A PINDARIC POEM

To the Reverend Doctor Burnet on the honor he did me of enquiring after me and my Muse [written after the Revolution].

When old Rome's candidates aspired to fame
  And did the people's suffrages obtain
For some great consul or a Caesar's name,
  The victor was not half so pleased and vain
As I when given the honor of your choice
And preference had in that one single voice;
  That voice from whence immortal wit still flows,
Wit that at once is solemn all and sweet,
  Where noblest eloquence and judgment shows
The inspiring mind, illustrious, rich, and great,
A mind that can inform your wondrous pen
  In all that's perfect and sublime,
And with an art beyond the wit of men,
  On whatere theme or on what great design,
It carries a commanding force like that of writ divine.

'Tis to your pen, great Sir, the nation owes
For all the good this mighty change has wrought;
Twas that the wondrous method did dispose
Ere the vast work was to perfection brought.

O, strange effect of a seraphic quill,
That can by unperceptible degrees
Change every notion, every principle
To any form its great dictator please.

Though I the wondrous change deplore
That makes me useless and forlorn,
Yet I the great design adore,
Though ruined in the universal turn.
Nor can my indigence and lost repose,
Those meager furies that surround me close,
Convert my sense and reason more
To this unprecedented enterprise,
Than that a man so great, so learned, so wise
The brave achievement owns and nobly justifies.
Tis you, great Sir, alone, by Heaven preserved,
Whose conduct has so well the nation served;
Tis you that to posterity shall give
This ages wonder and its history.
And Great Nassau shall in your annals live
To all futurity.
Your pen shall more immortalize his name
Than even his own renowned and celebrated fame.

ABRAHAM COWLEY

A published poet at the precocious age of fifteen, Cowley was the chief representative of the school of metaphysical wit to flourish anew after the Restoration. He did so partly by virtue of his Pindaric Odes, a popular genre which finds its high point in Dryden, but more by his essays and simpler verses written in Horatian retirement, after Charles refused to reward him for his services as an exiled Royalist.

Of Solitude

Nunquam minus solus, quam cum solus is now become a very vulgar saying. Every man and almost every boy for these seventeen hundred years has had it in his mouth. But it was at first spoken by the excellent Scipio, who was without question a most eloquent and witty person, as well as the most wise, most worthy, most happy, and the greatest of all mankind. His meaning no doubt was this, that he found more satisfaction to his mind and more improvement of it by solitude than by company, and to show that he spoke not this loosely or out of vanity, after he had made Rome mistress of almost the whole world, he retired himself from it by a voluntary exile, and at a private house in the middle of a wood near Linternum passed the remainder of his glorious life no less gloriously. This house Seneca went to see so long after with great veneration, and among other things describes his baths to have been of so mean a structure that now, says he, the basest of the people would despise them, and cry out, "Poor Scipio understood not how to live." What an authority is here for the credit of retreat! and happy had it been for Hannibal if adversity could have taught him as much wisdom as was learnt by Scipio from the highest prosperities. This would be no wonder if it were as truly as it is colorably and wittily said by Monsieur de Montaigne, that ambition itself might teach us to love solitude; there's nothing does so much hate to have companions. 'Tis true, it loves to have its elbows free, it detests to have company on either side, but it delights above all things in a train behind, ay, and ushers too before it. But the greatest part of men are so far from the opinion of that noble Roman that if they chance at any time to be without company, they're like a becalmed ship, they never move but by the wind of other men's breath, and have no oars of their own to steer withal. It is very fantastical and contradictory in human nature, that men should love themselves above all the rest of the world, and yet never endure to be with themselves. When they are in love with a mistress, all other persons are importunate and burdensome to them. *Tecum vivere amem, tecum obeam lubens*, they would live and die with her alone.

> With thee forever I in woods could rest,
> Where never human foot the ground has press'd;
> Thou from all shades the darkness canst exclude,
> And from a desert banish solitude.

And yet our dear self is so wearisome to us that we can scarcely support its conversation for an hour together. This is such an odd temper of mind as Catullus expresses towards one of his mistresses, whom we may suppose to have been of a very unsociable humor.

> I hate, and yet I love thee too;
> How can that be? I know not how;
> Only that so it is I know,
> And feel with torment that 'tis so.

It is a deplorable condition, this, and drives a man sometimes to pitiful shifts in seeking how to avoid himself.

The truth of the matter is that neither he who is a fop in the world is a fit man to be alone, nor he who has set his heart much upon the world, though he have never so much understanding; so that solitude can be well fitted and set right but upon a very few persons. They must have enough knowledge of the world to see the vanity of it, and enough virtue to despise all vanity; if the mind be possessed with any lust or passions, a man had better be in a fair than in a wood alone. They may, like petty thieves, cheat us perhaps and pick our pockets in the midst of company, but, like robbers, they use to strip and bind, or murder us when they catch us alone. This is but to retreat from men and fall into the hands of devils. 'Tis like the punishment of parricides among the Romans, to be sewed into a bag with an ape, a dog, and a serpent. The first work therefore that a man must do to make himself capable of the good of solitude is the very eradication of all lusts, for how is it possible for a man to enjoy himself while his affections are tied to things without himself? In the second place, he must learn the art and get the habit of thinking; for this too, no less than well speaking, depends upon much practice, and cogitation is the thing which distinguishes the solitude of a god from a wild beast. Now because the soul of man is not by its own nature or observation furnished with sufficient materials to work upon, it is necessary for it to have continual recourse to learning and books for fresh supplies, so that the solitary life will grow indigent, and be ready to starve without them; but if once we be thoroughly engaged in the love of letters, instead of being wearied with the length of any day we shall only complain of the shortness of our whole life.

O life, long to the fool, short to the wise!

The first minister of state has not so much business in public as a wise man has in private; if the one have little leisure to be alone, the other has less leisure to be in company; the one has but part of the affairs of one nation, the other all the works of God and Nature under his consideration. There is no saying shocks me so much as that which I hear very often, that a man does not know how to pass his time. 'Twould have been but ill spoken by Methusalem in the nine hundred sixty-ninth year of his life, so far it is from us, who have not time enough to attain to the utmost perfection of any part of any science, to have cause to complain that we are forced to be idle for want of work. But this you'll say is work only for the learned, others are not capable either of the employments or divertisements that arrive from letters. I know they are not; and therefore cannot much recommend solitude to a man totally illiterate. But if any man be so unlearned as to want entertainment of the little intervals of accidental solitude, which frequently occur in almost all conditions (except the very meanest of the people, who have business enough in the necessary provisions for life), it is truly a great shame both to his parents and himself, for a very small portion of any ingenious art will stop up all those gaps of our time, either music, or painting, or designing, or chemistry, or history, or gardening, or twenty other things will do it usefully and pleasantly; and if he happen to set his affections upon poetry (which I do not advise him too immoderately), that will over-do it; no wood will be thick enough to hide him from the importunities of company or business, which would abstract him from his beloved.

> Hail, old patrician trees, so great and good!
>   Hail ye plebeian under-wood!
>   Where the poetic birds rejoice,
> And for their quiet nests and plenteous food,
>   Pay with their grateful voice.

> Hail, the poor Muses' richest manor-seat!
>   Ye country houses and retreat,
>   Which all the happy gods so love,
> That for you oft they quit their bright and great
>   Metropolis above.

> Here Nature does a house for me erect,
>   Nature, the wisest architect,
>   Who those fond artists does despise
> That can the fair and living trees neglect;
>   Yet the dead timber prize.

> Here let me, careless and unthoughtful lying,
>   Hear the soft winds above me flying,
>   With all their wanton boughs dispute,
> And the more tuneful birds to both replying,
>   Nor be myself too mute.

A silver stream shall roll his waters near,
  Gilt with the sunbeams here and there,
  On whose enamel'd bank I'll walk,
And see how prettily they smile, and hear
  How prettily they talk.

Ah wretched, and too solitary he
  Who loves not his own company!
  He'll feel the weight of't many a day
Unless he call in sin or vanity
  To help to bear't away.

Oh solitude, first state of humankind!
  Which bless'd remain'd till man did find
  Even his own helper's company.
As soon as two (alas!) together join'd,
  The serpent made up three.

Thee God himself, through countless ages, thee
  His sole companion chose to be,
  Thee, sacred Solitude alone,
Before the branchy head of number's tree
  Sprang from the trunk of One.

Thou (though men think thine an unactive part)
  Dost break and tame th' unruly heart,
  Which else would know no settled pace,
Making it move, well manag'd by thy art,
  With swiftness and with grace.

Thou the faint beams of Reason's scatter'd light,
  Dost like a burning-glass unite,
  Dost multiply the feeble heat,
And fortify the strength, till thou dost bright
  And noble fires beget.

Whilst this hard truth I teach, methinks I see
  The monster London laugh at me;
  I should at thee too, foolish city,
If it were fit to laugh at misery,
  But thy estate I pity.

Let but thy wicked men from out thee go,
    And all the fools that crowd thee so,
    Ev'n thou, who dost thy millions boast,
A village less than Islington wilt grow,
    A solitude almost.

CHARLES COTTON

Cotton was a fisherman with Izaak Walton and spoke his language. His lyric poetry has the breath of the country in it, though he can write also like the city wits in their more wholesome moments.

The Morning Quatrains

The cock has crowed an hour ago;
'Tis time we now dull sleep forego:
Tired nature is by sleep redressed,
And labor's overcome by rest.

We have outdone the work of night;
'Tis time we rise t'attend the light,
And ere he shall his beams display,
To plot new business for the day.

None but the slothful or unsound
Are by the sun in feathers found;
Nor, without rising with the sun,
Can the world's business e'er be done.

Hark, hark! the watchful chanticleer
Tells us the day's bright harbinger
Peeps o'er the eastern hills to awe
And warn night's sovereign to withdraw.

The morning curtains now are drawn,
And now appears the blushing dawn;
Aurora has her roses shed
To strew the way Sol's steeds must tread.

Xanthus and Æthon harnessed are
To roll away the burning car,
And, snorting flame, impatient bear
The dressing of the charioteer.

The sable cheeks of sullen Night
Are streaked with rosy streams of light,
Whilst she retires away in fear
To shade the other hemisphere.

The merry lark now takes her wings,
And longed-for day's loud welcome sings,
Mounting her body out of sight
As if she meant to meet the light.

Now doors and windows are unbarred;
Each-where are cheerful voices heard,
And round about "good-morrows" fly
As if day taught humanity.

The chimneys now to smoke begin,
And the old wife sits down to spin;
Whilst Kate, taking her pail, does trip
Mull's swollen and straddling paps to strip.

Vulcan now makes his anvil ring,
Dick whistles loud, and Maud doth sing,
And Silvio with his bugle horn
Winds an imprime unto the morn.

Now through the morning doors behold!
Phœbus, arrayed in burning gold,
Lashing his fiery steeds, displays
His warm and all-enlightening rays.

Now each one to his work repairs:
All that have hands are laborers,
And manufactures of each trade
By opening shops are open laid.

Hob yokes his oxen to the team;
The angler goes unto the stream;
The woodman to the purlieus hies,
The laboring bees to load their thighs.

Fair Amaryllis drives her flocks,
All night safe folded from the fox,
To flowery downs, where Colin stays
To court her with his roundelays.

The traveller now leaves his inn
A new day's journey to begin,
As he would post it with the day,
And early rising makes good way.

The slick-faced schoolboy satchel takes,
And with slow pace small riddance makes;
For why, the haste we make, you know,
To knowledge and to virtue's slow.

The fore-horse jingles on the road;
The waggoner lugs on his load;
The field with busy people snies;
And city rings with various cries.

The world is now a busy swarm,
All doing good or doing harm;
But let's take heed our acts be true,
For heaven's eye sees all we do.

None can that piercing sight evade:
It penetrates the darkest shade;
And sin, though it should 'scape the eye,
Would be discovered by the cry.

Rondeau

Forbear, fair Phyllis, oh forbear
Those deadly, killing frowns, and spare
A heart so loving and so true,

By none to be subdued but you,
Who my poor life's sole princess are
You only can create my care;
But offend you, I all things dare:
Then, lest your cruelty you rue,
           Forbear;
And lest you kill that heart, beware,
To which there is some pity due,
If but because I humbly sue.
Your anger, therefore, sweetest fair,
Though mercy in your sex is rare,
           Forbear.

JOHN DRYDEN

Dryden wrote two odes for performance at the annual festival of St. Cecilia. The first and simpler of the two, A Song for St. Cecilia's Day (1687), describes in imitative language the contrasting emotional effect of different instruments.

> *"The trumpets wild clangor*
> *Excites us to arms*
> *With shrill notes of anger*
> *And mortal alarms."*

In Alexander's Feast, written ten years later, the poet dramatizes the idea with an even higher degree of virtuosity. But here it is (more sensibly) the words as well as the music which have so overpowering and so specific an effect.

St. Cecilia was a virgin martyr in Roman times. Later legend explained that the angel who visited her nightly and appeared in time to prevent the consummation of a marriage into which she had been forced was attracted to earth by the beauty of her singing. She has thus become the patron saint of music and is often represented as seated at the organ, which she was thought to have invented.

The Restoration period inherited its musical enthusiasms from the preceding age but there were changes in patronage and organization, as well as in style and in the kind of instruments employed. The diaries of both Pepys and Evelyn reflect a widespread interest in musical developments. Pepys was himself a composer. He taught his wife and servants to play and sing, and never missed the opportunity for a duet with Mrs. Knipp. On one occasion, he records a "Musique

Meeting" at the Post Office where the Royal Society was present to listen to a new instrument called the arched-viall. The Puritans had objected to organs and professional choirs in churches. There were therefore no trained boy-soprano singers available at the Restoration, and instruments were used for a time to replace them. Purcell, the greatest composer of the time, was organist at Westminster. The music for the two earliest St. Cecilia's Day odes is his. Alexander's Feast was originally set by Jeremiah Clarke. The composition by Handel which is sometimes performed today belongs to a later period.

Alexander's Feast;
Or, the Power of Music

A SONG IN HONOR OF ST. CECILIA'S DAY: 1697

'Twas at his royal feast for Persia won
    By Philip's warlike son:
      Aloft in awful state
      The godlike hero sate
      On his imperial throne;
  His valiant peers were plac'd around;
Their brows with roses and with myrtles bound:
    (So should desert in arms be crown'd).
The lovely Thais, by his side,
Sate like a blooming Eastern bride,
In flow'r of youth and beauty's pride.
    Happy, happy, happy pair!
      None but the brave,
      None but the brave,
  None but the brave deserves the fair.

Chorus

    Happy, happy, happy pair!
      None but the brave,
      None but the brave,
  None but the brave deserves the fair.

    Timotheus, plac'd on high
      Amid the tuneful choir,
With flying fingers touch'd the lyre:

The trembling notes ascend the sky,
And heav'nly joys inspire.
The song began from Jove,
Who left his blissful seats above,
(Such is the pow'r of mighty love).
A dragon's fiery form belied the god:
Sublime on radiant spires he rode,
When he to fair Olympia press'd:
And while he sought her snowy breast,
Then round her slender waist he curl'd,
And stamp'd an image of himself, a sov'reign of the world.
The list'ning crowd admire the lofty sound,
"A present deity," they shout around;
"A present deity," the vaulted roofs rebound:
With ravish'd ears
The monarch hears,
Assumes the god,
Affects to nod,
And seems to shake the spheres.

Chorus

With ravish'd ears
The monarch hears,
Assumes the god,
Affects to nod,
And seems to shake the spheres.

The praise of Bacchus then the sweet musician sung,
Of Bacchus ever fair, and ever young.
The jolly god in triumph comes;
Sound the trumpets, beat the drums;
Flush'd with a purple grace
He shows his honest face:
Now give the hautboys breath; he comes, he comes.
Bacchus, ever fair and young,
Drinking joys did first ordain;
Bacchus' blessings are a treasure,
Drinking is the soldier's pleasure;
Rich the treasure,
Sweet the pleasure,
Sweet is pleasure after pain.

Chorus

Bacchus' blessings are a treasure,
Drinking is the soldier's pleasure;
    Rich the treasure,
    Sweet the pleasure,
Sweet is pleasure after pain.

Sooth'd with the sound, the king grew vain;
    Fought all his battles o'er again;
And thrice he routed all his foes, and thrice he slew the slain.
    The master saw the madness rise,
    His glowing cheeks, his ardent eyes;
And while he Heav'n and earth defied,
Chang'd his hand, and check'd his pride.
        He chose a mournful Muse,
        Soft pity to infuse;
    He sung Darius great and good,
        By too severe a fate,
    Fallen, fallen, fallen, fallen,
        Fallen from his high estate,
    And welt'ring in his blood;
    Deserted at his utmost need
    By those his former bounty fed;
    On the bare earth expos'd he lies,
    With not a friend to close his eyes.
With downcast looks the joyless victor sate,
        Revolving in his alter'd soul
        The various turns of chance below;
        And, now and then, a sigh he stole,
        And tears began to flow.

Chorus

    Revolving in his alter'd soul
        The various turns of chance below;
    And, now and then, a sigh he stole,
        And tears began to flow.

The mighty master smil'd to see
That love was in the next degree;
'Twas but a kindred sound to move,

For pity melts the mind to love.
 Softly sweet, in Lydian measures,
 Soon he sooth'd his soul to pleasures.
"War," he sung, "is toil and trouble;
Honor but an empty bubble;
 Never ending still beginning,
Fighting still, and still destroying:
 If the world be worth thy winning,
Think, O think it worth enjoying:
 Lovely Thais sits beside thee,
 Take the good the gods provide thee."
The many rend the skies with loud applause;
So Love was crown'd, but Music won the cause.
 The prince, unable to conceal his pain,
  Gaz'd on the fair
  Who caus'd his care,
 And sigh'd and look'd, sigh'd and look'd,
 Sigh'd and look'd, and sigh'd again;
At length, with love and wine at once oppress'd,
The vanquish'd victor sunk upon her breast.

Chorus

 The prince, unable to conceal his pain,
  Gaz'd on the fair
  Who caus'd his care,
 And sigh'd and look'd, sigh'd and look'd,
 Sigh'd and look'd, and sigh'd again;
At length, with love and wine at once oppress'd,
The vanquish'd victor sunk upon her breast.

Now strike the golden lyre again;
A louder yet, and yet a louder strain.
Break his bands of sleep asunder,
And rouse him, like a rattling peal of thunder.
 Hark, hark, the horrid sound
  Has rais'd up his head;
  As wak'd from the dead,
 And amaz'd, he stares around.
"Revenge, revenge," Timotheus cries,
 "See the Furies arise;
 See the snakes that they rear,

How they hiss in their hair,
And the sparkles that flash from their eyes!
Behold a ghastly band,
Each a torch in his hand!
Those are Grecian ghosts, that in battle were slain,
And unburied remain
Inglorious on the plain:
Give the vengeance due
To the valiant crew.
Behold how they toss their torches on high,
How they point to the Persian abodes,
And glitt'ring temples of their hostile gods."
The princes applaud with a furious joy;
And the king seiz'd a flambeau with zeal to destroy;
Thais led the way,
To light him to his prey,
And, like another Helen, fir'd another Troy.

Chorus

And the king seiz'd a flambeau with zeal to destroy;
Thais led the way,
To light him to his prey,
And, like another Helen, fir'd another Troy.

Thus long ago,
Ere heaving bellows learn'd to blow
While organs yet were mute,
Timotheus, to his breathing flute
And sounding lyre,
Could swell the soul to rage, or kindle soft desire.
At last divine Cecilia came,
Inventress of the vocal frame;
The sweet enthusiast, from her sacred store,
Enlarg'd the former narrow bounds,
And added length to solemn sounds,
With Nature's mother-wit, and arts unknown before.
Let old Timotheus yield the prize,
Or both divide the crown:
He rais'd a mortal to the skies;
She drew an angel down.

Grand Chorus

At last divine Cecilia came,
Inventress of the vocal frame;
The sweet enthusiast, from her sacred store,
Enlarg'd the former narrow bounds,
And added length to solemn sounds,
With Nature's mother-wit, and arts unknown before.
Let old Timotheus yield the prize,
Or both divide the crown:
He rais'd a mortal to the skies;
She drew an angel down.

CHARLES SACKVILLE

*The name of Lord Buckhurst (later Earl of Dorset) is joined with
that of Rochester and Sedley in the book of Restoration misbehavior.
It was, however, the retrospective verdict of the age that he succeeded
better than his friends in being a rake without entirely losing the
character of a gentleman. "A Song Written at Sea" needs the air
to which it was once sung for its full effect, but its charms are otherwise undimmed by time. This tone of heartiness in gallantry is not
often heard in Restoration verse, though Colonel Lovelace, Cavalier
poet of a purer age, had sounded it in "To Lucasta on Going to the
Wars."*

Song

Written at Sea, in the First Dutch War, 1665, the Night Before the Engagement

To all you ladies now at land
    We men at sea indite,
But first would have you understand
    How hard it is to write:
The Muses now, and Neptune too,
We must implore to write to you,—
    With a fa, la, la, la, la!

For though the Muses should prove kind,
    And fill our empty brain,
Yet if rough Neptune rouse the wind
    To wave the azure main,
Our paper, pen, and ink, and we
Roll up and down our ships at sea,—
    With a fa, la, la, la, la!

Then if we write not by each post,
    Think not we are unkind;
Nor yet conclude our ships are lost
    By Dutchmen or by wind:
Our tears we'll send a speedier way;
The tide shall bring them twice a day,
    With a fa, la, la, la, la!

The King, with wonder and surprise,
    Will swear the seas grow bold,
Because the tides will higher rise
    Than e'er they used of old;
But let him know it is our tears
Brings floods of grief to Whitehall stairs,—
    With a fa, la, la, la, la!

Should foggy Opdam chance to know
    Our sad and dismal story,
The Dutch would scorn so weak a foe,
    And quit their fort at Goree;
For what resistance can they find
From men who've left their hearts behind?—
    With a fa, la, la, la, la!

Let wind and weather do its worst,
    Be you to us but kind;
Let Dutchmen vapor, Spaniards curse,
    No sorrow we shall find:
'Tis then no matter how things go,
Or who's our friend or who's our foe,—
    With a fa, la, la, la, la!

To pass our tedious hours away,
　　We throw a merry main,
Or else at serious ombre play;
　　But why should we in vain
Each other's ruin thus pursue?
We were undone when we left you,—
　　With a fa, la, la, la, la!

But now our fears tempestuous grow
　　And cast our hopes away,
Whilst you, regardless of our woe,
　　Sit careless at a play;
Perhaps permit some happier man
To kiss your hand or flirt your fan,—
　　With a fa, la, la, la, la!

When any mournful tune you hear,
　　That dies in every note,
As if it sighed with each man's care
　　For being so remote,
Think then how often love we've made
To you when all those tunes were played,—
　　With a fa, la, la, la, la!

In justice you cannot refuse
　　To think of our distress,
When we for hopes of honor lose
　　Our certain happiness:
All those designs are but to prove
Ourselves more worthy of your love,—
　　With a fa, la, la, la, la!

And now we've told you all our loves
　　And likewise all our fears,
In hopes this declaration moves
　　Some pity from your tears;
Let's hear of no inconstancy;
We have too much of that at sea,—
　　With a fa, la, la, la, la!

JOHN WILMOT, EARL OF ROCHESTER

From a portrait attributed to Jacob Huysmans. Reproduced by permission
of The National Portrait Gallery.

SIR ROBERT BOYLE

From a portrait by John Riley. Reproduced by permission of The Royal Society.

IV *Old and New Science*

~~~~~~~~~~~~~~~~~

The year 1660, which marks so dramatically the change from old to new in English politics, was no such turning point in science. Yet the most memorable deed of Charles's reign was the granting of a charter, in 1662, to a group of men already banded together in the common pursuit of knowledge according to the method of observation and experiment, which had been proclaimed by Sir Francis Bacon the only true way to its advancement. The pioneers in this movement—mathematicians, doctors, physicists, chemists, astronomers—had already some achievements to their credit, and such was their conviction that they would have gone on in any case. The backing which they now received from intelligent and highly placed well-wishers gave an immense stimulus to their activities and put England well in the lead of Europe in scientific progress.

We have already seen the loyalty of poets like Dryden and men of affairs like Pepys to the purposes of the Royal Society. Another poet, Abraham Cowley, had already published a parallel, though more ambitious, program for a research institution. John Evelyn, who several times refused the office of president, was both a patron and a contributor. It is evident from his diary that his regular contacts with his fellow members at their meetings and his successful efforts to house and equip the organization were among his greatest satisfactions. Never was a society better loved or more skillfully promoted. As early as 1667 its achievements were proudly reviewed and its basic philosophy persuasively set forth in a history by Thomas Sprat. This writer boldly says that the new philosophers are resolved to meddle not at all with divine matters, except only as the power and wisdom and goodness of God are displayed in the admirable order and workmanship of his creation. Everything was to be known but the unknowable, and the goal was mastery of nature for the good of man. In one chapter Sprat describes the principles of expression laid down by the society for the writing of scientific reports. "They have exacted from all their members a close, naked, natural way of speaking, positive expressions, clear senses, a native easiness; bringing things as near the mathematical plainness as they can, and preferring the language of artisans, countrymen and merchants before that of wits and scholars." The advantages of this philosophy of style made themselves felt beyond the bounds of science, and the modernization of English prose writing was the result.

The culmination of this epoch of scientific exploration was, of course, the work of Sir Isaac Newton, whose *Principia*, setting forth the law of gravity, appeared a year before its close. His discoveries in mathematics and his theories of light and color had previously been announced. The other great name is that of Robert Boyle, who had set up his laboratory at Oxford before the Restoration and ranks as the principal founder both of the Royal Society and of the Philosophical College which preceded it. Both these men knew where they were going and their methods and their work endured, while those of innumerable other projectors and experimenters came to nothing. But such achievements are really the work of many minds. With all its shortcomings, Restoration society afforded a climate favorable to the co-operation of human intelligence in at least one impersonal enterprise of noble aim.

It was not, however, to be expected that the scientific movement should go forward without oppositon. Thomas Hobbes, one of the greatest minds of his time, became embroiled with his rival mathematicians, tried foolishly to discredit Boyle's demonstrable conclusions, and was excluded from membership in the Royal Society. There were perennial bickerings from those who saw only the futile and ridiculous side of the activity, and there were the deep suspicion and resistance of men whose basic philosophy was challenged by the naturalistic point of view. Both the witty recreations at the expense of science and the fundamental clash between the theological and the scientific mind are represented in our selections, the latter appearing most interestingly in connection with the dying but still potent witchcraft delusion. The cases of Sir Thomas Browne, who testified that witches did exist, and of Joseph Glanvill, who defended the popular belief on philosophic grounds, are curious and instructive. Browne spent his own life in speculation, undertook the correction of vulgar errors, and was greatly interested in the work of the Royal Society of which his son was at one time president. He was even a discoverer of scientific fact. And Glanvill had written a Baconian book. But their judgments are determined by something other than inference from the observed facts.

For the new science itself we have chosen to give the words of a great pioneer in the art of healing. Physicians were among the most devoted workers in research from the beginning. William Harvey's discovery of the circulation of the blood, which belongs just before our period, is the most momentous incident in the history of the biological sciences. The advances which were made by others in the understanding and treatment of disease, though less familiar, are among the solidest as well as the most beneficent achievements of the age.

Far removed from such inquiry is the economic thought of Sir

A
TRYAL
OF
WITCHES,
AT THE
ASSIZES
HELD AT
Bury St. Edmonds for the County of *SVFFOLK*; on the Tenth Day of *March*, 1664.

BEFORE
Sir *MATTHEW HALE*, K^{t.}
THEN
Lord Chief Baron of His Majefty's Court of EXCHEQVER.

Taken by a Perfon then Attending the Court.

LONDON,
Printed for *D. Brown*, *J. Walthoe*, and *M. Wotton*. 1716.

William Petty with which we conclude this section. It is, however, equally an example of Baconian method applied to a department of knowledge then and for long afterward at the mercy of random guesswork and mistaken theory. One wonders how Petty got his figures, but granted their reliability his lucubrations have a modern ring. The man himself was a versatile enthusiast of the inventor type. Pepys reports his speculation on the difference between waking and dreaming and amusingly describes the King's laughing at him about his double-bottomed boat, "at which Petty was, I perceived, at some loss, but did argue discretely and bear the unreasonable follies of the King's objections and other bystanders with great discretion and did offer to take odds against the King's best boats." In a later age Petty might have narrowed his activity and become a rigorous economist. The necessity of specialization, as new vistas of knowledge opened up, was already becoming clear.

ANONYMOUS

This famous trial of 1662 belongs to a late stage in the history of witchcraft. It is not the last conviction in England, and the great outburst of persecution in Massachusetts occurred a whole generation later. But plenty of people were already skeptical and the validity of the evidence in any given case was likely to be sharply challenged. The significance of this trial lies not in the fact that a great and humane judge pronounced the sentence or that a man of science was willing to appear as witness for the prosecution. It lies rather in the effort which was made to put the alleged cause of the children's convulsions to an experimental test. The English statute against witchcraft was finally repealed in 1736. There were no witchcraft trials in New England in the eighteenth century. As to Sir Thomas Browne, it can only be said that if Joseph Addison had been put on oath in the sane and sober reign of Anne he would have been obliged in the name of conscience to subscribe to the same conviction. "I believe in general," Addison wrote in 1711, "that there is and has been such a thing as witchcraft; but at the same time can give no credit to any particular instance of it."

A Trial of Witches

At the assizes and general jail delivery held at Bury St. Edmunds for the county of Suffolk the tenth of March, 1664, before Matthew

Hale, Knight, Lord Chief Baron of His Majesty's Court of Exchequer, Rose Cullender and Amy Duny, widows, both of Leystoff in the county aforesaid, were severally indicted for bewitching Elizabeth and Ann Durent, Jane Bocking, Susan Chandler, William Durent, Elizabeth and Deborah Pacy. And the said Cullender and Duny, being arraigned upon the said indictment, pleaded "Not guilty," and afterwards, upon a long evidence were found guilty, and thereupon had judgment to die for the same.

Three of the parties above named, viz, Ann Durent, Susan Chandler, and Elizabeth Pacy, were brought to Bury to the assizes and were in reasonable good condition. But that morning they came into the hall to give instructions for the drawing of their bills of indictments the three persons fell into strange and violent fits, screeking out in the most sad manner, so that they could not in any wise give any instructions in the court who were the cause of their distemper. And though they did after some certain space recover out of their fits yet they were every one of them struck dumb, so that none of them could speak, neither at that time, nor during the assizes, until the conviction of the supposed witches.

As concerning William Durent, being an infant, his mother, Dorothy Durent, sworn and examined, deposed in open court that about the tenth of March, 1657, she having a special occasion to go from home and having none in her house to take care of her said child (it then sucking), desired Amy Duny, her neighbor, to look after her child during her absence, for which she promised to give her a penny. The same Dorothy Durent, however, desired the same Amy not to suckle her child and laid a great charge upon her not to do it. Upon which it was asked by the court, why did she give that direction, she being an old woman and not capable of giving suck? It was answered by the said Dorothy Durent that she very well knew that she did not give suck, but that for some years before she had gone under the reputation of a witch, which was one cause which made her give the caution. Another was that it was customary with old women that if they did look after a sucking child and nothing would please her but the breast, they did use to please the child to give it the breast and it did please the child but it sucked nothing but wind which did the child hurt. Nevertheless after the departure of this deponent, the said Amy did suckle the child. And after the return of the said Dorothy, the said Amy did acquaint her that she had given suck to the child contrary to her command. Whereupon the deponent was very angry with the said Amy for the same, at which the said Amy was much discontented and used many high expressions and threatening speeches toward her, telling her that she had as good to have done otherwise than to have found fault with her and so departed out of the house. And that very night her son fell into strange fits of swooning and was held in such terrible manner that she was much affrighted therewith and so continued for divers weeks. And the said examinant further said that she being exceedingly troubled at her child's distemper did go to a certain person named Doctor Jacob who lived at Yarmouth, who had the reputation in the country to help children that were bewitched. He advised her to hang up the child's blanket in the chimney corner all day and at night when she put the child to bed to put it into the said blanket and, if she found anything in it, she should not be afraid but to throw it into the fire. And this deponent did according to his direction. At night when she took down the blanket with an intent to put her child therein, there fell out of the same a great toad which ran up and down the hearth. She, having a young youth only with her in the house, desired him to catch the toad and throw it into the fire, which the youth did accordingly, and held it there with the tongs. As soon as it was in the fire it made a great and horrible noise and after a space there was a flashing in the fire like gun powder, making a noise like the discharge of a pistol, and thereupon the toad was no more seen nor heard. It was asked by the court, if that after the noise and flashing there was not the substance of the toad to be seen to continue in the fire? And it was answered by the said Dorothy Durent, that after the flashing and noise, there was no more seen than if there had been none there. The next day there came a young woman, a kinswoman of the said Amy, and a neighbor of this deponent, and told this deponent that her aunt (meaning the same Amy) was in a most lamentable condition, having her face all scorched with fire and that she was sitting alone in her house, in her smock without any fire. Thereupon, this deponent went unto the hearth of the said Amy Duny to see her, and found her in the same condition as was related to her. Her face, her legs and thighs, which this deponent saw, seemed very much scorched and burnt with fire, at which this deponent seemed much to wonder, and asked the said Amy how she came into that sad condition. And the said Amy replied she might thank her for it for that she (this deponent) was the cause thereof, but that she should live to see some of her children dead and she upon crutches. And this deponent further said that after the burning of the said toad, her child recovered and was well again and was living at the time of the Assizes. . . .

As concerning Elizabeth and Deborah Pacy, the first of the age of eleven years, the other of the age of nine years or thereabouts: as to the elder, she was brought into the court at the time of the instructions given to draw up the indictments, and afterwards at the time of trial of the said prisoners, but could not speak one word all the time. For the most part she remained as one wholly senseless, as one in a deep sleep, and could move no part of her body, and all the motions of life that appeared in her was that, as she lay upon cushions in the court upon her back, her stomach and belly, by the drawing of her breath, would arise to a great height. After the said Elizabeth had lain a long time on the table in the court, she came a little to herself and sat up, but could neither see nor speak but was sensible of what was said to her. After a while she laid her head on the bar of the court with a cushion under it and her hand and her apron on that and there she lay a good space of time. By the direction of the judge, Amy Duny was privately brought to Elizabeth Pacy, and she touched her hand; whereupon, the child, without so much as seeing her, for her eyes were closed all the while, suddenly leaped up, and catched Amy Duny by the hand and afterwards by the face and with her nails scratched her till blood came, and would by no means leave her till she was taken from her. Afterwards the child would still be pressing towards her, and making signs of anger conceived against her.

Deborah the younger daughter was held in such extreme manner that her parents wholly despaired of her life, and therefore could not bring her to the Assizes. . . .

At the hearing this evidence, there were divers known persons, such as Mr. Sergeant Keeling, Mr. Sergeant Earl, and Mr. Sergeant Barnard, present. Mr. Sergeant Keeling seemed much unsatisfied with it and thought it not sufficient to convict the prisoners. For admitting that the children were in truth bewitched, yet, said he, it can never be applied to the prisoners upon the imagination only of the parties afflicted. For if that might be allowed, no person whatsoever can be in safety, for perhaps they might fancy another person who might altogether be innocent in such matters.

There was also Dr. Brown of Norwich, a person of great knowledge, who after this evidence given and upon view of the three persons in court, was desired to give his opinion what he did conceive of them. And he was clearly of opinion that the persons were bewitched, and said that in Denmark there had been lately a great discovery of witches who used the very same way of afflicting persons by conveying pins into them, and crooked as these pins were, with needles and nails. And his opinion was that the Devil in such cases did work upon the bodies of men and women upon a natural foundation, that is, to stir up and excite such humors superabounding in their bodies to a great excess, whereby he did in an extraordinary manner afflict them with such distempers as their bodies were most subject to, as particularly appeared in these children. For he conceived that these swooning fits were natural and nothing else but that they call the Mother, but only heightened to a great excess by the subtlety of the Devil, co-operating with the malice of these which we term witches, at whose instance he does these villanies.

Besides the particulars above-mentioned touching the said persons bewitched, there were many other things objected against them for a further proof and manifestation that the said children were bewitched.

As first, during the time of the trial, there were some experiments made with the persons afflicted by bringing the persons to touch them. It was observed that when they were in the midst of their fits, to all men's apprehension wholly deprived of all sense and understanding, closing their fists in such manner as that the strongest man in the court could not force them open, yet by the least touch of one of those supposed witches, Rose Challender by name, they would suddenly shriek out, opening their hands, which accident would not happen by the touch of any other person.

And lest they might privately see when they were touched by the said Rolfe Challender, they were blinded with their own aprons and the touching took the same effect as before.

There was an ingenious person that objected that there might be a great fallacy in this experiment, and there ought not to be any stress put upon this to convict the parties, for the children might counterfeit this their distemper, and perceiving what was done to them they might in such manner suddenly alter the motion and gesture of their bodies on purpose to induce persons to believe that they were not natural but wrought strangely by the touch of the prisoners.

Wherefore, to avoid this scruple, it was privately desired by the judge that the Lord Cornwallis, Sir Edmund Bacon, and Mr. Sargeant Keeling and some other Gentlemen there in court, would attend one of the distempered persons in the farther part of the hall while she was in her fits, and then to send for one of the witches to try what would then happen, which they did accordingly. Amy Duny was conveyed from the Bar and brought to the maid. They put an apron before her eyes and then one other person touched her hand, which produced the same effect as the touch of the witch did in the court. Whereupon, the gentlemen returned, openly protesting that they did believe the whole transaction of this business was a mere imposture.

This put the court and all persons into a stand. But at length Mr. Pacy did declare that possibly the maid might be deceived by a suspicion that the witch touched her when she did not. For he had observed divers times that although they could not speak, but were deprived of the use of their tongues and limbs, their understandings were perfect for that they have related divers things which have been when they were in their fits after they were recovered out of them. This saying of Mr. Pacy was found to be true afterwards when his daughter was fully recovered (as she afterwards was), as shall in due time be related. For she was asked whether she did hear or understand anything that was done and acted in the court during the time that she lay as one deprived of her understanding. And she said she did. And by the opinions of some, this experiment (which others would have a fallacy) was rather a confirmation that the parties were really bewitched than otherwise. For, say they, it is not possible that any should counterfeit such distempers, being accompanied with such various circumstances, much less children, and for so long time and yet undiscovered by their parents and relations. For no man can suppose that they should all conspire together (being out of several families and, as they affirm, no way related one to the other, and scarce of familiar acquaintance) to do an act of this nature whereby no benefit or advantage could redound to any of the parties, but a guilty conscience for perjuring themselves in taking the lives of two poor simple women away, and there appears no malice in the case. For the prisoner themselves did scarce so much as object to it. Wherefore, say they, it is very evident that the parties were bewitched, and that, when they apprehend or understand by any means that the persons who have done them this wrong are near or touch them, then their spirits being more than ordinarily moved with rage and anger at them being present, they do use more violent gestures of their bodies and extend forth their hands as desirous to lay hold upon them, which at other times not having the same occasion, the instance there falls not out the same. . . .

This was the substance of the whole evidence given against the prisoners at the bar. Being demanded what they had to say for themselves, they replied "nothing material" to anything that was proved against them. Whereupon, the judge in giving his direction to the jury, told them that he would not repeat the evidence unto them lest by so doing he should wrong the evidence on the one side or on the other. Only this acquainted them, that they had two things to inquire after: first, whether or no these children were bewitched; second, whether the prisoners at the bar were guilty of it.

That there were such creatures as witches he made no doubt at all, for first, the Scriptures had affirmed so much; secondly, the wisdom of all nations had provided laws against such persons, which is an argument of their confidence of such a crime. Such has been the judgment of this Kingdom, as appears by that Act of Parliament which has proved punishments proportionable to the quality of the offense. And he desired them strictly to observe their evidence, and desired the great God of Heaven to direct their hearts in this weighty thing they had in hand. For to condemn the innocent, and to let the guilty go free, were both an abomination to the Lord.

With this short direction, the jury departed from the Bar, and within the space of half an hour returned and brought them in both guilty upon the several indictments, which were thirteen in number, whereupon they stood indicted.

JOSEPH GLANVILL

As a fellow of the Royal Society the Reverend Joseph Glanvill was thoroughly conversant with the temper and method of the new science. He had, indeed, commended himself to his experimental colleagues by a Baconian attack on the scholastic philosophy entitled The Vanity of Dogmatizing. *His scientific scepticism stopped far short, however, of denial of the reality of the supernatural. Sharing the interests of the Cambridge philosopher, Henry More, including the doctrine of the pre-existence of the soul, he associated a rationalistic attitude toward witchcraft with materialism generally. In the work from which the following extracts are taken, Glanvill presents a vast array of case histories to counterbalance the multiplying arguments of the modernists, writing what Lecky has called the ablest defense of the witch superstition ever published. The title is* Sadducismus Triumphatus, *the philosophy of the unbelieving Sadducees defeated. It precedes by a decade the great outbreak of witch persecution in New England in*

1692 and well illustrates the thinking which made it possible for intelligent men to succumb to the delusion.

The Case for Witchcraft: Objections Answered

But another prejudice against the belief of witches is a presumption upon the enormous force of melancholy and imagination, which without doubt can do wonderful things and beget strange persuasions; and to these causes some ascribe the presumed effects of sorcery and witchcraft. To which I briefly reply and yet I hope sufficiently: 1. that to resolve all the clear circumstances of fact which we find in well-attested and confirmed relations of this kind into the power of deceivable imagination is to make fancy the greater prodigy and to suppose that it can do stranger feats than are believed of any other kind of fascination. And to think that pins and nails, for instance, can by the power of imagination be conveyed within the skin, or that imagination should deceive so many as have been witnesses in objects of sense, in all the circumstances of discovery—this, I say, is to be infinitely more credulous than the assertors of sorcery and demoniac contracts. And by the same reason it may be believed that all the battles and strange events of the world which ourselves have not seen are but dreams and fond imaginations; and likewise those that are fought in the clouds, when the brains of the deluded spectators are the only theaters of those fancied transactions. And 2. to deny the evidence of act because their imaginations may deceive the relators, when we have no reason to think so but a bare presumption that there is no such thing as is related, is quite to destroy the credit of all human testimony and to make all men liars in a larger sense than the prophet concluded in his haste. For not only the melancholic and fanciful, but the grave and sober, whose judgments we have no reason to suspect to be tainted by their imaginations, have, from their own knowledge and experience, made reports of this nature.

To pass then to another prejudice. The frequent impostures that are met with in this kind beget in some a belief that all such relations are forgeries and tales. And if we urge the evidence of a story for the belief of witches or apparitions they will produce two, as seemingly strong and plausible, which shall conclude in mistake or design, inferring thence that all others are of the same quality and credit. But such arguers may please to consider: 1. that a single relation for an

affirmative, sufficiently confirmed and attested, is worth a thousand
tales of forgery and imposture, from whence an universal negative
cannot be concluded. And 2. it seems to me a belief sufficiently bold
and precarious that all these relations of forgery and mistake should
be certain, and not one amongst all those which attest the affirmative
reality, with circumstances as good as could be expected or wished,
should be true, but all fabulous and vain. And they have no reason
to object credulity to the assertors of sorcery and witchcraft that
can swallow so large a morsel.

And I desire such objectors to consider, 3., whether it is fair to
infer that, because there are some cheats and impostors, there are no
realities. Indeed, frequency of deceit and fallacy will warrant a greater
care in examining, and scrupulosity and shyness of assent to things
wherein fraud hath been practiced or may in the least degree be suspected. But to conclude, because that an old woman's fancy abused
her, or some knavish fellows put tricks upon the ignorant and timorous, that therefore whole Assizes have been a thousand times deceived in judgments upon matters of fact and numbers of sober
persons have been forsworn in things wherein perjury could not advantage them—I say such inferences are as void of reason as they are
of charity and good manners.

THOMAS HOBBES

Leviathan, *that great monument of rationalism in the interest of
autocratic government, was a legacy from the preceding age. Hobbes's
judgment regarding witchcraft is characteristic and the contrast with
Glanvill is symptomatic of the clash between two competing modes
of philosophic thought, both belonging to the time and both persist-
ing to the present, when witchcraft is no longer an issue. It may seem
odd that Hobbes, whose view of man and society is mechanistic, in spite
of his professed Christianity, should have been hostile to the scientific
work of the Royal Society, and Glanvill, the supernaturalist, a supporter of it. But one remembers that modern scientists like Sir
Oliver Lodge have been investigators of and believers in a world of
spirit. The typical experimental philosopher was, as we shall see, different in his attitude from either of these men.*

Religious Origins

From this ignorance of how to distinguish dreams and other strong
fancies from vision and sense did arise the greatest part of the reli-

gion of the Gentiles in times past, that worshipped satyrs, fawns, nymphs and the like, and nowadays the opinion that rude people have of fairies, ghosts, and goblins and of the power of witches. For, as for witches, I think not that their witchcraft is any real power but yet that they are justly punished for the false belief they have that they can do such mischief, joined with their purpose to do it if they can, their trade being nearer to a new religion than to a craft or science. And for fairies and walking ghosts, the opinion of them has, I think, been on purpose either taught or not confuted, to keep in credit the use of exorcism, of crosses, of holy water and other such inventions of ghostly men. Nevertheless, there is no doubt but God can make unnatural apparitions; but that he does it so often as men need to fear such things more than they fear the stay or change of the course of nature, which he also can stay and change, is no point of Christian faith. But evil men, under pretext that God can do anything, are so bold as to say anything when it serves their turn, though they think it untrue. It is the part of a wise man to believe them no further than right reason makes that which they say appear credible. If this superstitious fear of spirits were taken away, and with it prognostications from dreams, false prophecies, and many other things depending thereon by which crafty, ambitious persons abuse the simple people, men would be much more fitted than they are for civil obedience.

SIR THOMAS BROWNE

The convolved thought processes and polyphonic utterance of the author of Urn-Burial *may seem to be in strange company among the men of science, but they will serve to remind us that neither he nor his world had passed away. Browne was as curious as any of the virtuosos, his observations being often the stuff which Royal Society reports were made of. But he was not satisfied to see man and nature in the dry Baconian light, and his style was the very thing the new age intended to discard.* A Letter to a Friend *is an unpremeditated discourse which reveals the author, the artist and the man as one. It was afterwards elaborated into a treatise on Christian morals, the last work of its author's pen.*

Letter to a Friend

Give me leave to wonder that news of this nature should have such heavy wings that you should hear so little concerning your dearest friend, and that I must make that unwilling repetition to tell you, *ad portam rigidos calces extendit,* that he is dead and buried and by this time no puny among the mighty nations of the dead; for though he left this world not very many days past, yet every hour, you know, largely addeth unto that dark society; and considering the incessant mortality of mankind, you cannot conceive there dieth in the whole earth so few as a thousand an hour.

Although at this distance you had no early account or particular of his death, yet your affection may cease to wonder that you had not some secret sense or intimation thereof by dreams, thoughtful whisperings, mercurisms, airy nuncios or sympathetical insinuations, which many seem to have had at the death of their dearest friends; for since we find in that famous story, that spirits themselves were fain to tell their fellows at a distance that the great Antonio was dead, we have a sufficient excuse for our ignorance in such particulars, and must rest content with the common road and Appian way, of knowledge by information. Though the uncertainty of the end of this world hath confounded all human predictions, yet they who shall live to see the sun and moon darkened and the stars to fall from heaven will hardly be deceived in the advent of the last day; and therefore strange it is that the common fallacy of consumptive persons, who feel not themselves dying and therefore still hope to live, should also reach their friends in perfect health and judgment— that you should be so little acquainted with Plautus's sick complexion, or that almost an Hippocratical face should not alarum you to higher fears, or rather despair, of his continuation in such an emaciated state, wherein medical predictions fail not, as sometimes in acute diseases, and wherein 'tis as dangerous to be sentenced by a physician as a judge.

Upon my first visit I was bold to tell them who had not let fall all hopes of his recovery, that in my sad opinion he was not like to behold a grasshopper, much less to pluck another fig; and in no long time after seemed to discover that odd mortal symptom in him not mentioned by Hippocrates, that is, to lose his own face, and look like some of his near relations; for he maintained not his proper countenance, but looked like his uncle, the lines of whose face lay deep and invisible in his healthful visage before: for as from our beginning we run through variety of looks before we come to consistent and settled faces, so before our end, by sick and languishing alterations, we put on new visages; and in our retreat to earth may fall upon such looks which from community of seminal originals were before latent in us.

He was fruitlessly put in hope of advantage by change of air and imbibing the pure aerial nitre of these parts; and therefore, being so far spent, he quickly found Sardinia in Tivoli, and the most healthful air of little effect, where death had set his broad arrow; for he lived not unto the middle of May, and confirmed the observation of Hippocrates of that mortal time of the year when the leaves of the fig-tree resemble a daw's claw. He is happily seated who lives in places whose air, earth, and water, promote not the infirmities of his weaker parts, or is early removed into regions that correct them. He that is tabidly inclined were unwise to pass his days in Portugal; cholical persons will find little comfort in Austria or Vienna; he that is weak-legged must not be in love with Rome, nor an infirm head with Venice or Paris. Death hath not only particular stars in heaven, but malevolent places on earth, which single out our infirmities and strike at our weaker parts; in which concern, passager and migrant birds have the great advantages; who are naturally constituted for distant habitations, whom no seas nor places limit, but in their appointed seasons will visit us from Greenland and Mount Atlas, and, as some think, even from the Antipodes.

Though we could not have his life, yet we missed not our desires in his soft departure, which was scarce an expiration; and his end not unlike his beginning, when the salient point scarce affords a sensible motion, and his departure so like unto sleep, that he scarce needed the civil ceremony of closing his eyes; contrary unto the common way, wherein death draws up, sleep lets fall the eye-lids. With what strife and pains we came into the world we know not; but 'tis commonly no easy matter to get out of it: yet if it could be made out that such who have easy nativities have commonly hard deaths, and contrarily, his departure was so easy that we might justly suspect his birth was of another nature, and that some Juno sat cross-legged at his nativity.

Besides his soft death, the incurable state of his disease might somewhat extenuate your sorrow, who know that monsters but seldom happen, miracles more rarely in physic. Angelus Victorius gives a serious account of a consumptive, hectical, phthisical woman, who was suddenly cured by the intercession of Ignatius. We read not of any in scripture who in this case applied unto our Saviour, though some may be contained in that large expression that he went about Galilee healing all manner of sickness and all manner of diseases.

Amulets, spells, sigils, and incantations, practised in other diseases, are seldom pretended in this; and we find no sigil in the Archidoxis of Paracelsus to cure an extreme consumption or marasmus, which, if other diseases fail, will put a period unto long livers, and at last makes dust of all. And therefore the Stoics could not but think that the fiery principle would wear out all the rest, and at last make an end of the world, which notwithstanding without such a lingering period the Creator may effect at his pleasure; and to make an end of all things on earth and our planetical system of the world, he need but put out the sun. . . .

In this deliberate and creeping progress unto the grave, he was somewhat too young and of too noble a mind, to fall upon that stupid symptom observable in divers persons near their journey's end and which may be reckoned among the mortal symptoms of their last disease; that is, to become more narrow-minded, miserable, and tenacious, unready to part with anything, when they are ready to part with all, and afraid to want when they have no time to spend; meanwhile physicians, who know that many are mad but in a single depraved imagination and one prevalent decipience, and that beside and out of such single deliriums a man may meet with sober actions and good sense in bedlam, cannot but smile to see the heirs and concerned relations gratulating themselves on the sober departure of their friends; and though they behold such mad covetous passages, content to think they die in such good understanding and in their sober senses.

Avarice, which is not only infidelity but idolatry, either from covetous progeny or questuary education, had no root in his breast, who made good works the expression of his faith, and was big with desires unto public and lasting charities; and surely where good wishes and charitable intentions exceed abilities, theorical beneficency may be more than a dream. They build not castles in the air who would build churches on earth; and though they leave no such structures here, may lay good foundations in heaven. In brief, his life and death were such that I could not blame them who wished the like, and almost to have been himself; almost, I say, for though we may wish the prosperous appurtenances of others, or to be another in his happy accidents, yet so intrinsical is every man unto himself, that some doubt may be made, whether any would exchange his being, or substantially become another man. . . .

Though age had set no seal upon his face yet a dim eye might clearly discover fifty in his actions; and therefore, since wisdom is the grey hair, and an unspotted life old age, although his years came short, he might have been said to have held up with longer livers, and to have been Solomon's old man. And surely if we deduct all those days of our life which we might wish unlived and which abate the comfort of those we now live, if we reckon up only those days which God hath accepted of our lives, a life of good years will hardly be a span long. The son in this sense may out-live the father and none be climacterically old. He that early arriveth unto the parts and prudence of age, is happily old without the uncomfortable attendants of it; and 'tis superfluous to live unto grey hairs, when in a precocious temper we anticipate the virtues of them. In brief, he cannot be accounted young who out-liveth the old man. He that hath early arrived unto the measure of a perfect stature in Christ hath already fulfilled the prime and longest intention of his being; and one day lived after the perfect rule of piety, is to be preferred before sinning immortality.

Although he attained not unto the years of his predecessors, yet he wanted not those preserving virtues which confirm the thread of weaker constitutions. *Cautelous* chastity and *crafty* sobriety were far from him; those jewels were *paragon*, without flaw, hair, ice, or cloud in him. . . .

SIR WILLIAM TEMPLE

Besides being a diplomat of solid worth, Sir William Temple was a gentleman of taste and learning, master of an easy essay style which much commended itself to his own and later generations. His Discourse of Health and Long Life represents Temple at his most humane and well illustrates the medical pretensions of the well-informed and rational-minded amateur. The observations of Sydenham which follow are something very different.

Discourse of Health and Long Life

1.

NO HAPPINESS WITHOUT HEALTH

When I was young and in some idle company, it was proposed that everyone should tell what their three wishes should be, if they were sure to be granted. Some were very pleasant, and some very extravagant; mine were health, and peace, and fair weather; which, though out of the way among young men, yet perhaps might pass well enough among old. They are all of a strain, for health in the body is like peace in the state and serenity in the air. The sun, in our climate at least, has something so reviving, that a fair day is a kind of sensual pleasure, and of all others the most innocent.

Peace is a public blessing, without which no man is safe in his fortunes, his liberty, or his life. Neither innocence or laws are a guard of defence; no possessions are enjoyed but in danger or fear, which equally lose the pleasure and ease of all that fortune can give us. Health is the soul that animates all enjoyments of life, which fade and are tasteless, if not dead, without it. A man starves at the best and the greatest tables, makes faces at the noblest and most delicate wines, is old and impotent in seraglios of the most sparkling beauties, poor and wretched in the midst of the greatest treasures and fortunes. With common diseases strength grows decrepit, youth loses all vigor, and beauty all charms; music grows harsh; and conversation disagreeable; palaces are prisons, or of equal confinement; riches are useless, honor and attendance are cumbersome, and crowns themselves are a burden. But if diseases are painful and violent, they equal all conditions of life, make no difference between a prince and a beggar; and a fit of the stone or the colic puts a king to the rack, and makes him as miserable as he can do the meanest, the worst, and most criminal of his subjects.

To know that the passions or distempers of the mind make our lives unhappy, in spite of all accidents and favors of fortune, a man perhaps must be a philosopher; and requires much thought, and study and deep reflections. To be a Stoic, and grow insensible of pain, as well as poverty or disgrace, one must be perhaps something more or less than a man, renounce common nature, oppose common truth and constant experience. But there needs little learning or study, more than common thought and observation, to find out that ill health loses not only the enjoyments of fortune, but the pleasures of sense, and even of imagination, and hinders the common operations both of body and mind from being easy and free. Let the philosophers reason and differ about the chief good or happiness of man; let them find it where they can, and place it where they please; but there is no mistake so gross, or opinion so impertinent (how common soever), as to think pleasures arise from what is without us, rather than from what is within; from the impression given us of objects, rather than from the disposition of the organs that receive them. The various effects of the same objects upon different persons, or upon the same persons at different times, make the contrary most evident. Some distempers make things look yellow, others double what we see; the commonest alter our tastes and our smells, and the very foulness of ears changes sounds. The difference of tempers, as well as of age, may have the same effect, by the many degrees of perfection or imperfection in our original tempers, as well as of strength or decay, from the differences of health and of years. From all which 'tis easy, without being a great naturalist, to conclude, that our perceptions are formed, and our imaginations raised upon them, in a very great measure, by the dispositions of the organs through which the several objects make their impressions; and that these vary according to the different frame and temper of the others; as the sound of the same breath passing through an open pipe, a flute, or a trumpet.

But to leave philosophy, and return to health. Whatever is true in point of happiness depending upon the temper of the mind, 'tis certain that pleasures depend upon the temper of the body; and that, to enjoy them, a man must be well himself, as a vessel must be sound to have your wine sweet; for otherwise, let it be never so pleasant and so generous, it loses the taste; and pour in never so much, it all turns sour, and were better let alone. Whoever will eat well, must have a stomach; who will relish the pleasure of drinks, must have his mouth in taste; who will enjoy a beautiful woman, must be in vigor himself; nay, to find any felicity, or take any pleasure in the greatest advantages of honor and fortune, a man must be in health. Who would not be covetous, and with reason, if this could be purchased with gold? Who not ambitious, if it were at the command of power, or restored by honor? But alas! a white staff will not help gouty feet to walk better than a common cane; nor a blue ribband bind up a wound so well as a fillet; the glitter of gold or of diamonds will but hurt sore eyes, instead of curing them; and an aching head will be no more eased by wearing a crown than a common night-cap.

2.

INGREDIENTS OF HEALTH

If health be such a blessing, and the very source of all pleasure, it may be worth the pains to discover the regions where it grows, the springs that feed it, the customs and methods by which 'tis best cultivated and preserved. Towards this end, it will be necessary to consider the examples or instances we meet with of health and long life; which is the consequence of it; and to observe the places, the customs, and the conditions of those who enjoyed them in any degree extraordinary; from whence we may best guess at the causes, and make the truest conclusions.

Of what passed before the Flood, we know little from Scripture itself, besides the length of their lives; so as I shall only observe upon that period of time that men are thought neither to have eat flesh nor drunk wine before it ended. For to Noah first seems to have been given the liberty of feeding upon living creatures, and the prerogative of planting the vine. Since that time we meet with little mention of very long lives in any stories either sacred or profane, besides the Patriarchs of the Hebrews, the Brachmans among the old Indians, and the Brazilians at the time that country was discovered by the Europeans. Many of these were said then to have lived two hundred, some three hundred years. The same terms of life are attributed to the old Brachmans; and how long those of the Patriarchs were is recorded in Scripture. Upon all these I shall observe, that the Patriarchs' abodes were not in cities, but in open countries and fields: that their lives were pastoral, or employed in some sorts of agriculture: that they were of the same race to which their marriages were generally confined: that their diet was simple, as that of the ancients is generally represented, among whom flesh or wine was seldom used but at sacrifices or solemn feasts. The Brachmans were all of the same races, lived in fields and in woods, after the course of their studies were ended, and fed only upon rice, milk, or herbs. The Brazilians, when first discovered, lived the most natural original lives of mankind, so frequently described in ancient countries, before laws, or property, or arts made entrance among them; and so their customs may be concluded to have been yet more simple than either of the other two. They lived without business or labor, further than for their necessary food, by gathering fruits, herbs, and plants. They knew no drink but water; were not tempted to eat nor drink beyond common thirst or appetite; were not troubled with either public or domestic cares, nor knew any pleasures but the most simple and natural.

From all these examples and customs it may probably be concluded, that the common ingredients of health and long life (where births are not impaired from the conception by any derived infirmities of the race they come from) are great temperance, open air, easy labor, little care, simplicity of diet, rather fruits and plants than flesh, which easier corrupts; and water, which preserves the radical moisture, without too much increasing the radical heat: whereas sickness, decay, and death proceed commonly from the one preying too fast upon the other, and at length wholly extinguishing it.

I have sometimes wondered that the regions of so much health and so long lives were all under very hot climates; whereas the most temperate are allowed to produce the strongest and most vigorous bodies. But weaker constitutions may last as long as the strong, if better preserved from accidents; so Venice glass, as long as an earthen pitcher, if carefully kept; and, for one life that ends by mere decay of nature or age, millions are intercepted by accidents from without or diseases within; by untimely deaths or decays; from the effects of excess and luxury, immoderate repletion or exercise; the preying of our minds upon our bodies by long passions or consuming cares, as well as those accidents which are called violent. Men are perhaps most betrayed to all these dangers by great strength and vigor of constitution, by more appetite and larger fare in colder climates: in the warm, excesses are found more pernicious to health, and so more avoided; and, if experience and reflection do not cause temperance among them, yet it is forced upon them by the faintness of the appetite. I can find no better account of a story Sir Francis Bacon tells, of a very old man, whose customs and diet he inquired; but he said he observed none besides eating before he was hungry and drinking before he was dry; for by that rule he was sure never to eat nor drink much at a time. Besides, the warmth of air keeps the pores open, and by continual perspiration breathes out those humors, which breed most diseases, if in cooler climates it be not helped by exercise. And this I take to be the reason of our English constitutions finding so much benefit by the air of Montpelier, especially in long colds or consumptions, or rather lingering diseases; though I have known some who attributed the restoring of their health there as much to the fruits as the air of that place. . . .

3.

EXAMPLES OF LONG LIFE IN BRITAIN

For the honor of our climate, it has been observed by ancient authors, that the Britons were longer-lived than any other nation to them known. And in modern times there have been more and greater examples of this kind than in any other countries of Europe. The story of old Parr is too late to be forgotten by many now alive, who was brought out of Derbyshire to the court in King Charles I's time, and lived to a hundred and fifty-three years old; and might have, as was thought, gone further, if the change of country air and diet for that of the town had not carried him off, perhaps untimely, at that very age. The late Robert Earl of Leicester, who was a person of great learning and observation, as well as of truth, told me several stories very extraordinary upon this subject; one, of a Countess of Desmond, married out of England in Edward IV's time, and who lived far in King James's reign, and was counted to have died some years above a hundred and forty; at which age she came from Bristol to London to beg some relief at court, having long been very poor by the ruin of that Irish family into which she was married.

Another he told me was of a beggar at a bookseller's shop, where he was some weeks after the death of Prince Henry; and observing those that passed by, he was saying to his company, that never such a mourning had he seen in England. This beggar said, No, never since the death of Prince Arthur. My Lord Leicester, surprised, asked what she meant, and whether she remembered it. She said, Very well; and upon his more curious inquiry, told him that her name was Rainsford, of a good family in Oxfordshire: that, when she was about twenty years old, upon the falseness of a lover, she fell distracted; how long she had been so, nor what passed in that time, she knew not; that, when she was thought well enough to go abroad, she was fain to beg for her living; that she was some time at this trade before she recovered any memory of what she had been, or where bred; that, when this memory returned, she went down into her country, but hardly found the memory of any of her friends she had left there; and so returned to a parish in Southwark, where she had some allowance among other poor, and had been for many years; and once a week walked into the city, and took what alms were given her. My Lord Leicester told me he sent to inquire at the parish, and found their account agree with the woman's: upon which he ordered her to call at his house once a week, which she did for some time; after which he heard no more of her. This story raised some discourse upon a remark of some in the company that mad people are apt to live long. They alleged examples of their own knowledge: but the result was, that, if it were true, it must proceed from the natural vigor of their tempers, which disposed them to passions so violent as ended in frenzies; and from the great abstinence and hardships of diet they are forced upon by the methods of their cure, and severity of those who had them in care; no other drink but water being allowed them, and very little meat.

The last story I shall mention from that noble person, upon this subject, was of a morrice-dancer in Herefordshire; whereof, he said, he had a pamphlet still in his library, written by a very ingenious gentleman of that county, and which gave an account how such a year of King James's reign, there went about the country a set of morrice-dancers, composed of ten men who danced, a Maid Marian, and a tabor and pipe: and how these twelve, one with another, made up twelve hundred years. It is not so much that so many in one small county should live to that age as that they should be in vigor and in humor to travel and to dance.

I have, in my life, met with two of above a hundred and twelve; whereof the woman had passed her life in service, and the man in common labor, till he grew old, and fell upon the parish. But I met with one who had gone a much greater length, which made me more curious in my inquiries. 'Twas an old man, who begged usually at a lonely inn upon the road in Staffordshire, who told me he was a hundred twenty-four years old; that he had been a soldier in the Calais voyage, under the Earl of Essex, of which he gave me a sensible account. That, after his return, he fell to labor in his own parish, which was about a mile from the place where I met him; that he continued to work till a hundred and twelve, when he broke one of his ribs by a fall from a cart, and being thereby disabled, he fell to beg. This agreeing with what the master of the house told me was reported and believed by all his neighbors, I asked him what his usual food was; he said, milk, bread, and cheese, and flesh when it was given him. I asked him what he used to drink; he said, O, Sir, we have the best water in our parish that is in all the neighborhood. Whether he never drank anything else? he said, Yes, if anybody gave it him, but not otherwise. And the host told me, he had got many a pound in his house, but never spent one penny. I asked if he had any neighbors as old as he; and he told me but one, who had been his fellow-soldier at Calais, and was three years older; but he had been most of his time in a good service, and had something to live on now he was old.

I have heard, and very credibly, of many in my life, above a hundred years old, brought as witnesses upon trials of titles, and bounds of land: but I have observed most of them have been of Derbyshire, Staffordshire, or Yorkshire, and none above the rank of common farmers. The oldest I ever knew any persons of quality, or indeed any gentleman, either at home or abroad, was fourscore and twelve. This, added to all the former recites or observations, either of long-lived races or persons in any age or country, makes it easy to conclude, that health and long life are usually blessings of the poor, not of the rich, and the fruits of temperance rather than of luxury and excess. And, indeed, if a rich man does not in many things live like a poor, he will certainly be the worse for his riches: if he does not use exercise, which is but voluntary labor; if he does not restrain appetite by choice, as the others do by necessity. If he does not practise sometimes even abstinence and fasting, which is the last extreme of want and poverty: if his cares and troubles increase with his riches, or his passions with his pleasures, he will certainly impair in health whilst he improves his fortunes, and lose more than he gains by the bargain; since health is the best of all human possessions, and without which the rest are not relished or kindly enjoyed. . . .

4.

FASHION IN DISEASES AND REMEDIES

In the course of my life I have often pleased or entertained myself with observing the various and fantastical changes of the diseases generally complained of, and of the remedies in common vogue, which were like birds of passage, very much seen or heard of at one season, and disappeared at another, and commonly succeeded by some of a very different kind. When I was very young nothing was so much feared or talked of as rickets among children, and consumptions among young people of both sexes. After these the spleen came in play, and grew a formal disease: then the scurvy, which was the general complaint, and both were thought to appear in many various guises. After these, and for a time, nothing was so much talked of as the ferment of the blood, which passed for the cause of all sorts of ailments that neither physicians nor patients knew well what to make of. And to all these succeeded vapors, which serve the same turn, and furnish occasion of complaint among persons whose bodies or minds ail something, but they know not what; and, among the Chinese, would pass for mists of the mind or fumes of the brain, rather than indispositions of any other parts. Yet these employ our physicians perhaps more than other diseases, who are fain to humor such patients in their fancies of being ill, and to prescribe some remedies, for fear of losing their practice to others that pretend more skill in finding out the cause of diseases, or care in advising remedies, which neither they nor their patients find any effect of, besides some gains to one, and amusement to the other. This, I suppose, may have contributed much to the mode of going to the waters either cold or hot, upon so many occasions, or else upon none besides that of entertainment, and which commonly may have no other effect. And it is well if this be the worst of the frequent use of those waters, which, though commonly innocent, yet are sometimes dangerous, if the temper of the person or cause of the indisposition be unhappily mistaken, especially in people of age.

As diseases have changed vogue, so have remedies, in my time and observation. I remember at one time the taking of tobacco, at another the drinking of warm beer, proved for universal remedies; then swallowing of pebble stones, in imitation of falconers curing hawks. One doctor pretended to help all heats and fevers, by drinking as much cold spring water as the patient could bear; at another time, swallowing up a spoonful of powder of sea-biscuit after meals was infallible for all indigestion, and so preventing diseases: then coffee and tea began their successive reigns. The infusions of powder of steel have had their turns, and certain drops, of several names and compositions; but none that I find have established their authority, either long or generally, by any constant and sensible successes of their reign, but have rather passed like a mode, which everyone is apt to follow, and finds the most convenient or graceful while it lasts; and begins to dislike in both those respects when it goes out of fashion.

5.

DUBIOUS PRACTICES IN PHYSIC

Thus men are apt to play with their healths and their lives, as they do with their clothes; which may be the better excused since both are so transitory, so subject to be spoiled with common use, to be torn by accidents, and at best to be so soon worn out. Yet the usual practice of physic among us runs still the same course, and turns, in a manner, wholly upon evacuation, either by bleeding, vomits, or some sorts of purgation; though it be not often agreed among physicians in what cases or what degrees any of these are necessary; nor among other men, whether any of them are necessary or no. Montaigne questions whether purging ever be so, and from

many ingenious reasons: the Chinese never let blood; and, for the
other, it is very probable that nature knows her own wants and times
so well, and so easily finds her own relief that way, as to need little
assistance, and not well to receive the common violences that are
offered her. I remember three in my life and observation who were
downright killed with vomits, as they could have been with daggers;
and I can say for myself, upon an accident very near mortal, when I
was young, that, sending for the two best physicians of the town,
the first prescribed me a vomit, and immediatèly sent it me: I had
the grace or sense to refuse it till the other came, who told me, if I
had taken it, I could not have lived half an hour. I observed a consult of physicians, in a fever of one of my near friends, perplexed to
the last degree whether to let him blood or no, and not able to resolve, till the course of the disease had declared itself, and thereby
determined them. Another of my friends was so often let blood, by
his first physician, that a second who was sent for questioned whether
he would recover it; the first persisted the blood must be drawn till
some good appeared; the other affirmed that in such diseases the
whole mass was corrupted, but would purify again when the accident
was past, like wine after a fermentation, which makes all in the vessel
thick and foul for a season; but, when that is past, grows clear again
of itself. So much is certain, that it depends a great deal upon the
temper of the patient, the nature of the disease in its first causes,
upon the skill and care of the physician to decide whether any of
these violences upon nature are necessary or no, and whether they
are like to do good or harm.

The rest of our common practice consists in various compositions
of innocent ingredients, which feed the hopes of the patient, and the
apothecary's gains, but leave nature to her course, who is the sovereign
physician in most diseases, and leaves little for others to do, further
than to watch accidents; where they know no specific remedies, to
prescribe diets; and, above all, to prevent disorders from the stomach,
and take care that nature be not employed in the kitchen, when she
should be in the field to resist her enemy; and that she should not
be weakened in her spirits and strength, when they are most necessary
to support and relieve her. It is true, physicians must be in danger of
losing their credit with the vulgar, if they should often tell a patient
he has no need of physic, and prescribe only rules of diet or common
use; most people would think they had lost their fee; but the excellence of a physician's skill and care is discovered by resolving first
whether it be best in the case to administer any physic or none, to

trust to nature or to art; and the next, to give such prescriptions, as, if they do no good, may be sure to do no harm.

In the midst of such uncertainties of health and of physic, for my own part I have, in the general course of my life, and of many acute diseases, as well as some habitual, trusted to God Almighty, to nature, to temperance, or abstinence, and the use of common remedies, either vulgarly known and approved like proverbs by long observation and experience, either of my own or such persons as have fallen in the way of my observation or inquiry.

Among the plants of our soil and climate, those I esteem of greatest virtue and most friendly to health, are sage, rue, saffron, alehoof, garlic, and elder. . . .

6.

GARLIC FOR THE GOUT

Garlic has of all our plants the greatest strength, affords most nourishment, and supplies most spirits to those who eat little flesh, as the poorer people seldom do in the hotter, and especially the more eastern climates; so that the labor of the world seems to be performed by the force and virtue of garlic, leeks, and onions, no other food of herbs or plants yielding strength enough for much labor. Garlic is of great virtue in all colics, a great strengthener of the stomach upon decays of appetite or indigestion, and I believe is (if at least there be any such) a specific remedy of the gout. I have known great testimonies of this kind within my acquaintance, and have never used it myself upon this occasion, without an opinion of some success or advantage. But I could never long enough bear the constraint of a diet I found not very agreeable myself, and at least fancied offensive to the company I conversed with.

Besides, this disease is to me so hereditary, and comes into my veins from so many ancestors, that I have reason to despair of any cure but the last, and content myself to fence against it by temperance and patience, without hopes of conquering such an inveterate enemy. Therefore I leave the use of garlic to such as are inveigled into the gout by the pleasure of too much drinking, the ill effects whereof are not more relieved by any other diet than by this plant, which is so great a drier and opener, especially by perspiration. Nor is it less used in many parts abroad as physic than as food. In several provinces of France it is usual to fall into a diet of garlic for a fortnight of three weeks, upon the first fresh butter of the spring; and the common people esteem it a preservative against the diseases of the ensuing year; and a broth of garlic or onions is so generally used the next day after a debauch as to be called *soupe à l'ivrogne*. This is enough to show the use as well as virtues of this northern spice, which is in mighty request among the Indians themselves, in the midst of so many others that enrich and perfume those noble regions.

7.

VARIOUS SPECIFICS

Elder is of great virtue of all indispositions arising from any watery humors; and not only the flowers and berries, but even the green bark, are used with effect and perhaps equal success in their seasons. I have been told of some great cures of the gout by the succeeding use of all three throughout the year; but I have been always too libertine, for any great and long subjections, to make the trials. The spirit of elder is sovereign in colics; and the use of it, in general, very beneficial in scurvies and dropsies: though, in the last, I esteem broom yet of more virtue, either brewed in common drink, or the ashes taken in white wine every morning: which may perhaps pass for a specific remedy; whereof we may justly complain, that, after so long experience of so learned a profession as physic, we yet know so very few.

That which has passed of latter years for the most allowed in this kind, has been the quinquina, or Jesuits' powder, in fevers, but especially agues. I can say nothing of it upon any experience of my own, nor any within my knowledge. I remember its entrance upon our stage with some disadvantage, and the repute of leaving no cures without danger of worse returns. But the credit of it seems now to be established by common use and prescription, and to be improved by new and singular preparations; whereof I have very good and particular reasons to affirm that they are all amusements; and that what virtue there is in this remedy lies in the naked simple itself, as it comes over from the Indies, and in the choice of that which is least dried, or perished by the voyage.

The next specific I esteem to be that little insect called millepedes: the powder whereof, made up into little balls with fresh butter, I never knew fail of curing any sore throat: it must lie at the root of the tongue, and melt down at leisure upon going to bed. I have been assured that Doctor Mayerne used it as a certain cure for all cancers in the breast; and should be very tedious if I should tell here how much the use of it has been extolled by several within my knowledge, upon the admirable effects for the eyes, the scurvy, and the gout; but there needs no more to value it, than what the ancient physicians affirm of it in those three words:

Digerit,	*Aperit,*	*Abstergit.*
It digests,	It opens,	It cleanses.

For rheums in the eyes and the head, I take a leaf of tobacco, put into the nostrils for an hour each morning, to be a specific medicine: or betony, if the other be too strong or offensive. The effect of both is to draw rheums off the head, through their proper and natural channel. And, as old Prince Maurice of Nassau told me, he had by this preserved his eyes, to so great an age, after the danger of losing them at thirty years old; and I have ever since used it with the same success, after great reasons near that age to apprehend the loss or decays of mine.

In times and places of great contagion, the strongest preservative yet known is a piece of myrrh held in the mouth when or where the danger is most apprehended; which I have both practised and taught many others with success, in several places where cruel plagues have raged: though in such cases, after all, the best and safest is to run away as soon as one can. Yet, upon this occasion, I think myrrh may pass for a specific in prevention; and may, for aught I know, be of use in remedies, as the greatest remedy of corruption; which is known by the use of embalmings in the East.

For all illnesses of stomach, or indigestions, proceeding from hot or sharp humors, to which my whole family has been much subject, as well as very many of my acquaintance, and for which, powder of crabs' eyes and claws and burnt egg-shells are often prescribed as sweeteners of any sharp humors, I have never found anything of much or certain effect, besides the eating of strawberries, common cherries, white figs, soft peaches, or grapes, before every meal during their seasons; and when those are past, apples after meals; but all must be very ripe. And this, by my own and all my friends' experience who have tried it, I reckon for a specific medicine in this illness, so frequently complained of; at least, for the two first I never knew them fail; and the usual quantity is about forty cherries, without swallowing either skin or stone. I observe this the rather, because the recourse commonly made in this case to strong waters I esteem very pernicious, and which inevitably destroys the stomach with frequent use. The best, at least most innocent of all distilled liquors, is milk water, made with balm, carduus, mint, and wormwood; which has many good effects in illnesses of the stomach, and none ill. The best and safest strong water, if any be so, for common use, I esteem to be that made of juniper berries especially in accidents of stone or colic.

Of all cordials, I esteem my Lady Kent's powder the best, the most innocent, and the most universal; though the common practice of physic abounds in nothing more, and the virtue seems to be little else, besides an allusion of the name to the heart.

Upon the gout I have writ what I had known or practised, in an essay of moxa; and upon the spleen, what I had observed, in a chapter upon the dispositions of the people in the Netherlands. I shall only add for the help of my fellow-sufferers in the first, that, besides what is contained in the former essay, and since those pains have grown more diffused, and less fixed in one point, so as to be burned with moxa, which never failed of giving me present ease, I have found the most benefit from three methods. The first is, that of moving the joint where the pain begins as long as I am in my bed; which I have often done, and counted five or six hundred times or more, till I found first a great heat, and then perspiration, in the part; the heat spends or disperses the humor within, and the perspiration drives it out; and I have escaped many threats of ill fits by these motions. If they go on, the only poultice or plaster I have dealt with is wool from the belly of a fat sheep, which has often given me ease in a very little time. If the pains grow sharp and the swellings so diffused as not to be burned with moxa, the best remedy I have found is a piece of scarlet dipped in scalding brandy, laid upon the afflicted part, and the heat often renewed by dropping it upon the scarlet as hot as can be endured. And from this I have often found the same success as from moxa, and without breaking the skin or leaving any sore.

8.

DANGERS OF THE SPLEEN

To what I have said in another place of the spleen, I shall only add here, that whatever the spleen is, whether a disease of the part so called, or of people that ail something, but they know not what; it is certainly a very ill ingredient into any other disease, and very

SIR CHRISTOPHER WREN

From a portrait by Sir Godfrey Kneller. Reproduced by permission of
The Royal Society.

LONDON REBUILT AFTER THE FIRE

From an old print. By permission of Magdalene College, Cambridge.

often dangerous. For, as hope is the sovereign balsam of life, and the best cordial in all distempers both of body or mind; so fear, and regret, and melancholy apprehensions, which are the usual effects of the spleen, with the distractions, disquiets, or at least intranquillity they occasion, are the worst accidents that can attend any diseases; and make them often mortal, which would otherwise pass, and have had but a common course. I have known the most busy ministers of state, most fortunate courtiers, most vigorous youths, most beautiful virgins, in the strength or flower of their age, sink under common distempers, by the force of such weights, and the cruel damps and disturbances thereby given their spirits and their blood. It is no matter what is made the occasion, if well improved by spleen and melancholy apprehensions; a disappointed hope, a blot of honor, a strain of conscience, an unfortunate love, an aching jealousy, a repining grief, will serve the turn, and all alike.

I remember an ingenious physician, who told me, in the fanatic times, he found most of his patients so disturbed by troubles of conscience that he was forced to play the divine with them, before he could begin the physician; whose greatest skill perhaps often lies in the infusing of hopes, and inducing some composure and tranquillity of mind, before they enter upon the other operations of their art; and this ought to be the first endeavor of the patient too; without which, all other medicines may lose their virtue.

The two greatest blessings of life are, in my opinion, health and good humor; and none contribute more to one another. Without health, all will allow life to be but a burden, and the several conditions of fortune to be all wearisome, dull, or disagreeable, without good humor; nor does any seem to contribute towards the true happiness of life but as it serves to increase that treasure or to preserve it. Whatever other differences are commonly apprehended in the several conditions of fortune, none perhaps will be found so true or so great as what is made by those two circumstances, so little regarded in the common course of pursuits of mortal men.

Whether long life be a blessing or no, God Almighty only can determine, who alone knows what length it is like to run, and how it is like to be attended. Socrates used to say that it was pleasant to grow old with good health and a good friend; and he might have reason. A man may be content to live while he is no trouble to himself or his friends; but, after that, it is hard if he be not content to die. I knew and esteemed a person abroad, who used to say, a man must be a mean wretch that desired to live after threescore years old. But so much, I doubt, is certain, that in life, as in wine, he that will drink it good must not draw it to dregs.

Where this happens, one comfort of age may be that whereas younger men are usually in pain when they are not in pleasure, old men find a sort of pleasure whenever they are out of pain. And, as young men often lose or impair their present enjoyments by raving after what is to come, by vain hopes, or fruitless fears, so old men relieve the wants of their age, by pleasing reflections upon what is past. Therefore men in the health and vigor of their age should endeavor to fill their lives with reading, with travel, with the best conversation, and the worthiest actions, either in their public or their private stations; that they may have something agreeable left to feed on when they are old, by pleasing remembrances.

But, as they are only the clean beasts which chew the cud, when they have fed enough; so they must be clean and virtuous men that can reflect with pleasure upon the past accidents or courses of their lives. Besides, men who grow old with good sense, or good fortunes, and good nature, cannot want the pleasure of pleasing others, by assisting with their gifts, their credit, and their advice, such as deserve it; as well as their care of children, kindness to friends, and bounty to servants.

But there cannot indeed live a more unhappy creature than an ill-natured old man, who is neither capable of receiving pleasures, nor sensible of doing them to others; and, in such a condition, it is time to leave them.

9.

GAUDEANT BENE NATI

Thus have I traced in this essay whatever has fallen in my way or thoughts to observe concerning life and health, and which I conceived might be of any public use to be known or considered. The plainness wherewith it is written easily shows there could be no other intention; and it may at least pass like a Derbyshire charm, which is used among sick cattle, with these words, If it does thee no good, it will do thee no harm.

To sum up all, the first principle of health and long life is derived from the strength of our race or our birth; which gave occasion to that saying, *Gaudeant bene nati,* Let them rejoice that are happily born. Accidents are not in our power to govern; so that the best cares or provisions for life and health that are left us consist in the discreet and temperate government of diet and exercise: in both which all excess is to be avoided, especially in the common use of wine, whereof the first glass may pass for health, the second for good humor, the third for our friends, but the fourth is for our enemies.

For temperance in other kinds, or in general, I have given its character and virtues in the essay of moxa, so as to need no more upon that subject here.

When, in default or despite of all these cares, or by the effect of ill airs and seasons, acute or strong diseases may arise, recourse must be had to the best physicians that are in reach, whose success will depend upon thought and care, as much as skill. In all diseases of body or mind, it is happy to have an able physician for a friend, or discreet friend for a physician; which is so great a blessing that the wise man will have it to proceed only from God, where he says, "A faithful friend is the medicine of life, and he that fears the Lord shall find him."

THOMAS SYDENHAM

Thomas Sydenham, more than any other single figure, is the father of English medicine. He was not himself a member of the Royal Society but he worked in the tradition of a devoted group, including Jonathan Goddard and Francis Glisson, who pursued the methods of observation and experiment and helped undermine the barbaric pedantry which before their times had made the doctor more dangerous than the disease. His works were republished for the use of American students by Dr. Benjamin Rush of Philadelphia and it is from his edition that our text is drawn.

The Improvement of Physic

The improvement of physic, in my opinion, depends (1) upon collecting a genuine and natural description or history of all diseases as can be procured; and (2) laying down a fixed and complete method of cure. It is easy enough to describe diseases unskillfully, but to write such a full and accurate history of them as to escape the censure that Lord Bacon has passed upon some great promisers in another way is a much more difficult task. "We are not to learn," says the noble author, "that we have a voluminous natural history which is agreeable to the variety of its matter and, by the pains bestowed upon it, rendered curious and entertaining in many places; but if it were stripped of its fables, quotations, trifling disputes, philology and other ornaments that are fitter for the conversation of learned men at their hours of relaxation than for institutes of philosophy, the matter of it would be brought into a narrow compass. Such a history falls far short of our design." And thus the cure of diseases is easily delivered according to the common method; but to do it in a masterly scientifical manner will appear a much harder task to those who know that there are abundance of distempers to be met with in practical writers that were and still continue incurable.

But with regard to the history of diseases, whoever considers the undertaking deliberately, will easily perceive that the author must attend to several more particulars than are ordinarily minded; a few of which I shall mention at present.

(1) All diseases, then, ought to be reduced to certain and determinate kinds with the same exactness as we see it done by botanic writers in their treatises of plants. For there are diseases that come under the same genus, bear the same name, and have some symptoms in common, which, notwithstanding, being of a different nature, require a different treatment.—Thus it is generally known that the word "carduus" is applied to several kinds of herbs and yet a botanist would be guilty of inaccuracy who should content himself with giving a general description of the plant and enumerating the marks wherein it differs from all others, and in the mean time take no notice of the peculiar characteristics of every species which distinguish them from one another. In like manner, it is not enough for a writer to give us only the common signs or appearances of any disease; for though the same variety does not happen in all distempers, yet I hope to make it plainly appear in the following sheets that there are several which, notwithstanding their being treated of by authors under the same name, without any distinction of kind, are extremely different.

Furthermore, where we meet with this distribution of distempers into kinds it is commonly done to serve some hypothesis founded upon the true phenomena; and thence this distinction is rather adapted to the bent of the author and his manner of philosophizing than to the nature of the disorder. How much the improvement of physic has been obstructed by this erroneous procedure appears in not a few diseases, the cure of which would not have been undiscovered at this day, if the benevolent writers of experiments and observations had not been deceived by taking one disease for another. And to this cause I esteem it owing that the materia medica is so immensely enlarged and yet with little advantage to the diseased.

(2) In writing, therefore, a history of diseases every philosophical hypothesis which has prepossessed the writer in its favor ought to be totally laid aside, and then the manifest and natural phenomena of diseases, however minute, must be noted with the utmost accuracy, imitating in this the great exactness of painters who in their pictures copy the smallest spots or moles in the originals; for it is difficult to give a detail of the numerous errors that spring from hypothesis, while writers, misled by false appearances, assign such phenomena for diseases as never existed but in their own brains; whereas they ought to appear clearly, if the truth of their favorite hypothesis, which they esteem incontestable, were well established. Again, if any symptom properly suiting their hypothesis does in reality belong to the disease they are about to describe, they lay too much stress upon it as if nothing more was wanting to confirm it; whereas, on the contrary, if it does not agree with their hypothesis, their manner is either take no notice at all of it or but barely to mention it unless they can, by means of some philosophical subtility, adjust it thereto and bring it in some measure to answer their end.

(3) Again, in describing any disease, it is necessary to enumerate both the peculiar and constant phenomena or symptoms and the accidental ones separately; of which latter kind are those which differ occasionally by reason of the age and constitution of the patient and the different method of cure. For the appearance or aspect of a disorder often varies according to the different method of cure, some symptoms being rather occasioned by the physician than the disorder itself; so that persons laboring under the same illness being differently treated have different symptoms. And hence, unless great caution be used in this point, our notions of the symptoms of diseases must necessarily be very loose and uncertain; not to mention that uncommon cases do not more properly belong to the history of diseases than the biting of the palmer worm in describing sage is to be reckoned amongst the characteristic marks of that plant.

Observations on the Gout

There is no doubt but men will conclude either that the nature of the disease which is my present subject is in a manner incomprehensible, or that I, who have been afflicted with it for these thirty-four years past, am a person of very slender abilities, inasmuch as my observations concerning this distemper and the cure thereof fall short of answering their expectations. But notwithstanding this, I will faithfully deliver the remarks I have hitherto made concerning the difficulties and intricacies respectively occurring in the history of the disease and the method of cure; leaving the illustration thereof to time, the discoverer of the truth.

The gout generally attacks those aged persons who have spent most part of their lives in ease, voluptuousness, high living, and too free a use of wine, and other spirituous liquors and at length, by reason of the common inability to motion in old age, entirely left off those exercises which young persons commonly use. And farther, such as are liable to this disease have large heads and are generally of a plethoric, moist, and lax habit of body and withal of a strong and vigorous constitution and possessed of the best stamina vitae.

The gout, however, does not only seize the gross and corpulent but sometimes, though less frequently, attacks lean and slender persons: neither does it always wait till old age comes, but sometimes attacks such as are in the prime of life, when they have received the seeds of it from gouty parents or have otherwise occasioned it by an over-early use of venery, or the leaving off such exercises as they formerly indulged to a great degree; and who besides have had a voracious appetite and used spirituous liquors immoderately and afterwards quitted them of a sudden for those of a thin and cooling kind.

When it seizes a person far advanced in years for the first time it never has such stated periods, nor proves so violent, as when it attacks a younger person, because 1. he generally perishes before the disease, accompanied with its natural symptoms, comes to its height; and 2. because the natural heat and vigor of the body being abated, it cannot be so constantly and powerfully thrown off upon the joints. But when it comes on sooner, though it may not yet fix on one part, nor prove so severe, but affect the patient occasionally keeping no certain period, giving only a little pain for a few days and coming on and going off without any order; yet it increases gradually and goes on regularly, both with respect to the time of its coming and the continuance of the fit and rages more violently in its progress than in its beginning.

I will first treat of the regular gout, and next of the irregular one; whether occasioned by an unadvised use of improper remedies or the weakness of the subject. The regular gout generally seizes in the following manner: it comes on a sudden towards the close of January or the beginning of February, giving scarce any sign of its approach, except that the patient has been afflicted for some weeks before with a bad digestion, crudities of the stomach, and much flatulency and heaviness, that gradually increase till the fit at length begins; which however is proceeded for a few days by a numbness of the thighs, and a sort of descent of flatulencies through the fleshy parts thereof, along with convulsive motions; and the day preceding the fit the appetite is sharp but preternatural. The patient goes to bed and sleeps quietly till about two in the morning when he is awakened by a pain, which usually seizes the great toe, but sometimes the heel, the calf of the leg or the ankle. The pain resembles that of a dislocated bone and is attended with a sensation as if water just warm were poured upon the membranes of the part affected; and these symptoms are immediately succeeded by a chillness, shivering, and a slight fever. The chillness and shivering abate in proportion as the pain increases, which is mild in the beginning but grows gradually more violent every hour and comes to its height towards evening, adapting itself to the numerous bones of the tarsus and metatarsus, the ligaments whereof it affects; sometimes resembling a tension or laceration of those ligaments, sometimes the gnawing of a dog and sometimes a weight and coarctation, or contraction, of the membranes of the parts affected, which become so exquisitely painful as not to endure the weight of the cloths, nor the shaking of the room from a person's walking briskly therein. And hence the night is not only passed in pain, but likewise with a restless removal of the part affected from one place to another and a continual change of its posture. Nor does the perpetual restlessness of the whole body, which always accompanies the fit and especially in the beginning, fall short of the agitation and pain of the gouty limb. Hence numberless fruitless endeavors are used to ease the pain by continually changing the situation of the body and the part affected, which, notwithstanding, abates not till two or three in the morning, that is, till after twenty-four hours from the first approach of the fit;

when the patient is suddenly relieved by means of a moderate digestion and some dissipation of the peccant matter, though he falsely judges the case to proceed from the last position of the part affected. And being now in a breathing sweat he falls asleep, and upon waking finds the pain much abated and the part affected to be then swelled, whereas before only a remarkable swelling of the veins thereof appeared, as is usual in all gouty fits.

The next day and perhaps two or three days afterwards, if the gouty matter be copious, the part affected will be somewhat pained and the pain increase towards evening and remit about break of day. In a few days it seizes the other foot in the same manner; and if the pain be violent in this, and that which was first seized be quite easy, the weakness thereof soon vanishes and it becomes as strong and healthy as if it had never been indisposed. Nevertheless, the gout affects the foot just seized, as it did the former, both in respect of the vehemence and duration of the pain; and sometimes when there is so copious a peccant matter in the beginning of the fit that one foot is unable to contain it, it affects both at the same time with equal violence; but it generally attacks the feet successively, as above remarked. When it has seized both feet the following fits are irregular, both with respect to the time of seizure and their continuance, but the pain always increases in the evening and remits in the morning; and what we call a fit of the gout, which goes off sooner or later, according to the age of the patient, is made up of a number of these small fits. For when this disease lasts two or three months it is not to be esteemed one continued fit, but rather a series or assemblage of little fits, the last of which prove milder and shorter, till the peccant matter being at length quite expelled, the patient recovers; which, in strong constitutions, and such as seldom have the gout, often happens in fourteen days; and in the aged and those that have frequent returns of the disease, in two months; but in such as are more debilitated, whether with age or the long duration of the distemper, it does not go off till summer advances, which drives it away.

During the first fourteen days the urine is high-colored and after separation lets fall a kind of red gravelly sediment and not above a third part of the liquids taken in is voided by urine and the body is generally costive during this time. The fit is accompanied throughout with loss of appetite, chillness of the whole body towards the evening and a heaviness and uneasiness even of those parts that are not affected by the disease. When the fit is going off, a violent itching seizes the foot, especially between the toes, whence the skin peels off as if the patient had taken poison. The disease being over, the appetite and strength return sooner or later, according as the immediately preceding fit has been more or less severe, and in consequence of this the following fit comes on a shorter or longer space of time; for if the last fit proves very violent, the next will not attack the patient till the same season of the year returns again.

In this manner does the regular gout, accompanied with its genuine and proper symptoms, appear; but when it is exasperated, either by wrong management or long continuance so that the substance of the body is in a manner changed into supplies for the disease and nature unable to expel it according to her usual way, the symptoms differ considerably from those just described.

SAMUEL BUTLER

The Elephant and the Moon

Members of a learned society, observing the moon through a telescope, see what they believe to be two armies in battle. The phenomenon is interpreted as a conflict between the moon's surface dwellers and the underground. As they watch, an elephant detaches himself from one side and moves swiftly from West to East across the disk. The virtuosos hypothesize about moon elephants and are writing their report when a hitherto unobserved fact is brought to their attention.

> But while they were diverted all
> With wording the Memorial,
> The foot-boys, for diversion too,
> As having nothing else to do,
> Seeing the telescope at leisure,
> Turned virtuosos for their pleasure,
> Began to gaze upon the Moon
> As those they waited on had done,
> With monkeys' ingenuity
> That love to practise what they see.
> When one, whose turn it was to peep,
> Saw something in the engine creep,
> And, viewing well, discovered more
> Than all the learned had done before.
> Quoth he, "A little thing is slunk

Into the long star-gazing trunk
And now is gotten down so nigh
I have him just against mine eye."
    This being overheard by one
Who was not so far overgrown
In any virtuous speculation
To judge with mere imagination,
Immediately he made a guess
At solving all appearances,
A way far more significant
Than all their hints of the Elephant,
And found, upon a second view,
His own hypothesis most true,
For he had scarce applied his eye
To the engine but immediately
He found a mouse was gotten in
The hollow tube, and, shut between
The two glass windows in restraint,
Was swelled into an Elephant,
And proved the virtuous occasion
Of all this learned dissertation;
And as a mountain heretofore
Was great with child, they say, and bore
A silly mouse, this mouse, as strange,
Brought forth a mountain in exchange. . . .

*The philosophers are thrown into tumult by this discovery. One of
them suggests, and all agree, that not truth but only novelty is the
object of their concern.*

For what has mankind gained by knowing
His little truth but his undoing,
Which wisely was by nature hidden
And only for his good forbidden?
And therefore with great prudence does
The world still strive to keep it close;
For if all secret truths were known,
Who would not be once more undone?

*Fortified with this pragmatic argument the gentlemen return to their
investigation. The conclusion of the narrative is as follows.*

This being resolved, they, one by one,
Reviewed the tube, the Mouse, and Moon;
But still the narrower they pried,
The more they were unsatisfied,
In no one thing they saw agreeing,
As if they'd several faiths of seeing.
Some swore, upon a second view,
That all they'd seen before was true;
And that they never would recant
One syllable of th' Elephant;
Avowed his snout could be no Mouse's,
But a true Elephant's proboscis.
Others began to doubt and waver,
And knew not whether to espouse
The cause of th' Elephant or Mouse.
Some held no way so orthodox
To try it, as the ballot-box,
And like the nation's patriots,
To find, or make, the truth by votes;
Others conceived it much more fit
To unmount the tube, and open it
And, for their private satisfaction,
To re-examine th' "Transaction,"
And after explicate the rest,
As they should find cause for the best.
To this, as the only expedient,
The whole assembly gave consent,
But ere the tube was half let down,
It cleared the first phenomenon;
For, at the end, prodigious swarms
Of flies and gnats, like men in arms,
Had all passed muster, by mischance,
Both for the Sub- and Pri-volvans.
This being discovered, put them all
Into a fresh and fiercer brawl,
Ashamed that men so grave and wise
Should be chaldesed by gnats and flies,
And take the feeble insects' swarms
For mighty troops of men at arms;
As vain as those who, when the Moon
Bright in a crystal river shone,

Threw casting-nets as subtly at her,
To catch and pull her out of the water.
   But when they had unscrewed the glass
To find out where th' impostor was
And saw the Mouse that, by mishap,
Had made the telescope a trap,
Amazed, confounded, and afflicted,
To be so openly convicted,
Immediately they get them gone,
With this discovery alone:
   That those who greedily pursue
Things wonderful instead of true,
That in their speculations choose
To make discoveries strange news
And natural history a Gazette
Of tales stupendous and far-fet,
Hold no truth worthy to be known
That is not huge and overgrown
And explicate appearances
Not as they are but as they please—
In vain strive Nature to suborn,
And, for their pains, are paid with scorn.

THOMAS SHADWELL

Shadwell's Grub Street capitalization of the joke about the Baconian fanatics is well below the level of Butler's satire. It is, however, sufficiently amusing to be quoted. Dryden pilloried this writer for all time in Mac Flecknoe:

> *"The rest to some faint learning make pretense*
> *But Shadwell never deviates into sense."*

The Virtuoso

Lady Gimcrack. Yet I confess, Sir Nicholas is a fine solitary philosophical person. But my nature more affects the vigorous gaiety and jollity of youth than the fruitless speculations of age.

Longvil. Those are fitter for your youth and blood. But may we not have the honor we were promised of seeing Sir Nicholas?

Lady Gimcrack. The truth is, he is within, but upon some private business. But nothing shall be reserved from such accomplished persons as you are. The truth is, he's learning to swim.

Longvil. Is there any water hereabouts, Madam?

Lady Gimcrack. He does not learn to swim in the water, Sir.

Bruce. Not in the water, Madam! How then?

Lady Gimcrack. In his laboratory, a spacious room where all his instruments and fine knicknacks are.

Bruce. A swimming master! This is beyond all precedent. (*Aside*) He is the most curious coxcomb breathing.

Lady Gimcrack. He has a frog in a bowl of water, tied with a packthread by his loins; which packthread Sir Nicholas holds in his teeth, lying upon his belly on a table. As the frog strikes, he strikes, and his swimming master stands by to tell him when he does well or ill.

Longvil. This is the rarest fop that ever was heard of.

Bruce. Few virtuosos can arrive to this pitch, Madam. This is the most curious invention I ever heard of.

Lady Gimcrack. Alas! He has many such. He is a rare mechanic philosopher. The College indeed refused him; they envied him.

Longvil. Were it not possible to have the favor of seeing this experiment?

Lady Gimcrack. I cannot deny anything to such persons. I'll introduce you. (*Exeunt*)

Scene opens and discovers Sir NICHOLAS *learning to swim on a table,* Sir FORMAL *and the swimming master standing by.*

Sir Formal. In earnest, this is very fine. I doubt not, Sir, but in a short space of time you will arrive at that superiority in this watery science that not a frog breathing will exceed you. Though I confess it is the most curious of all amphibious animals in the art, shall I say, or rather nature, of swimming.

Swimming Master. Ah! Well struck, Sir Nicholas. That was admirable. That was as well swum as any man in England can. Observe the frog. Draw up your arms a little nearer, and then thrust them out strongly. Gather up your legs a little more. So, very well. Incomparable.

Enter BRUCE, LONGVIL, *and* Lady GIMCRACK.

Bruce. Let's not interrupt them, Madam, yet but observe a little this great curiosity.

Longvil. 'Tis a noble invention.

Lady Gimcrack. 'Tis a thing the College never thought of.

Sir Nicholas. Let me rest a little to respire. So, it is wonderful, my noble friend, to observe the agility of this pretty animal which, notwithstanding I impede its motion by the detention of this filium or thread within my teeth, which makes a ligature about its loins, and though by many sudden stops I cause the animal sometimes to sink or immerse, yet with indefatigable activity it rises and keeps almost its whole body upon the superficies or surface of this humid element.

Sir Formal. True, noble Sir. Nor do I doubt but your genius will make art equal, if not exceed, nature. Nor will this or any other frog upon the face of the earth out-swim you.

Sir Nicholas. Nay, I doubt not, Sir, in a very little time to become amphibious. A man, by art, may appropriate any element to himself. You know a great many virtuosos that can fly, but I am so much advanced in the art of flying that I can already out-fly that ponderous animal called a buzzard. Nor should any greyhound in England catch me in the calmest day before I got upon wing. Nay, I doubt not but in a little time to improve the art so far that it will be as common to buy a pair of wings to fly to the world in the moon as to buy a pair of wax boots to ride into Sussex with.

Sir Formal. Nay, doubtless, Sir, if you proceed in those swift gradations you have hitherto prospered in, there will be no difficulty in the noble enterprise which is devoutly to be efflagitated by all ingenious persons since the intelligence with that lunary world would be of infinite advantage to us in the improvement of our politics.

Sir Nicholas. Right, for the moon being *Domina Humidorum,* that is, the governess of moist bodies, has, no doubt the superior government of all islands. And its influence is the cause so many of us are delirious and lunatic in this. But having sufficiently refrigerated my lungs by way of respiration, I will return to my swimming.

Swimming Master. Admirably well struck! Rarely swum! He shall swim with any man in Europe.

Sir Formal. Hold, Sir Nicholas. Here are those noble gentlemen and philosophers whom I invited to kiss your hand. And I am not a little proud of the honor of being the grateful and happy instrument of the necessitude and familiar communication which is like to intervene between such excellent virtuosos.

Bruce. We are Sir Nicholas's and your most humble servants.

Longvil. We shall think ourselves much honored with the knowledge of so celebrated a virtuoso.

Sir Nicholas. You are right welcome into my poor laboratory. And if in aught I can serve you in the way of science, my nature is diffusive and I shall be glad of communicating with such eminent virtuosos as I am let to know you are.

Longvil. We pretend to nothing more than to be your humble admirers.

Sir Formal. All the ingenious world is proud of Sir Nicholas for his physico-mechanical excellencies.

Sir Nicholas. I confess I have some felicity that way, but were I as praecelling in physico-mechanical investigations as you in tropical rhetorical flourishes, I would yield to none.

Longvil. How the asses claw to one another (*aside*).

Bruce. We are both your admirers. But of all quaint inventions, none ever came near this of swimming.

Sir Formal. Truly, I opine it to be a most compendious method that in a fortnight's prosecution has advanced him to be the best swimmer of Europe. Nay, it were possible to swim with any fish of his inches.

Longvil. Have you ever tried in the water, Sir?

Sir Nicholas. No, Sir, but I swim most exquisitely on land.

Bruce. Do you intend to practice in the water, Sir?

Sir Nicholas. Never, Sir. I hate the water. I never come upon the water, Sir.

Longvil. Then there will be no use of swimming.

Sir Nicholas. I content myself with the speculative part of swimming. I care not for the practice. I seldom bring anything to use. 'Tis not my way. Knowledge is my ultimate end.

JOHN EVELYN

Evelyn's diary is filled with the record of his contacts with famous and interesting men and women. The following characterization of Sir William Petty marks a high point in his connoisseurship of genius, and is expressive of a kind of enthusiasm which he reserved for virtuosos, both in the seventeenth century and the modern sense. In Sir William Petty, a fellow member of the Royal Society, Evelyn found a man after his own heart, a great inventive genius whose actual achievements in cartography, economic theory and statistical research were second to none, even in that age of intellectual advancement. Evelyn was present at the launching of the double-bottomed boat, which the King cheerfully christened The Experiment.

Sir William Petty

March 22. Supped at Sir William Petty's with the Bishop of Salisbury and divers honorable persons. We had a noble entertainment in a house gloriously furnished. The master and mistress of it were extraordinary persons. Sir William was the son of a mean man somewhere in Sussex, and sent from School to Oxford where he studied philosophy but was most eminent in mathematics and mechanics, proceeded Doctor of Physic, and was grown famous as for his learning so for his recovering a poor wench that had been hanged for felony. And her body having been begged, as the custom is, for the anatomy lecture, he bled her, put her to bed with a warm woman, and with spirits and other means restored her to life. The young scholars joined and made her a little portion, and married her to a man who had several children by her, she living fifteen years after, as I have been assured. Sir William came from Oxford to be a tutor to a neighbor of mine. Thence, when the rebels were dividing their conquests in Ireland, he was employed by them to measure and set out the land, which he did on an easy contract, so much per acre. This he effected so exactly that it not only furnished him with a great sum of money but enabled him to purchase an estate worth £4000 a year. He afterwards married the daughter of Sir Hardresse Waller. She was an extraordinary wit as well as beauty and a prudent woman.

Sir William, among other inventions, was author of the double-bottomed ship which, though it perished and he was censured for rashness, being lost in the Bay of Biscay in a storm when, I think, fifteen other vessels miscarried. The vessel was flat-bottomed, of exceeding use to put into shallow ports and ride over small depths of water. It consisted of two distinct keels cramped together with huge timbers, etc., so as that a violent stream ran between. It bore a monstrous broad sail, and he still persists that it is practicable and of exceeding use, and he has often told me he would adventure himself in such another, could he procure sailors and his Majesty's permission to make a second Experiment, which name the King gave it at the launching.

The Map of Ireland made by Sir William Petty is believed to be the most exact that ever yet was made of any country. He did promise to publish it, and I am told it has cost him near £1,000 to have it engraved at Amsterdam. There is not a better Latin poet living when he gives himself that diversion, nor is his excellence less in Council and prudent matters of state, but he is so exceeding nice in sifting and examining all possible contingencies that he adventures at nothing which is not demonstration. There were not in the whole world his equal for a superintendent of manufacture and improvement of trade, or to govern a plantation. If I were a prince, I should make him my second Counsellor, at least. There is nothing difficult to him. He is besides courageous, on which account I cannot but note a true story of him, that when Sir Aleyn Brodrick sent him a challenge upon a difference between them in Ireland, Sir William, though exceedingly purblind, accepted the challenge, and it being his part to propound the weapon, desired his antagonist to meet him with a hatchet or axe in a dark cellar, which the other of course refused. Sir William was, with all this, facetious and of easy conversation, friendly and courteous, and had such a faculty of imitating others that he would take a text and preach, now like a brave orthodox divine, then falling into the Presbyterian way, then to the fanatical, the Quaker, the monk and friar, the Popish priest, with such admirable action and alteration of voice and tone as it was not possible to abstain from wonder, and one would swear to hear several persons or forbear to think he was not in good earnest an enthusiast and almost beside himself. Then he would fall out of it into a serious discourse, but it was very rarely he would be prevailed on to oblige the company with this faculty, and that only among most intimate friends. My Lord Duke of Ormond once obtained it of him, and was almost ravished with admiration. But by and by he fell upon a serious reprimand of the faults and miscarriages of some princes and governors, which though he named none, did so sensibly touch the Duke, who was then Lieutenant of Ireland, that he began to be very uneasy and wished the spirit laid which he had raised, for he was neither able to endure such truths nor could he but be delighted. At last he melted his discourse to a ridiculous subject and came down from the joint stool on which he had stood, but my Lord would not have him preach any more. He never could get favor at Court because he outwitted all the projectors that came near him. Having never known such another genius, I cannot but mention these particulars amongst a multitude of others which I could produce. When I who knew him in mean circumstances have been in his splendid palace, he would himself be in admiration how he arrived at it. Nor was it his value or inclination for splendid furniture and the curiosities of the age, but his elegant lady could endure nothing mean or that was not magnificent. He was very negligent himself and rather so of his person and of a philosophic temper. "What a to-do is here!" would he say, "I can lie in straw with as much satisfaction."

He is the author of the ingenious deductions from the bills of mortality which go under the name of Mr. Grant; also of that useful discourse of the manufacture of wool and several others in the register of the Royal Society. He was also author of that paraphrase on the 104th Psalm in Latin verse, which goes about in MS. and is inimitable. In a word, there is nothing impenetrable to him.

SIR WILLIAM PETTY

Political Arithmetic
Or
A Discourse
Concerning

The extent and value of Lands, People, Buildings; Husbandry, Manufacture, Commerce, Fishery, Artisans, Seamen, Soldiers; Public Revenues, Interest, Taxes, Superlucration, Registries, Banks; Valuation of Men, Increasing of Seamen, of Militias, Harbours, Situation, Shipping, Power at Sea, etc.: as the same relates to every country in general, but more particularly to the territories of His Majesty of Great Britain, and his neighbors of Holland, Zealand, and France.

1.

A PROGRAM OF ECONOMIC INQUIRY

Forasmuch as men who are in a decaying condition or who have but an ill opinion of their own concernments, instead of being, as some think, the more industrious to resist the evils they apprehend, do, contrariwise, become the more languid or ineffectual in all their endeavors, neither caring to attempt or prosecute even the *probable* means of their relief. Upon this consideration, as a member of the Commonwealth, next to knowing the precise truth in what condition the common interest stands, I would in all doubtful cases think the best, and consequently not despair without strong and manifest reasons, carefully examining whatever tends to lessen my hopes of the public welfare.

I have therefore thought fit to examine the following persuasions which I find too current in the world and too much to have affected the minds of some to the prejudice of all, viz.:

That the rents of lands are generally fallen; that therefore and for many other reasons the whole Kingdom grows every day poorer and poorer. That formerly it abounded with gold but now there is a great scarcity both of gold and silver. That there is no trade nor employment for the people and yet that the land is underpeopled. That taxes have been many and great. That Ireland and the plantations in America and other additions to the Crown are a burden to England. That Scotland is of no advantage. That trade in general does lamentably decay. That the Hollanders are at our heels in the race for naval power; the French grow too fast upon both and appear so rich and potent that it is but their clemency that they do not devour their neighbors. And finally, that the Church and State of England are in the same danger with the trade of England. With many other dismal suggestions which I had rather stifle than repeat.

It is true, the expense of foreign commodities has of late been too great. Much of our plate, had it remained money, would have better served trade. Too many matters have been regulated by laws, which nature, long custom, and general consent ought only to have governed. The slaughter and destruction of men by the late civil wars and plague have been great. The fire at London and disaster at Chatham have begotten opinions in the *vulgus* of the world, to our prejudice. The Nonconformists increase. The people of Ireland think long of their settlement. The English there apprehend themselves to be aliens and are forced to seek a trade with foreigners, which they might as well maintain with their own relations in England.

But notwithstanding all this, the like whereof was always in all places, the buildings of London grow great and glorious. The American plantations employ 400 sail of ships. Actions [i.e., shares] in the East India Company are nearly double the principal money. Those who can give good security may have money under statute interest.

Materials for building, even oak timber, are little the dearer (some cheaper) for [i.e., in spite of] the rebuilding of London. The Exchange seems as full of merchants as formerly. No more beggars in the streets nor executed for thieves than heretofore. The number of coaches and splendor of equipage exceeds former times. The public theatres are very magnificent. The King has a greater navy and stronger guards than before our calamities. The clergy are rich and the cathedrals in repair. Much land has been improved and the price of food is so reasonable as that men refuse to have it cheaper by admitting of Irish cattle.

And, in brief, no man needs to want that will take moderate pains. That some are poorer than others, ever was and ever will be, and that many are naturally querulous and envious is an evil as old as the world.

These general observations and that men eat and drink and laugh as they used to do, have encouraged me to try if I could also comfort others, being satisfied myself that the interest and affairs of England are in no deplorable condition.

The method I take to do this is not yet very usual. For, instead of using only comparative and superlative words and intellectual arguments, I have taken the course (as a specimen of the Political Arithmetic I have long aimed at) to express myself in terms of number, weight, or measure; to use only arguments of sense and to consider only such causes as have visible foundations in nature, leaving those that depend upon the mutable minds, opinions, appetites, and passions of particular men to the consideration of others. Really professing myself as unable to speak satisfactorily upon those grounds (if they may be called grounds!) as to foretell the cast of a die, to play well at tennis, billiards, or bowls (without long practice) by virtue of the most elaborate conceptions that ever have been written *de projectilibus et missilibus* or of the angles of incidence and reflection.

Now the observations or positions expressed by number, weight, and measure upon which I bottom the ensuing discourses are either true or not apparently false. And which if they are not already true, certain, and evident yet may be made so by the Sovereign Power, *Nam id certum est quod certum reddi potest*. And if they are false, not so false as to destroy the arguments they are brought for, but at the worst are sufficient as suppositions to show the way to that knowledge I aim at.

And I have, withal, for the present, confined myself to the ten principal conclusions hereafter particularly handled, which if they shall be judged material and worthy of a better discussion, I hope all ingenious and candid persons will rectify the errors, defects, and imperfections which probably may be found in any of the propositions upon which these ratiocinations were grounded. Nor would it misbecome authority itself to clear the truth of those matters which private endeavors cannot reach to.

2.

ENGLISH CAPITAL AND THE WORLD'S TRADE

That the King of England's subjects have stock competent and convenient to drive the trade of the whole commercial world.

Now for the further encouragement of trade, as we have shown that there is money enough in England to manage the affairs thereof, so we shall now offer to consideration whether there be not a competent and convenient stock to drive the trade of the whole commercial world.

To which purpose, it is to be remembered that all the commodities yearly exported out of every part of the last-mentioned world may be bought for 45,000,000 pounds and that the shipping employed in the same world are not worth above 15,000,000 pounds more, and consequently that 60,000,000 pounds at most would drive the whole trade above mentioned without any trust [i.e., credit] at all.

But forasmuch as the growers of commodities do commonly trust them to such merchants or factors as are worth but such part of the full value of their commodities as may possibly be lost upon the sale of them, whereas gain is rather to be expected, it follows that less than a stock of 60,000,000 pounds—nay, less than half that sum —is sufficient to drive the trade above mentioned, it being well known that any tradesman of good reputation, worth 500 pounds, will be trusted with above 1,000 pounds worth of commodities.

Wherefore, less than 30,000,000 pounds will suffice for the said purpose, of which sum the coin, shipping, and stock already in the trade do at least make one-half.

And it has been shown how, by the policy of a bank, any sum of money may be equivalent in trade unto nearly double the same. By all of which, it seems that even at present much is not wanting to perform what is propounded.

But suppose 20,000,000 or more were wanting, it is not improbable that since the generality of gentlemen and some noblemen do put their younger sons to merchandise, they will see it reasonable, as they increase in the number of merchants so to increase the magnitude of trade and consequently to increase stock. Which may effectually be done by inbanking 20,000,000 pounds worth of land (not being above a sixth or seventh of the whole territory of England)—that is to say, by making a fund of such value to be security for all commodities bought and sold upon the account of the universal trade here mentioned.

And thus, it having appeared that England has in it as much land like Holland and Zealand as the said two provinces do themselves contain, with abundance of other land not inconvenient for trade; and that there are spare hands enough to earn many millions of money more than they now do; and that there is employment to earn several millions even from the consumption of England itself, —it follows from thence and from what has been said in the last paragraph about enlarging of stock, both of money and land, that it is not impossible—nay, a very feasible matter—for the King of England's subjects to gain the universal trade of the whole commercial world.

Nor is it unseasonable to intimate this matter. Forasmuch as the younger brothers of the good families of England cannot otherwise be provided for so as to live according to their birth and breeding.

For if the lands of England are worth 8,000,000 pounds per annum, there be, at a medium, about 10,000 families of about 800 pounds per annum, in each of which, one with another, we may suppose there is a younger brother whom less than 200 pounds or 300 pounds per annum will not maintain suitable to his relations.

Now I say that neither the offices at Court nor commands in our ordinary army and navy, nor Church preferments, nor the usual gains by the profession of the Law or of Physic, nor the employments under noblemen and prelates, will, all of them put together, furnish livelihoods of above 300 pounds per annum to 3,000 of the said 10,000 younger brothers, wherefore it remains that trade alone must supply the rest.

But if the said 7,000 gentlemen be applied to trade without increasing of trade; or if we hope to increase trade without increasing of stock (which, for ought appears, is only to be done by inbanking a due proportion of lands and money), we must necessarily be disappointed.

Where note that selling of lands to foreigners for gold and silver would enlarge the stock of the kingdom, whereas doing the same between one another doth effect nothing. For he that turns all his land into money, disposes himself for trade and he that parts with his money for land, does the contrary; but to sell land to foreigners increases both money and people and consequently trade.

Wherefore it is to be thought that when the laws denying strangers to purchase and not permitting them to trade without paying extraordinary duties were made, that then the public state of things and interest of the nation were far different from what they now are.

Having handled these ten principal conclusions, I might go on with others *ad infinitum*. But to what has been already said I look upon as sufficient for to show what I mean by Political Arithmetic and to show

1. The uses of knowing the true state of the people, land, stock, trade, etc.
2. That the King's subjects are not in so bad a condition as discontented men would make them.
3. The great effect of unity, industry, and obedience in order to the common safety and each man's peculiar happiness.

V *Grace Abounding*

GEORGE FOX

Fox, the founder of the Society of Friends, bore witness to the truth in a remarkable journal covering the whole period of his ministry from his first preaching and imprisonment under the Commonwealth to his last sickness in 1691. Whether considered as a purely human document or as a revelation of the deepest realities of the spiritual life, the Journal illustrates the incredible durability of what was at once the most intransigent and the most pacific form of Puritan dissent.

Margaret Fell

Upon my being taken and forcibly carried away from Margaret Fell's house, and charged with things of so high a nature, she was concerned, as looking upon it to be an injury offered to herself. Whereupon she writ the following lines and sent them abroad, directed thus:

To all Magistrates concerning the wrong taking up and imprisoning of George Fox at Lancaster.

I do inform the governors of this nation, that Henry Porter, mayor of Lancaster, sent a warrant with four constables to my house, for which he had no authority or order. And they searched my house, and apprehended a man in it, which was not guilty of the breach of any law, nor guilty of any offence to any in the nation. And after they had apprehended him and brought him before Porter, there was bail offered, what he would demand, for his appearance to answer what could be laid to his charge; but he (contrary to law, if he had taken him lawfully) denied any bail and clapped him up in close prison. After he was in prison a copy of his mittimus was demanded, which ought not to be denied to any prisoner, nor no lawful magistrate will, that so he may see what is laid to his charge. But it was denied him; a copy of it he could not have, only they were suffered to read it over. And every word that was there charged against him was utterly false; and he was not guilty of any one charge in it. This will be proved and manifested to the nation. So let the governors consider of it. I am concerned in the thing, inasmuch as he was apprehended in my house; and if he be guilty I am so too. So I desire to have this searched out.

And Margaret Fell went to London and spoke with the King about my taking, and showed him the manner of it and offered up her life to the King to stand as a pledge for the peace and quietness of all Friends and for their faith. . . .

I had seen from the Lord a considerable time before that I should take Margaret Fell to be my wife. And when I first mentioned it to her she felt the answer of life from God thereunto. But though the Lord had opened this thing unto me, yet I had not received a command from the Lord for the accomplishment of it then. Wherefore I let the thing rest, and went on in the work and service of the Lord as before, according as the Lord let me, travelling up and down in this nation and through the nation of Ireland. But now, after I was come back from Ireland and was come to Bristol and found Margaret Fell there, it opened in me from the Lord that the thing should be now accomplished.

And after we had discoursed the thing together I told her if she also was satisfied with the accomplishing of it now she should first send for her children, which she did. And when the rest of her daughters were come I was moved to ask the children and her sons-in-law whether they were all satisfied and whether Margaret had answered them according to her husband's will to her children, she being a widow, and if her children had left anything to her for the assistance of her children, in which if she married they might suffer loss, whether she had answered them in lieu of that and all other things. And the children made answer and said she had doubled it, and would not have me to speak of those things. I told them I was plain and would have all things done plainly, for I sought not any outward advantage to myself.

And so when I had thus acquainted the children with it, and when it had been laid before several meetings both of the men and women, assembled together for that purpose, and all were satisfied, there was a large meeting appointed of purpose in the meeting house at Broad Mead in Bristol, the Lord joining us together in the honourable marriage in the everlasting covenant and immortal Seed of life, where there were several large testimonies borne by Friends. Then was a certificate, relating both the proceedings and the marriage, openly read and signed by the relations and by most of the ancient Friends of that city, besides many other Friends from divers parts of the nation.

And before we were married I was moved to write forth a paper to all the meetings in England both of men and women and elsewhere, for all meetings of Friends which were begotten to the Lord were but as one meeting to me.

After this I stayed in Bristol about a week and then passed with Margaret into the country to Olveston, where Margaret passed homewards towards the north and I passed on in the work of the Lord into Wiltshire, where I had many large and precious meetings. . . .

And there was one Walter Newton, a neighbour to my relations, who had been an ancient Puritan, said unto me he heard I was married, and asked the reason. And I told him, as a testimony, that all might come up into the marriage as was in the beginning, and as a testimony that all might come up out of the wilderness to the marriage of the Lamb. And he said he thought marriage was only for the procreation of children, and I told him I never thought of any such thing but only in obedience to the power of the Lord. And I judged such things below me, though I saw such things and established marriages; but I looked on it as below me. And though I saw such a thing in the Seed yet I had no command to do such a thing till a half year before, though people had long talked of it, and there was some jumble in some minds about it, but the Lord's power came over all and laid all their spirits; and some after confessed it.

Fox in New England

And on the 30th day of the 4th month (June), we had a meeting at Providence, very large, and all sorts and sects of people were there. I had a great travail concerning the meeting, in having and preserving it quiet, and for the bringing the Truth over them and in them, and so set the power of God and his Seed above all and in them and over them, for they were above the priests in high notions. And the Lord set his Seed over all and above all and they went away mightily satisfied and said that they never heard the like and did much desire another meeting. And some came a-purpose to dispute, but all were silent and the power of the Lord was over all, praised be the Lord. And many came to me for more meetings and people came far and near to it, and it was of great service and to the honour of God. And from Rhode Island it was about threescore miles by water backwards and forwards; and the governor went with me, and many others. And there were two justices of the peace and other officers there, and the glorious power of the Lord shined over all, glory to the great Lord for ever.

A great barn was so full of people and I was so hot with sweat as though I had been sodden, but all was well. The blessed Seed was over all. There was a priest did threaten, but his mouth was stopped. There was a woman that was bad and scoffed, and she went away and was struck sick and sent for one to look to her; and she told of her scoffing and her badness and would not look to her, and this was at Providence. . . .

In New England there was an Indian king that said he saw that there were many of their people of the Indians turned to the New England professors. He said they were worse since than they were before they left their own religion; and of all religions he said the Quakers were the best. And if they should turn to the New England professors' religion, that made the people worse than they were before, and if should turn to the Quakers, which was the best, then the professors would hang him and put them to death and banish them as they did the Quakers, and therefore he thought it was the best to be as he was.

WILLIAM PENN

Little evidence has been given in the materials included in this book of the importance of America in the consciousness of seventeenth-century England. The first epoch of Virginia and New England settlement was indeed over, but the problem and the hope of a world-wide England was very much present under both Charles and James and events of great importance were occurring. The facts are sufficiently familiar. Confirmation of English possession of New York, seized by James's fleet in 1664, was one of the results (indeed, as we see it, it was the great result) of the first war with Holland. By the Treaty of Breda in 1667, the Dutch withdrew their claim to any part of North America. The Carolinas had been founded in 1663; John Locke, who became secretary to the Lords Proprietors, gave in his constitution a simple answer to the problems of religious rivalry which had proved insoluble in England. It was in this period that Massachusetts lost its charter and it was in this period, finally, that William Penn, under royal proprietary charter, set up the Quaker Commonwealth of Pennsylvania.

The logic of circumstances and personalities which led to this last extension of the imperium of Britain is apparent in the materials already before us. Penn's father, a fair specimen of Restoration public man, who drank and went to plays with Samuel Pepys, was entitled to reward for his services as an English admiral. The son, inconveniently inclined to nonconformity from boyhood, joined

*the Quakers in 1667, after which the Restoration could have nothing
of him. Both he and the troublesome and yet appealing sect were
taken care of by a stroke of the royal pen. The determination which
led him to choose imprisonment rather than yield to the pressure of
his family and class was with him in the work of colonization. His
heart was in the new world but, except for brief periods of residence
there, he remained an English gentleman and, perforce, a politician.
His writings are voluminous*—No Cross No Crown, The Sandy Foundations Shaken, Some Fruits of Solitude—*and help form the image
of a spiritual hero as competent in the ways of this world as he was
committed to its transformation into a better.*

Letter to the Indians, Dated October 18, 1681

My Friends,

There is one great God and power that hath made the world and
all things therein, to whom you and I, and all people owe their
being and well being, and to whom you and I must one day give an
account, for all that we do in the world. This great God hath written
his law in our hearts, by which we are taught and commanded to
love, and help, and do good to one another and not do harm and
mischief to one another.

Now this great God hath been pleased to make me concerned in
your parts of the world, and the king of the country where I live,
hath given unto me a great province; but I desire to enjoy it with
your love and consent, that we may always live together as neighbours and friends, else what would the great God say to us, who hath
made us not to devour and destroy one another but to live soberly
and kindly together in the world? Now I would have you well observe, that I am sensible of the unkindness and injustice that hath
been too much exercised toward you by the people of these parts
of the world, who sought themselves, and to make great advantages
by you, rather than be examples of justice and goodness unto you,
which I hear hath been matter of trouble to you, and caused great
grudgings and animosities, sometimes to the shedding of blood, which
hath made the great God angry. But I am not such a man, as is well
known in my own country. I have great love and regards towards you,
and I desire to win and gain your love and friendship, by a kind,
just, and peaceable life; and the people I send are of the same mind,
and shall in all things behave themselves accordingly; and if in anything any shall offend you or your people, you shall have a full and

speedy satisfaction for the same, by an equal number of just men on both sides, that by no means you may have just occasion of being offended against them.

I shall shortly come to you myself. At which time we may more largely and freely confer and discourse of these matters. In the meantime, I have sent my commissioners to treat with you about land and a firm league of peace. Let me desire you to be kind to them and the people, and receive these presents and tokens which I have sent to you, as a testimony of my good will to you, and my resolution to live justly, peaceably, and friendly with you.

I am your loving friend,
WILLIAM PENN

Prayer for Philadelphia, August 1684

And thou, Philadelphia, the virgin settlement of this province, named before thou wert born, what love, what care, what service, and what travail has there been to bring thee forth and preserve thee from such as would abuse and defile thee!

O that thou mayst be kept from the evil that would overwhelm thee: that, faithful to the God of thy mercies, in the life of righteousness, thou mayst be preserved to the end! My soul prays to God for thee, that thou mayst stand in the day of trial, that thy children may be blessed of the Lord, and thy people saved by his power. My love to thee has been great, and the remembrance of thee affects my heart and mine eye. The God of eternal strength keep and preserve thee to his glory and thy peace.

THOMAS ELLWOOD

Ellwood is a very simple fellow and better represents the average Quaker convert than does William Penn. He is best remembered for his contact with John Milton. The lines of the austere portrait soften when we read of the kindness that was between the poet and his admiring friend. Whether the idea of Paradise Regained *was really suggested to his mind by Ellwood is a question. But it at least pleased the young man to think so, and Milton did nothing to disabuse him. Ellwood stood for the moment for the "fit audience though few," without the thought of whom it would have been hard for even the inspired poet to go on.*

Father and Son

Next day we parted, he for London, I for home, under a very great weight and exercise upon my spirit. For I now saw, in and by the farther openings of the Divine Light in me, that the enemy, by his false reasonings, had beguiled and misled me with respect to my carriage towards my father. For I now clearly saw that the honor due to parents did not consist in uncovering the head and bowing the body to them, but in a ready obedience to their lawful commands, and in performing all needful services unto them. Wherefore, as I was greatly troubled for what I already had done in that case, though it was through ignorance, so I plainly felt I could no longer continue therein without drawing on myself the guilt of willful disobedience, which I well knew would draw after it divine displeasure and judgment.

Hereupon the enemy assaulted me afresh, setting before me the danger I should run myself into of provoking my father to use severity towards me, and perhaps to the casting me utterly off. But over this temptation the Lord, whom I cried unto, supported me, and gave me faith to believe that He would bear me through whatever might befall me on that account. Wherefore I resolved, in the strength which He should give me, to be faithful to His requirings, whatever might come of it.

Thus laboring under various exercises on the way, I at length got home, expecting I should have but a rough reception from my father. But when I came home, I understood my father was from home; wherefore I sat down by the fire in the kitchen, keeping my mind retired to the Lord, with breathings of spirit to Him that I might be preserved from falling.

After some time I heard the coach drive in, which put me into a little fear, and a sort of shivering came over me. But by that time he was alighted and come in, I had pretty well recovered myself; and as soon as I saw him, I rose up and advanced a step or two towards him, with my head covered, and said, "Isaac Penington and his wife remember their loves to thee."

He made a stop to hear what I said, and observing that I did not stand bare and that I used the word *thee* to him, he, with a stern countenance, and tone that spake high displeasure, only said, "I shall talk with you, sir, another time"; and so hastening from me went into the parlor, and I saw him no more that night.

Though I foresaw there was a storm arising, the apprehension of which was uneasy to me, yet the peace which I felt in my own breast raised in me a return of thanksgiving to the Lord for His gracious supporting hand, which had thus far carried me through this exercise, with humble cries in spirit to Him that He would vouchsafe to stand by me in it to the end, and uphold me, that I might not fall.

My spirit longed to be among friends, and to be at some meeting with them on the first day, which now drew on, this being the sixth-day night. Wherefore I purposed to go to Oxford on the morrow, which was the seventh day of the week, having heard there was a meeting there. Accordingly, having ordered my horse to be made ready betimes, I got up in the morning and made myself ready also. Yet before I would go, that I might be as observant to my father as possibly I could, I desired my sister to go up to him in his chamber and acquaint him that I had a mind to go to Oxford and desired to know if he pleased to command me any service there. He bid her tell me he would not have me go till he had spoken with me; and getting up immediately, he hastened down to me before he was quite dressed.

As soon as he saw me standing with my hat on, his passion transporting him, he fell upon me with both his fists, and having by that means somewhat vented his anger, he plucked off my hat and threw it away. Then stepping hastily out to the stable and seeing my borrowed nag stand ready saddled and bridled, he asked his man whence that horse came; who telling him he fetched it from Mr. Such-an-one's, "Then ride him presently back," said my father, "and tell Mr. —— I desire he will never lend my son a horse again unless he brings a note from me."

The poor fellow, who loved me well, would fain have made excuses and delays; but my father was positive in his command, and so urgent that he would not let him stay so much as to take his breakfast, though he had five miles to ride, nor would he himself stir from the stable till he had seen the man mounted and gone.

Then coming in, he went up into his chamber to make himself more fully ready, thinking he had me safe enough now my horse was gone; for I took so much delight in riding that I seldom went on foot.

But while he was dressing himself in his chamber, I, who understood what had been done, changing my boots for shoes, took another hat, and acquainting my sister, who loved me very well, and whom I could confide in, whither I meant to go, went out privately and walked away to Wycombe, having seven long miles thither, which yet seemed little and easy to me from the desire I had to be among friends.

As thus I travelled all alone, under a load of grief from the sense I had of the opposition and hardship I was to expect from my father, the enemy took advantage to assault me again, casting a doubt into my mind whether I had done well in thus coming away from my father without his leave or knowledge.

I was quiet and peaceable in my spirit before this question was darted into me; but after that, disturbance and trouble seized upon me, so that I was at a stand what to do—whether to go forward or backward. Fear of offending inclined me to go back, but desire of the meeting, and to be with friends, pressed me to go forward.

I stood still awhile to consider and weigh as well as I could the matter. I was sensibly satisfied that I had not left my father with any intention of undutifulness or disrespect to him, but merely in obedience to that drawing of spirit which I was persuaded was of the Lord, to join with His people in worshipping Him; and this made me easy.

But then the enemy, to make me uneasy again, objected, "But how could that drawing be of the Lord which drew me to disobey my father?"

I considered thereupon the extent of paternal power, which I found was not wholly arbitrary and unlimited, but had bounds set unto it; so that as in civil matters it was restrained to things lawful, so in spiritual and religious cases it had not a compulsory power over conscience, which ought to be subject to the heavenly Father. And therefore, though obedience to parents be enjoined to children, yet it is with this limitation [*in the Lord*]: "Children, obey your parents in the Lord; for this is right" (I Pet. 6.1).

This turned the scale for going forward, and so on I went. And yet I was not wholly free from some fluctuations of mind, from the besettings of the enemy. Wherefore, although I knew that outward signs did not properly belong to the gospel dispensation, yet for my better assurance I did, in fear and great humility, beseech the Lord that he would be pleased so far to condescend to the weakness of His servant as to give me a sign by which I might certainly know whether my way was right before Him or not.

The sign which I asked was, "That if I had done wrong in coming as I did, I might be rejected or but coldly received at the place I was going to; but if this mine undertaking was right in His sight, He would give me favor with them I went to, so that they should receive me with hearty kindness and demonstrations of love." Accordingly, when I came to John Rance's house (which, being so much a stranger to all, I chose to go to, because I understood the meeting was commonly held there), they received me with more than ordinary kindness, especially Frances Rance, John Rance's then wife, who was both a grave and motherly woman and had a hearty love to truth and tenderness towards all that in sincerity sought after it. And this so kind reception, confirming me in the belief that my undertaking was approved of by the Lord, gave great satisfaction and ease to my mind; and I was thankful to the Lord therefor.

Thus it fared with me there; but at home it fared otherwise with my father. He, supposing I had betaken myself to my chamber when he took my hat from me, made no inquiry after me till evening came; and then, sitting by the fire and considering that the weather was very cold, he said to my sister, who sat by him: "Go up to your brother's chamber, and call him down; it may be he will sit there else in a sullen fit till he has caught cold." "Alas! sir," said she, "he is not in his chamber, nor in the house neither." At that my father, startling, said: "Why, where is he then?"—"I know not, sir," said she, "where he is; but I know that when he saw you had sent away his horse, he put on shoes and went out on foot, and I have not seen him since. And indeed, sir," added she, "I don't wonder at this going away, considering how you used him." This put my father into a great fright doubting I was gone quite away; and so great a passion of grief seized on him that he forebore not to weep and to cry out aloud, so that the family heard him: "Oh, my son! I shall never see him more; for he is of so bold and resolute a spirit that he will run himself into danger and so may be thrown into some gaol or other, where he may lie and die before I can hear of him." Then bidding her light him up to his chamber, he went immediately to bed, where he lay restless and groaning, and often bemoaning himself and me, for the greatest part of the night.

A Visit to John Milton

After I was well enough to go abroad with respect to my own health and the safety of others, I went up, in the beginning of the twelfth month, 1661, to my friend Isaac Penington's at Chalfont, and

abode there some time for the airing myself more fully that I might
be more fit for conversation.

I mentioned before that when I was a boy I had made some good
progress in learning and lost it all again before I came to be a man;
nor was I rightly sensible of my loss therein until I came amongst
the Quakers. But then I both saw my loss and lamented it, and
applied myself with utmost diligence at all leisure times to recover
it; so false I found that charge to be which in those times was cast
as a reproach upon the Quakers that they despised and decried all
human learning because they denied it to be essentially necessary to
a gospel ministry, which was one of the controversies of those times.

But though I toiled hard and spared no pains to regain what once
I had been master of, yet I found it a matter of so great difficulty
that I was ready to say as the noble eunuch to Philip in another case,
"How can I, unless I had some man to guide me?"

This I had formerly complained of to my especial friend, Isaac
Penington, but now more earnestly, which put him upon considering and contriving a means for my assistance.

He had an intimate acquaintance with Dr. Paget, a physician of
note in London, and he, with John Milton, a gentleman of great
note for learning throughout the learned world for the accurate
pieces he had written on various subjects and occasions.

This person, having filled a public station in the former times, lived
now a private and retired life in London, and having wholly lost his
sight, kept always a man to read to him, which usually was the son
of some gentleman of his acquaintance, whom in kindness he took to
improve in his learning.

Thus by the mediation of my friend Isaac Penington with Dr.
Paget and of Dr. Paget with John Milton was I admitted to come
to him, not as a servant to him, which at that time he needed not,
nor to be in the house with him, but only to have the liberty of
coming to his house at certain hours when I would, and to read to
him what books he should appoint me, which was all the favor I
desired.

But this being a matter which would require some time to bring
it about, I in the meanwhile returned to my father's house in Oxfordshire.

I had before received direction by letters from my eldest sister,
written by my father's command, to put off what cattle he had left
about his house and to discharge his servants; which I had done at
the time called Michaelmas before. So that all that winter, when I

was at home, I lived like an hermit, all alone, having a pretty large house and nobody in it but myself, a nights especially; but an elderly woman, whose father had been an old servant to the family, came every morning and made my bed, and did what else I had occasion for her to do, till I fell ill of the smallpox, and then I had her with me and the nurse. But now, understanding by letter from my sister that my father did not intend to return to settle there, I made off those provisions which were in the house that they might not be spoiled when I was gone; and because they were what I should have spent if I had tarried there, I took the money made of them to myself for my support at London if the project succeeded for my going thither.

This done, I committed the care of the house to a tenant of my father's who lived in the town, and taking my leave of Crowell, went up to my sure friend Isaac Penington again; where understanding that the mediation used for my admittance to John Milton had succeeded so well that I might come when I would, I hastened to London and in the first place went to wait upon him.

He received me courteously, as well for the sake of Dr. Paget, who introduced me, as of Isaac Penington, who recommended me; to both whom he bore a good respect. And having inquired divers things of me with respect to my former progression in learning, he dismissed me to provide myself of such accommodations as might be most suitable to my future studies.

I went therefore and took myself a lodging as near to his house— which was then in Jewyn Street—as conveniently I could, and from thenceforward went every day in the afternoon, except on the first days of the week, and, sitting by him in his dining-room, read to him in such books in the Latin tongue as he pleased to hear me read.

At my first sitting to read to him, observing that I used the English pronunciation, he told me, if I would have the benefit of the Latin tongue, not only to read and understand Latin authors but to converse with foreigners either abroad or at home, I must learn the foreign pronunciation. To this I consenting, he instructed me how to sound the vowels; so different from the common pronunciation used by the English, who speak Anglice their Latin, that—with some few other variations in sounding some consonants in particular cases, as c before e or i like ch, sc before i like sh, etc.—the Latin thus spoken seemed as different from that which was delivered, as the English generally speak it, as if it was another language.

I had before, during my retired life at my father's, by unwearied diligence and industry, so far recovered the rules of grammar, in which I had once been very ready, that I could both read a Latin author and after a sort hammer out his meaning. But this change of pronunciation proved a new difficulty to me. It was now harder to me to read than it was before to understand when read. But

> *Labor omnia vincit*
> *Improbus:*
> Incessant pains,
> The end obtains.

And so did I. Which made my reading the more acceptable to my master. He, on the other hand, perceiving with what earnest desire I pursued learning, gave me not only all the encouragement but all the help he could; for, having a curious ear, he understood by my tone when I understood what I read and when I did not, and accordingly would stop me, examine me, and open the most difficult passages to me.

Thus went I on for about six weeks' time, reading to him in the afternoons; and exercising myself with my own books in my chamber in the forenoons, I was sensible of an improvement.

But, alas! I had fixed my studies in a wrong place. London and I could never agree for health; my lungs, as I suppose, were too tender to bear the sulphurous air of that city, so that I soon began to droop; and in less than two months' time I was fain to leave both my studies and the city and return into the country to preserve life; and much ado I had to get thither. . . .

Some little time before I went to Aylesbury prison, I was desired by my quondam master, Milton, to take an house for him in the neighborhood where I dwelt, that he might get out of the city for the safety of himself and his family, the pestilence then growing hot in London. I took a pretty box for him in Giles Chalfont, a mile from me, of which I gave him notice, and intended to have waited on him and seen him well settled in it but was prevented by that imprisonment.

But now being released and returned home, I soon made a visit to him, to welcome him into the country.

After some common discourses had passed between us, he called for a manuscript of his; which, being brought, he delivered to me, bidding me take it home with me and read it at my leisure, and when I had so done, return it to him with my judgment thereupon.

When I came home and had set myself to read it, I found it was that excellent poem which he entitled "Paradise Lost." After I had, with the best attention, read it through, I made him another visit and returned him his book, with due acknowledgement of the favor he had done me in communicating it to me. He asked me how I liked it and what I thought of it, which I modestly but freely told him, and after some further discourse about it, I pleasantly said to him, "Thou hast said much here of 'Paradise Lost,' but what hast thou to say of 'Paradise Found'?" He made me no answer, but sat some time in a muse; then brake off that discourse and fell upon another subject.

After the sickness was over and the City well cleansed and become safely habitable again, he returned thither. And when afterwards I went to wait on him there, which I seldom failed of doing whenever my occasions drew me to London, he showed me his second poem, called "Paradise Regained," and in a pleasant tone said to me, "This is owing to you, for you put it into my head by the question you put to me at Chalfont, which before I had not thought of." But from this digression I return to the family I then lived in.

JOHN BUNYAN

Of all the great mass of writing which grew out of the Puritan preoccupation with sin, repentance and redemption through Jesus Christ, the work of John Bunyan stands alone in the universality of its appeal. He was a man of the people; he spoke the common language and no other. His grasp of the realities of human life and his unrivaled power of dramatizing the hopes and fears of men arose from the intensity of his own experience, interpreted and fortified by devoted study of a single book, the English Bible. Grace Abounding is the realistic record of his conversion, a kind of testimony in which Puritan literature abounds. The Pilgrim's Progress externalizes the conflicts and the triumphs of the Christian life in the familiar form of an allegorical journey. Bunyan's narrative has the vividness of direct vision, which indeed it was. The characters, though bearing the names of good and evil, are no abstractions but living men and women; the setting is the daily scene of rural England, in which, however, every act and circumstance is weighted with an immense significance. The reader is made to share Christian's breathless eagerness, to struggle with him in the slough of despondency, to stand at his side against the fiend and to exult as he goes in at the gate and beholds the city shining like the sun.

Bunyan grew up in a small town and followed his father's trade

*as tinker. He served in the Parliamentary army at the age of seven-
teen, joined one of the small independent congregations and became
a lay preacher of the Baptist persuasion. He refused to be silenced at
the Restoration and lay twelve years in prison—until the temporary
relaxation of the laws against dissenting ministers in 1672. It was
there that he poured forth his personal experience of the terrors of
sin, the hardship of repentance and the recurrent ecstasy of knowing
that he was saved by the blood of Christ.* Grace Abounding *is the
culmination of a series of religious works written between 1661 and
1666.* Pilgrim's Progress *belongs to a second period of imprisonment
in 1675. It has been reprinted hundreds of times and translated into
innumerable languages.*

Grace Abounding to the Chief of Sinners;
Or, a Brief Relation of the Exceeding Mercy of God
in Christ, to His Poor Servant John Bunyan

In this my relation of the merciful working of God upon my soul,
it will not be amiss, if, in the first place, I do, in a few words, give
you a hint of my pedigree, and manner of bringing up; that thereby
the goodness and bounty of God towards me may be the more advanced and magnified before the sons of men.

For my descent then, it was, as is well known by many, of a low
and inconsiderable generation; my father's house being of that rank
that is meanest and most despised of all the families in the land.
Wherefore I have not here, as others, to boast of noble blood, or of a
high-born state, according to the flesh; though, all things considered,
I magnify the heavenly Majesty, for that by this door He brought me
into this world, to partake of the grace and life that is in Christ by
the Gospel.

But yet, notwithstanding the meanness and inconsiderableness of
my parents, it pleased God to put it into their hearts to put me to
school, to learn both to read and write; the which I also attained,
according to the rate of other poor men's children; though, to my
shame I confess, I did soon lose that little I learned, and that even
almost utterly, and that long before the Lord did work His gracious
work of conversion upon my soul.

As for my own natural life, for the time that I was without God in
the world, it was indeed according to the course of this world, and
"the spirit that now worketh in the children of disobedience" (Eph.
ii. 2, 3). It was my delight to be "taken captive by the Devil at his

will" (2 Tim. ii. 26). Being filled with all unrighteousness: the which did also so strongly work and put forth itself, both in my heart and life, and that from a child, that I had but few equals, especially considering my years, which were tender, being few, both for cursing, swearing, lying, and blaspheming the holy name of God.

Yea, so settled and rooted was I in these things that they became as a second nature to me; the which, as I also have with soberness considered since, did so offend the Lord that even in my childhood He did scare and affright me with fearful dreams, and did terrify me with dreadful visions; for often, after I had spent this and the other day in sin, I have in my bed been greatly afflicted, while asleep, with the apprehensions of devils and wicked spirits, who still, as I then thought, labored to draw me away with them, of which I could never be rid.

Also I should, at these years, be greatly afflicted and troubled with the thoughts of the day of judgment, and that both night and day, and should tremble at the thoughts of the fearful torments of hell-fire; still fearing that it would be my lot to be found at last amongst those devils and hellish fiends who are there bound down with the chains and bonds of eternal darkness, "unto the judgment of the great day."

These things, I say, when I was but a child but nine or ten years old, did so distress my soul that when in the midst of my many sports and childish vanities, amidst my vain companions, I was often much cast down and afflicted in my mind therewith, yet could I not let go my sins. Yea, I was also then so overcome with despair of life and Heaven, that I should often wish either that there had been no Hell, or that I had been a devil—supposing they were only tormentors; that if it must needs be that I went thither, I might be rather a tormentor than be tormented myself.

A while after, these terrible dreams did leave me, which also I soon forgot; for my pleasures did quickly cut off the remembrance of them, as if they had never been: wherefore, with more greediness, according to the strength of nature, I did still let loose the reins to my lusts, and delighted in all transgression against the law of God: so that, until I came to the state of marriage, I was the very ringleader of all the youth that kept me company, into all manner of vice and ungodliness.

Yea, such prevalency had the lusts and fruits of the flesh in this poor soul of mine that, had not a miracle of precious grace prevented, I had not only perished by the stroke of eternal justice, but had also laid myself open even to the stroke of those laws which bring some to disgrace and open shame before the face of the world.

In these days, the thoughts of religion were very grievous to me; I could neither endure it myself, nor that any other should; so that, when I have seen some read in those books that concerned Christian piety, it would be as it were a prison to me. Then I said unto God, "Depart from me, for I desire not the knowledge of Thy ways" (Job xxi. 14). I was now void of all good consideration, Heaven and Hell were both out of sight and mind; and as for saving and damning, they were least in my thoughts. O Lord, Thou knowest my life, and my ways were not hid from Thee.

Yet this I well remember, that though I could myself sin with the greatest delight and ease, and also take pleasure in the vileness of my companions; yet, even then, if I have at any time seen wicked things, by those who professed goodness, it would make my spirit tremble. As once, above all the rest, when I was in my height of vanity, yet hearing one to swear that was reckoned for a religious man, it had so great a stroke upon my spirit that it made my heart to ache.

But God did not utterly leave me, but followed me still, not now with convictions, but judgments; yet such as were mixed with mercy. For once I fell into a creek of the sea, and hardly escaped drowning. Another time I fell out of a boat into Bedford river, but mercy yet preserved me alive. Besides, another time, being in the field with one of my companions, it chanced that an adder passed over the highway; so I, having a stick in my hand, struck her over the back; and having stunned her, I forced open her mouth with my stick, and plucked her sting out with my fingers; by which act, had not God been merciful unto me, I might, by my desperateness, have brought myself to mine end.

This also have I taken notice of with thanksgiving; when I was a soldier, I, with others, were drawn out to go to such a place to besiege it; but when I was just ready to go, one of the company desired to go in my room; to which, when I had consented, he took my place; and coming to the siege, as he stood sentinel, he was shot into the head with a musket bullet, and died.

Here, as I said, were judgments and mercy, but neither of them did awaken my soul to righteousness; wherefore I sinned still, and grew more and more rebellious against God, and careless of mine own salvation.

Presently after this, I changed my condition into a married state, and my mercy was to light upon a wife whose father was counted godly. This woman and I, though we came together as poor as poor might be, not having so much household stuff as a dish or spoon betwixt us both, yet this she had for her part, *The Plain Man's Pathway to Heaven*, and *The Practice of Piety*, which her father had left her when he died. In these two books I should sometimes read with her, wherein I also found some things that were somewhat pleasing to me; but all this while I met with no conviction. She also would be often telling of me what a godly man her father was, and how he would reprove and correct vice, both in his house, and amongst his neighbors; what a strict and holy life he lived in his day, both in word and deed.

Wherefore these books with this relation, though they did not reach my heart, to awaken it about my sad and sinful state, yet they did beget within me some desires to religion: so that, because I knew no better, I fell in very eagerly with the religion of the times; to wit, to go to church twice a day, and that too with the foremost; and there should very devoutly both say and sing as others did, yet retaining my wicked life; but withal, I was so overrun with a spirit of superstition that I adored, and that with great devotion, even all things, both the high place, priest, clerk, vestment, service, and what else belonging to the church; counting all things holy that were therein contained, and especially the priest and clerk most happy, and without doubt greatly blessed, because they were the servants, as I then thought, of God, and were principal in the holy temple, to do His work therein.

This conceit grew so strong in little time upon my spirit that, had I but seen a priest, though never so sordid and debauched in his life, I should find my spirit fall under him, reverence him, and knit unto him; yea, I thought for the love I did bear unto them, supposing they were the ministers of God, I could have lain down at their feet, and have been trampled upon by them; their name, their garb, and work did so intoxicate and bewitch me.

After I had been thus for some considerable time, another thought came into my mind; and that was, whether we were of the Israelites, or no? For finding in the Scriptures that they were once the peculiar people of God, though I, if I were one of this race, my soul must needs be happy. Now, again, I found within me a great longing to be resolved about this question, but could not tell how I should. At last I asked my father of it; who told me, No, we were not. Wherefore then I fell in my spirit as to the hopes of that, and so remained.

But all this while, I was not sensible of the danger and evil of sin; I was kept from considering that sin would damn me, what religion soever I followed, unless I was found in Christ. Nay, I never thought of him, nor whether there was one, or no. Thus man, while blind, doth wander, but wearieth himself with vanity for he knoweth not the way to the city of God (Eccles. x. 15).

But one day, amongst all the sermons our parson made, his subject was, to treat of the Sabbath day, and of the evil of breaking that, either with labor, sports, or otherwise. Now I was, notwithstanding my religion, one that took much delight in all manner of vice, and especially that was the day that I did solace myself therewith, wherefore I fell in my conscience under his sermon, thinking and believing that he made that sermon on purpose to show me my evil doing; and at that time I felt what guilt was, though never before, that I can remember; but then I was, for the present, greatly loaden therewith, and so went home when the sermon was ended, with a great burden upon my spirit.

This, for that instant, did benumb the sinews of my best delights, and did embitter my former pleasures to me; but behold, it lasted not, for before I had well dined, the trouble began to go off my mind, and my heart returned to its old course: but oh! how glad was I that this trouble was gone from me, and that the fire was put out, that I might sin again without control! Wherefore, when I had satisfied nature with my food, I shook the sermon out of my mind, and to my old custom of sports and gaming I returned with great delight.

But the same day, as I was in the midst of a game at cat, and having struck it one blow from the hole, just as I was about to strike it the second time, a voice did suddenly dart from Heaven into my soul, which said, "Wilt thou leave thy sins and go to Heaven, or have thy sins and go to Hell?" At this I was put to an exceeding maze; wherefore, leaving my cat upon the ground, I looked up to Heaven, and was, as if I had, with the eyes of my understanding, seen the Lord Jesus looking down upon me, as being very hotly displeased with me, and as if he did severely threaten me with some grievous punishment for these and other my ungodly practices.

I had no sooner thus conceived in my mind but suddenly this conclusion was fastened on my spirit, for the former hint did set my sins again before my face, that I had been a great and grievous sinner, and that it was now too late for me to look after Heaven; for Christ would not forgive me, nor pardon my transgressions. Then I fell to musing upon this also; and while I was thinking on it, fearing lest it should be so, I felt my heart sink in despair, concluding it was too late; and therefore I resolved in my mind I would go on in sin: for, thought I, if the case be thus, my state is surely miserable; miserable if I leave my sins, and but miserable if I follow them; I can but be damned, and if I must be so, I had as good be damned for many sins as to be damned for few.

Thus I stood in the midst of my play, before all that then were present; but yet I told them nothing: but I say, I having made this conclusion, I returned desperately to my sport again; and I well remember that presently this kind of despair did so possess my soul that I was persuaded I could never attain to other comfort than what I should get in sin; for Heaven was gone already, so that on that I must not think; wherefore I found within me a great desire to take my fill of sin, still studying what sin was yet to be committed, that I might taste the sweetness of it; and I made as much haste as I could to fill my belly with its delicates, lest I should die before I had my desire; for that I feared greatly. In these things, I protest before God, I lie not, neither do I feign this sort of speech; these were really, strongly, and with all my heart, my desires; the good Lord, whose mercy is unsearchable, forgive me my transgressions.

And I am very confident that this temptation of the Devil is more usual amongst poor creatures than many are aware of, even to overrun their spirits with a scurvy and seared frame of heart, and benumbing of conscience; which frame, he stilly and slyly supplieth with such despair that though not much guilt attendeth the soul, yet they continually have a secret conclusion within them that there is no hopes for them; for they have loved sins, "therefore after them they will go" (Jer. ii. 25; xviii. 12).

Now therefore I went on in sin with great greediness of mind, still grudging that I could not be so satisfied with it as I would. This did continue with me about a month, or more; but one day, as I was standing at a neighbor's shop-window, and there cursing and swearing, and playing the madman, after my wonted manner, there sat within the woman of the house, and heard me, who, though she was a very loose and ungodly wretch, yet protested that I swore and cursed at that most fearful rate that she was made to tremble to hear me; and told me further that I was the ungodliest fellow for swearing that ever she heard in all her life; and that I, by thus doing, was able to spoil all the youth in a whole town, if they came but in my company.

At this reproof I was silenced, and put to secret shame, and that too, as I thought, before the God of Heaven; wherefore, while I stood there, and hanging down my head, I wished with all my heart that I might be a little child again, that my father might learn me to speak without this wicked way of swearing; for, thought I, I am so accustomed to it that it is in vain for me to think of a reformation, for I thought it could never be.

But how it came to pass, I know not; I did from this time forward so leave my swearing that it was a great wonder to myself to observe it; and, whereas before I knew not how to speak unless I put an oath before, and another behind, to make my words have authority, now I could, without it, speak better, and with more pleasantness than ever I could before. All this while I knew not Jesus Christ, neither did I leave my sports and plays. . . .

Now I shall go forward to give you a relation of other of the Lord's dealings with me, of his dealings with me at sundry other seasons, and of the temptations I then did meet withal. I shall begin with what I met with when I first did join in fellowship with the people of God in Bedford. After I had propounded to the church that my desire was to walk in the order and ordinances of Christ with them, and was also admitted by them; while I thought of that blessed ordinance of Christ, which was his last supper with his Disciples before his death, that Scripture, "This do in remembrance of me" (Luke xxii. 19), was made a very precious word unto me; for by it the Lord did come down upon my conscience with the discovery of his death for my sins; and as I then felt, did as if he plunged me in the virtue of the same. But, behold, I had not been long a partaker at that ordinance, but such fierce and sad temptations did attend me at all times therein, both to blaspheme the ordinance, and to wish some deadly thing to those that then did eat thereof; that, lest I should at any time be guilty of consenting to these wicked and fearful thoughts, I was forced to bend myself all the while to pray to God to keep me from such blasphemies; and also to cry to God to bless the bread and cup to them as it went from mouth to mouth. The reason of this temptation I have thought since was, because I did not, with that reverence as became me, at first approach to partake thereof.

Thus I continued for three-quarters of a year, and could never have rest nor ease; but at last the Lord came in upon my soul with that same Scripture by which my soul was visited before; and after that I have been usually very well and comfortable in the partaking of that blessed ordinance, and have, I trust, therein discerned the Lord's body as broken for my sins, and that his precious blood hath been shed for my transgressions.

Upon a time I was somewhat inclining to a consumption, wherewith, about the spring, I was suddenly and violently seized with much weakness in my outward man, insomuch that I thought I could not live. Now began I afresh to give myself up to a serious examination after my state and condition for the future, and of my evidences for that blessed world to come; for it hath, I bless the name of God, been my usual course, as always, so especially in the day of affliction, to endeavor to keep my interest in the life to come clear before my eye.

But I had no sooner begun to recall to mind my former experience of the goodness of God to my soul, but there came flocking into my mind an innumerable company of my sins and transgressions, amongst which these were at this time most to my affliction, namely, my deadness, dulness, and coldness in holy duties; my wanderings of heart, of my wearisomeness in all good things, my want of love to God, His ways, and people, with this at the end of all, Are these the fruits of Christianity? are these the tokens of a blessed man?

At the apprehension of these things my sickness was doubled upon me, for now was I sick in my inward man, my soul was clogged with guilt; now also was my former experience of God's goodness to me quite taken out of my mind, and hid as if it had never been, nor seen. Now was my soul greatly pinched between these two considerations, Live I must not, die I dare not; now I sunk and fell in my spirit, and was giving up all for lost; but as I was walking up and down in the house, as a man in a most woeful state, that word of God took hold of my heart, Ye are "justified freely by His grace, through the redemption that is in Christ Jesus" (Rom. iii. 24). But oh, what a turn it made upon me!

Now was I as one awakened out of some troublesome sleep and dream, and listening to this heavenly sentence, I was as if I had heard it thus expounded to me: Sinner, thou thinkest that because of thy sins and infirmities I cannot save thy soul, but behold my Son is by me, and upon him I look, and not on thee, and will deal with thee according as I am pleased with him. At this I was greatly lightened in my mind, and made to understand that God could justify a sinner at any time; it was but His looking upon Christ, and imputing of his benefits to us, and the work was forthwith done.

And as I was thus in a muse, that Scripture also came with great power upon my spirit, "Not by works of righteousness which we have done, but according to His mercy He saved us," etc. (Tit. iii, 5, 2 Tim. i. 9). Now was I got on high; I saw myself within the arms of

grace and mercy; and though I was before afraid to think of a dying
hour, yet now I cried, Let me die. Now death was lovely and beautiful in my sight; for I saw we shall never live indeed till we be gone
to the other world. Oh, methought, this life is but a slumber in
comparison of that above; at this time also I saw more in those words,
"Heirs of God" (Rom. viii. 17), than ever I shall be able to express
while I live in this world. "Heirs of God"! God himself is the portion
of the saints. This I saw and wondered at, but cannot tell you what
I saw.

Again, as I was at another time very ill and weak, all that time also
the tempter did beset me strongly, for I find he is much for assault-
ing the soul when it begins to approach towards the grave, then is
his opportunity, laboring to hide from me my former experience of
God's goodness; also setting before me the terrors of death and the
judgment of God, insomuch that at this time, through my fear of
miscarrying forever, should I now die, I was as one dead before death
came, and was as if I had felt myself already descending into the
pit; methought, I said, there was no way, but to Hell I must; but
behold, just as I was in the midst of those fears, these words of the
angels carrying Lazarus into Abraham's bosom darted in upon me, as
who should say, So it shall be with thee when thou dost leave this
world. This did sweetly revive my spirit, and help me to hope in
God; which, when I had with comfort mused on a while, that word
fell with great weight upon my mind, "O death, where is thy sting?
O grave, where is thy victory?" (1 Cor. xv. 55). At this I became
both well in body and mind at once, for my sickness did presently
vanish, and I walked comfortably in my work for God again.

At another time, though just before I was pretty well and savory
in my spirit, yet suddenly there fell upon me a great cloud of darkness, which did so hide from me the things of God and Christ that
I was as if I had never seen or known them in my life; I was also so
overrun in my soul, with a senseless, heartless frame of spirit, that I
could not feel my soul to move or stir after grace and life by Christ;
I was as if my loins were broken, or as if my hands and feet had been
tied or bound with chains. At this time also I felt some weakness to
seize upon my outward man, which made still the other affliction
the more heavy and uncomfortable to me.

After I had been in this condition some three or four days, as I was
sitting by the fire, I suddenly felt this word to sound in my heart,
I must go to Jesus; at this my former darkness and atheism fled away,
and the blessed things of Heaven were set within my view. While I

was on this sudden thus overtaken with surprise, "Wife," said I, "is there ever such a Scripture, I must go to Jesus?" She said she could not tell; therefore I sat musing still to see if I could remember such a place; I had not sat above two or three minutes but that came bolting in upon me, "And to an innumerable company of angels," and withal, Hebrews the twelfth, about the mount Sion, was set before mine eyes (ver. 22-4).

Then with joy I told my wife, "Oh now I know, I know!" But that night was a good night to me, I never had but few better; I longed for the company of some of God's people that I might have imparted unto them what God had showed me. Christ was a precious Christ to my soul that night; I could scarce lie in my bed for joy, and peace, and triumph, through Christ; this great glory did not continue upon me until morning, yet that twelfth of the author to the Hebrews (ver. 22-4) was a blessed Scripture to me for many days together after this.

The words are these, "Ye are come unto Mount Sion, and unto the city of the living God, the heavenly Jerusalem, and to an innumerable company of angels, to the general assembly and church of the firstborn, which are written in Heaven, and to God the Judge of all, and to the spirits of just men made perfect, and to Jesus the mediator of the new covenant, and to the blood of sprinkling, that speaketh better things than that of Abel." Through this blessed sentence the Lord led me over and over, first to this word, and then to that, and showed me wonderful glory in every one of them. These words also have oft since this time been great refreshment to my spirit. Blessed be God for having mercy on me.

The Pilgrim's Progress in the Similitude of a Dream

CHRISTIAN FLIES THE WRATH TO COME

As I walked through the wilderness of this world, I lighted on a certain place where was a Den, and I laid me down in that place to sleep: and, as I slept, I dreamed a dream. I dreamed, and behold, I saw a man clothed with rags, standing in a certain place, with his face from his own house, a book in his hand, and a great burden upon his back. (Isa. lxiv. 6; Luke xiv. 33; Psa. xxxviii. 4; Hab. ii. 2.)

I looked, and saw him open the book, and read therein; and, as he read, he wept and trembled; and, not being able longer to contain, he brake out with a lamentable cry, saying, "What shall I do?" (Acts ii. 37; xvi. 30, 31.)

In this plight, therefore, he went home and refrained himself as long as he could, that his wife and children should not perceive his distress; but he could not be silent long, because that his trouble increased. Wherefore at length he brake his mind to his wife and children; and thus he began to talk to them. O my dear wife, said he, and you the children of my bowels, I, your dear friend, am in myself undone by reason of a burden that lieth hard upon me; moreover, I am for certain informed that this our city will be burned with fire from heaven; in which fearful overthrow, both myself, with thee my wife, and you my sweet babes, shall miserably come to ruin, except (the which yet I see not) some way of escape can be found, whereby we may be delivered. At this his relations were sore amazed; not for that they believed that what he had said to them was true, but because they thought that some frenzy distemper had got into his head; therefore, it drawing towards night, and they hoping that sleep might settle his brains, with all haste they got him to bed. But the night was as troublesome to him as the day; wherefore, instead of sleeping, he spent it in sighs and tears. So, when the morning was come, they would know how he did. He told them, Worse and worse: he also set to talking to them again; but they began to be hardened. They also thought to drive away his distemper by harsh and surly carriages to him; sometimes they would deride, sometimes they would chide, and sometimes they would quite neglect him. Wherefore he began to retire himself to his chamber, to pray for and pity them, and also to condole his own misery; he would also walk solitarily in the fields, sometimes reading, and sometimes praying: and thus for some days he spent his time.

Now, I saw, upon a time, when he was walking in the fields, that he was, as he was wont, reading in his book, and greatly distressed in his mind; and as he read, he burst out, as he had done before, crying, "What shall I do to be saved?"

I saw also that he looked this way and that way, as if he would run; yet he stood still, because, as I perceived, he could not tell which way to go. I looked then, and saw a man named Evangelist coming to him, who asked, Wherefore dost thou cry?

He answered, Sir, I perceive by the book in my hand, that I am

condemned to die, and after that to come to judgment (Heb. ix.
27); and I find that I am not willing to do the first (Job xvi. 11), nor
able to the second. (Ezek. xxii. 14.)

Then said Evangelist, Why not willing to die, since this life is
attended with so many evils? The man answered, Because I fear that
this burden that is upon my back will sink me lower than the grave,
and I shall fall into Tophet. (Isa. xxx. 33.) And, sir, if I be not fit to
go to prison, I am not fit, I am sure, to go to judgment, and from
thence to execution; and the thoughts of these things make me cry.

Then said Evangelist, If this be thy condition, why standest thou
still? He answered, Because I know not whither to go. Then he gave
him a parchment roll, and there was written within, "Flee from the
wrath to come." (Matt. iii. 7.)

The man, therefore, read it, and looking upon Evangelist very
carefully, said, Whither must I fly? Then said Evangelist, pointing
with his finger over a very wide field, Do you see yonder wicket-
gate? (Matt. vii. 13, 14.) The man said, No. Then said the other,
Do you see yonder shining light? (Psa. cxix. 105; 2 Pet. i. 19.) He
said, I think I do. Then said Evangelist, Keep that light in your eye,
and go up directly thereto; so shalt thou see the gate; at which, when
thou knockest, it shall be told thee what thou shalt do. So I saw
in my dream that the man began to run. Now, he had not run far
from his own door, but his wife and children, perceiving it, began to
cry after him to return; but the man put his fingers in his ears, and
ran on, crying, Life! life! Eternal life! (Luke xiv. 26.) So he looked
not behind him, but fled towards the middle of the plain. (Gen. xix.
17.)

The neighbours also came out to see him run (Jer. xx. 10); and,
as he ran, some mocked, others threatened, and some cried after him
to return; and, among those that did so, there were two that resolved
to fetch him back by force. The name of the one was Obstinate,
and the name of the other Pliable. Now, by this time, the man was
got a good distance from them; but, however, they were resolved to
pursue him, which they did, and in a little time they overtook him.
Then said the man, Neighbours, wherefore are ye come? They said,
To persuade you to go back with us. But he said, That can by no
means be; you dwell, said he, in the City of Destruction, the place
also where I was born: I see it to be so; and, dying there, sooner or
later, you will sink lower than the grave, into a place that burns with
fire and brimstone: be content, good neighbours, and go along with
me.

OBST. What! said Obstinate, and leave our friends and our comforts behind us?

CHR. Yes, said Christian, for that was his name, because that ALL which you shall forsake is not worthy to be compared with a little of that which I am seeking to enjoy (2 Cor. v. 17); and, if you will go along with me, and hold it, you shall fare as I myself; for there, where I go, is enough and to spare (Luke xv. 17). Come away, and prove my words.

OBST. What are the things you seek, since you leave all the world to find them?

CHR. I seek an inheritance incorruptible, undefiled, and that fadeth not away (1 Pet. i. 4), and it is laid up in heaven, and safe there (Heb. xi. 16), to be bestowed, at the time appointed, on them that diligently seek it. Read it so, if you will, in my book.

OBST. Tush! said Obstinate, away with your book; will you go back with us or no?

CHR. No, not I, said the other, because I have laid my hand to the plough (Luke ix. 62).

OBST. Come, then, neighbour Pliable, let us turn again, and go home without him; there is a company of these crazy-headed coxcombs, that, when they take a fancy by the end, are wiser in their own eyes than seven men that can render a reason (Prov. xxvi. 16).

PLI. Then said Pliable, Don't revile; if what the good Christian says is true, the things he looks after are better than ours: my heart inclines to go with my neighbour.

OBST. What! more fools still! Be ruled by me, and go back; who knows whither such a brain-sick fellow will lead you? Go back, go back, and be wise.

CHR. Nay, but do thou come with thy neighbour, Pliable; there are such things to be had which I spoke of, and many more glories besides. If you believe me not, read here in this book; and for the truth of what is expressed therein, behold, all is confirmed by the blood of Him that made it (Heb. ix. 17-22; xiii. 20).

PLI. Well, neighbour Obstinate, saith Pliable, I begin to come to a point; I intend to go along with this good man, and to cast in my lot with him: but, my good companion, do you know the way to this desired place?

CHR. I am directed by a man, whose name is Evangelist, to speed me to a little gate that is before us, where we shall receive instructions about the way.

PLI. Come, then, good neighbour, let us be going. Then they went both together.

OBST. And I will go back to my place, said Obstinate; I will be no companion of such misled fantastical fellows.

Now, I saw in my dream, that, when Obstinate was gone back, Christian and Pliable went talking over the plain; and thus they began their discourse.

CHR. Come, neighbour Pliable, how do you do? I am glad you are persuaded to go along with me. Had even Obstinate himself but felt what I have felt of the powers and terrors of what is yet unseen, he would not thus lightly have given us the back.

PLI. Come, neighbour Christian, since there are none but us two here, tell me now further what the things are, and how to be enjoyed, whither we are going.

CHR. I can better conceive of them with my mind, than speak of them with my tongue: but yet, since you are desirous to know, I will read of them in my book.

PLI. And do you think that the words of your book are certainly true?

CHR. Yes, verily; for it was made by Him that cannot lie (Tit. i. 2).

PLI. Well said; what things are they?

CHR. There is an endless kingdom to be inhabited, and everlasting life to be given us, that we may inhabit that kingdom for ever (Isa. xlv. 17; John x. 28, 29).

PLI. Well said; and what else?

CHR. There are crowns of glory to be given us, and garments that will make us shine like the sun in the firmament of heaven (2 Tim. iv. 8; Rev. iii. 4; Matt. xiii. 43).

PLI. This is very pleasant; and what else?

CHR. There shall be no more crying, nor sorrow: for He that is owner of the place will wipe all tears from our eyes (Isa. xxv. 6-8; Rev. vii. 17; xxi. 4).

PLI. And what company shall we have there?

CHR. There we shall be with seraphims and cherubims, creatures that will dazzle your eyes to look on them (Isa. vi. 2). There also you shall meet with thousands and ten thousands that have gone before us to that place; none of them are hurtful, but loving and holy; every one walking in the sight of God, and standing in His presence with acceptance for ever (1 Thess. iv. 16, 17; Rev. v. 11). In a word, there we shall see the elders with their golden crowns (Rev.

iv. 4); there we shall see the holy virgins with their golden harps (Rev. xiv. 1-5); there we shall see men that by the world were cut in pieces, burnt in flames, eaten of beasts, drowned in the seas, for the love that they bare to the Lord of the place, all well, and clothed with immortality as with a garment (John xii. 25; 2 Cor. v. 4).

PLI. The hearing of this is enough to ravish one's heart. But are these things to be enjoyed? How shall we get to be sharers thereof?

CHR. The Lord, the Governor of the country, hath recorded that in this book; the substance of which is, If we be truly willing to have it; he will bestow it upon us freely. (Isa. lv. 1, 2; John vi. 37; vii. 37; Rev. xxi. 6; xxii. 17.)

PLI. Well, my good companion, glad am I to hear of these things: come on, let us mend our pace.

CHR. I cannot go so fast as I would, by reason of this burden that is on my back.

THE SLOUGH OF DESPOND

Now, I saw in my dream, that just as they had ended this talk they drew near to a very miry slough, that was in the midst of the plain; and they, being heedless, did both fall suddenly into the bog. The name of the slough was Despond. Here, therefore, they wallowed for a time, being grievously bedaubed with the dirt; and Christian, because of the burden that was on his back, began to sink in the mire.

PLI. Then said Pliable, Ah! neighbour Christian, where are you now?

CHR. Truly, said Christian, I do not know.

PLI. At this Pliable began to be offended, and angrily said to his fellow, Is this the happiness you have told me all this while of? If we have such ill speed at our first setting out, what may we expect betwixt this and our journey's end? May I get out again with my life, you shall possess the brave country alone for me. And, with that, he gave a desperate struggle or two, and got out of the mire on that side of the slough which was next to his own house: so away he went, and Christian saw him no more.

Wherefore Christian was left to tumble in the Slough of Despond alone: but still he endeavoured to struggle to that side of the slough that was still further from his own house, and next to the wicket-gate; the which he did, but could not get out, because of the burden that was upon his back: but I beheld in my dream, that a man came to him, whose name was Help, and asked him, What he did there?

CHR. Sir, said Christian, I was bid go this way by a man called Evangelist, who directed me also to yonder gate, that I might escape the wrath to come; and as I was going thither I fell in here.

HELP. But why did not you look for the steps?

CHR. Fear followed me so hard, that I fled the next way, and fell in.

HELP. Then said he, Give me thy hand: so he gave him his hand, and he drew him out, and set him upon sound ground, and bid him go on his way. (Psa. xl. 2.)

Then I stepped to him that plucked him out, and said, Sir, wherefore, since over this place is the way from the City of Destruction to yonder gate, is it that this plat is not mended, that poor travellers might go thither with more security? And he said unto me, This miry slough is such a place as cannot be mended; it is the descent whither the scum and filth that attends conviction for sin doth continually run, and therefore it is called the Slough of Despond; for still, as the sinner is awakened about his lost condition, there ariseth in his soul many fears, and doubts, and discouraging apprehensions, which all of them get together, and settle in this place. And this is the reason of the badness of this ground. . . .

THE FIGHT WITH THE FIEND

Then he began to go forward; but Discretion, Piety, Charity, and Prudence, would accompany him down to the foot of the hill. So they went on together, reiterating their former discourses, till they came to go down the hill. Then said Christian, As it was difficult coming up, so, so far as I can see, it is dangerous going down. Yes, said Prudence, so it is, for it is a hard matter for a man to go down into the Valley of Humiliation, as thou art now, and to catch no slip by the way; therefore, said they, are we come out to accompany thee down the hill. So he began to go down, but very warily; yet he caught a slip or two.

Then I saw in my dream that these good companions, when Christian was gone to the bottom of the hill, gave him a loaf of bread, a bottle of wine, and a cluster of raisins; and then he went on his way.

But now, in this Valley of Humiliation, poor Christian was hard put to it; for he had gone but a little way before he espied a foul fiend coming over the field to meet him; his name is Apollyon. Then did Christian begin to be afraid, and to cast in his mind whether to go back or to stand his ground. But he considered again that he had no armour for his back; and therefore thought that to turn the back to him might give him the greater advantage with ease to pierce him with his darts. Therefore he resolved to venture and stand his ground; for, thought he, had I no more in mine eye than the saving of my life, it would be the best way to stand.

So he went on, and Apollyon met him. Now the monster was hideous to behold; he was clothed with scales, like a fish (and they are his pride), he had wings like a dragon, feet like a bear, and out of his belly came fire and smoke, and his mouth was as the mouth of a lion. When he was come up to Christian, he beheld him with a disdainful countenance, and thus began to question him.

APOL. Whence come you? and whither are you bound?

CHR. I am come from the City of Destruction, which is the place of all evil, and am going to the City of Zion.

APOL. By this I perceive thou art one of my subjects, for all that country is mine, and I am the prince and god of it. How is it, then, that thou hast run away from thy king? Were it not that I hope thou mayest do me more service, I would strike thee now, at one blow, to the ground.

CHR. I was born, indeed, in your dominions, but your service was hard, and your wages such as a man could not live on, "for the wages of sin *is* death" (Rom. iv. 23); therefore, when I was come to years, I did as other considerate persons do, look out, if, perhaps, I might mend myself.

APOL. There is no prince that will thus lightly lose his subjects, neither will I as yet lose thee; but since thou complainest of thy service and wages, be content to go back: what our country will afford, I do here promise to give thee.

CHR. But I have let myself to another, even to the King of Princes; and how can I, with fairness, go back with thee?

APOL. Thou hast done in this according to the proverb, "Changed a bad for a worse;" but it is ordinary for those that have professed themselves his servants, after a while to give him the slip, and return again to me. Do thou so too, and all shall be well.

CHR. I have given him my faith, and sworn my allegiance to him; how, then, can I go back from this, and not be hanged as a traitor?

APOL. Thou didst the same to me, and yet I am willing to pass by all, if now thou wilt yet turn again and go back.

CHR. What I promised thee was in my nonage; and, besides, I

count the Prince under whose banner now I stand is able to absolve me; yea, and to pardon also what I did as to my compliance with thee; and, besides, O thou destroying Apollyon! to speak truth, I like his service, his wages, his servants, his government, his company and country, better than thine; and, therefore, leave off to persuade me further; I am his servant, and I will follow him.

APOL. Consider, again, when thou art in cool blood, what thou art like to meet with in the way that thou goest. Thou knowest that, for the most part, his servants come to an ill end, because they are transgressors against me and my ways. How many of them have been put to shameful deaths; and, besides, thou countest his service better than mine, whereas he never came yet from the place where he is to deliver any that served him out of our hands; but as for me, how many times, as all the world very well knows, have I delivered, either by power, or fraud, those that have faithfully served me, from him and his, though taken by them; and so I will deliver thee.

CHR. His forbearing at present to deliver them is on purpose to try their love, whether they will cleave to him to the end; and as for the ill end thou sayest they come to, that is most glorious in their account; for, for present deliverance, they do not much expect it, for they stay for their glory, and then they shall have it, when their Prince comes in his and the glory of the angels.

APOL. Thou hast already been unfaithful in thy service to him; and how dost thou think to receive wages of him?

CHR. Wherein, O Apollyon! have I been unfaithful to him?

APOL. Thou didst faint at first setting out, when thou wast almost choked in the Gulf of Despond; thou didst attempt wrong ways to be rid of thy burden, whereas thou shouldest have stayed till thy Prince had taken it off; thou didst sinfully sleep and lose thy choice thing; thou wast, also, almost persuaded to go back at the sight of the lions; and when thou talkest of thy journey, and of what thou hast heard and seen, thou art inwardly desirous of vain-glory in all thou sayest or doest.

CHR. All this is true, and much more which thou hast left out; but the Prince whom I serve and honour is merciful, and ready to forgive; but, besides, these infirmities possessed me in thy country, for there I sucked them in; and I have groaned under them, been sorry for them, and have obtained pardon of my Prince.

APOL. Then Apollyon broke out into a grievous rage, saying, I am an enemy to this Prince; I hate his person, his laws, and people; I am come out on purpose to withstand thee.

CHR. Apollyon, beware what you do; for I am in the king's highway, the way of holiness; therefore take heed to yourself.

APOL. Then Apollyon straddled quite over the whole breadth of the way, and said, I am void of fear in this matter; prepare thyself to die; for I swear by my infernal den, that thou shalt go no further; here will I spill thy soul.

And with that he threw a flaming dart at his breast; but Christian had a shield in his hand with which he caught it, and so prevented the danger of that.

Then did Christian draw, for he saw it was time to bestir him: and Apollyon as fast made at him, throwing darts as thick as hail; by the which, notwithstanding all that Christian could do to avoid it, Apollyon wounded him in his head, his hand, and foot. This made Christian give a little back; Apollyon, therefore, followed his work amain, and Christian again took courage, and resisted as manfully as he could. This sore combat lasted for above half a day, even till Christian was almost quite spent; for you must know that Christian, by reason of his wounds, must needs grow weaker and weaker.

Then Apollyon, espying his opportunity, began to gather up close to Christian, and wrestling with him, gave him a dreadful fall; and with that Christian's sword flew out of his hand. Then said Apollyon, I am sure of thee now. And with that he had almost pressed him to death, so that Christian began to despair of life: but as God would have it, while Apollyon was fetching of his last blow, thereby to make a full end of this good man, Christian nimbly stretched out his hand for his sword, and caught it, saying, "Rejoice not against me, O mine enemy: when I fall I shall arise" (Micah vii. 8); and with that gave him a deadly thrust, which made him give back, as one that had received his mortal wound. Christian perceiving that, made at him again, saying, "Nay, in all these things we are more than conquerors through him that loved us" (Rom. viii. 37). And with that Apollyon spread forth his dragon's wings and sped him away, that Christian for a season saw him no more (James iv. 7).

In this combat no man can imagine, unless he had seen and heard as I did, what yelling and hideous roaring Apollyon made all the time of the fight—he spake like a dragon; and, on the other side, what sighs and groans burst from Christian's heart. I never saw him all the while give so much as one pleasant look, till he perceived he had wounded Apollyon with his two-edged sword; then, indeed, he did smile, and look upward; but it was the dreadfullest sight that ever I saw.

So when the battle was over, Christian said, "I will here give thanks to him that delivered me out of the mouth of the lion, to him that did help me against Apollyon." And so he did, saying,—

> Great Beelzebub, the captain of this fiend,
> Design'd my ruin; therefore to this end
> He sent him harness'd out: and he with rage
> That hellish was, did fiercely me engage.
> But blessed Michael helped me, and I,
> By dint of sword, did quickly make him fly.
> Therefore to him let me give lasting praise,
> And thank and bless his holy name always.

Then there came to him a hand, with some of the leaves of the tree of life, the which Christian took, and applied to the wounds that he had received in the battle, and was healed immediately. He also sat down in that place to eat bread, and to drink of the bottle that was given him a little before; so, being refreshed, he addressed himself to his journey, with his sword drawn in his hand; for he said, I know not but some other enemy may be at hand. But he met with no other affront from Apollyon quite through this valley. . . .

VANITY FAIR

Then I saw in my dream, that when they were got out of the wilderness, they presently saw a town before them, and the name of that town is Vanity; and at the town there is a fair kept, called Vanity Fair; it is kept all the year long; it beareth the name of Vanity Fair, because the town where it is kept is lighter than vanity; and also because all that is there sold, or that cometh thither, is vanity. As is the saying of the wise, "all that cometh is vanity" (Eccles. i.; ii. 11, 17; xi. 8; Isa. xi. 17).

This fair is no new-erected business, but a thing of ancient standing; I will show you the original of it.

Almost five thousand years agone, there were pilgrims walking to the Celestial City, as these two honest persons are: and Beelzebub, Apollyon, and Legion, with their companions, perceiving by the path that the pilgrims made, that their way to the city lay through this town of Vanity, they contrived here to set up a fair; a fair wherein should be sold all sorts of vanity, and that it should last all the year long; therefore at this fair are all such merchandise sold, as houses, lands, trades, places, honours, preferments, titles, countries, kingdoms, lusts, pleasures, and delights of all sorts, as whores, bawds, wives, husbands, children, masters, servants, lives, blood, bodies, souls, silver, gold, pearls, precious stones, and what not.

And, moreover, at this fair there is at all times to be seen juggling, cheats, games, plays, fools, apes, knaves, and rogues, and that of every kind.

Here are to be seen, too, and that for nothing, thefts, murders, adulteries, false swearers, and that of a blood-red colour.

And as in other fairs of less moment, there are the several rows and streets, under their proper names, where such and such wares are vended; so here likewise you have the proper places, rows, streets (viz. countries and kingdoms), where the wares of this fair are soonest to be found. Here is the Britain Row, the French Row, the Italian Row, the Spanish Row, the German Row, where several sorts of vanities are to be sold. But, as in other fairs, some one commodity is as the chief of all the fair, so the ware of Rome and her merchandise is greatly promoted in this fair; only our English nation, with some others, have taken a dislike thereat.

Now, as I said, the way to the Celestial City lies just through this town where this lusty fair is kept; and he that will go to the City, and yet not go through this town, must needs "go out of the world" (1 Cor. v. 10). The Prince of princes himself, when here, went through this town to his own country, and that upon a fair day too; yea, and as I think, it was Beelzebub, the chief lord of this fair, that invited him to buy of his vanities; yea, would have made him lord of the fair, would he have but done him reverence as he went through the town (Matt. iv. 8; Luke iv. 5-7). Yea, because he was such a person of honour, Beelzebub had him from street to street, and showed him all the kingdoms of the world in a little time, that he might, if possible allure the Blessed One to cheapen and buy some of his vanities; but he had no mind to the merchandise, and therefore left the town, without laying out so much as one farthing upon these vanities. This fair, therefore, is an ancient thing, of long standing, and a very great fair.

THE HEAVENLY CITY

Now, I further saw, that betwixt them and the gate was a river, but there was no bridge to go over: the river was very deep. At the sight, therefore, of this river, the Pilgrims were much stunned; but the men that went with them said, You must go through, or you cannot come at the gate.

The Pilgrims then began to inquire if there was no other way to the gate; to which they answered, Yes; but there hath not any, save two, to wit, Enoch and Elijah, been permitted to tread that path, since the foundation of the world, nor shall, until the last trumpet shall sound (1 Cor. xv. 51, 52). The Pilgrims then, especially Christian, began to despond in their minds, and looked this way and that, but no way could be found by them, by which they might escape the river. Then they asked the men if the waters were all of a depth. They said, No; yet they could not help them in that case; for, said they, you shall find it deeper or shallower, as you believe in the King of the place.

They then addressed themselves to the water; and entering, Christian began to sink, and crying out to his good friend Hopeful, he said, I sink in deep waters; the billows go over my head, all his waves go over me! Selah.

Then said the other, Be of good cheer, my brother, I feel the bottom, and it is good. Then said Christian, Ah! my friend "the sorrows of death have compassed me about;" I shall not see the land that flows with milk and honey; and with that a great darkness and horror fell upon Christian, so that he could not see before him. Also here he in great measure lost his senses, so that he could neither remember, nor orderly talk of any of those sweet refreshments that he had met with in the way of his pilgrimage. But all the words that he spake still tended to discover that he had horror of mind, and heart fears that he should die in that river, and never obtain entrance in at the gate. Here also, as they that stood by perceived, he was much in the troublesome thoughts of the sins that he had committed, both since and before he began to be a pilgrim. It was also observed that he was troubled with apparitions of hobgoblins and evil spirits, for ever and anon he would intimate so much by words. Hopeful, therefore, here had much ado to keep his brother's head above water; yea, sometimes he would be quite gone down, and then, ere a while, he would rise up again half dead. Hopeful also would endeavour to comfort him, saying, Brother, I see the gate, and men standing by to receive us; but Christian would answer, It is you, it is you they wait for; you have been Hopeful ever since I knew you. And so have you, said he to Christian. Ah, brother! said he, surely if I was right he would now arise to help me; but for my sins he hath brought me into the snare, and hath left me. Then said Hopeful, My brother, you have quite forgot the text, where it is said of the wicked, "There are no bands in their death, but their strength is firm. They are not troubled as other men, neither are they plagued like other men" (Ps. lxxiii. 4, 5). These troubles and distresses that you go through in these waters are no sign that God hath forsaken you; but are sent to try you, whether you will call to mind that which heretofore you have received of his goodness, and live upon him in your distresses.

Then I saw in my dream, that Christian was as in a muse a while. To whom also Hopeful added this word, Be of good cheer, Jesus Christ maketh thee whole; and with that Christian brake out with a loud voice, Oh! I see him again, and he tells me, "When thou passest through the waters, I will be with thee; and through the rivers, they shall not overflow thee" (Isa. xliii. 2). Then they both took courage, and the enemy was after that as still as a stone, until they were gone over. Christian therefore presently found ground to stand upon, and so it followed that the rest of the river was but shallow. Thus they got over. Now, upon the bank of the river, on the other side, they saw the two shining men again, who there waited for them; wherefore, being come out of the river, they saluted them saying, We are ministering spirits, sent forth to minister for those that shall be heirs of salvation. Thus they went along towards the gate.

Now you must note that the city stood upon a mighty hill, but the Pilgrims went up that hill with ease, because they had these two men to lead them up by the arms; also, they had left their mortal garments behind them in the river, for though they went in with them, they came out without them. They, therefore, went up here with much agility and speed, though the foundation upon which the city was framed was higher than the clouds. They therefore went up through the regions of the air, sweetly talking as they went, being comforted, because they safely got over the river, and had such glorious companions to attend them.

The talk they had with the Shining Ones was about the glory of the place; who told them that the beauty and glory of it was inexpressible. There, said they, is the "Mount Zion, the heavenly Jerusalem, the innumerable company of angels, and the spirits of just men made perfect" (Heb. xii. 22-24). You are going now, said they, to the paradise of God, wherein you shall see the tree of life, and eat of the never-fading fruits thereof; and when you come there, you shall have white robes given you, and your walk and talk shall be every day with the King, even all the days of eternity (Rev. ii. 7; iii. 4; xxii. 5). There you shall not see again such things as you saw when you were in the lower region upon the earth, to wit, sorrow, sickness, affliction, and death, "for the former things are passed away." You are now going to Abraham, to Isaac, and Jacob, and to the prophets —men that God hath taken away from the evil to come, and that are now resting upon their beds, each one walking in his righteousness (Isa. lvii. 1, 2; lxv. 17). The men then asked, What must we do in the holy place? To whom it was answered, You must there receive the comforts of all your toil, and have joy for all your sorrow; you must reap what you have sown, even the fruit of all your prayers, and tears, and sufferings for the King by the way (Gal. vi. 7). In that place you must wear crowns of gold, and enjoy the perpetual sight and vision of the Holy One, for "there you shall see him as he is" (1 John iii. 2). There also you shall serve him continually with praise, with shouting, and thanksgiving, whom you desired to serve in the world, though with much difficulty, because of the infirmity of your flesh. There your eyes shall be delighted with seeing, and your ears with hearing the pleasant voice of the Mighty One. There you shall enjoy your friends again, that are gone thither before you; and there you shall with joy receive, even every one that follows into the holy place after you. There also shall you be clothed with glory and majesty, and put into an equipage fit to ride out with the King of Glory. When he shall come with sound of trumpet in the clouds, as upon the wings of the wind, you shall come with him; and when he shall sit upon the throne of judgment, you shall sit by him; yea, and when he shall pass sentence upon all the workers of iniquity, let them be angels or men, you also shall have a voice in that judgment, because they were his and your enemies (1 Thes. iv. 13-17; Jude 14; Dan. vii. 9, 10; 1 Cor. vi, 2, 3). Also, when he shall again return to the city, you shall go too, with sound of trumpet, and be ever with him.

Now while they were thus drawing towards the gate, behold a company of the heavenly host came out to meet them; to whom it was said by the other two Shining Ones, These are the men that have loved our Lord when they were in the world, and that have left all for his holy name; and he hath sent us to fetch them, and we have brought them thus far on their desired journey, that they may go in and look their Redeemer in the face with joy. Then the heavenly host gave a great shout, saying, "Blessed are they which are called unto the marriage supper of the Lamb" (Rev. xix. 9). There came out also at this time to meet them, several of the King's trumpeters, clothed in white and shining raiment, who, with melodious noises, and loud, made even the heavens to echo with their sound. These trumpeters saluted Christian and his fellow with ten thousand welcomes from the world; and this they did with shouting, and sound of trumpet.

This done, they compassed them round on every side; some went before, some behind, and some on the right hand, some on the left (as it were to guard them through the upper regions), continually sounding as they went, with melodious noise, in notes on high: so that the very sight was to them that could behold it as if heaven itself was come down to meet them. Thus, therefore, they walked on together; and as they walked ever and anon these trumpeters, even with joyful sound, would, by mixing their music with looks and gestures, still signify to Christian and his brother, how welcome they were into their company, and with what gladness they came to meet them; and now were these two men, as it were, in heaven, before they came at it, being swallowed up with the sight of angels, and with hearing of their melodious notes. Here also they had the city itself in view, and they thought they heard all the bells therein to ring, to welcome them thereto. But above all, the warm and joyful thoughts that they had about their own dwelling there, with such company, and that for ever and ever. Oh, by what tongue or pen can their glorious joy be expressed! And thus they came up to the gate.

Now, when they were come up to the gate, there was written over it in letters of gold, "Blessed are they that do his commandments, that they may have right to the tree of life, and may enter in through the gates into the city" (Rev. xxii. 14).

Then I saw in my dream, that the Shining Men bid them call at the gate; the which, when they did, some looked from above over the gate, to wit, Enoch, Moses, and Elijah, &c., to whom it was said: These pilgrims are come from the City of Destruction, for the love that they bear to the King of this place; and then the pilgrims gave in unto them each man his certificate, which they had received in the beginning; those, therefore, were carried in to the King, who, when he had read them, said, Where are the men? To whom it was answered, They are standing without the gate. The King then commanded to open the gate, "That the righteous nation," said he, "which keepeth the truth, may enter in" (Isa. xxvi. 2).

Now I saw in my dream that these two men went in at the gate:

and lo, as they entered, they were transfigured, and they had raiment put on that shone like gold. There was also that met them with harps and crowns, and gave them to them—the harps to praise withal, and the crowns in token of honour. Then I heard in my dream that all the bells in the city rang again for joy, and that it was said unto them, "ENTER YE INTO THE JOY OF YOUR LORD." I also heard the men themselves, that they sang with a loud voice, saying, "BLESSING, AND HONOUR, AND GLORY, AND POWER, BE UNTO HIM THAT SITTETH UPON THE THRONE, AND UNTO THE LAMB, FOR EVER AND EVER" (Rev. v. 13).

Now, just as the gates were opened to let in the men, I looked in after them, and, behold, the City shone like the sun; the streets also were paved with gold, and in them walked many men, with crowns on their heads, palms in their hands, and golden harps to sing praises withal.

There were also of them that had wings, and they answered one another without intermission, saying, "Holy, holy, holy is the Lord" (Rev. iv. 8). And after that they shut up the gates; which, when I had seen, I wished myself among them.

Now while I was gazing upon all these things, I turned my head to look back, and saw Ignorance come up to the river side; but he soon got over, and that without half that difficulty which the other two men met with. For it happened that there was then in that place one Vain-hope, a ferryman, that with his boat helped him over; so he, as the others I saw, did ascend the hill, to come up to the gate, only he came alone; neither did any man meet him with the least encouragement. When he was come up to the gate, he looked up to the writing that was above, and then began to knock, supposing that entrance should have been quickly administered to him; but he was asked by the men that looked over the top of the gate, Whence came you? and what would you have? He answered, I have ate and drank in the presence of the King, and he has taught in our streets. Then they asked him for his certificate, that they might go in and show it to the King; so he fumbled in his bosom for one, and found none. Then said they, Have you none? But the man answered never a word. So they told the King, but he would not come down to see him, but commanded the two Shining Ones that conducted Christian and Hopeful to the City, to go out and take Ignorance, and bind him hand and foot, and have him away. Then they took him up, and carried him through the air, to the door that I saw in the side of the hill, and put him in there. Then I saw that there was a way to hell, even from the gates of heaven, as well as from the City of Destruction. So I awoke, and behold it was a dream.

THOMAS TRAHERNE

The "spirit of the age" does not control the thought and expression of every man of genius who is environed by it. Thomas Traherne, in his lyrics and prose meditations, belongs to no particular time or place. His religious mysticism is as alien to the experience of a Bunyan or a Milton as it is to that of such an Anglican as Jeremy Taylor. The author was almost entirely unknown in his own time and would no doubt have been little regarded even if his work had appeared in print. When the manuscripts were discovered and published in the twentieth century, the theme on which they were composed was already familiar through Wordsworth's "Intimations of Immortality from Recollections of Early Childhood," a poem which owes a debt to Traherne's predecessor in the early seventeenth century, the metaphysical, Henry Vaughn.

Centuries of Meditation

THE THIRD CENTURY

I

Will you see the infancy of this sublime and celestial greatness? Those pure and virgin apprehensions I had from the womb, and that divine light wherewith I was born are the best unto this day, wherein I can see the Universe. By the gift of God they attended me into the world, and by His special favor I remember them till now. Verily they seem the greatest gifts His wisdom could bestow, for without them all other gifts had been dead and vain. They are unattainable by book, and therefore I will teach them by experience. Pray for them earnestly; for they will make you angelical, and wholly celestial. Certainly Adam in Paradise had not more sweet and curious apprehensions of the world than I when I was a child.

II

All appeared new, and strange at first, inexpressibly rare and delightful and beautiful. I was a little stranger, which at my entrance into the world was saluted and surrounded with innumerable joys.

My knowledge was divine. I knew by intuition those things which
since my apostasy I collected again by the highest reason. My very
ignorance was advantageous. I seemed as one brought into the Estate
of Innocence. All things were spotless and pure and glorious: yea,
and infinitely mine, and joyful and precious. I knew not that there
were any sins, or complaints, or laws. I dreamed not of poverties,
contentions, or vices. All tears and quarrels were hidden from mine
eyes. Everything was at rest, free and immortal. I knew nothing of
sickness or death or rents or exaction, either for tribute or bread. In
the absence of these I was entertained like an angel with the works
of God in their splendor and glory, I saw all in the peace of Eden;
Heaven and earth did sing my Creator's praises, and could not make
more melody to Adam than to me. All time was eternity, and a perpetual Sabbath. Is it not strange that an infant should be heir of
the whole world, and see those mysteries which the books of the
learned never unfold?

III

The corn was orient and immortal wheat, which never should be
reaped, nor was ever sown. I thought it had stood from everlasting
to everlasting. The dust and stones of the street were as precious as
gold: the gates were at first the end of the world. The green trees
when I saw them first through one of the gates transported and ravished me, their sweetness and unusual beauty made my heart to leap,
and almost mad with ecstasy, they were such strange and wonderful
things. The men! Oh what venerable and reverend creatures did the
aged seem! Immortal Cherubims! And young men glittering and
sparkling angels, and maids strange seraphic pieces of life and beauty!
Boys and girls tumbling in the street, and playing, were moving
jewels. I knew not that they were born or should die; but all things
abided eternally as they were in their proper places. Eternity was
manifest in the light of the day, and something infinite behind everything appeared: which talked with my expectation and moved my
desire. The city seemed to stand in Eden, or to be built in Heaven.
The streets were mine, the temple was mine, the people were mine,
their clothes and gold and silver were mine, as much as their sparkling eyes, fair skins and ruddy faces. The skies were mine, and so
were the sun and moon and stars, and all the world was mine; and
I the only spectator and enjoyer of it. I knew no churlish proprieties,
nor bounds, nor divisions: but all proprieties and divisions were
mine; all treasures and the possessors of them. So that with much ado

I was corrupted, and made to learn the dirty devices of this world. Which now I unlearn, and become, as it were, a little child again that I may enter into the Kingdom of God.

Wonder

1.

How like an angel came I down!
How bright are all things here!
When first among His works I did appear,
Oh how their glory me did crown?
The world resembled His *Eternity*,
In which my soul did walk;
And ev'rything that I did see,
Did with me talk.

2.

The skies in their magnificence,
The lively, lovely air;
Oh how divine, how soft, how sweet, how fair!
The stars did entertain my sense,
And all the works of God so bright and pure,
So rich and great did seem,
As if they ever must endure,
In my esteem.

3.

A native health and innocence
Within my bones did grow,
And while my God did all His glories show,
I felt a vigor in my sense
That was all spirit. I within did flow
With seas of life, like wine;
I nothing in the world did know,
But 'twas divine.

4.

Harsh ragged objects were conceal'd,
Oppressions, tears, and cries,
Sins, griefs, complaints, dissensions, weeping eyes

Were hid: and only things reveal'd,
Which heav'nly spirits, and the angels prize.
The state of innocence
And bliss, not trades and poverties,
Did fill my sense.

5.

The streets were pav'd with golden stones,
The boys and girls were mine,
Oh how did all their lovely faces shine!
The sons of men all holy ones
In joy, and beauty, then appear'd to me,
And ev'rything which here I found,
While like an angel I did see,
Adorn'd the ground.

6.

Rich diamond and pearl and gold
In ev'ry place was seen;
Rare splendors, yellow, blue, red, white, and green,
Mine eyes did ev'rywhere behold.
Great wonders cloth'd with glory did appear,
Amazement was my bliss.
That and my wealth was ev'rywhere:
No joy to this!

7.

Curs'd and devis'd proprieties,
With envy, avarice,
And fraud, those fiends that spoil ev'n Paradise,
Fled from the splendor of mine eyes.
And so did hedges, ditches, limits, bounds,
I dream'd not aught of those,
But wander'd over all men's grounds,
And found repose.

8.

Proprieties themselves were mine,
And hedges ornaments;
Walls, boxes, coffers, and their rich contents
Did not divide my joys, but all combine.

> Clothes, ribbons, jewels, laces, I esteem'd
> My joys by others worn;
> For me they all to wear them seem'd
> When I was born.

VI *Hic Jacet*